FLASH MEMORIES

Edited by **Igor S. Stievano**

Flash Memories
Edited by Igor S. Stievano

Published by InTech
Janeza Trdine 9, 51000 Rijeka, Croatia

Publishing Process Manager Ivana Lorkovic

Technical Editor Teodora Smiljanic

Cover Designer InTech Design Team

Additional hard copies can be obtained from orders@intechopen.com

Flash Memories, Edited by Igor S. Stievano
p. cm.
ISBN 978-953-307-272-2

For EU product safety concerns:
IN TECH d.o.o., Prolaz Marije Krucifikse Kozulić 3, 51000 Rijeka, Croatia,
info@intechopen.com or visit our website at intechopen.com.

Meet the editor

Igor S. Stievano received the Laurea degree and the Ph.D. degree in electronic engineering from the Politecnico di Torino, Torino, Italy, in 1996 and in 2001, respectively. Currently he is an Associate Professor of Circuit Theory with the ElectroMagnetc Compatibility (EMC) group at the Dipartimento di Elettronica, Politecnico di Torino. His research interests are in the field of Electromagnetic Compatibility, where he works on the macromodeling of linear and nonlinear circuit elements, with specific application to the behavioral modeling of digital integrated circuits, transmission lines and linear junctions. He is Author of more than 90 papers published in international journals and conference proceedings. He is Senior Member of the Institute of Electrical and Electronics Engineers (IEEE). He has been a reviewer for several IEEE journals and since 2007 he has been member of the Scientific Steering Committee of the IEEE International Workshop on Electromagnetic Compatibility of Integrated Circuits, EMC Compo.

Contents

Preface

In recent years, the ICT market has quickly moved toward the integration of a large variety of functions into a single portable electronic equipment. The boundaries among different devices like music players, digital cameras or mobile phones are going to vanish. In this trend, one of the key factors is played by data storage, since all these devices require a large amount of memory to store either audio or visual data. Also, the energy consumption needs to be reduced to further extend battery duration and the functionality of the devices.

In this setting, Flash memories provide an effective solution, as they offer impressive features, including low noise, reliability, low energy consumption, small size and weight, and robustness to mechanical stresses. Flash memories are thus actively contributing to a new generation of devices. The technology is mature and this class of devices is massively used in a wide range of applications. The performances of Flash memories also contribute to the growing interest in solid-state disks, that are currently replacing traditional hard drives in ubiquitous notebook PCs, netbooks and PC tablets. The research on memories and their applications, therefore, will be of paramount importance for the development of future electronic products.

This book is aimed at presenting the state-of-the-art technologies and the research studies related, but not limited, to flash memories. The book consists of fourteen Chapters organized into three Parts, which guide the reader through the different aspects of the subject.

Part 1 focuses on the contributions related to modeling, algorithms and programming techniques. The first Chapter provides a comprehensive overview of file management with specific interest on native flash file systems. The second and third chapters address the important problem of error correction and coding. The fourth Chapter discusses the features and performances of both the automatic and the semi-automatic block cleaning processes. Finally, the last Chapter provides an overview of the state-of-the-art methods to build behavioral models of Flash memories for signal and power integrity simulations.

Part 2 is mainly dedicated to contributions with emphasis on applications. The first Chapter addresses the problem of storage in battery-powered devices operating in a distributed wireless sensor network, thus highlighting the importance of flash memory chips in a sensor node. The second Chapter presents the design of a peripheral controller reconfigurable system based on the FPGA Dynamic Partial Reconfiguration technology, which enables more efficient run-time resource management. The last Chapter focuses on practical examples of in-circuit programming of commercial flash memory devices.

Part 3 collects results on the technology, materials and design topics. The first three Chapters deal with alternative improved technologies and innovative materials for enhancing the performance of memories along with a detailed discussion of features, strengths and limitations of the proposed solutions. The last Chapter concludes the book by discussing a method for molecular dynamic simulations. This simulation is aimed at assessing the strengths of these new materials and their possible application to the future technology of Flash memories.

Enjoy the book!

Igor Simone Stievano
Politecnico di Torino
Dipartimento di Elettronica
Italy

Part 1

Modeling, Algorithms and Programming Techniques

1

Design Issues and Challenges of File Systems for Flash Memories

Stefano Di Carlo[1], Michele Fabiano[1], Paolo Prinetto[1] and Maurizio Caramia[2]
[1]*Department of Control and Computer Engineering, Politecnico di Torino*
[2]*Command Control and Data Handling, Thales Alenia Space*
Italy

1. Introduction

The increasing demand for high-speed storage capability both in consumer electronics (e.g., USB flash drives, digital cameras, MP3 players, solid state hard-disks, etc.) and mission critical applications, makes NAND flash memories a rugged, compact alternative to traditional mass-storage devices such as magnetic hard-disks.

The NAND flash technology guarantees a non-volatile high-density storage support that is fast, shock-resistant and very power-economic. At higher capacities, however, flash storage can be much more costly than magnetic disks, and some flash products are still in short supply. Furthermore, the continuous downscaling allowed by new technologies introduces serious issues related to yield, reliability, and endurance of these devices (Cooke, 2007; IEEE Standards Department, 1998; Jae-Duk et al., 2002; Jen-Chieh et al., 2002; Ielmini, 2009; Mincheol et al., 2009; Mohammad et al., 2000). Several design dimensions, including flash memory technology, architecture, file management, dependability enhancement, power consumption, weight and physical size, must be considered to allow a widespread use of flash-based devices in the realization of high-capacity mass-storage systems (Caramia et al., 2009a).

Among the different issues to consider when designing a flash-based mass-storage system, the file management represents a challenging problem to address. In fact, flash memories store and access data in a completely different manner if compared to magnetic disks. This must be considered at the Operating System (OS) level to grant existing applications an efficient access to the stored information. Two main approaches are pursuit by OS and flash memory designers: (i) block-device emulation, and (ii) development of native file systems optimized to operate with flash-based devices (Chang & Kuo, 2004).

Block-device emulation refers to the development of a hardware/software layer able to emulate the behavior of a traditional block device such as a hard-disk, allowing the OS to communicate with the flash using the same primitives exploited to communicate with magnetic-disks. The main advantage of this approach is the possibility of reusing available file systems (e.g., FAT, NTFS, ext2) to access the information stored in the flash, allowing maximum compatibility with minimum intervention on the OS. However, traditional file systems do not take into account the specific peculiarities of the flash memories, and the emulation layer alone may be not enough to guarantee maximum performance.

The alternative to the block-device emulation is to exploit the hardware features of the flash device in the development of a *native flash file system*. An end-to-end flash-friendly solution can be more efficient than stacking a file system designed for the characteristics of magnetic hard-disks on top of a device driver designed to emulate disks using flash memories (Gal & Toledo, 2005). For efficiency reasons, this approach is becoming the preferred solution whenever embedded NAND flash memories are massively exploited.
The literature is rich of strategies involving block-device emulation, while, to the best of our knowledge, a comprehensive comparison of available native file systems is still missing. This chapter discusses how to properly address the issues of using NAND flash memories as mass-memory devices from the native file system standpoint. We hope that the ideas and the solutions proposed in this chapter will be a valuable starting point for designers of NAND flash-based mass-memory devices.

2. Flash memory issues and challenges

Although flash memories are a very attractive solution for the development of high-end mass storage devices, the technology employed in their production process introduces several reliability challenges (IEEE Standards Department, 1998; Jen-Chieh et al., 2002; Mohammad et al., 2000). Native flash file systems have to address these problems with proper strategies and methodologies in order to efficiently manage the flash memory device. Fig. 1 shows a possible partial taxonomy of such strategies that will be discussed in the sequel of this section.

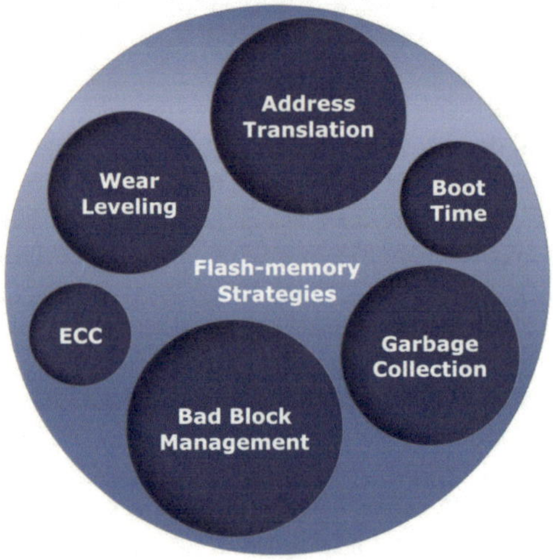

Fig. 1. A possible taxonomy of the management strategies for flash memories

2.1 Technology

The target memory technology is the first parameter to consider when designing a native flash file system. The continuous technology downscaling strongly affects the reliability of the flash memory cells, while the reduction of the distance among cells may lead to several types of cell interferences (Jae-Duk et al., 2002; Mincheol et al., 2009).
From the technology standpoint, two main families of flash memories do exist: (i) NOR flash memories and (ii) NAND flash memories. A deep analysis of the technological aspects of NOR and NAND flash memories is out of the scope of this chapter (the reader may refer to

(Ielmini, 2009) for additional information). Both technologies use floating-gate transistors to realize non-volatile storing cells. However, the NAND technology allows denser layout and greater storage capacity per unit of area. It is therefore the preferred choice when designing mass-storage systems, and it will be the only technology considered in this chapter.
NAND flash memories can be further classified based on the number of bit per cell the memory is able to store. Single Level Cell (SLC) memories store a single bit per cell, while Multiple Level Cell (MLC) memories allow to store multiple bits per memory cell. Fig. 2 shows a comparison between SLC and MLC NAND flash memories (Lee et al., 2009) considering three main characteristics: capacity, performance and endurance.

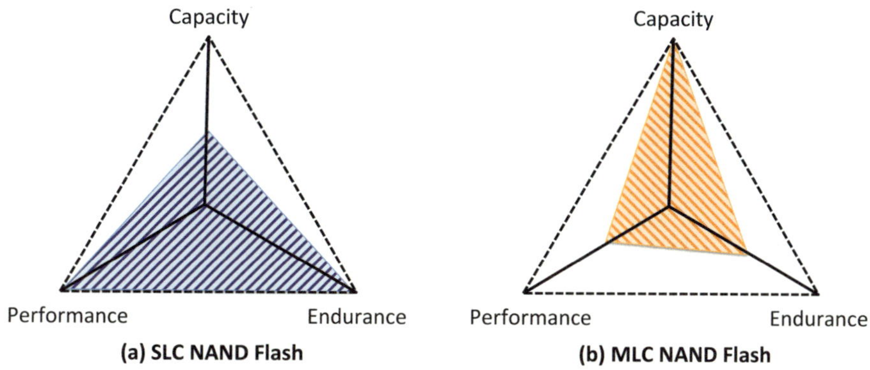

Fig. 2. Comparison of SLC and MLC flash memories

The MLC technology offers higher capacity compared to the SLC technology at the same cost in terms of area. However, MLC memories are slightly slower than SLC memories. MLC memories are more complex, cells are closer, there are multiple voltage references and highly-dependable analog circuitry is requested (Brewer & Gill, 2008). The result is an increased bit error rate (BER) that reduces the overall endurance and reliability (Mielke et al., 2008), thus requiring proper error correction mechanisms at the chip and/or file system level. Consumer electronic products, that continuously demand for increased storage capacity, are nowadays mainly based on MLC NAND flash memories, while mission-critical applications that require high reliability mainly adopt SLC memories (Yuan, 2008).

2.2 Architecture

A native flash file system must be deeply coupled with the hardware architecture of the underlying flash memory. A NAND flash memory is usually a hierarchical structure organized into pages, blocks and planes.
A page groups a fixed number of memory cells. It is the smallest storage unit when performing read and programming operations. Each page includes a data area where actual data are stored and a spare area. The spare area is typically used for system level management, although there is no physical difference from the rest of the page. Pages already written with data must be erased prior to write new values. A typical page size can be 2KB plus 64B spare, but the actual trend is to increase the page size up to 4KB+128B and to exploit the MLC technology.
A block is a set of pages. It is the smallest unit when performing erase operations. Therefore, a page can be erased only if its corresponding block is totally erased. A block typically contains 64 pages, with a trend to increase this number to 128 pages per block, or even more. Since flash

memories wear out after a certain number of erasure cycles (endurance), if the erasure cycles of a block exceed this number, the block cannot be considered anymore reliable for storing data. A typical value for the endurance of an SLC flash memory is about 10^5 erasure cycles. Finally, blocks are grouped into planes. A flash memory with N planes can read/write and erase N pages/blocks at the same time (Cooke, 2007).

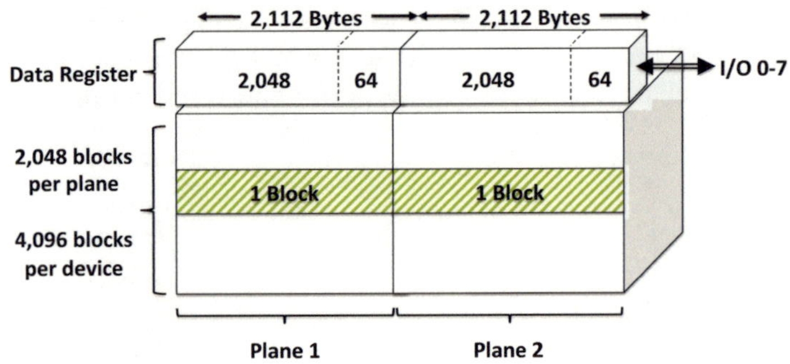

Fig. 3. A Dual Plane 2KB-Page SLC NAND Flash memory

Fig. 3 shows an example of a 512MB dual plane SLC NAND flash memory architecture proposed in (Cooke, 2007). Each plane can store 256MB with pages of 2KB+64B. A data register able to store a full page is provided for each plane, and an 8-bit data bus (i.e., I/O 0-7) is used to access stored information.

Several variations of this basic architecture can be produced, with main differences in performance, timing and available set of commands (Cooke, 2007). To allow interoperability among different producers, the Open NAND Flash Interface (ONFI) Workgroup is trying to provide an open specification (ONFI specification) to be used as a reference for future designs (ONFI, 2010).

2.3 Address translation and boot time

Each page of a flash is identified by both a logical and physical address. Logical addresses are provided to the user to identify a given data with a single address, regardless if the actual information is moved to different physical locations to optimize the use of the device. The *address translation* mechanism that maps logical addresses to the corresponding physical addresses must be efficient to generate a minor impact on the performance of the memory. The address translation information must be stored in the non-volatile memory to guarantee the integrity of the system. However, since frequent updates are performed, a translation lookup table is usually stored in a (battery-backed) RAM, while the flash memory stores the metadata to build this table. The size of the table is a trade-off between the high cost of the RAM and the performance of the storage system.

Memories with a large page size require less RAM, but they inefficiently handle small writes. In fact, since an entire page must be written into the flash with every flush, larger pages cause more unmodified data to be written for every (small) change. Small page sizes efficiently handles small writes, but the resulting RAM requirements can be unaffordable. At the file system level, the translation table can be implemented both at the level of pages or blocks thus allowing to trade-off between the table size and the granularity of the table.

2.4 Garbage collection

Data stored in a page of a flash memory cannot be overwritten unless an erasure of the full block is performed. To overcome this problem, when the content of a page must be updated, the new data are usually saved in a new free page. The new page is marked as *valid* while the old page is marked as *invalid*. The address translation table is then updated to allow the user to access the new data with the same logical address. This process introduces several challenges at the file system level.

At a certain point, free space is going to run out. When the amount of free blocks is less than a given threshold, invalidated pages must be erased in order to free some space. The only way to erase a page is to erase the whole block it belongs to. However, a block selected for erasure may contain both valid and invalid pages. As a consequence, the valid pages of the block must be copied into other free pages. The old pages can be then marked as invalid and the selected block can be erased and made available for storage.

This cleaning activity is referred to as *garbage collection*. Garbage collection decreases the flash memory performance and therefore represents a critical aspect of the design of a native flash file system. Moreover, as described in the next subsection, it may impact on the endurance of the device. The key objective of an efficient garbage collection strategy is to reduce garbage collection costs and evenly erase all blocks.

2.5 Memory wearing

As previously introduced, flash memories wear out after a certain number of erasure cycles (usually between 10^4 and 10^5 cycles). If the number of erasures of a block exceeds this number, the block is marked as a *bad block* since it cannot be considered anymore reliable for storing data. The overall life time of a flash memory therefore depends on the number of performed erasure cycles. *Wear leveling* techniques are used to distribute data evenly across each block of the entire flash memory, trying to level and to minimize the number of erasure cycles of each block.

There are two main wear leveling strategies: dynamic and static wear leveling. The *dynamic* wear leveling only works on those data blocks that are going to be written, while the *static* wear leveling works on all data blocks, including those that are not involved in a write operation. Active data blocks are in general wear-leveled dynamically, while static blocks (i.e., blocks where data are written and remain unchanged for long periods of time) are wear-leveled statically. The dynamic and static blocks are usually referred as *hot* and *cold* data, respectively. In MLC memories it is important to move cold data to optimize the wear leveling. If cold data are not moved then the related pages are seldom written and the wear is heavily skewed to other pages. Moreover, every read to a page has the potential to disturb data on other pages in the same block. Thus continuous read-only access to an area can cause corruption, and cold data should be periodically rewritten.

Wear leveling techniques must be strongly coupled with garbage collection algorithms at the file system level. In fact, the two tasks have in general conflicting objectives and the good trade-off must be found to guarantee both performance and endurance.

2.6 Bad block management

As discussed in the previous sections, when a block exceeds the maximum number of erasure cycles, it is marked as a *bad block*. Bad blocks can be detected also in new devices as a result of blocks identified as faulty during the end of production test.

Bad blocks must be detected and excluded from the active memory space. In general, simple techniques to handle bad blocks are commonly implemented. An example is provided by the Samsung's XSR (Flash Driver) and its Bad Block Management scheme (Samsung, 2007). The flash memory is initially split into a reserved and a user area. The reserved blocks in the reserved area represent a *Reserve Block Pool* that can be used to replace bad blocks. Samsung's XSR basically remaps a bad block to one of the reserved blocks so that the data contained in a bad block is not lost and the bad block is not longer used.

2.7 Error correcting codes

Fault tolerance mechanisms and in particular Error Correcting Codes (ECCs) are systematically applied to NAND flash devices to improve their level of reliability. ECCs are cost-efficient and allow detecting or even correcting a certain number of errors.

ECCs have to be fast and efficient at the same time. Several ECC schema have been proposed based on linear codes like Hamming codes or Reed-Solomon codes (Chen et al., 2008; Micron, 2007). Among the possible solutions, Bose-Chaudhuri-Hocquenghem (BCH) codes are linear codes widely adopted with flash memories (Choi et al., 2010; Junho & Wonyong, 2009; Micheloni et al., 2008). They are less complex than other ECC, providing also a higher code efficiency. Moreover, manufacturers' and independent studies (Deal, 2009; Duann, 2009; Yaakobi et al., 2009) have shown that flash memories tend to manifest non-correlated bit errors. BCH are particularly efficient when errors are randomly distributed, thus representing a suitable solution for flash memories.

The choice of the characteristics of the ECC is a trade-off between reliability requirements and code complexity, and strongly depends on the target application (e.g. consumer electronics vs mission-critical applications) (Caramia et al., 2009b).

ECC can be implemented both at the software-level, or resorting to hardware facilities. Software implemented ECC allow to decouple the error correction mechanisms from the specific hardware device. However, the price to pay for a software-based ECC solution is a drastic performance reduction. For this reason, available file systems tend to delegate the code computation tasks to a dedicate hardware limiting the amount of operations performed in software, at the cost of additional resources (e.g., hardware, power consumption, etc.) and reduced flexibility.

3. File systems for flash memories

As shortly described in the introduction of this chapter, at the OS level the common alternatives to manage flash based mass-storage devices are block-device emulation and native flash file systems (Chang & Kuo, 2004). Both approaches try to address the issues discussed in Section 2. Fig. 4 shows how the two solutions can be mapped in a generic OS.

The block-device emulation approach hides the presence of a flash memory device, by emulating the behavior of a traditional magnetic hard-disk. The flash device is seen as a contiguous array of storage blocks. This emulation mechanism is achieved by inserting at the OS level a new layer, referred to as *Flash Translation Layer* (FTL). Different implementations of FTL have been proposed (Chang et al., 2007; Intel, 1998; Jen-Wei et al., 2008). The advantage of using an FTL is that existing file systems, such as NTFS, Ext2 and FAT, usually supported by the majority of modern OS, can be directly used to store information in the flash. However, this approach has many performance restrictions. In fact, existing file systems do not take into account the critical issues imposed by the flash technology (see Section 2) and in several situations they may behave in contrast with these constraints. Very sophisticated FTL must

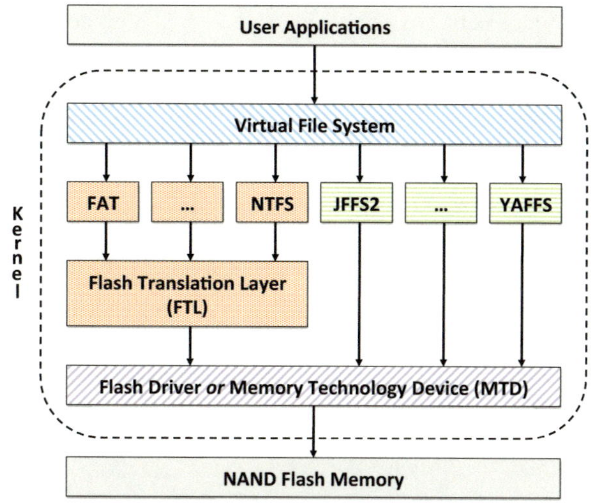

Fig. 4. Flash Translation Layer and Flash File Systems

be therefore designed with heavy consequences on the performance of the system. Moreover, the typical block size managed by traditional file systems usually does not match the block size of a flash memory. This imposes the implementation of complex mechanisms to properly manage write operations (Gal & Toledo, 2005).

The alternative solution, to overcome the limitation of using an FTL, is to expose the hardware characteristics of the flash memory to the file system layer, demanding to this module the full management of the device. These new file systems, specifically designed to work with flash memories, are usually referred to as Flash File Systems (FFS). This approach allows the file system to fully exploit the potentiality of a flash memory guaranteeing increased performance, reliability and endurance of the device. In other words, if efficiency is more important than compatibility, FFS is the best option to choose.

The way FFS manage the information is somehow derived from the model of *journaled* file systems. In a journaled file system, each metadata modification is written into a journal (i.e., a log) before the actual block of data is modified. This in general helps recovering information in case of crash. In particular log-structured file systems (Aleph One Ltd., 2011; Rosenblum & Ousterhout, 1992; Woodhouse, 2001) take the journaling approach to the limit since the journal *is* the file system. The disk is organized as a log consisting of fixed-sized segments of contiguous areas of the disk, chained together to form a linked list. Data and metadata are always written to the end of the log, never overwriting old data. Although this organization has been in general avoided for traditional magnetic disks, it perfectly fits the way information can be saved into a flash memory since data cannot be overwritten in these devices, and write operations must be performed on new pages. Furthermore, log-structuring the file system on a flash does not influence the read performance as in traditional disks, since the access time on a flash is constant and does not depend on the position where the information is stored (Gal & Toledo, 2005).

FFS are nowadays mainly used whenever so called Memory Technology Devices (MTD) are available in the system, i.e., embedded flash memories that do not have a dedicated hardware controller. Removable flash memory cards and USB flash drives are in general provided with a

built-in controller that in fact behaves as an FTL and allows high compatibility and portability of the device. FFS have therefore limited benefits on these devices.
Several FFS are available. A possible approach to perform a taxonomy of the available FFS is to split them into three categories: (i) experimental FFS documented in scientific and technical publications, (ii) open source projects and (iii) proprietary products.

3.1 Flash file systems in the technical and scientific literature

Several publications proposed interesting solutions for implementing new FFS (Kawaguchi et al., 1995; Lee et al., 2009; Seung-Ho & Kyu-Ho, 2006; Wu & Zwaenepoel, 1994). In general each of these solutions aims at optimizing a subset of the issues proposed in Section 2.
Although these publications in general concentrate on algorithmic aspects, and provide reduced information about the real implementation, they represent a good starting point to understand how specific problems can be solved in the implementation of a new FFS.

3.1.1 eNVy

Fig. 5 describes the architecture of a system based on eNVy, a large non-volatile main memory storage system built to work with flash memories (Wu & Zwaenepoel, 1994).

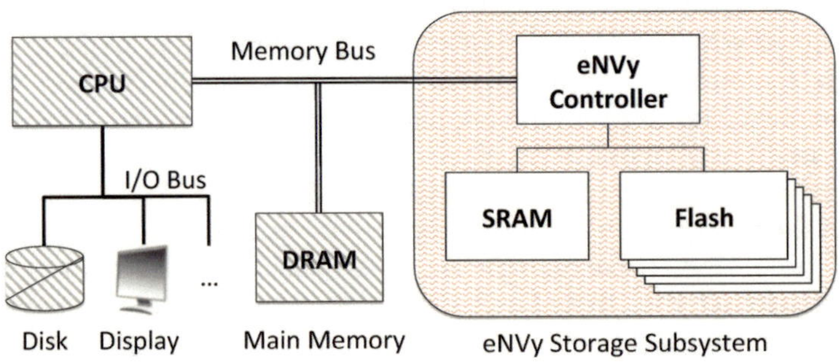

Fig. 5. Architecture of eNVy

The main goal of eNVy is to present the flash memory to a host computer as a simple linear array of non-volatile memory. The additional goal is to guarantee an access time to the memory array as close as possible to those of an SRAM (about 100us) (Gal & Toledo, 2005). The reader may refer to (Wu, 1994) for a complete description of the eNVy FFS.

Technology

eNVy adopts an SLC NAND flash memory with page size of 256B.

Architecture

The eNVy architecture combines an SLC NAND flash memory with a small and fast battery-backed static RAM. This small SRAM is used as a very fast write buffer required to implement an efficient copy-on-write strategy.

Address translation

The physical address space is partitioned into pages of 256B that are mapped to the pages of the flash. A page table stored in the SRAM maintains the mapping between the linear logical address space presented to the host and the physical address space of the flash. When performing a write operation, the target flash page is copied into the SRAM (if not already loaded), the page table is updated and the actual write request is performed into this fast memory. As long as the page is mapped into the SRAM, further read and write requests are performed directly using this buffer. The SRAM is managed as a FIFO, new pages are inserted at the end, while pages are flushed from the tail when their number exceeds a certain threshold (Gal & Toledo, 2005).

Garbage collection

When the SRAM write buffer is full, eNVy attempts to flush pages from the SRAM to the flash. This in turn requires to allocate a set of free pages in the flash. If there is no free space, the eNVy controller starts a garbage collection process called cleaning in the eNVy terminology (see Fig. 6).

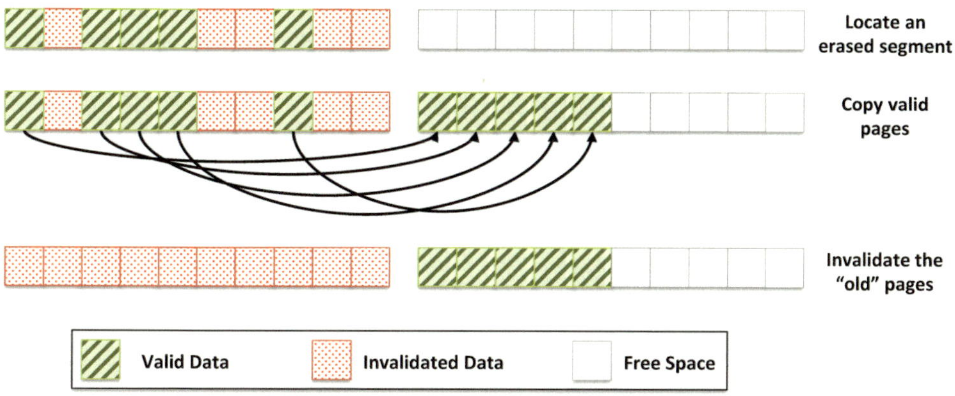

Fig. 6. Steps of the eNVy cleaning process

When eNVy cleans a block (segment in the eNVy terminology), all of its live data (i.e., valid pages) are copied into an empty block. The original block is then erased and reused. The new block will contain a cluster of valid pages at its head, while the remaining space will be ready to accept new pages. A clean (i.e., completely erased) block must be always available for the next cleaning operation.

The policy for deciding which block to clean is an hybrid between a *greedy* and a *locality gathering* method. Both methods are based on the concept of "flash cleaning cost", defined as $\frac{\mu}{1-\mu}$ where μ is the utilization of the block. Since after about 80% utilization the cleaning cost reaches unreasonable levels, μ in can not exceed this threshold.

The *greedy* method cleans the block with the majority of invalidated pages in order to maximize the recovered space. This method lowers cleaning costs for uniform distributions (i.e., it tends to clean blocks in a FIFO order), but performance suffers as the locality of references increases.

The *locality gathering* algorithm attempts to take advantage from high locality of references. Since hot blocks are cleaned more often than cold blocks, their cleaning cost can be lowered by redistributing data among blocks. However, for uniform access distributions, this technique prevents cleaning performance from being improved. In fact, if all data are accessed with the same frequency, the data distribution procedure allocates the same amount of data to each segment. Since pages are flushed back to their original segments to preserve locality, all blocks always stay at $\mu = 80\%$ utilization, leading to a fixed cleaning cost of 4.

eNVy adopts an hybrid approach, which combines the good performance of the FIFO algorithm for uniform access distributions and the good results of the locality gathering algorithm for higher locality of references.
The high performance of the system is guaranteed by adopting a wide bus between the flash and the internal RAM, and by temporarily buffering accessed flash pages. The wide bus allows pages stored in the flash to be transferred to the RAM in one cycle, while buffering pages in RAM allows to perform several updates to a single page with a single RAM-to-flash page transfer. Reducing the number of flash writes reduces the number of unit erasures, thereby improving performance and extending the lifetime of the device (Gal & Toledo, 2005). However, using a wide bus has a significant drawback. To build a wide bus, several flash chips are used in parallel (Wu & Zwaenepoel, 1994). This increases the effective size of each erase unit. Large erase units are harder to manage and, as a result, they are prone to accelerated wear (Gal & Toledo, 2005). Finally, although (Wu & Zwaenepoel, 1994) states that a cleaning algorithm is designed to evenly wear the memory and to extend its lifetime, the work does not present any explicit wear leveling algorithm. The bad block management and the ECC strategies are missing as well.

3.1.2 Core flash file system (CFFS)

(Seung-Ho & Kyu-Ho, 2006) proposes the Core Flash File System (CFFS) for NAND flash-based devices. CFFS is specifically designed to improve the booting time and to reduce the garbage collection overhead.
The reader may refer to (Seung-Ho & Kyu-Ho, 2006) for a complete description of CFFS. While concentrating on boot time and garbage collection optimizations, the work neither presents any explicit bad block management nor any error correction code strategy.

Address translation

CFFS is a log-structured file system. Information items about each file (e.g., file name, file size, timestamps, file modes, index of pages where data are allocated, etc.) are saved into a spacial data structure called inode. Two solutions can be in general adopted to store inodes in the flash: (i) storing several inodes per page, thus optimizing the available space, or (ii) storing a single inode per page. CFFS adopts the second solution. Storing a single inode per page introduces a certain overhead in terms of flash occupation, but, at the same time, it guarantees enough space to store the index of pages composing a file, thus reducing the flash scan time at the boot.
CFFS classifies inodes in two classes as reported in Fig. 7. *i-class1* maintains direct indexing for all index entries except the final one, while *i-class2* maintains indirect indexing for all index entries except the final one. The final index entry is indirectly indexed for i-class1 and double indirectly indexed for i-class2. This classification impacts the file size range allowed by the file system. Let us assume to have 256B of metadata for each inode and a flash page size of 512B. The inode will therefore contain 256B available to store index pointers. A four-byte pointer is sufficient to point to an individual flash page. As a consequence, $256/4 = 64$ pointers fit the page. This leads to:

- ***i-class1***: 63 pages are directly indexed and 1 page is indirectly indexed, which in turn can directly index $512/4 = 128$ pages; as a consequence the maximum allowed file size is $(63 + 128) \times 512B = 96KB$
- ***i-class2***: 63 pages are indirectly indexed, each of which can directly index $512/4 = 128$ pages, thus they can address an overall amount of $63 \times 128 = 8064$ pages. 1 page is

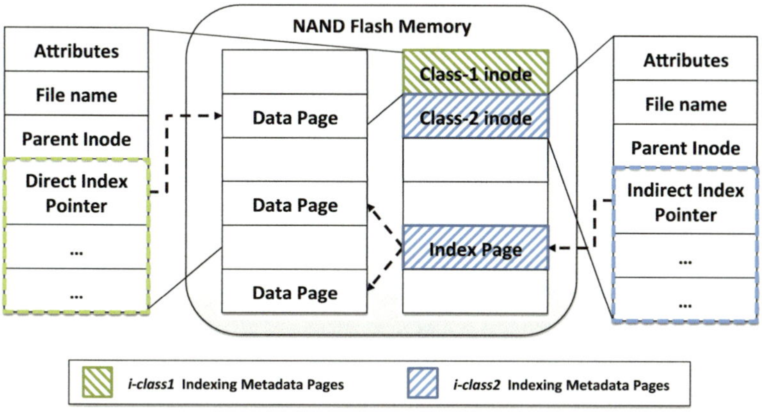

Fig. 7. An example of direct (*i-class1*) and indirect (*i-class2*) indexing for a NAND flash

double indirectly indexed, which in turn can indirectly index up to $(512/4)^2 = 16384$ pages. Therefore, the maximum allowed file size is $(8064 + 16384) \times 512B = 12MB$

If the flash page is $2KB$, the maximum file size is $1916KB$ for i-class1 and $960MB$ for i-class2. The reason CFFS classifies inodes into two types is the relationship between the file size and the file usage patterns. In fact, most files are small and most write accesses are to small files. However, most storage is also consumed by large files that are usually only accessed for reading (Seung-Ho & Kyu-Ho, 2006). The *i-class1* requires one additional page consumption for the inode[1], but can address only pretty small files. Each writing into an indirect indexing entry of *i-class2* causes the consumption of two additional pages, but it is able to address bigger files.
When a file is created in CFFS, the file is first set to *i-class1* and it is maintained in this state until all index entries are allocated. As the file size grows, the inode class is altered from *i-class1* to *i-class2*. As a consequence, most files are included in *i-class1* and most write accesses are concentrated in *i-class1*. In addition, most read operations involve large files, thus inode updates are rarely performed and the overhead for indirect indexing in *i-class2* files is not significant.

Boot time

An *InodeMapBlock* stores the list of pages containing the inodes in the first flash memory block. In case of clean unmounting of the file system (i.e., unmount flag *UF* not set) the *InodeMapBlock* contains valid data that are used to build an *InodeBlockHash* structure in RAM used to manage the inodes until the file system is unmounted. When the file system is unmounted, the *InodeBlockHash* is written back into the *InodeMapBlock*. In case of unclean unmounting (i.e., unmount flag *UF* set), the *InodeMapBlock* does not contain valid data. A full scan of the memory is therefore required to find the list of pages storing the inodes.

Garbage collection

The garbage collection approach of CFFS is based on a sort of hot-cold policy. Hot data have high probability of being updated in the near future, therefore, pages storing hot data have

[1] in general, the number of additional flash pages consumed due to updating the inode index information is proportional to the degree of the indexing level

higher chance to be invalidated than those storing cold data. Metadata (i.e., inodes) are hotter than normal data. Each write operation on a file surely results in an update of its inode, but other operations may result in changing the inode, as well (e.g., renaming, etc.). Since CFFS allocates different flash blocks for metadata and data without mixing them in a single block, a pseudo-hot-cold separation already exists. Hot inode pages are therefore stored in the same block in order to minimize the amount of hot-live pages to copy, and the same happens for data blocks.

Wear leveling

The separation between inode and data blocks leads to an implicit hot-cold separation which is efficiently exploited by the garbage collection process. However, since the inode blocks are hotter and are updated more frequently, they probably may suffer much more erasures than the data blocks. This can unevenly wear out the memory, thus shortening the life-time of the device. To avoid this problem, a possible wear-leveling strategy is to set a sort of "swapping flag". When a data block must be erased, the flag informs the allocator that the next time the block is allocated it must be used to store an inode, and vice versa.

3.1.3 FlexFS

FlexFS is a flexible FFS for MLC NAND flash memories. It takes advantage from specific facilities offered by MLC flash memories. FlexFS is based on the JFFS2 file system (Woodhouse, 2001; 2009), a file system originally designed to work with NOR flash memories. The reader may refer to (Lee et al., 2009) for a detailed discussion on the FlexFS file system. However, the work does not tackle neither bad block management, not error correction codes.

Technology

In most MLC flash memories, each cell can be programmed at runtime to work either as an SLC or an MLC cell (*flexible cell programming*). Fig. 8 shows an example for an MLC flash storing 2 bits per cell.

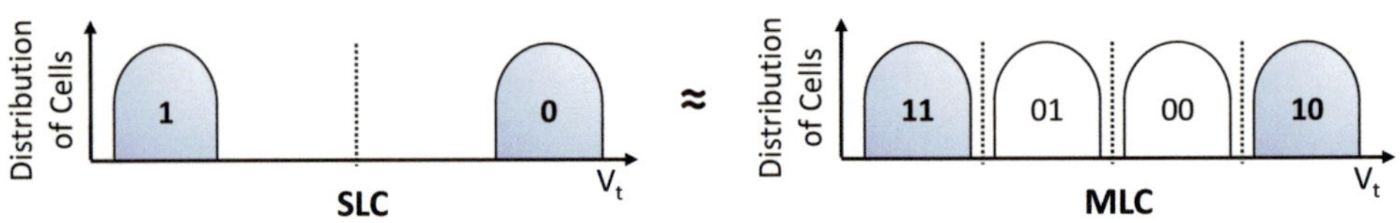

Fig. 8. Flexible Cell Programming

When programmed in MLC mode, the cell uses all available configurations to store data (2 bits per cell). This configuration provides high capacity but suffers from the reduced performance intrinsic to the MLC technology (see Fig. 2). When programmed in SLC mode, only two out of the four configurations are in fact used. The information is stored either in the LSB or in the MSB of the cell. This specific configuration allows information to be stored in a more robust way, as typical in SLC memories, and, therefore, it allows to push the memory at higher performance. The flexible programming therefore allows to choose between the high performance of SLC memories and the high capacity of MLC memories.

Data allocation

FlexFS splits the MLC flash memory into SLC and MLC regions and dynamically changes the size of each region to meet the changing requirements of applications. It handles heterogeneous cells in a way that is transparent to the application layer. Fig. 9 shows the layout of a flash memory block in FlexFS.

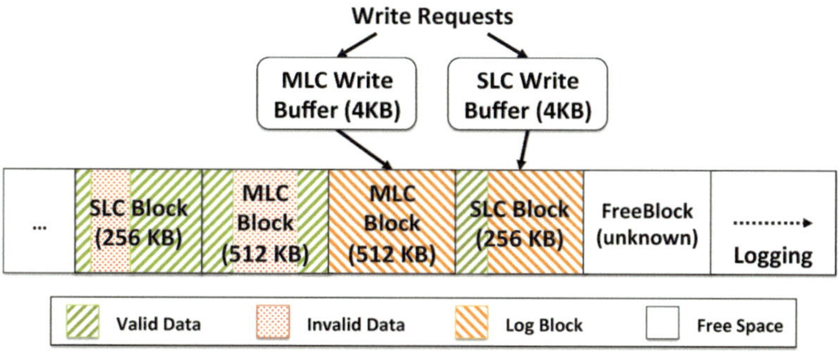

Fig. 9. The layout of flash blocks in FlexFS

There are three types of flash memory blocks: SLC blocks, MLC blocks and free blocks. FlexFS manages them as an SLC region, an MLC region and one free blocks pool. A free block does not contain any data. Its type is decided at the allocation time.
FlexFS allocates data similarly to other log-structured file systems, with the exception of two log blocks reserved for writing. When data are evicted from the write buffer, FlexFS writes them sequentially from the first page to the last page of the corresponding region's log block. When the free pages in the log block run out, a new log block is allocated.
The baseline approach for allocating data can be to write as much data as possible into SLC blocks to maximize I/O performances. In case there are no SLC blocks available, a data migration from the SLC to the MLC region is triggered to create more free space. Fig. 10 shows an example of data migration.

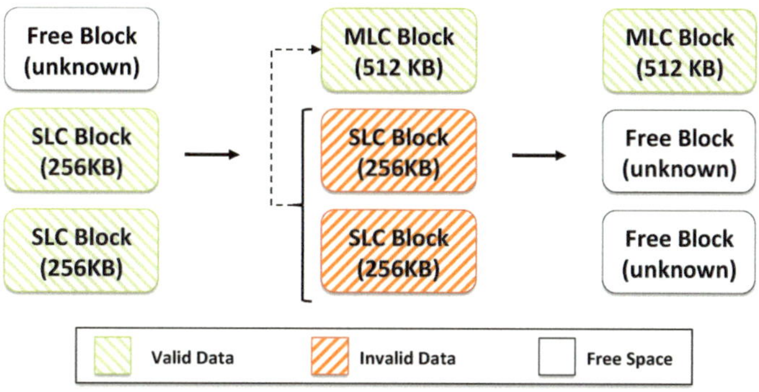

Fig. 10. An example of Data Migration

Assuming to have two SLC blocks with valid data, the data migration process converts the free block into an MLC block and then copies the 128 pages of the two SLC blocks into this MLC block. Finally, the two SLC blocks are erased, freeing this space.
This simple approach has two main drawbacks. First of all, if the amount of data stored in the flash approaches to half of its maximum capacity, the migration penalty becomes very high and reduces I/O performance. Second, since the flash has limited erasure cycles, the number of erasures due to data migration have to be controlled to meet a given lifetime requirement. Proper techniques are therefore required to address these two problems.

Three key techniques are adopted to leverage the overhead associated with data migrations: *background migration*, *dynamic allocation* and *locality-aware data management*.

The *background migration* technique exploits the idle time of the system (T_{idle}) to hide the data migration overhead. During T_{idle} the background migrator moves data from the SLC region to the MLC region, thus freeing many blocks that would be compulsory erased later. The first drawback of this technique is that, if an I/O request arrives during a background migration, it will be delayed of a certain time T_{delay} that must be minimized by either monitoring the I/O subsystem or suspending the background migration in case of an I/O request. This problem can be partially mitigated by reducing the amount of idle time devoted to background migration, and by triggering the migration at given intervals (T_{wait}) in order to reduce the probability of an I/O request during the migration.

The background migration is suitable for systems with enough idle time (e.g., mobile phones). With systems with less idle time, the *dynamic allocation* is adopted. This method dynamically redirects part of the incoming data directly to the MLC region depending on the idleness of the system. Although this approach reduces the performance, it also reduces the amount of data written in the SLC region, which in turn reduces the data migration overhead. The dynamic allocator determines the amount of data to write in the SLC region. This parameter depends on the idle time, which dynamically changes, and, therefore, must be carefully forecast. The time is divided into several windows. Each window represents the period during which N_p pages are written into the flash. FlexFS evaluates the predicted T_{idle}^{pred} as a weighted average of the idle times of the last 10 windows. Then, an allocation ratio α is calculated in function of T_{idle}^{pred} as $\alpha = T_{idle}^{pred}/(N_p{\cdot}T_{copy})$, where T_{copy} is the time required to copy a single page from SLC to MLC. If $T_{idle}^{pred} \geqslant N_p \cdot T_{copy}$, there is enough idle time for data migration, thus $\alpha = 1$. Fig. 11 shows an example of dynamic allocation. The dynamic allocator distributes the incoming data across the MLC and SLC regions depending on α. In this case, according to the previous $N_p = 10$ windows and to T_{idle}^{pred}, $\alpha = 0.6$. Therefore, for the next $N_p = 10$ pages 40%, of the incoming data will be written in the MLC, and 60% in the SLC region, respectivelly. After writing all 10 pages, the dynamic allocator calculates a new value of α for the next N_p pages.

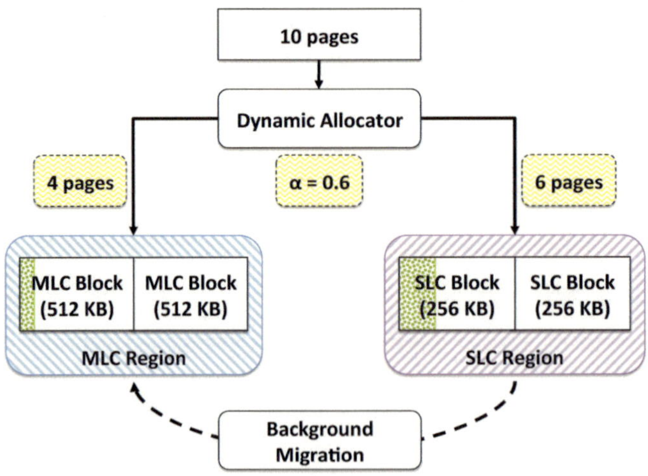

Fig. 11. An example of Dynamic Allocation

The *locality-aware data management* exploits the locality of I/O accesses to improve the efficiency of data migration. Since hot data have a higher update rate compared to cold data, they will be invalidated frequently, potentially causing several unnecessary page migrations. In the case of a locality-unaware approach, pages are migrated from SLC to MLC based on the available idle time T_{idle}. If hot data are allowed to migrate before cold data during T_{idle}, the new copy of the data in the MLC region will be invalidated in a short time. Therefore, a new copy of this information will be written in the SLC region. This results in unnecessary migrations, reduction of the SLC region and a consequent decrease of α to avoid a congestion of the SLC region.
If locality of data is considered, the efficiency of data migration can be increases. When performing data migration cold data have the priority. Hot data have a high temporal locality, thus data migration for them is not required. Moreover, the value of α can be adjusted as $\alpha = T_{idle}^{pred} / [(N_p - N_p^{hot}) \cdot T_{copy}]$ where N_p^{hot} is the number of page writes for hot pages stored in the SLC region.
In order to detect hot data, FlexFS adopts a two queues-based locality detection technique. An hot and a cold queue maintain the inodes of frequently and infrequently modified files. In order to understand which block to migrate from MLC to SLC, FlexFS calculates the average hotness of each block and chooses the block whose hotness is lower than the average. Similar to the approach of idle time prediction, N_p^{hot} counts how many hot pages were written into the SLC region during the previous 10 windows. Their average hotness value will be the N_p^{hot} for the next time window.

Garbage collection

There is no need for garbage collection into the SLC region. In fact, cold data in SLC will be moved by the data migrator to the MLC region and hot data are not moved for high locality. However, the data migrator cannot reclaim the space used by invalid pages in the MLC region. This is the job of the garbage collector. It chooses a victim block V in the MLC region with as many invalidated pages as possible. Then, it copies all the valid pages of V into a different MLC block. Finally, it erases the block V, which becomes part of the free block pool. The garbage collector also exploits idle times to hide the overhead of the cleaning from the users, however only limited information on this mechanism is provided in (Lee et al., 2009).

Wear leveling

The use of FlexFS implies that each block undergoes more erasure cycles because of data migration. To improve the endurance and to prolong the lifetime, it would be better to write data to the MLC region directly, but this would reduce the overall performance. To address this trade-off, FlexFS adopts a novel wear-leveling approach to control the amount of data to write to the SLC region depending on a given storage lifetime. In particular, L_{min} is the minimum guaranteed lifetime that must be ensured by the file system. It can be expressed as $L_{min} \approx C_{total} \cdot E_{cycles} / WR$, where C_{total} is the size of the flash memory, and E_{cycles} is the number of erasure cycles allowed for each block. The writing rate WR is the amount of data written in the unit of time (e.g., per day). FlexFS controls the wearing rate so that the total erase count is close to the *maximum number of erase cycles* N_{erase} at a given L_{min}.
The wearing rate is directly proportional to the value of α. In fact, if $\alpha = 1.0$ then only SLC blocks are written, thus if 2 SLC blocks are involved, data migration will involve 1 MLC block, using 3 overall blocks (see Fig. 10). If $\alpha = 0$, then only MLC blocks are written, no data migration occurs and only 1 block is exploited. Fig. 12 shows an example of wearing rate control.

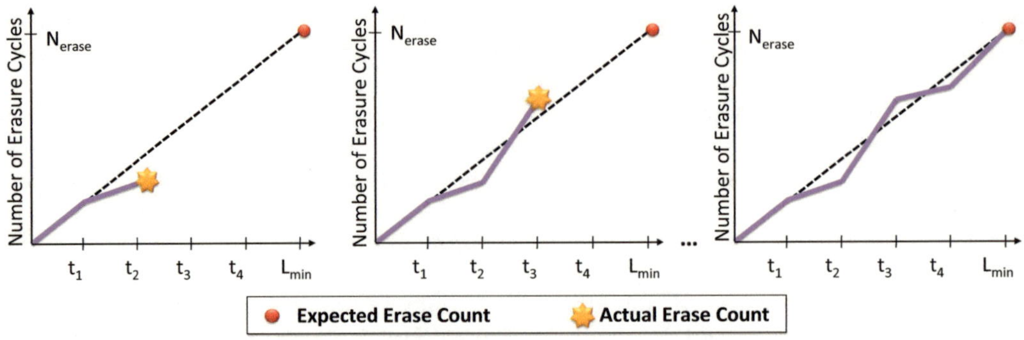

Fig. 12. An example of Wearing Rate Control

At first, the actual erase count of Fig. 12 is lower than the expected one, thus the value of α must be increased. After some time, the actual erase count is higher than expected, thus α is decreased. At the end, the actual erase count becomes again smaller than the expected erase count, thus another increase of the value of α is required.

3.2 Open source flash file systems

Open source file systems are widely used in multiple applications using a variety of flash memory devices and are in general provided with a full and detailed documentation. The large open source community of developers ensures that any issue is quickly resolved and the quality of the file system is therefore high. Furthermore, their code is fully available for consulting, modifications, and practical implementations. Nowadays, YAFFS represents the most promising open-source project for the the development of an open FFS. For this reason we will concentrate on this specific file system.

3.2.1 Yet Another Flash File System (YAFFS)

YAFFS (Aleph One Ltd., 2011) is a robust log-structured file system specifically designed for NAND flash memories, focusing on data integrity and performance. It is licensed both under the General Public License (GPL) and under per-product licenses available from Aleph One. There are two versions of YAFFS: YAFFS1 and YAFFS2. The two versions of the file system are very similar, they share part of the code and provide support for backward compatibility from YAFFS2 to YAFFS1. The main difference between the two file systems is that YAFFS2 is designed to deal with the characteristics of modern NAND flash devices. In the sequel, without losing of generality, we will address the most recent YAFFS2, unless differently specified. We will try to introduce YAFFS's most important concepts. We strongly suggest the interested readers to consult the related documentation documentation (Aleph One Ltd., 2010; 2011; Manning, 2010) and above all the code implementation, which is the most valuable way to thoroughly understand this native flash file system.

Portability

Since YAFFS has to work in multiple environments, *portability* is a key requirement. YAFFS has been successfully ported under Linux, WinCE, pSOS, eCos, ThreadX, and various special-purpose OS. Portability is achieved by the absence of OS or compiler-specific features in the main code and by the proper use of abstract types and functions to allow Unicode or ASCII operations.

Technology

Both YAFFS1 and YAFFS2 are designed to work with NAND flash memories. YAFFS1 was designed for devices with page size of 512B plus 16B of spare information. YAFFS1 exploited the possibility of performing multiple write cycles per page available in old generations of NAND flash devices. YAFFS2 is the successor of YAFFS1 designed to work with the contemporary generation of NAND flash chips designed with pages equal or greater than 2KB + 64B. For sake of reliability, new devices do not allow page overwriting and pages of a block must be written sequentially.

Architecture and data allocation

YAFFS is designed with a modular architecture to provide flexibility for testing and development. YAFFS modules include both kernel and user space code, as summarized in Fig. 13.

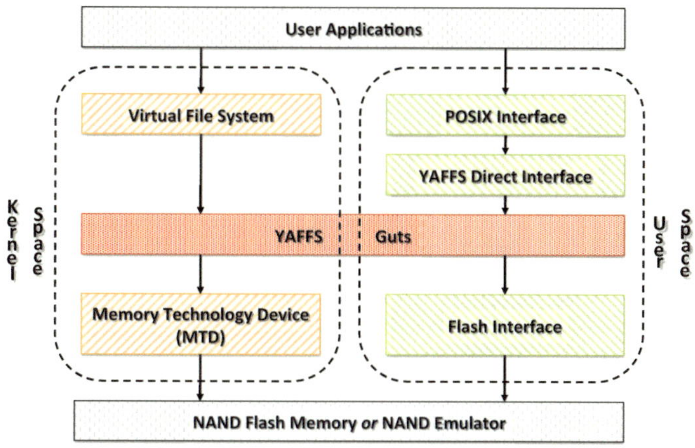

Fig. 13. The YAFFS Architecture

Since developing and debugging code in user space is easier than working in kernel mode, the core of the file system, namely the *guts* algorithms, is implemented as user code. This code is also shared with the kernel of the OS. If a full interface at the OS level is required (e.g., implementation of specific system calls), it must be implemented inside the Virtual File System (VFS) layer. Otherwise, YAFFS can be used at the application level. In this configuration, information can be accessed through the YAFFS Direct Interface. This is the typical case for applications without OS, embedded OS or bootloaders (Aleph One Ltd., 2010).
YAFFS also includes an emulation layer that provides an excellent way to debug the file system even when no flash devices are available (Manning, 2010).
File systems are usually designed to store information organized into files. YAFFS is instead designed to store *Objects*. An object is anything a file system can store: regular data files, directories, hard/symbolic links, and special objects. Each object is identified by a unique *objectId*. Although the NAND flash is arranged in pages, the allocation unit for YAFFS is the *chunk*. Typically, a chunk is mapped to a single page, but there is flexibility to use chunks that span over multiple pages[2]. Each chunk is identified by its related *objectId* and by a *ChunkId*: a progressive number identifying the position of the chunk in the object.

[2] in the sequel, the terms page and chunk will be considered as synonymous unless stated otherwise

YAFFS writes data in the form of a sequential log. Each entry of the log corresponds to a single chunk. Chunks are of two types: *Object Headers* and *Data Chunks*. An Object Header is a descriptor of an object storing metadata information including: the *Object Type* (i.e., whether the object is a file, a directory, etc.) and the *File Size* in case of an object corresponding to a file. Object headers are always identified by $ChunkId = 0$. Data chunks are instead used to old the actual data composing a file.

Fig. 14 shows a simple example of how YAFFS behaves considering two blocks each composed of four chunks.

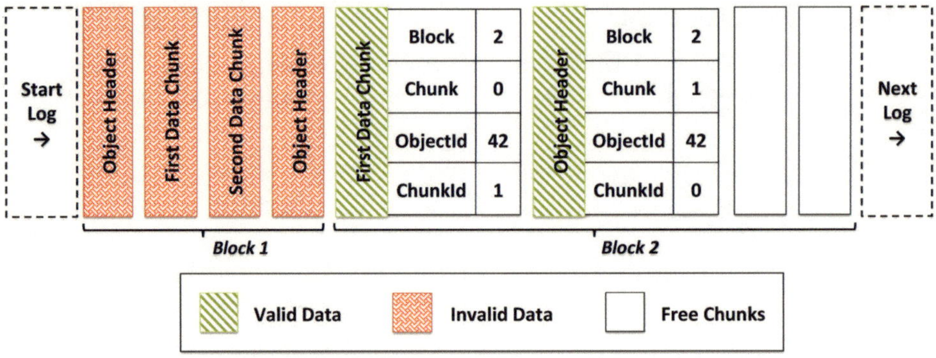

Fig. 14. An Example of YAFFS Operations

The situation depicted in Fig. 14 shows the data allocation for a file with ObjectId 42 that was first created allocating two data chunks, and then modified deleting the second data chunk and updating the first chunk. The chunks corresponding to the initial creation of the file are those saved in Block 1. When a new file is created, YAFFS first allocates an Object Header (Chunk 1 of Block 1). It then writes the required data chunks (Chunks 2 and 3 of Block 1), and, finally, when the file is closed, it invalidates the first header and allocates an new updated header (Chunk 4 of Block 1). When the file is updated, according to the requested modifications, Chunk 3 of Block 1 is invalidated and therefore deleted, while Chunk 2 of Block 1 is invalidated and the updated copy is written in Chunk 2 of Block 2 (the first available Chunk). Finally, the object header is invalidated (Chunk 4 of Block 1) and the updated copy is written in Chunk 2 of Block 2.

At the end of this process, all chunks of Block 1 are invalidated while Block 2 still has two free chunks that will be used for the next allocations. As will be described later in this section, to improve performance YAFFS stores control information including the validity of each chunk in RAM. In case of power failure, it must therefore be able to recover the set of valid chunks where data are allocated. This is achieved by the use of a global *sequence number*. As each block is allocated, YAFFS increases the *sequence number* and uses this counter to mark each chunk of the block. This allows to organize the log in a chronological order. Thanks to the sequence number, YAFFS is able to determine the sequence of events and to restore the file system state at boot time.

Address translation

The data allocation scheme proposed in Fig. 14 requires several data structures to properly manage information. To increase performance, YAFFS does not store this information in the flash, but it provides several data structures stored in RAM. The most important structures are:

- *Device partition*: it holds information related to a YAFFS partition or mount point, providing support for multiple partitions. It is fundamental for all the other data structures which are usually part of, or accessed via this structure.
- *Block info*: each device has an array of block information holding the current state of the NAND blocks.
- *Object*: each object (i.e., regular file, directory, etc.) stored in the flash has its related object structure in RAM which holds the state of the object.
- *File structure*: an object related to a data file stores a tree of special nodes called *Tnodes*, providing a mechanism to find the actual data chunks composing the file.

Among all the other information, each file object stores the depth and the pointer to the top of Tnode tree. The Tnode tree is made up of Tnodes arranged in levels. At *Level 0* a Tnode holds 2^4=16 NAND *ChunkId* which identify the location of the chunks in the NAND flash. At levels greater than 0, a Tnode holds 2^3=8 pointers to other Tnodes in the following level. Powers-of-two make look-ups simpler by just applying bitmasks (Manning, 2010).

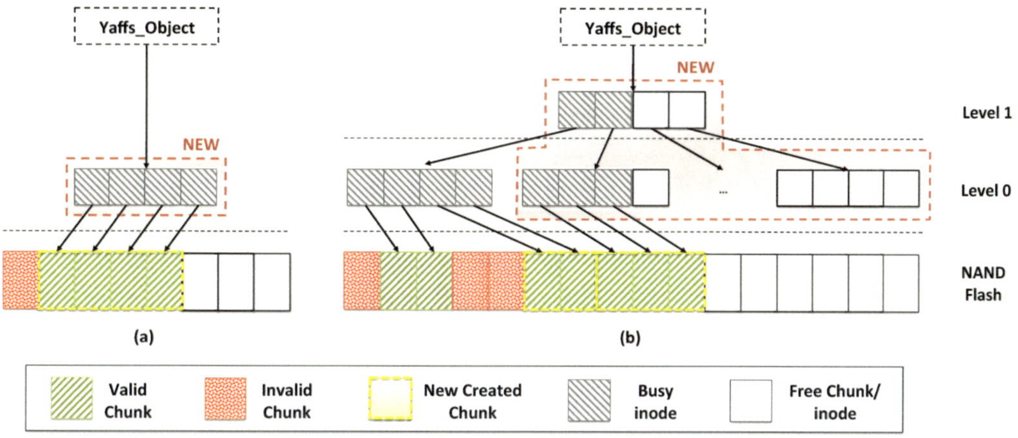

Fig. 15. An example of Tnode tree for data file

Fig. 15 shows an example of Tnode for a file object. For the sake of simplicity, only 4 entries are shown for each Tnode. Fig. 15(a) shows the creation of an object composed of 4 chunks, thus only one Level-0 Tnode is requested. In Fig. 15(b) the object's size starts to grow up, thus a Level-1 Tnode is added. This Level-1 Tnode can point to other Level-0 Tnodes which in turn will point to the physical NAND chunks. In particular, Fig. 15(b) shows how two of the previous chunks can be rewritten and three new chunks can be added. When the object's size will become greater than the 16 chunks of Fig. 15(b), then a Level-2 Tnode will be allocated and so on.

For sake of brevity, we will not address the structures used to manage directories, hard/symbolic links and other objects. Interested readers can refer to (Manning, 2010) for a detailed discussion.

Boot time

The mounting process of a YAFFS partition requires to scan the entire flash. Scanning is the process in which the state of the file system is rebuilt from scratch. It reads the metadata (tags) associated with all the active chunks and may take a considerable amount of time.

During the mounting process, YAFFS2 adopts the so called *backwards* scanning to identify the most current chunks. This process exploits the sequence numbers introduced in the previous paragraphs. First, a pre-scan of the blocks is required to determine their sequence number. Second, they are sorted to make a chronologically ordered list. Finally, a *backwards* scanning (i.e., from the highest to the lowest sequence number) of the blocks is performed. The first occurrence of any pair *ObjectId:ChunkId* is the most current one, while all following matchings are obsolete and thus treated as deleted.
YAFFS provides several optimizations to improve boot performance. YAFFS2 supports the *checkpointing* which bypasses normal mount scanning, allowing very fast mount times. Mount times are variable, but 3 sec for 2 GB have been reported. Checkpoint is a mechanism to speed up the mounting process by taking a snapshot of the YAFFS runtime state at unmount and then rebuilding the runtime state on re-mounting. Using this approach, only the structure of the file system (i.e., directory relationships, Tnode trees, etc.) must be created at boot, while much of the details such as filename, permissions, etc. can be lazy-loaded on demand. This will happen when the object is looked up (e.g., by a file open or searching for a file in the directory). However, if the checkpoint is not valid, it is ignored and the state is scanned again. Scanning needs extra information (i.e., parent directory, object type, etc.) to be stored in the tags of the object headers in order to reduce the amount of read operations during the scan. YAFFS2 extends the tags in the object headers with extra fields to improve the mount scanning performance. A way to store them without enlarging the tags size is to exploit the "useless" fields of the object headers (i.e., *chunkId* and *nbytes*) to cleverly pack the most important data. These physical information items are called *packed tags*.

Garbage collection

YAFFS actually calls the garbage collector before writing each chunk of data to the flash memory. It adopts a pretty simple garbage collection strategy. First of all, it checks how many erased blocks are available. In case there are *several* erased blocks, there is no need for a strong intervention. A *passive* garbage collection can be performed on blocks with very few chunks in use. In case of *very few* erased blocks, a harder work is required to recover space. The garbage collector identifies the set of blocks with more chunks in use, performing an ***aggressive*** garbage collection.
The rationale behind this strategy is to delay garbage collection whenever possible, in order to spread and reduce the "stall" time for cleaning. This has the benefit of increasing the average system performance. However, spreading the garbage collection may lead to possible fluctuations in the file system throughput (Manning, 2010).
The YAFFS garbage collection algorithm is under constant review to reduce "stall" time and to increase performance. Charles Manning, the inventor of YAFFS, recently provided a new *background garbage collector*. It should significantly reduce foreground garbage collection in many usage scenarios, particularly those where writing is "bursty" such as a cell phones or similar applications. This could make writing a lot faster, and applications more responsive. Furthermore, YAFFS has included the idea of "block refreshing" in the garbage collector. YAFFS will periodically select the oldest block by exploiting the sequence number and perform garbage collection on it even if it has no garbage. This operation basically rewrites the block to new areas, thus performing a sort of *static wear leveling*.

Wear leveling

YAFFS does not have an explicit set of functions to actively perform wear leveling. In fact, being a log structured file system, it implicitly spreads out the wear by performing all writes in sequence on different chunks. Each partition has a free *allocation block*. Chunks are allocated sequentially from the allocation block. When the allocation block is full, another empty block is selected to become the allocation block by searching upwards from the previous allocation block. Moreover, blocks are allocated serially from the erased blocks in the partition, thus the process of erasing tends to evenly use all blocks as well. In conclusion, in spite of the absence of a specific code, wear leveling is performed as a side effect of other activities (Manning, 2010).

Bad block management

Although YAFFS1 was actively marking bad blocks, YAFFS2 delegates this problem to driver functions. A block is in general marked as bad if a read or write operation fails or three ECC errors are detected. Even if this is a suitable policy for the more reliable SLC memories, alternative strategies for MLC memories are under investigation (Manning, 2010).

Error correction code

YAFFS1 can work with existing software or hardware ECC logic or provide built-in error correction codes, while YAFFS2 does not provide ECC internally, but, requires that the driver provides the ECC. The ECC code supplied with YAFFS is the fastest C code implementation of a Smart Media compatible ECC algorithm with Single Error Correction (SEC) and Double Error Detection (DED) on a 256-byte data block (Manning, 2010).

3.3 Proprietary FFS

Most of the native FFS are proprietary, i.e., they are under exclusive legal rights of the copyright holder. Some of them can be licensed under certain conditions, but restricted from other uses such as modification, further distribution, or reverse engineering. Although the adopted strategies are usually hidden or expressed from a very high-level point of view, it is important to know the main commercial FFS and the related field of application, even if details on the implementation are not available.

3.3.1 exFAT (Microsoft)

The Extended File Allocation Table (exFAT), often incorrectly called FAT64, is the Microsoft proprietary patent-pending file system intended for USB flash drives (Microsoft, 2009). exFAT can be used where the NTFS or FAT file systems are not a feasible solution, due to data structure overhead or to file size restrictions.

The main advantages of exFAT over previous FAT file systems include the support for larger disk size (i.e., up to 512 TB recommended max), a larger cluster size up to 32 MB, a bigger file size up to 16 TB, and several I/O improvements. However, there is limited or absent support outside Microsoft OS environment. Moreover, exFAT looks less reliable than FAT, since it uses a single mapping table, the subdirectory size is limited to 256MB, and Microsoft has not released the official exFAT file specification, requiring a license to make and distribute exFAT implementations (Microsoft, 2011a). A comparison among exFAT and other three MS Windows based file systems can be found in (Microsoft, 2011b).

3.3.2 XCFiles (Datalight)

XCFiles is an exFAT-compatible file system implementation by Datalight for Wind River VxWorks and other embedded OS. XCFiles was released in June 2010 to target consumer devices. It allows embedded systems to support SDXC, the SD Card Association standard for extended capacity storage cards (SD Association, 2011). XCFiles is intended to be portable to any 32-bit platform which meets certain requirements (Datalight, 2010).

3.3.3 TrueFFS (M-Systems)

True flash file system (TrueFFS) is a low level file system designed to run on a raw solid-state drive. TrueFFS implements error correction, bad block re-mapping and wear leveling. Externally, TrueFFS presents a normal hard disk interface. TrueFFS was created by M-Systems (Ban, 1995) on the "DiskOnChip 2000" product line, later acquired by Sandisk in 2006. TFFS or TFFS-lite is a derivative of TrueFFS. It is available in the VxWorks OS, where it works as a FTL, not as a fully functional file system (SanDisk, 2011b).

3.3.4 ExtremeFFS (SanDisk)

ExtremeFFS is an internal file system for SSD developed by SanDisk allowing for improved random write performance in flash memories compared to traditional systems such as TrueFFS. The company plans on using ExtremeFFS in an upcoming MLC implementation of NAND flash memory (SanDisk, 2011a).

3.3.5 OneFS (Isilon)

The OneFS file system is a distributed networked file system designed by Isilon Systems for use in its Isilon IQ storage appliances. The maximum size of a file is 4TB, while the maximum volume size is 2304TB. However, only the OneFS OS is supported (Isilon, 2011).

3.3.6 emFile (Segger Microcontroller Systems)

emFile is a file system for deeply embedded devices supporting both NAND and NOR flashes. It implements wear leveling, fast read and write operations, and very low RAM usage. Moreover, it implements a JTAG emulator that allows to interface the Segger's patented flash breakpoint software to a Remote Debug Interface (RDI) compliant debugger. This software allows program developers to set multiple breakpoints in the flash thus increasing the capability of debugging applications developed over this file system. This feature is however only available for systems based on an ARM microprocessor (Segger, 2005; 2010).

4. Comparisons of the presented FFS

Table 1 summarizes the analysis proposed in this chapter by providing an overall comparison among the proposed FFS, taking into account the aspects proposed in Section 2[3]. Proprietary FFS are excluded from this comparison given the reduced available documentation.

Considering the technology, eNVy represents the worst choice since it was designed for old flash NAND devices that are rather different from modern chips. Similarly, CFFS was only adopted on the SLC 64MB SmartMedia^{TM} Card that is a pretty small device compared to the modern ones. Both FFS do not offer support for MLC memories. FlexFS is the only FFS providing support for a reliable NAND MLC at the cost of under-usage of the memory capacity. YAFFS supports modern SLC NAND devices with pages equal or greater than 2KB, however the MLC support is still under development.

[3] The symbol "–" denotes that no information is available

	eNVy (Wu & Zwaenepoel, 1994)		**CFFS** (Seung-Ho & Kyu-Ho, 2006)		**FlexFS** (Lee et al., 2009)		**YAFFS** (Aleph One Ltd., 2011)	
	Pro	**Cons**	**Pro**	**Cons**	**Pro**	**Cons**	**Pro**	**Cons**
Technology	–	Old devices	SLC support	No MLC, Small devices	MLC support	Capacity Waste	SLC $\geqslant 2KB$ support	No MLC support
Architecture	Simple	Extra resources	–	–	$4KB$ Pages	Pages Flexibility	Easy port & debug	–
Address Translation	Fast	Expensive (Bus&RAM)	Hot-Cold Separation	Moderate file size	–	–	Robust, fail-safe	Extra resources
Boot Time	–	–	Fast	Extra Resources	–	–	Fast	Extra resources
Garbage Collection	Simple	Throughput Fluctuations	Efficient		Only for MLC	Poor detailed	Simple, Block refresh	Throughput Fluctuations
Wear Leveling	–	Accelerated wear	Simple	No Static	Static and Dynamic	Response-time Overhead	Simple	Alternative policies unfeasible
Bad Block	–	–	–	–	–	–	Simple & Cheap	Unsuitable for MLC
(Integrated) ECC	–	–	–	–	–	–	Simple & Cheap	Unsuitable for MLC

Table 1. Comparison among the strategies of the presented FFS

Excluding YAFFS, details about the architecture of the examined FFS are rather scarce. The architecture of eNVy is quite simple but it requires a considerable amount of extra resources to perform well. FlexFS supports MLC devices with 4KB pages, but no details are given about the portability to other page dimensions. YAFFS modular architecture provides easy portability, development, and debug, but the log-structure form can limit some design aspects.
The address translation process of eNVy is very fast, but, at the sam time, it is very expensive due to the use of the wide bus and the battery-backed SRAM. The implicit hot-cold data separation of CFFS improves addressing, but leads to very moderate maximum file size. The log-structure and the consistency of tags of YAFFS lead to a very robust strategy for addressing at the cost of some overhead.
CFFS is designed to minimize the boot time, but extra resources are required. Moreover experimental data are only available from its use on a very small device (i.e., 64MB). Since FlexFS is JFFS2-based, the boot will be reasonably slower compared to the other file systems. YAFFS has low boot time thanks to the mechanism of checkpointing, that in turn requires extra space in the NAND flash.
The pretty simple garbage collection strategy of eNVy may suffer throughput fluctuations with particular patterns of data. CFFS is designed for minimizing the garbage collection overhead. The big advantage of FlexFS is that the garbage collection is limited to the MLC area, but its performance depends on the background migration. The smooth loose/hard garbage collection strategy of YAFFS is also able to refresh older blocks, but may suffer throughput fluctuations.
Wear leveling is one of the most critical aspects when dealing with flash memories. eNVy uses multiple flash chips in parallel, thus being prone to accelerated wear. CFFS has a simple dynamic wear leveling strategy, but no block refreshing is explicitly provided. FlexFS has both static and dynamic wear leveling, buy delays in response times may occur. Since in YAFFS the wear leveling is a side effect of other activities, it is very simple but evaluating alternative wear leveling strategies can be very tough.
YAFFS is the only FFS that explicitly address bad blocks management and ECC. Since they are usually customized to the needs of the user, the integrated strategies are very simple and cheap, but are not suitable for MLC flash.
An additional comparison among the performance of the different file systems is provided in Table 2. In this table, power-fail safe refers to the file system capability of recovering from unexpected crashes.

	eNVy Wu & Zwaenepoel (1994)	**CFFS** (Seung-Ho & Kyu-Ho, 2006)	**FlexFS** (Lee et al., 2009)	**YAFFS** (Aleph One Ltd., 2011)
Power-fail Safe	No	No details	No details	Yes
Resource Overhead	High	Medium	High	Low
Performance	Medium-High	Medium	High	High

Table 2. Performance comparison among the presented FFS

The comparisons performed in this section clearly show that a single solution able to efficiently address all challenges of using NAND flash memories to implement high-hand

mass-storage systems is still missing. A significant effort both from the research and developers community will be required in the next years to cover this gap. Current solutions already propose several interesting solutions. Open-source projects such as YAFFS have, in our opinion, the potential to quickly integrate specific solutions identified by the research community into a product that can be easily distributed to the users in a short term. In particular, YAFFS is one of the most interesting solutions in the world of the FFS. However, there are many things that need to be improved. In fact, although the support for SLC technology is well-established, the support for MLC devices is still under research. This is especially linked with the lower reliability of MLC NAND flash devices. At the end, YAFFS is efficiently linking theory and practice, thus resulting in being today the most complete solution among the possible open source flash-based file system.
Since the FFS and the related management techniques are continuously evolving, we hope that this chapter can be a valuable help both to an easier analysis of these strategies and to a more efficient development of new algorithms and methodologies for flash-based mass memory devices.

5. Acknowledgments

The authors would like to thank Charles Manning for the valuable comments and advices at various stages of this manuscript and the FP7 HiPEAC network of excellence (Grant Agreement no ICT-217068).

6. References

Aleph One Ltd. (2010). Yaffs Direct Interface (YDI), Retrieved April 6, 2011 from the World Wide Web `http://www.yaffs.net/files/yaffs.net/YaffsDirect.pdf`.

Aleph One Ltd. (2011). Yet Another Flash File System 2 (YAFFS2), Retrieved April 6, 2011 from the World Wide Web `http://www.yaffs.net/`.

Ban, A. (1995). Flash file system, u.s. patent 5404485, apr. 4, Retrieved April 6, 2011 from the World Wide Web `http://www.freepatentsonline.com/5404485.pdf`.

Brewer, J. & Gill, M. (2008). *Nonvolatile Memory Technologies with Emphasis on Flash: A Comprehensive Guide to Understanding and Using Flash Memory Devices*, IEEE Press.

Caramia, M., Di Carlo, S., Fabiano, M. & Prinetto, P. (2009a). FLARE: A design environment for flash-based space applications, *Proceedings of IEEE International High Level Design Validation and Test Workshop*, HLDVT '09, San Francisco, CA, USA, pp. 14–19.

Caramia, M., Di Carlo, S., Fabiano, M. & Prinetto, P. (2009b). Flash-memories in space applications: Trends and challenges, *Proceedings of the 7th IEEE East-West Design & Test Symposium*, EWDTS '09, Moscow, Russian Federation, pp. 429–432.

Chang, L.-P. & Kuo, T.-W. (2004). An efficient management scheme for large-scale flash-memory storage systems, *Proceedings of the ACM Symposium on Applied Computing*, SAC '04, ACM, Nicosia, Cyprus, pp. 862–868.

Chang, Y.-H., Hsieh, J.-W. & Kuo, T.-W. (2007). Endurance enhancement of flash-memory storage systems: an efficient static wear leveling design, *Proceedings of the 44th annual Design Automation Conference*, DAC '07, ACM, San Diego, California, pp. 212–217.

Chen, B., Zhang, X. & Wang, Z. (2008). Error correction for multi-level NAND flash memory using Reed-Solomon codes, *Proceedings of the IEEE Workshop on Signal Processing Systems*, Washington, DC, USA, pp. 94–99.

Choi, H., Liu, W. & Sung, W. (2010). VLSI implementation of BCH error correction for multilevel cell NAND flash memory, *IEEE Transactions on Very Large Scale Integration (VLSI) Systems* **18**(6): 843–847.

Cooke, J. (2007). The inconvenient truths of NAND flash memory, Retrieved April 6, 2011 from the World Wide Web `http://download.micron.com/pdf/presentations/events/flash_mem_summit_jcooke_inconvenient_truths_nand.pdf`.

Datalight (2010). XCFiles File System for Next Generation Removable Storage, Retrieved April 6, 2011 from the World Wide Web `http://www.datalight.com/products/filesystems/xcfiles`.

Deal, E. (2009). Trends in NAND flash memory error correction, Retrieved April 6, 2011 from the World Wide Web `http://www.cyclicdesign.com/whitepapers/Cyclic_Design_NAND_ECC.pdf`.

Duann, N. (2009). Error correcting techniques for future NAND flash memory in SSD applications, Retrieved April 6, 2011 from the World Wide Web `http://www.bswd.com/FMS09/FMS09-201-Duann.pdf`.

Gal, E. & Toledo, S. (2005). Algorithms and data structures for flash memories, *ACM Comput. Surv.* **37**: 138–163.

IEEE Standards Department (1998). IEEE standard definitions and characterization of floating gate semiconductor arrays, *IEEE Std 1005-1998* .

Intel (1998). Understanding the Flash Translation Layer (FTL) specification, AP-684 (order 297816), Retrieved April 6, 2011 from the World Wide Web `http://www.cse.ust.hk/~yjrobin/reading_list/%5BFlash%20Disks%5DUnderstanding%20the%20flash%20translation%20layer%20(FTL)%20specification.pdf`.

Isilon (2011). OneFS, Retrieved April 6, 2011 from the World Wide Web `http://www.isilon.com/onefs-operating-system`.

Jae-Duk, L., Sung-Hoi, H. & Jung-Dal, C. (2002). Effects of floating-gate interference on NAND flash memory cell operation, *IEEE Electron Device Letters* **23**(5): 264–266.

Jen-Chieh, Y., Chi-Feng, W., Kuo-Liang, C., Yung-Fa, C., Chih-Tsun, H. & Cheng-Wen, W. (2002). Flash memory built-in self-test using march-like algorithms, *Proceedings of the First IEEE International Workshop on Electronic Design, Test and Applications*, Christchurch , New Zealand, pp. 137–141.

Jen-Wei, H., Yi-Lin, T., Tei-Wei, K. & Tzao-Lin, L. (2008). Configurable flash-memory management: Performance versus overheads, *IEEE Trans. on Computers* **57**(11): 1571–1583.

Junho, C. & Wonyong, S. (2009). Efficient software-based encoding and decoding of BCH codes, *IEEE Transactions on Computers* **58**(7): 878–889.

Kawaguchi, A., Nishioka, S. & Motoda, H. (1995). A flash-memory based file system, *Proceedings of the USENIX Annual Technical Conference*, TCON'95, USENIX Association, New Orleans, Louisiana, pp. 13–13.

Lee, S., Ha, K., Zhang, K., Kim, J. & Kim, J. (2009). FlexFS: a flexible flash file system for MLC NAND flash memory, *Proceedings of the USENIX Annual Technical Conference*, USENIX'09, USENIX Association, San Diego, California, pp. 9–9.

Ielmini, D. (2009). Reliability issues and modeling of flash and post-flash memory (invited paper), *Microelectronic Engineering* **86**(7–9): 1870–1875.

Manning, C. (2010). How YAFFS works, Retrieved April 6, 2011 from the World Wide Web `http://www.yaffs.net/files/yaffs.net/HowYaffsWorks.pdf`.

Micheloni, R., Marelli, A. & Ravasio, R. (2008). *Error Correction Codes for Non-Volatile Memories*, Springer Publishing Company, Incorporated.

Micron (2007). Hamming codes for NAND flash-memory devices overview, Retrieved April 6, 2011 from the World Wide Web `http://download.micron.com/pdf/technotes/nand/tn2908.pdf`.

Microsoft (2009). Description of the exFAT file system driver update package, Retrieved April 6, 2011 from the World Wide Web `http://support.microsoft.com/kb/955704/en-us`.

Microsoft (2011a). exFAT file system, Retrieved April 6, 2011 from the World Wide Web `http://www.microsoft.com/about/legal/en/us/IntellectualProperty/IPLicensing/Programs/exFATFileSystem.aspx`.

Microsoft (2011b). File system functionality comparison, Retrieved April 6, 2011 from the World Wide Web `http://msdn.microsoft.com/en-us/library/ee681827(v=vs.85).aspx`.

Mielke, N., Marquart, T., Wu, N., Kessenich, J., Belgal, H., Schares, E., Trivedi, F., Goodness, E. & Nevill, L. (2008). Bit error rate in NAND flash memories, *Proceedings of the IEEE International Reliability Physics Symposium*, Phoenix, AZ, USA, pp. 9–19.

Mincheol, P., Keonsoo, K., Jong-Ho, P. & Jeong-Hyuck, C. (2009). Direct field effect of neighboring cell transistor on cell-to-cell interference of nand flash cell arrays, *IEEE Electron Device Letters* **30**(2): 174–177.

Mohammad, M., Saluja, K. & Yap, A. (2000). Testing flash memories, *Proceeding of the Thirteenth International Conference on VLSI Design*, IEEE Computer Society, Calcutta, India, pp. 406–411.

ONFI (2010). Open NAND Flash interface (ONFi) specification, Retrieved April 6, 2011 from the World Wide Web `http://onfi.org/wp-content/uploads/2009/02/ONFI%202_2%20Gold.pdf`.

Rosenblum, M. & Ousterhout, J. K. (1992). The design and implementation of a log-structured file system, *ACM Trans. Comput. Syst.* **10**: 26–52.

Samsung (2007). XSR1.5 bad block management, Retrieved April 6, 2011 from the World Wide Web `http://www.samsung.com/global/business/semiconductor/products/flash/downloads/applicationnote/xsr_v15_badblockmgmt_application_note.pdf`.

SanDisk (2011a). Sandisk's know-how strengthens the SSD industry, Retrieved April 6, 2011 from the World Wide Web `http://www.sandisk.com/business-solutions/ssd/technical-expertise--metrics`.

SanDisk (2011b). TrueFFS, Retrieved April 6, 2011 from the World Wide Web `http://www.sandisk.nl/Assets/File/OEM/Manuals/pu/mdoc/PU0301.pdf`.

SD Association (2011). SDXC, Retrieved April 6, 2011 from the World Wide Web `http://www.sdcard.org/developers/tech/sdxc`.

Segger (2005). J-link flash breakpoints, Retrieved April 6, 2011 from the World Wide Web `http://www.segger.com/cms/jlink-flash-breakpoints.html`.

Segger (2010). emFile file system, Retrieved April 6, 2011 from the World Wide Web `http://www.segger.com/cms/emfile.html`.

Seung-Ho, L. & Kyu-Ho, P. (2006). An efficient NAND flash file system for flash memory storage, *IEEE Transactions on Computers* **55**(7): 906–912.

Woodhouse, D. (2001). JFFS : The Journalling Flash File System, *Proceedings of the Ottawa Linux Symposium*, Ottawa, Ontario Canada.
URL: *http://sources.redhat.com/jffs2/jffs2.pdf*

Woodhouse, D. (2009). JFFS2: The Journalling Flash File System, version 2, Retrieved April 6, 2011 from the World Wide Web `http://sourceware.org/jffs2/`.

Wu, M. (1994). *The architecture of eNVy, a non-volatile, main memory storage system*, Master's thesis, Rice University.

Wu, M. & Zwaenepoel, W. (1994). eNVy: a non-volatile, main memory storage system, *SIGOPS Oper. Syst. Rev.* **28**: 86–97.

Yaakobi, E., Ma, J., Caulfield, A., Grupp, L., Swanson, S., Siegel, P. & J.K., W. (2009). Error correction coding for flash memories, Retrieved April 6, 2011 from the World Wide Web `http://www.flashmemorysummit.com/English/Collaterals/Proceedings/2009/20090813_S201_Yaakobi.pdf`.

Yuan, C. (2008). Flash memory reliability NEPP 2008 task final report, Retrieved April 6, 2011 from the World Wide Web `http://trs-new.jpl.nasa.gov/dspace/bitstream/2014/41262/1/09-9.pdf`.

2

Error Control Coding for Flash Memory

Haruhiko Kaneko
Tokyo Institute of Technology
Japan

1. Introduction

Error control code (ECC) is extensively used in high-speed wireless/wired communication system, magnetic disk, and optical disc (Lin & Costello, 2004). Also the ECC can efficiently improve data reliability of semiconductor memory system (Fujiwara, 2006). This chapter presents error control coding techniques for flash memory and solid-state drive (SSD). This chapter begins with brief introduction of error sources in the flash memory, and then provides fundamental mathematics of the ECC, followed by constructions of practical ECCs.

2. Errors in flash memory

Efficient ECC should be designed based on the analysis of error characteristics/statistics in the flash memory. This section outlines error sources of the flash memory, and presents a channel model based on a Gaussian-distribution approximation of the threshold voltage.

2.1 Errors sources in flash memory

2.1.1 Physical defect

Similar to general LSI circuits, flash memory suffers from wafer process defect (Muroke, 2006), such as short circuit between drain contact and control gate, adjacent poly lines, metal lines, poly and metal lines, or two metal levels. Other major defects in the flash memory are observed in tunnel oxide and peripheral circuit.
Many of the above defects can be detected by memory chip test (Mohammad et al., 2001), and thus a moderate number of defects can be masked by a redundant hardware design, while faulty chips with an excessive number of defects are discarded. Hence, the above physical defects do not affect ECC design significantly.

2.1.2 Trapping / detrapping in tunnel oxide

Stress on the tunnel oxide by program/erase (P/E) cycles causes generation of traps, such as positive-charge, neutral, and electron traps. The positive-charge and neutral traps induce leakage current, as explained in **2.1.3**, and the electron traps lengthen the charge time in programming phase. Also, detrapping of electrons trapped in the tunnel oxide causes lowered threshold voltage.

2.1.3 Leakage current

Leakage of electrons stored in the floating gate causes alteration of the threshold voltage, which results in errors in readout data. Stress induced leakage current (SILC) is caused by

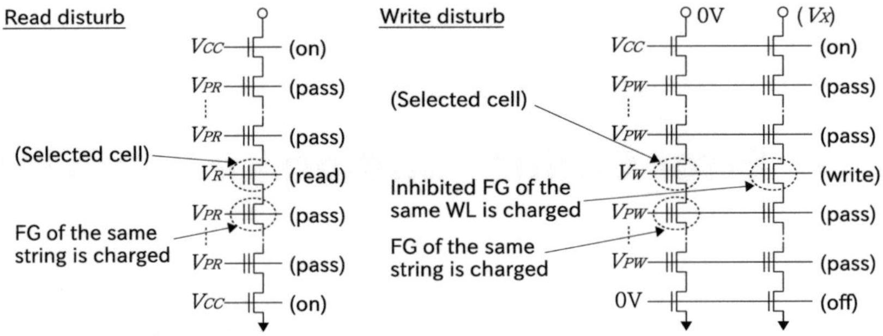

Fig. 1. Read/write disturb in NAND flash memory.

deterioration of the tunnel oxide after many P/E cycles, that is, positive-charge and neutral traps generated in the tunnel oxide causes leakage of electrons from the FG (Mielke et al., 2008). The leakage current significantly increases when multiple traps in the tunnel oxide form a path through which the FG is discharged (Ielmini et al., 2005). In multilevel cell (MLC) memory, the highest level cells are affected by the SILC more severely compared to lower level cells because of the largest electric field in the tunnel oxide.

2.1.4 Read/write disturb

High voltages applied to the CG in the read/write process cause insertion of electrons into the FG. Figure 1 illustrates the following read/write disturb in NAND flash memory.

- Read disturb: FG in the same string of a selected cell is charged.
- Write disturb in selected string: FG in the same string of a selected cell is charged.
- Write disturb in selected WL: Inhibited FG in the same WL of a selected cell is charged.

2.1.5 Overprogramming / overerase

The FG could be excessively charged in the programming phase because of, for example, random telegraph noise in verify step and erratic tunneling caused by positive charges in the tunnel oxide (Mielke et al., 2008). The overprogramming results in error due to an elevated threshold voltage. Some errors caused by overprogramming might be accidentally recovered by detrapping of electrons trapped in the tunnel oxide.

Overerase phenomena is also observed in the flash memory cell (Chimenton et al., 2003), where the threshold voltage is excessively dropped by the erasing. Overerased bits are classified into two classes, that is, tail bit and fast bit. The tail bit has a slightly lower threshold compared to normal bits, while the fast bit has a much lower threshold. It is predicted that the tail and fast bits are caused by statistical fluctuations of cell charges and physical nature of the cell, respectively.

2.1.6 Ionizing radiation

In a radiation harsh environment, such as spacecraft, aircraft, and nuclear plant, errors in the flash memory could be induced by radiation of ionizing particles (e.g., α-particle, β-particle, neutron, and cosmic rays) and high-energy electromagnetic wave (e.g., ultraviolet, X-ray, and γ-ray). The ionizing radiation causes lattice displacement in crystal, which changes the property of the semiconductor junctions, and thus results in errors. Effects of the total ionization dose (TID) on the flash memory have been extensively examined (Claeys et al., 2002; Oldham et al., 2007), and some experiments show that memory cells fail at the TID of

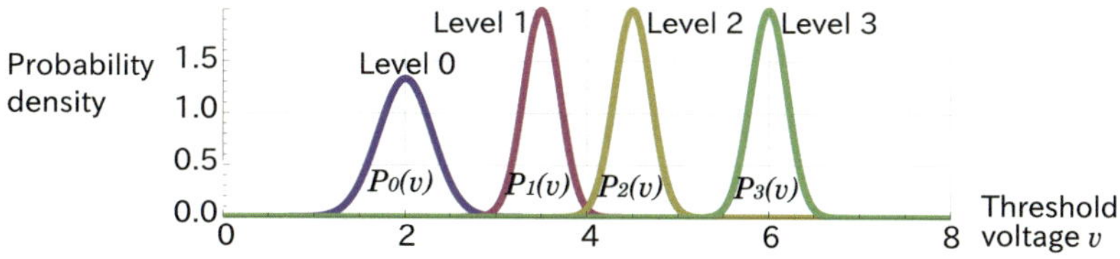

Fig. 2. Example of PDF $P_i(v)$ of threshold voltage.

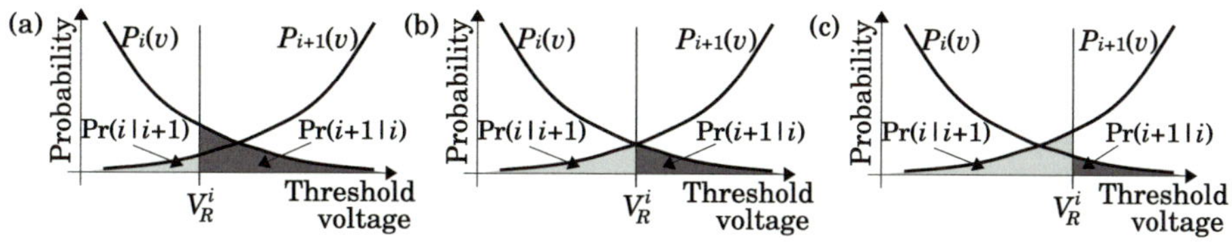

Fig. 3. Probabilities $\Pr(i|i+1)$ and $\Pr(i+1|i)$.

around 100 [Krad]. The TID affects the functions of the charge pump and row decoder, as well as the cell array (Bagatin et al., 2009).

2.2 Channel model

Since error sources of the flash memory are various as described in **2.1**, it is difficult to establish a precise channel model of the flash memory. Therefore, an approximated channel model is derived based on a Gaussian approximation of the threshold voltage distribution. In the following, we assume a b-bit MLC having $Q = 2^b$ charge levels of the FG. Let $P_i(v)$ be the probability density function (PDF) representing the probability that the threshold voltage of level-i cell is equal to v, where $i \in \{0, 1, \ldots, Q-1\}$. The PDF $P_i(v)$ is approximated by the Gaussian distribution as $P_i(v) = \frac{1}{\sqrt{2\pi}\sigma_i} \exp\left(-\frac{(x-\mu_i)^2}{2\sigma_i^2}\right)$, where μ_i and σ_i are the mean and standard deviation of the threshold voltage of level-i cell, respectively. Figure 2 illustrates an example of $P_i(v)$ for 2-bit/cell memory, where $b = 2, Q = 2^b = 4, \mu_0 = 2.0, \mu_1 = 3.5, \mu_2 = 4.5, \mu_3 = 6.0, \sigma_0 = 0.3$, and $\sigma_1 = \sigma_2 = \sigma_3 = 0.2$. In general, the standard deviation of level-0 cell is larger than that of higher level cells.

Let V_R^i be the read (verify) voltage of control gate which discriminates level-i and level-$(i+1)$ cells, where $i \in \{0, 1, \ldots, Q-2\}$ and $\mu_i < V_R^i < \mu_{i+1}$. For a given PDF $P_i(v)$ and a read voltage V_R^i, the probability that level-i cell is identified as level-j is given by

$$\Pr(j|i) = \begin{cases} \int_{-\infty}^{V_R^0} P_i(v)dv & (j = 0) \\ \int_{V_R^{j-1}}^{V_R^j} P_i(v)dv & (1 \le j \le Q-2) \\ \int_{V_R^{Q-2}}^{\infty} P_i(v)dv & (j = Q-1) \end{cases} .$$

Figures 3 (a), (b), and (c) illustrate the probabilities $\Pr(i|i+1)$ and $\Pr(i+1|i)$ for three read voltages. Here, the dark and light shaded areas represent the probabilities $\Pr(i+1|i)$ and $\Pr(i+1|i)$, respectively. It is obvious from Fig. 3(b) that error probability between level-i and level-$(i+1)$ cells is minimized when V_R^i is determined such that $P_i(V_R^i) = P_{i+1}(V_R^i)$. For example, for the 4-level cell shown in Fig. 2, the optimum read voltages satisfying this equation are determined as $V_R^0 = 2.288$, $V_R^1 = 4.000$, and $V_R^2 = 5.250$.

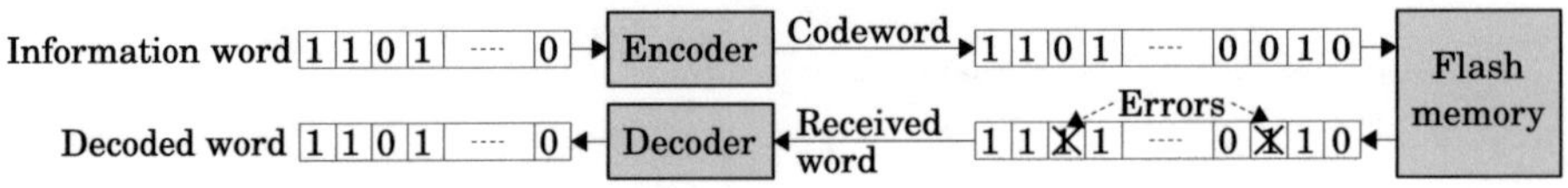

Fig. 4. Error control coding using a block code.

If the spatial and temporal correlations of errors are negligible in the flash memory, the errors can be described by a Q-ary stationary memoryless channel, whose channel matrix is given as

$$P = \begin{bmatrix} p_{0,0} & \cdots & p_{0,Q-1} \\ \vdots & \ddots & \vdots \\ p_{Q-1,0} & \cdots & p_{Q-1,Q-1} \end{bmatrix} = \begin{bmatrix} \Pr(0|0) & \ldots & \Pr(Q-1|0) \\ \vdots & \ddots & \vdots \\ \Pr(0|Q-1) & \ldots & \Pr(Q-1|Q-1) \end{bmatrix},$$

where $p_{i,j} = \Pr(j|i)$.

3. Introduction to linear block code

Figure 4 illustrates an error control coding scheme for the flash memory, where a block code is employed to correct/detect errors. In the write process, an information word is encoded to a codeword by the encoder, and then the codeword is written to the flash memory. In the read process, a received word (i.e., a readout codeword possibly having errors) is decoded by the decoder, wherein the errors are corrected or detected. Since many of practical ECCs are classified into linear block code, this section provides fundamentals of the linear block codes.

3.1 Galois field

Practical linear block codes are usually defined over Galois field. This subsection covers definition and construction of Galois field.

3.1.1 Definition

Galois Field $\mathrm{GF}(q)$ is defined as a finite set having q elements on which two binary operations, namely, addition $(+)$ and multiplication $(\cdot)$, are defined, where q is a prime number or a power of a prime number. Galois field is defined such that the following axioms hold.

Axioms of Galois field

1. Closure under addition: $\forall x, y \in \mathrm{GF}(q),\ x + y \in \mathrm{GF}(q)$.
2. Commutativity of addition: $\forall x, y \in \mathrm{GF}(q),\ x + y = y + x$.
3. Associativity of addition: $\forall x, y, z, \in \mathrm{GF}(q),\ (x + y) + z = x + (y + z)$.
4. Additive identity: $\forall x \in \mathrm{GF}(q), \exists 0 \in \mathrm{GF}(q),\ x + 0 = 0 + x = x$.
5. Additive inverse: $\forall x \in \mathrm{GF}(q), \exists(-x) \in \mathrm{GF}(q),\ x + (-x) = (-x) + x = 0$.
6. Closure under multiplication: $\forall x, y \in \mathrm{GF}(q),\ x \cdot y \in \mathrm{GF}(q)$.
7. Commutativity of multiplication: $\forall x, y \in \mathrm{GF}(q),\ x \cdot y = y \cdot x$.
8. Associativity of multiplication: $\forall x, y, z \in \mathrm{GF}(q),\ (x \cdot y) \cdot z = x \cdot (y \cdot z)$.
9. Multiplicative identity: $\forall x \in \mathrm{GF}(q), \exists 1 \in \mathrm{GF}(q),\ x \cdot 1 = 1 \cdot x = x$.
10. Multiplicative inverse: $\forall x \in \mathrm{GF}(q) - \{0\}, \exists x^{-1},\ x \cdot x^{-1} = x^{-1} \cdot x = 1$.
11. Distributivity: $\forall x, y, z \in \mathrm{GF}(q),\ x \cdot (y + z) = x \cdot y + x \cdot z$.

In the above notation, 0 and 1 are referred to as *zero* and *unity*, respectively. The set of axioms says that the four arithmetic operations (addition, substitution, multiplication, and division) can be applied to elements in $\mathrm{GF}(q)$. There exist two types of Galois field, that is, *prime field* $\mathrm{GF}(q)$ and *extension field* $\mathrm{GF}(q^m)$, where q is a prime number and $m \geq 2$ is an integer.

Addition table

+	0	1	2	3	4
0	0	1	2	3	4
1	1	2	3	4	0
2	2	3	4	0	1
3	3	4	0	1	2
4	4	0	1	2	3

Multiplication table

·	0	1	2	3	4
0	0	0	0	0	0
1	0	1	2	3	4
2	0	2	4	1	3
3	0	3	1	4	2
4	0	4	3	2	1

Table 1. Addition and multiplication tables of GF(5).

3.1.2 Prime field

Prime field is defined as $\mathrm{GF}(q) = \{0, 1, \ldots, q-1\}$, where q is a prime, and addition and multiplication of elements $x, y \in \mathrm{GF}(q)$ are defined as

$$(x + y) \bmod q \quad \text{and} \quad (x \cdot y) \bmod q,$$

respectively. Here, "$a \bmod q$" indicates the remainder of a divided by q. Table 1 presents an example of addition and multiplication tables of GF(5).

3.1.3 Extension field

Extension field $\mathrm{GF}(q^m)$ is constructed using a polynomial defined over $\mathrm{GF}(q)$. Let

$$f(x) = \sum_{i=0}^{m} f_i x^i = f_m x^m + f_{m-1} x^{m-1} + \cdots + f_1 x + f_0$$

be a polynomial over $\mathrm{GF}(q)$ of degree m, where $f_i \in \mathrm{GF}(q)$ for $0 \le i \le m$ and $f_m \neq 0$. Addition and multiplication of polynomials over $\mathrm{GF}(q)$ is defined in the same manner as polynomials over the real number except that addition and multiplication of coefficients are performed according to the definitions of $\mathrm{GF}(q)$. *Period* of a polynomial $f(x)$ is defined as the minimum positive integer e satisfying $f(x)|(x^e - 1)$, where $f(x)|g(x)$ indicates that $g(x)$ is divisible by $f(x)$.

Irreducible polynomial is a polynomial which cannot be factorized to polynomials over $\mathrm{GF}(q)$. For example, $x^2 + 1$ over GF(2) is not irreducible because $x^2 + 1 = (x+1)(x+1)$, whereas $x^2 + x + 1$ over GF(2) is irreducible. *Primitive polynomial* $p(x)$ is an irreducible polynomial whose period is $q^m - 1$. List of primitive polynomials is provided in various ECC text books, such as in (Lin & Costello, 2004).

Let $p(x) = \sum_{i=0}^{m} p_i x^i$ be a primitive polynomial of degree m over $\mathrm{GF}(q)$, where $p_m = 1$, and let α be a root of $p(x)$, that is $p(\alpha) = 0$. Since α satisfies $\alpha^m = -\sum_{i=0}^{m-1} p_i \alpha^i$, α^s is expressed as a polynomial of α of degree less than m for any non-negative integer s, that is,

$$\alpha^s = \sum_{i=0}^{m-1} a_i \alpha^i, \tag{1}$$

where $a_i \in \mathrm{GF}(q)$. The left-hand side and the right-hand side of Eq.(1) are referred to as the power and polynomial representations of α^s, respectively, and its coefficient vector

$$\mathrm{vec}(\alpha^s) = (a_{m-1}, a_{m-2}, \ldots, a_0)$$

is referred to as the vector representation of α^s.

Example 1. *Let α be a root of primitive polynomial $p(x) = x^3 + x + 1$ over GF(2). Table 2 shows the polynomial and vector representations of the powers of α. (Note that $-x = x$ in GF(2).)*

Power	Polynomial	Vector	Power	Polynomial	Vector
α^0	1	$(0,0,1)$	α^5	$\alpha^3+\alpha^2=\alpha^2+\alpha+1$	$(1,1,1)$
α^1	α	$(0,1,0)$	α^6	$\alpha^3+\alpha^2+\alpha=\alpha^2+1$	$(1,0,1)$
α^2	α^2	$(1,0,0)$	α^7	$\alpha^3+\alpha=1$	$(0,0,1)$
α^3	$\alpha+1$	$(0,1,1)$	$\vdots$	$\vdots$	$\vdots$
α^4	$\alpha^2+\alpha$	$(1,1,0)$			

Table 2. Polynomial and vector representation of powers of a root α of primitive polynomial $p(x)=x^3+x+1$ over GF(2).

Addition table

$+$	0	α^0	α^1	α^2	α^3	α^4	α^5	α^6
0	0	α^0	α^1	α^2	α^3	α^4	α^5	α^6
α^0	α^0	0	α^3	α^6	α^1	α^5	α^4	α^2
α^1	α^1	α^3	0	α^4	α^0	α^2	α^6	α^5
α^2	α^2	α^6	α^4	0	α^5	α^1	α^3	α^0
α^3	α^3	α^1	α^0	α^5	0	α^6	α^2	α^4
α^4	α^4	α^5	α^2	α^1	α^6	0	α^0	α^3
α^5	α^5	α^4	α^6	α^3	α^2	α^0	0	α^1
α^6	α^6	α^2	α^5	α^0	α^4	α^3	α^1	0

Multiplication table

$\cdot$	0	α^0	α^1	α^2	α^3	α^4	α^5	α^6
0	0	0	0	0	0	0	0	0
α^0	0	α^0	α^1	α^2	α^3	α^4	α^5	α^6
α^1	0	α^1	α^2	α^3	α^4	α^5	α^6	α^0
α^2	0	α^2	α^3	α^4	α^5	α^6	α^0	α^1
α^3	0	α^3	α^4	α^5	α^6	α^0	α^1	α^2
α^4	0	α^4	α^5	α^6	α^0	α^1	α^2	α^3
α^5	0	α^5	α^6	α^0	α^1	α^2	α^3	α^4
α^6	0	α^6	α^0	α^1	α^2	α^3	α^4	α^5

Table 3. Addition and multiplication tables of GF(2^3).

Theorem 1. *Let α be a root of primitive polynomial $p(x)$ of degree m over* GF(q). *The following relation holds for non-negative integers i and j:*

$$\alpha^i = \alpha^j \quad \Leftrightarrow \quad i \equiv j \ (\mathrm{mod}\ q^m - 1).$$

An extension field GF(q^m) of degree m is generated from a ground field GF(q) as GF(q^m) $= \{0, \alpha^0, \alpha^1, \ldots, \alpha^{q^m-2}\}$, where α is a root of primitive polynomial of degree m over GF(q), and the vector representation of 0 is $(0, \ldots, 0)$. Here, the additive and multiplicative identities are 0 and $\alpha^0 = 1$, respectively, and the addition and multiplication of α^i and α^j are defined as

$$\alpha^i + \alpha^j = \alpha^k$$

and

$$\alpha^i \cdot \alpha^j = \alpha^{(i+j) \bmod q^m - 1},$$

where $\mathrm{vec}(\alpha^i) + \mathrm{vec}(\alpha^j) = \mathrm{vec}(\alpha^k)$ over GF(q). In short, the addition is defined on the vector representation, and the multiplication on the power representation.

Example 2. *Let α be a root of primitive polynomial $p(x) = x^3 + x + 1$ over* GF(2). *Extension field* GF(2^3) *is defined as* GF(2^3) $= \{0, \alpha^0, \alpha^1, \ldots, \alpha^6\}$, *where the non-zero elements are listed in Table 2. The addition and multiplication tables of* GF(2^3) *are presented in Table 3.*

3.2 Linear space

3.2.1 Definition

Let $\mathbf{u} = (u_0, u_1, \ldots, u_{n-1})$ and $\mathbf{v} = (v_0, v_1, \ldots, v_{n-1})$ be vectors of length n over GF(q), where $u_i, v_i \in$ GF(q) for $0 \le i \le n-1$ and GF(q) is either prime field or extension field. For the vectors over GF(q), addition, inner product, and scalar multiplication are defined as

$$\mathbf{u} + \mathbf{v} = (u_0 + v_0, u_1 + v_1, \ldots, v_{n-1} + u_{n-1}),$$
$$\mathbf{u} \cdot \mathbf{v} = u_0 \cdot v_0 + u_1 \cdot v_1 + \cdots + u_{n-1} \cdot v_{n-1}, \quad \text{and}$$
$$a \cdot \mathbf{v} = (a \cdot v_0, a \cdot v_1, \ldots, a \cdot v_{n-1}),$$

respectively, where the addition and multiplication of vector components are defined on GF(q). For simplicity, the multiplication operator '$\cdot$' will be omitted hereafter. Let $\mathbf{V}$ be a set of vectors of length n over GF(q). The set $\mathbf{V}$ is a linear space if the following conditions hold.

1. Closure under addition: $\forall \mathbf{u}, \mathbf{v} \in \mathbf{V},\ \mathbf{u} + \mathbf{v} \in \mathbf{V}$.
2. Commutativity of addition: $\forall \mathbf{u}, \mathbf{v} \in \mathbf{V},\ \mathbf{u} + \mathbf{v} = \mathbf{v} + \mathbf{u}$.
3. Associativity of addition: $\forall \mathbf{u}, \mathbf{v}, \mathbf{w} \in \mathbf{V},\ (\mathbf{u} + \mathbf{v}) + \mathbf{w} = \mathbf{u} + (\mathbf{v} + \mathbf{w})$.
4. Zero vector: $\forall \mathbf{u} \in \mathbf{V}, \exists \mathbf{o} \in \mathbf{v},\ \mathbf{u} + \mathbf{o} = \mathbf{o} + \mathbf{u} = \mathbf{u}$.
5. Inverse vector: $\forall \mathbf{u} \in \mathbf{V}, \exists -\mathbf{u} \in \mathbf{V},\ \mathbf{u} + (-\mathbf{u}) = \mathbf{o}$.
6. Closure under scalar multiplication: $\forall \mathbf{u} \in \mathbf{V}, \forall a \in \mathrm{GF}(q),\ a\mathbf{u} \in \mathbf{V}$.
7. Distributivity (scalar addition): $\forall \mathbf{u} \in \mathbf{V}, \forall a, b \in \mathrm{GF}(q),\ (a + b)\mathbf{u} = a\mathbf{u} + b\mathbf{u}$.
8. Distributivity (vector addition): $\forall \mathbf{u}, \mathbf{v} \in \mathbf{V}, \forall a \in \mathrm{GF}(q),\ a(\mathbf{u} + \mathbf{v}) = a\mathbf{u} + a\mathbf{v}$.
9. Associativity of scalar multiplication: $\forall \mathbf{u} \in \mathbf{V}, \forall a, b \in \mathrm{GF}(q),\ (ab)\mathbf{u} = a(b\mathbf{u})$.
10. Identity of scalar multiplication: $\forall \mathbf{u} \in \mathbf{V},\ 1\mathbf{u} = \mathbf{u}$.

Example 3. *The following set of all vectors over* GF(2) *of length* 4 *is a linear space:*

$$\begin{aligned}\mathbf{V} = \{&(0,0,0,0),(0,0,0,1),(0,0,1,0),(0,0,1,1),(0,1,0,0),(0,1,0,1),(0,1,1,0),(0,1,1,1),\\ &(1,0,0,0),(1,0,0,1),(1,0,1,0),(1,0,1,1),(1,1,0,0),(1,1,0,1),(1,1,1,0),(1,1,1,1)\}.\end{aligned}$$

A subset $\mathbf{S}$ of a linear space $\mathbf{V}$ is a linear subspace if the following conditions hold:

1. Closure under addition: $\forall \mathbf{u}, \mathbf{v} \in \mathbf{S},\quad \mathbf{u} + \mathbf{v} \in \mathbf{S}$.
2. Closure under scalar multiplication: $\forall \mathbf{u} \in \mathbf{S}, \forall a \in \mathrm{GF}(q),\quad a\mathbf{u} \in \mathbf{S}$.

Example 4. *One example of the linear subspace of* $\mathbf{V}$ *in Example 3 is* $\mathbf{S} = \{(0,0,0,0),(0,0,1,1),(1,1,0,0),(1,1,1,1)\}$.

3.2.2 Basis vector and dimension

Linear space $\mathbf{V}$ can be specified by a set of *basis vectors* as follows:

$$\mathbf{V} = \{\mathbf{v} = a_0\mathbf{v}_0 + a_1\mathbf{v}_1 + \cdots + a_{k-1}\mathbf{v}_{k-1} \mid a_i \in \mathrm{GF}(q), \mathbf{v}_i\text{: basis vector}\},$$

where $\mathbf{v}_0, \mathbf{v}_1, \ldots, \mathbf{v}_{k-1}$ are linearly independent vectors of length n over GF(q). Here, the basis vectors satisfy the following condition:

$$a_0\mathbf{v}_0 + a_1\mathbf{v}_1 + \cdots + a_{k-1}\mathbf{v}_{k-1} = \mathbf{o} \quad \Leftrightarrow \quad a_0 = a_1 = \cdots = a_{k-1} = 0,$$

where $\mathbf{o}$ is the zero-vector.

Example 5. *The followings are examples of basis vectors of* $\mathbf{V}$ *and* $\mathbf{S}$ *of Examples 3 and 4, respectively.*
One example of basis vectors of $\mathbf{V}$*:* $\{(0,0,0,1),(0,0,1,0),(0,1,0,0),(1,0,0,0)\}$.
Another example of basis vectors of $\mathbf{V}$*:* $\{(0,0,1,1),(1,1,0,0),(0,0,0,1),(0,1,1,0)\}$.
An example of basis vectors of $\mathbf{S}$*:* $\{(0,0,1,1),(1,1,0,0)\}$.

For a given vector space $\mathbf{V}$, there exists a number of combinations of basis vectors, while the number of basis vectors in each combination is identical. The *dimension* k of vector space $\mathbf{V}$ is defined as the number of basis vectors of $\mathbf{V}$.

Example 6. *The dimensions of* $\mathbf{V}$ *and* $\mathbf{S}$ *in Examples 3 and 4 are* $k = 4$ *and* 2*, respectively.*

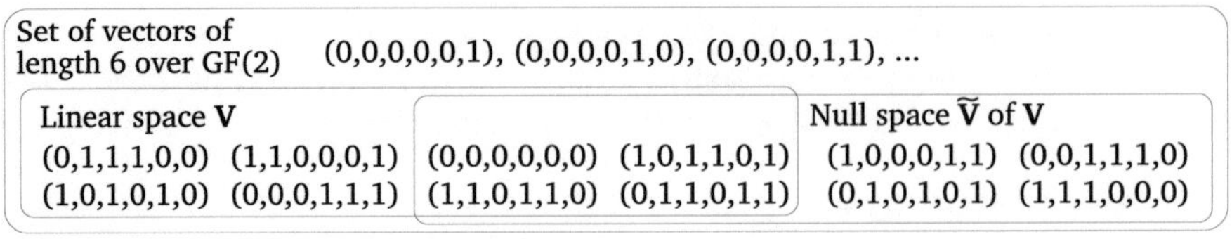

Fig. 5. Example of null space over GF(2).

3.2.3 Null space

Let $\mathbf{V}$ be a linear space of dimension k defined as

$$\mathbf{V} = \{\mathbf{v} = a_0\mathbf{v}_0 + a_1\mathbf{v}_1 + \cdots + a_{k-1}\mathbf{v}_{k-1} \mid a_i \in \mathrm{GF}(q), \mathbf{v}_i \text{ is basis vector}\},$$

where $\mathbf{v}_i$ is a vector of length n over GF(q). The *null space* of $\mathbf{V}$ is defined as

$$\widetilde{\mathbf{V}} = \{\widetilde{\mathbf{v}} = (\widetilde{v}_0, \widetilde{v}_1, \ldots, \widetilde{v}_{n-1}) \mid \forall \mathbf{v} \in \mathbf{V}, \mathbf{v} \cdot \widetilde{\mathbf{v}} = 0, \widetilde{v}_i \in \mathrm{GF}(q)\}.$$

Equivalently, the null space $\widetilde{\mathbf{V}}$ is defined using the basis vectors of $\mathbf{V}$ as

$$\widetilde{\mathbf{V}} = \{\widetilde{\mathbf{v}} = (\widetilde{v}_0, \widetilde{v}_1, \ldots, \widetilde{v}_{n-1}) \mid \forall i \in \{0, 1, \ldots, k-1\}, \mathbf{v}_i \cdot \widetilde{\mathbf{v}} = 0, \widetilde{v}_i \in \mathrm{GF}(q)\}.$$

It can be proved that the null space is a linear space.

Example 7. *Figure 5 presents an example of linear space* $\mathbf{V}$ *and its null space* $\widetilde{\mathbf{V}}$ *over* GF(2).

3.3 Linear block code

3.3.1 Definition

Let $\mathbf{F}^n$ be a linear space defined as a set of all vectors of length n over GF(q), that is,

$$\mathbf{F}^n = \{\mathbf{u} = (u_0, u_1, \ldots, u_{n-1}) \mid u_i \in \mathrm{GF}(q)\}.$$

A *block code* of length n over GF(q) is defined as a subset of $\mathbf{F}^n$, and a *linear block code* $\mathbf{C}$ of length n over GF(q) is defined as a linear subspace of $\mathbf{F}^n$. A code $\mathbf{C}$ of length n with dimension k is denoted as (n,k) code. Encoding by a linear block code $\mathbf{C}$ is defined as a bijective mapping from $\mathbf{F}^k$ to $\mathbf{C}$. Vectors in $\mathbf{C}$ and $\mathbf{F}^k$ are referred to as codeword and information word, respectively.

Example 8. *From the linear subspace* $\mathbf{V}$ *shown in Fig. 5, (6,3) linear block code* $\mathbf{C}$ *over* $\mathbf{F} = \mathrm{GF}(2)$ *is generated as*

$$\mathbf{C} = \{(0,1,1,1,0,0), (1,0,1,0,1,0), (1,1,0,0,0,1), (0,0,0,1,1,1), \\ (0,0,0,0,0,0), (1,1,0,1,1,0), (1,0,1,1,0,1), (0,1,1,0,1,1)\}.$$

Encoding by $\mathbf{C}$ *is defined as an arbitrarily bijective mapping from* $\mathbf{F}^3$ *to* $\mathbf{C}$. *The following is one example of the bijective mapping:*

$$(0,0,0) \to (0,0,0,0,0,0) \quad (0,0,1) \to (1,1,0,0,0,1) \quad (0,1,0) \to (1,0,1,0,1,0) \quad (0,1,1) \to (0,1,1,0,1,1)$$
$$(1,0,0) \to (0,1,1,1,0,0) \quad (1,0,1) \to (1,0,1,1,0,1) \quad (1,1,0) \to (1,1,0,1,1,0) \quad (1,1,1) \to (0,0,0,1,1,1)$$

Systematic encoding is an encoding in which each bit in the information word appears in a fixed position of the codeword. The above encoding example is a systematic encoding because an information word $\mathbf{d} = (d_0, d_1, d_2) \in \mathbf{F}^3$ is mapped to a codeword $\mathbf{u} = (u_0, u_1, u_2, u_3, u_4, u_5) \in \mathbf{C}$, where $d_0 = u_3, d_1 = u_4$, and $d_2 = u_5$.

3.3.2 Generator matrix

Since linear block code $\mathbf{C}$ of length n over GF(q) is a linear subspace, $\mathbf{C}$ can be specified by a set of basis vectors $\{\mathbf{g}_0, \mathbf{g}_1, \ldots, \mathbf{g}_{k-1}\}$, where $\mathbf{g}_i$ is a row vector of length n over GF(q). Generator matrix $\mathbf{G}$ of an (n,k) linear block code $\mathbf{C}$ is defined as a $k \times n$ matrix over GF(q) whose row vectors are basis vectors of $\mathbf{C}$, that is,

$$\mathbf{G} = \begin{bmatrix} g_{0,0} & \cdots & g_{0,n-1} \\ \vdots & \ddots & \vdots \\ g_{k-1,0} & \cdots & g_{k-1,n-1} \end{bmatrix} = \begin{bmatrix} \mathbf{g}_0 \\ \vdots \\ \mathbf{g}_{k-1} \end{bmatrix},$$

where $g_{i,j} \in \mathrm{GF}(q)$ for $0 \le i \le k-1$ and $0 \le j \le n-1$. The code $\mathbf{C}$ is defined using the generator matrix $\mathbf{G}$ as follows:

$$\mathbf{C} = \{\mathbf{u} = (u_0, u_1, \ldots, u_{n-1}) = \mathbf{dG} \mid \mathbf{d} = (d_0, d_1, \ldots, d_{k-1}), d_i \in \mathrm{GF}(q)\}.$$

From this definition, linear code $\mathbf{C}$ is equivalent to the row space of $\mathbf{G}$.

Example 9. *A generator matrix of the linear block code* $\mathbf{C}$ *shown in Example 8 is given as*

$$\mathbf{G} = \begin{bmatrix} 0\,1\,1\,1\,0\,0 \\ 1\,0\,1\,0\,1\,0 \\ 1\,1\,0\,0\,0\,1 \end{bmatrix}.$$

3.3.3 Parity-check matrix

Let $\widetilde{\mathbf{C}}$ be the null space of linear code $\mathbf{C}$, and let $\{\mathbf{h}_0, \mathbf{h}_1, \ldots, \mathbf{h}_{r-1}\}$ be the set of basis vectors of $\widetilde{\mathbf{C}}$, where $\mathbf{h}_i$ is a row vector of length n over GF(q), and $r = n - k$. Parity-check matrix $\mathbf{H}$ of the linear code $\mathbf{C}$ is defined as the following $r \times n$ matrix over GF(q):

$$\mathbf{H} = \begin{bmatrix} h_{0,0} & \cdots & h_{0,n-1} \\ \vdots & \ddots & \vdots \\ h_{r-1,0} & \cdots & h_{r-1,n-1} \end{bmatrix} = \begin{bmatrix} \mathbf{h}_0 \\ \vdots \\ \mathbf{h}_{r-1} \end{bmatrix},$$

where $h_{i,j} \in \mathrm{GF}(q)$ for $0 \le i \le r-1$ and $0 \le j \le n-1$. The code $\mathbf{C}$ is defined by the parity-check matrix as follows:

$$\mathbf{C} = \{\mathbf{u} = (u_0, u_1, \ldots, u_{n-1}) \mid \mathbf{Hu}^T = \mathbf{o}^T = (0, \ldots, 0)^T, u_i \in \mathrm{GF}(q)\}.$$

In this definition, the code $\mathbf{C}$ is equivalent to the null space of the row space of $\mathbf{H}$.

Example 10. *An example parity-check matrix of the code* $\mathbf{C}$ *shown in Example 8 is given as*

$$\mathbf{H} = \begin{bmatrix} 1\,0\,0\,0\,1\,1 \\ 0\,1\,0\,1\,0\,1 \\ 0\,0\,1\,1\,1\,0 \end{bmatrix}.$$

3.3.4 Minimum distance

Let $\mathbf{u} = (u_0, u_1, \ldots, u_{n-1})$ and $\mathbf{v} = (v_0, v_1, \ldots, v_{n-1})$ be vectors of length n over GF(q). Hamming weight of $\mathbf{u}$ is defined as

$$w(\mathbf{u}) = (\text{the number of nonzero elements in } \mathbf{u}),$$

and Hamming distance between $\mathbf{u}$ and $\mathbf{v}$ is defined as $d(\mathbf{u},\mathbf{v}) = w(\mathbf{u}-\mathbf{v})$. In other words, Hamming distance $d(\mathbf{u},\mathbf{v})$ is the number of component positions in which the two vectors differ. Minimum distance of a block code $\mathbf{C}$ is defined as

$$d_{\min}(\mathbf{C}) = \min_{\mathbf{u},\mathbf{v}\in\mathbf{C},\mathbf{u}\neq\mathbf{v}} d(\mathbf{u},\mathbf{v}).$$

In general, it is hard to determine the minimum distance from the above definition if the cardinality of $\mathbf{C}$ is large. The following theorems are useful to determine the minimum distance of a linear block code.

Theorem 2. *For a linear block code* $\mathbf{C}$*, it holds that* $d_{\min}(\mathbf{C}) = \min_{\mathbf{u}\in\mathbf{C},\mathbf{u}\neq\mathbf{o}} w(\mathbf{u})$.

Proof. Since $\mathbf{C}$ is a linear block code, the following relation holds:

$$d_{\min}(\mathbf{C}) = \min_{\mathbf{u},\mathbf{v}\in\mathbf{C},\mathbf{u}\neq\mathbf{v}} d(\mathbf{u},\mathbf{v}) = \min_{\mathbf{u},\mathbf{v}\in\mathbf{C},\mathbf{u}\neq\mathbf{v}} w(\mathbf{u}-\mathbf{v}) = \min_{\mathbf{w}\in\mathbf{C},\mathbf{w}\neq\mathbf{o}} w(\mathbf{w}).$$

□

The above theorem says that the minimum distance of a linear block code $\mathbf{C}$ is equal to the minimum Hamming weight of non-zero codeword of $\mathbf{C}$. The minimum Hamming weight of non-zero codeword can be determined from the parity-check matrix as follows.

Theorem 3. *Let* $\mathbf{H}$ *be a parity-check matrix of linear block code* $\mathbf{C}$*. If there exist* d *column vectors in* $\mathbf{H}$ *which are linearly dependent, and also* $d-1$ *or fewer column vectors in* $\mathbf{H}$ *are linearly independent, then the minimum Hamming weight of non-zero codeword of* $\mathbf{C}$ *is* d*.*

Proof. Since $\mathbf{H}$ has d column vectors which are linearly dependent, there exists a codeword $\mathbf{u}$ of Hamming weight d satisfying $\mathbf{H}\mathbf{u}^T = \mathbf{o}^T$. Also, since $d-1$ or fewer column vectors in $\mathbf{H}$ are linearly independent, any vector $\mathbf{x}$ of Hamming weight $1 \leq w(\mathbf{x}) \leq d-1$ does not satisfy $\mathbf{H}\mathbf{x}^T = \mathbf{o}$, which means that $\mathbf{C}$ does not have non-zero codeword of Hamming weight less than or equal to $d-1$. Therefore, the minimum Hamming weight of non-zero codeword of $\mathbf{C}$ is d. □

Combining Theorems 2 and 3, the following theorem is obtained.

Theorem 4. *Let* $\mathbf{H}$ *be a parity-check matrix of linear block code* $\mathbf{C}$*. If there exist* d *column vectors in* $\mathbf{H}$ *which are linearly dependent, and also* $d-1$ *or fewer column vectors in* $\mathbf{H}$ *are linearly independent, then the minimum distance of* $\mathbf{C}$ *is* d*.*

3.3.5 Error control capability of bounded distance decoding

Let $\mathbf{u} = (u_0, u_1, \ldots, u_{n-1})$ be a codeword over GF(q), and let

$$\mathbf{r} = (r_0, r_1, \ldots, r_{n-1}) = \mathbf{u} + \mathbf{e} = (u_0, u_1, \ldots, u_{n-1}) + (e_0, e_1, \ldots, e_{n-1})$$

be a received word, that is, a readout word from flash memory, where $\mathbf{e}$ is an error vector over GF(q). The number of errors in $\mathbf{r}$ is defined as $d(\mathbf{u},\mathbf{r}) = w(\mathbf{u}-\mathbf{r}) = w(\mathbf{e})$.

Theorem 5. *A block code of minimum distance* d *is capable of correcting* t *errors and detecting* s *errors by the bounded distance decoding, where* $d \geq t+s+1$ *and* $t \leq s$*.*

Figure 6 illustrates the relation between t, s and d under the bounded distance decoding.

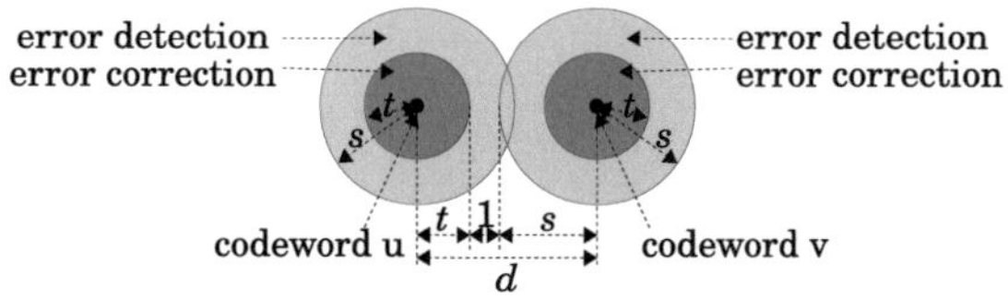

Fig. 6. Relation between the minimum distance and error correction/detection capabilities under the bounded distance decoding.

3.4 Cyclic code

3.4.1 Construction

Cyclic code **C** is a subclass of linear block code satisfying the following condition:

$$\mathbf{u} = (u_0, u_1, \ldots, u_{n-2}, u_{n-1}) \in \mathbf{C} \quad \Rightarrow \quad \mathbf{u}' = (u_{n-1}, u_0, \ldots, u_{n-3}, u_{n-2}) \in \mathbf{C}.$$

That is, if **u** is a codeword of **C**, then a cyclic shift of **u** is also a codeword. Cyclic code is usually defined using polynomials over GF(q). Let $\mathbf{u} = (u_0, u_1, \ldots, u_{n-1})$ and $\mathbf{v} = (v_0, v_1, \ldots, v_{n-1})$ be codewords of **C**. Polynomial representations of $\mathbf{u} \in \mathbf{C}$ and $\mathbf{v} \in \mathbf{C}$ are given as follows:

$$\mathbf{u}(x) = u_0 + u_1x + u_2x^2 + \ldots + u_{n-1}x^{n-1}, \quad \mathbf{v}(x) = v_0 + v_1x + v_2x^2 + \ldots + v_{n-1}x^{n-1},$$

where $u_i, v_i \in \mathrm{GF}(q)$. Addition of two codewords $\mathbf{u}(x) \in \mathbf{C}$ and $\mathbf{v}(x) \in \mathbf{C}$ is expressed as

$$\mathbf{u}(x) + \mathbf{v}(x) = (u_0 + v_0) + (u_1 + v_1)x + (u_2 + v_2)x^2 + \cdots + (u_{n-1} + v_{n-1})x^{n-1},$$

and right cyclic shift of $\mathbf{u}(x) \in \mathbf{C}$ as

$$x\mathbf{u}(x) \bmod (x^n - 1) = u_{n-1} + u_0x + u_1x^2 + \cdots + u_{n-2}x^{n-1} \in \mathbf{C}. \tag{2}$$

By recursively applying the relation of Eq.(2), we obtain $x^i\mathbf{u}(x) \bmod (x^n - 1) \in \mathbf{C}$ for any non-negative integer i. Since **C** is a linear block code, $(x^i + x^j)\mathbf{u}(x) \bmod (x^n - 1) \in \mathbf{C}$ for any pair of non-negative integers i and j. This implies that, if $\mathbf{u}(x)$ is a codeword of **C**, then $\mathbf{f}(x)\mathbf{u}(x) \bmod (x^n - 1)$ is also a codeword of **C**, where $\mathbf{f}(x)$ is a polynomial over GF(q).

Definition 1. *Let $\mathbf{g}(x)$ be a factor of $(x^n - 1)$, that is, $(x^n - 1) = \mathbf{g}(x)\mathbf{h}(x)$, where the degree of $\mathbf{g}(x)$ is r. Cyclic code **C** over GF(q) of length n is defined using $\mathbf{g}(x)$ as the generator polynomial, that is,*

$$\begin{aligned}\mathbf{C} &= \{\mathbf{f}(x)\mathbf{g}(x) \bmod (x^n - 1) \mid \mathbf{f}(x)\text{: polynomial over GF}(q)\} \\ &= \{\mathbf{d}(x)\mathbf{g}(x) \mid \mathbf{d}(x)\text{: polynomial over GF}(q) \text{ of degree less than } n - r\}.\end{aligned}$$

The following theorem is obvious from the above definition.

Theorem 6. *Let **C** be a cyclic code generated by $\mathbf{g}(x)$. Polynomial $\mathbf{u}(x)$ is a codeword of **C** if and only if*

$$\mathbf{u}(x) \bmod \mathbf{g}(x) = 0.$$

Example 11. *Polynomial $(x^7 - 1)$ over GF(2) is factorized as*

$$(x^7 - 1) = (x^3 + x + 1)(x^3 + x^2 + 1)(x + 1).$$

Let $\mathbf{g}(x) = x^3 + x + 1$ be the generator polynomial of cyclic code of length $n = 7$. Table 4 lists codewords of the cyclic code generated by $\mathbf{g}(x)$. This code is referred to as $(7, 4)$ cyclic Hamming code.

Example 12. *Cyclic redundancy check (CRC) codes are used as error detecting code. Table 5 shows generator polynomials of standardized CRC codes (Lin & Costello, 2004; Witzke & Leung, 1985).*

$\mathbf{d}(x)$	$\mathbf{u}(x) = \mathbf{d}(x)\mathbf{g}(x)$	(vector)	$\mathbf{d}(x)$	$\mathbf{u}(x) = \mathbf{d}(x)\mathbf{g}(x)$	(vector)
0	0	(0000000)	x^3	$x^3 + x^4 + x^6$	(0001101)
1	$1 + x + x^3$	(1101000)	$1 + x^3$	$1 + x + x^4 + x^6$	(1100101)
x	$x + x^2 + x^4$	(0110100)	$x + x^3$	$x + x^2 + x^3 + x^6$	(0111001)
$1 + x$	$1 + x^2 + x^3 + x^4$	(1011100)	$1 + x + x^3$	$1 + x^2 + x^6$	(1010001)
x^2	$x^2 + x^3 + x^5$	(0011010)	$x^2 + x^3$	$x^2 + x^4 + x^5 + x^6$	(0010111)
$1 + x^2$	$1 + x + x^2 + x^5$	(1110010)	$1 + x^2 + x^3$	$1+x+x^2+x^3+x^4+x^5+x^6$	(1111111)
$x + x^2$	$x + x^3 + x^4 + x^5$	(0101110)	$x + x^2 + x^3$	$x + x^5 + x^6$	(0100011)
$1+x+x^2$	$1 + x^4 + x^5$	(1000110)	$1+x+x^2+x^3$	$1 + x^3 + x^5 + x^6$	(1001011)

Table 4. $(7,4)$ Cyclic Hamming code generated by $g(x) = x^3 + x + 1$.

Standard	Generator polynomial	Standard	Generator polynomial
CRC-12	$x^{12} + x^{11} + x^3 + x^2 + x + 1$	CRC-16	$x^{16} + x^{15} + x^2 + 1$
IBM-SDLC	$x^{16} + x^{15} + x^{13} + x^7 + x^4 + x^2 + x + 1$	CCITT X-25	$x^{16} + x^{12} + x^5 + 1$
CD-ROM	$x^{32} + x^{31} + x^{16} + x^{15} + x^4 + x^3 + x + 1$	DVD-ROM	$x^{32} + x^{31} + x^4 + 1$
IEC TC57	$x^{16} + x^{14} + x^{11} + x^8 + x^6 + x^5 + x^4 + 1$		
IEEE 802.3	$x^{32}+x^{26}+x^{23}+x^{22}+x^{16}+x^{12}+x^{11}+x^{10}+x^8+x^7+x^5+x^4+x^2+x+1$		

Table 5. Example of standardized CRC code.

3.4.2 Systematic encoding

Let $\mathbf{C}$ be a cyclic code of length n, and let $\mathbf{g}(x)$ be a degree-r generator polynomial of $\mathbf{C}$. Systematic encoding of an information word $\mathbf{d}(x)$ of degree $k = n - r$ by $\mathbf{C}$ is defined as

$$\mathbf{u}(x) = x^r \mathbf{d}(x) - \rho(x),$$

where $\rho(x) = x^r \mathbf{d}(x) \bmod \mathbf{g}(x)$. It can be easily verified that $\mathbf{u}(x)$ is a codeword of $\mathbf{C}$ because the following relation holds.

$$\begin{aligned}\mathbf{u}(x) \bmod \mathbf{g}(x) &= (x^r \mathbf{d}(x) - \rho(x)) \bmod \mathbf{g}(x) \\ &= (x^r \mathbf{d}(x) - x^r \mathbf{d}(x) \bmod \mathbf{g}(x)) \bmod \mathbf{g}(x) \\ &= (x^r \mathbf{d}(x) - x^r \mathbf{d}(x)) \bmod \mathbf{g}(x) = 0.\end{aligned}$$

This systematic encoding generates a codeword

$$\mathbf{u}(x) = u_0 + u_1 x + \cdots + u_{r-1} x^{r-1} + u_r x^r + u_{r+1} x^{r+1} + \ldots u_{n-1} x^{n-1},$$

where the first r terms correspond to the check part $\rho(x)$, and the remaining $k = n - r$ terms to the information word $\mathbf{d}(x)$.

Example 13. *Table 6 presents the systematic encoding of the (7,4) cyclic Hamming code generated by* $g(x) = x^3 + x + 1$. *Although this code is identical to the code shown in Table 4, the mapping from* $\mathbf{d}(x)$ *to* $\mathbf{u}(x)$ *is systematic, that is,* $\mathbf{d}(x) = d_0 + d_1 x + d_2 x^2 + d_3 x^3$ *corresponds to* $u_3 x^3 + u_4 x^4 + u_5 x^5 + u_6 x^6$.

4. Basic error control codes

This section introduces basic error control codes which have been applied to various digital systems. All codes presented in this section are linear codes of length n defined over GF(2^m), where m is a positive integer. That is, a codeword is expressed as $\mathbf{u} = (u_0, u_1, \ldots, u_{n-1})$, where $u_i \in \mathrm{GF}(2^m)$ for $0 \le i \le n-1$. Here, u_i is referred to as *bit* (for $m = 1$) or *symbol* (for $m \ge 2$). Example of codeword structure of a systematic code is shown in Fig. 7(a), where the

$\mathbf{d}(x)$	$\mathbf{u}(x)$	(vector)	$\mathbf{d}(x)$	$\mathbf{u}(x)$	(vector)
0	0	(0000000)	x^3	$1+x^2+x^6$	(1010001)
1	$1+x+x^3$	(1101000)	$1+x^3$	$x+x^2+x^3+x^6$	(0111001)
x	$x+x^2+x^4$	(0110100)	$x+x^3$	$1+x+x^4+x^6$	(1100101)
$1+x$	$1+x^2+x^3+x^4$	(1011100)	$1+x+x^3$	$x^3+x^4+x^6$	(0001101)
x^2	$1+x+x^2+x^5$	(1110010)	x^2+x^3	$x+x^5+x^6$	(0100011)
$1+x^2$	$x^2+x^3+x^5$	(0011010)	$1+x^2+x^3$	$1+x^3+x^5+x^6$	(1001011)
$x+x^2$	$1+x^4+x^5$	(1000110)	$x+x^2+x^3$	$x^2+x^4+x^5+x^6$	(0010111)
$1+x+x^2$	$x+x^3+x^4+x^5$	(0101110)	$1+x+x^2+x^3$	$1+x+x^2+x^3+x^4+x^5+x^6$	(1111111)

Table 6. Systematic encoding of $(7,4)$ cyclic Hamming code generated by $g(x) = x^3 + x + 1$.

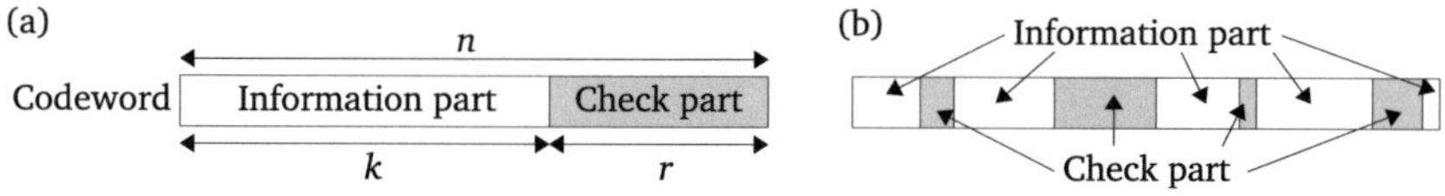

Fig. 7. Example of systematic codeword structure.

codeword consists of information and check parts of length k and r, respectively. Note that the check part can be divided and distributed over the codeword, as illustrated in Fig, 7(b).

4.1 Parity-check code

4.1.1 Definition

Parity-check code is a single-bit error detecting code over GF(2) whose codeword is expressed as $\mathbf{u} = (u_0, u_1, \ldots, u_{n-1})$, where $u_i \in \mathrm{GF}(2)$ for $0 \leq i \leq n-1$ and $\sum_{i=0}^{n-1} u_i = 0$. Here, the information length is $k = n - r = n - 1$ and the minimum distance is $d_{\min} = 2$. The parity-check and generator matrices are given as

$$\mathbf{H} = \begin{bmatrix} 1 \; 1 \; \ldots \; 1 \end{bmatrix}_{1\times n} \quad \text{and} \quad \mathbf{G} = \left[\begin{array}{c|c} \mathbf{I}_k & \begin{matrix} 1 \\ \vdots \\ 1 \end{matrix} \end{array} \right] = \left[\begin{array}{ccc|c} 1 & & 0 & 1 \\ & \ddots & & \vdots \\ 0 & & 1 & 1 \end{array} \right]_{k\times n},$$

respectively, where $\mathbf{I}_k$ is the $k \times k$ identity matrix.

4.1.2 Encoding/decoding

Encoding: Let $\mathbf{d} = (d_0, d_1, \ldots, d_{k-1})$ be an information word of length k. Codeword $\mathbf{u}$ for the information word $\mathbf{d}$ is determined as $\mathbf{u} = (u_0, u_1, \ldots, u_{n-2}, u_{n-1}) = (d_0, d_1, \ldots, d_{k-1}, p)$, where $n = k+1$ and $p = \sum_{i=0}^{k-1} d_i$.

Decoding: Let $\mathbf{r} = (r_0, r_1, \ldots, r_{n-1})$ be a received word, where $r_i \in \mathrm{GF}(2)$ for $0 \leq i \leq n-1$. Syndrome s is calculated as $s = \sum_{i=0}^{n-1} r_i$. If $s = 0$ holds, $\mathbf{r}$ is assumed to have no error; otherwise $\mathbf{r}$ has an odd number of errors.

4.2 Hamming SEC code

4.2.1 Definition

Hamming code is a single-bit error correcting (SEC) code over GF(2) defined by a parity-check matrix $\mathbf{H}$ whose column vectors are nonzero and distinct. The code length n of the Hamming code is upper bounded by $n \leq 2^r - 1$, where r is the number of check bits. Table 7 presents the maximum code length and information length of the Hamming code for $2 \leq r \leq 10$. Systematic parity-check matrix $\mathbf{H}$ of $(n, n-r)$ Hamming SEC code is expressed as $\mathbf{H} = \left[\mathbf{Q} | \mathbf{I}_r \right]$, where $\mathbf{Q}$ is an $r \times (n-r)$ matrix whose column vectors have Hamming weight ≥ 2,

Check length: r	2	3	4	5	6	7	8	9	10
Maximum code length: $n = 2^r - 1$	3	7	15	31	63	127	255	511	1023
Information length: $k = n - r$	1	4	11	26	57	120	247	502	1013

Table 7. Maximum code length n and information length k of Hamming code.

and $\mathbf{I}_r$ is the $r \times r$ identity matrix. Generator matrix of the code is $\mathbf{G} = \left[\,\mathbf{I}_k \middle| \mathbf{Q}^T\,\right]$, where $\mathbf{Q}^T$ indicates the transpose of $\mathbf{Q}$.

Example 14. *The following shows the parity-check and generator matrices of* $(7,4)$ *Hamming code:*

$$\mathbf{H} = \left[\,\mathbf{Q} \middle| \mathbf{I}_3\,\right] = \left[\begin{array}{cccc|ccc} 0 & 1 & 1 & 1 & 1 & 0 & 0 \\ 1 & 0 & 1 & 1 & 0 & 1 & 0 \\ 1 & 1 & 0 & 1 & 0 & 0 & 1 \end{array}\right] \quad \text{and} \quad \mathbf{G} = \left[\,\mathbf{I}_4 \middle| \mathbf{Q}^T\,\right] = \left[\begin{array}{cccc|ccc} 1 & 0 & 0 & 0 & 0 & 1 & 1 \\ 0 & 1 & 0 & 0 & 1 & 0 & 1 \\ 0 & 0 & 1 & 0 & 1 & 1 & 0 \\ 0 & 0 & 0 & 1 & 1 & 1 & 1 \end{array}\right].$$

4.2.2 Encoding

Encoding using generator matrix

Let $\mathbf{G}$ be a $k \times n$ generator matrix of (n,k) Hamming code. Information word $\mathbf{d} = (d_0, d_1, \ldots, d_{k-1})$ of length k is encoded as $\mathbf{u} = (u_0, u_1, \ldots, u_{n-1}) = \mathbf{dG}$.

Example 15. *Let* $\mathbf{G}$ *be the generator matrix of Example 14. Information word* $\mathbf{d} = (0,1,1,0)$ *is encoded as*

$$\mathbf{u} = \mathbf{dG} = (0,1,1,0) \left[\begin{array}{cccc|ccc} 1 & 0 & 0 & 0 & 0 & 1 & 1 \\ 0 & 1 & 0 & 0 & 1 & 0 & 1 \\ 0 & 0 & 1 & 0 & 1 & 1 & 0 \\ 0 & 0 & 0 & 1 & 1 & 1 & 1 \end{array}\right] = (0,1,1,0,0,1,1).$$

Encoding using systematic parity-check matrix

Let $\mathbf{H} = \left[\,\mathbf{Q} \middle| \mathbf{I}_r\,\right]$ be an $r \times n$ systematic parity-check matrix of $(n, n-r)$ Hamming code, and let $\mathbf{d} = (d_0, d_1, \ldots, d_{k-1})$ be an information word of length $k = n - r$. This information word $\mathbf{d}$ is encoded as $\mathbf{u} = (\mathbf{d}, \mathbf{p}) = (d_0, d_1, \ldots, d_{k-1}, p_0, p_1, \ldots, p_{r-1})$, where the check part $\mathbf{p}$ is determined as $\mathbf{p} = (p_0, p_1, \ldots, p_{r-1}) = \mathbf{dQ}^T$.

Example 16. *Let* $\mathbf{H} = \left[\,\mathbf{Q} \middle| \mathbf{I}_3\,\right]$ *be the systematic parity-check matrix of Example 14. The check part* $\mathbf{p}$ *for information word* $\mathbf{d} = (0,1,1,0)$ *is calculated as*

$$\mathbf{p} = \mathbf{dQ}^T = (0,1,1,0) \begin{bmatrix} 0 & 1 & 1 \\ 1 & 0 & 1 \\ 1 & 1 & 0 \\ 1 & 1 & 1 \end{bmatrix} = (0,1,1).$$

Thus, codeword is generated as $\mathbf{u} = (\mathbf{d}, \mathbf{p}) = (0,1,1,0,\ 0,1,1)$.

4.2.3 Decoding

Let $\mathbf{u}' = (u'_0, u'_1, \ldots, u'_{n-1})$ be a received word expressed as

$$\mathbf{u}' = \mathbf{u} + \mathbf{e} = (u_0, u_1, \ldots, u_{n-1}) + (e_0, e_1, \ldots, e_{n-1}),$$

where $\mathbf{u}$ is an original codeword and $\mathbf{e}$ is an error vector. If $\mathbf{e}$ is the zero-vector, $\mathbf{u}'$ has no error. Hamming SEC code can recover $\mathbf{u}$ from $\mathbf{u}'$ when $w(\mathbf{e}) \leq 1$. Decoding is based on the following relation:

$$\mathbf{s} = \mathbf{H}{\mathbf{u}'}^T = \mathbf{H}(\mathbf{u} + \mathbf{e})^T = \mathbf{H}\mathbf{u}^T + \mathbf{H}\mathbf{e}^T = \mathbf{H}\mathbf{e}^T.$$

Check length: r	3	4	5	6	7	8	9	10	11
Maximum code length: $n = 2^{r-1}$	4	8	16	32	64	128	256	512	1024
Information length: $k = n - r$	1	4	11	26	57	120	247	502	1013

Table 8. Maximum code length n and information length k of OWC SEC-DED code.

This relation says that, if $\mathbf{u}'$ has a single bit error in the i-th bit, the syndrome $\mathbf{s}$ is equal to the i-th column vector of $\mathbf{H}$, where $0 \le i \le n-1$. The received word $\mathbf{u}'$ is decoded as follows:

1. The syndrome $\mathbf{s}$ is calculated as $\mathbf{s} = \mathbf{H}\mathbf{u}'^T$.
2. If $\mathbf{s}$ is the zero-vector, then $\mathbf{u}'$ is assumed to have no error, and thus decoded word is determined as $\widetilde{\mathbf{u}} = \mathbf{u}'$.
3. If $\mathbf{s}$ is equal to the i-th column vector of $\mathbf{H}$, the received word $\mathbf{u}'$ is assumed to have an error in the i-th bit. Decoded word is determined as $\widetilde{\mathbf{u}} = \mathbf{u}' + \mathbf{i}_i$, where $\mathbf{i}_i$ is a binary vector whose i-th element is 1 and the other elements are 0.
4. If $\mathbf{s}$ is nonzero and is not equal to any column vector of $\mathbf{H}$, the received word $\mathbf{u}'$ has multiple-bit error. Decoding result of this case is *uncorrectable error detection*.

Example 17. *Let* $\mathbf{u} = (0,1,1,0,0,1,1)$ *be the codeword generated in Example 16, and let* $\mathbf{e} = (0,0,1,0,0,0,0)$ *be the error vector. Received word is given as*

$$\mathbf{u}' = (0,1,1,0,0,1,1) + (0,0,1,0,0,0,0) = (0,1,0,0,0,1,1).$$

The syndrome of $\mathbf{u}'$ *is calculated as*

$$\mathbf{s} = \mathbf{H}\mathbf{u}'^T = \left[\begin{array}{cccc|ccc} 0&1&1&1&1&0&0 \\ 1&0&1&1&0&1&0 \\ 1&1&0&1&0&0&1 \end{array}\right] (0,1,0,0,0,1,1)^T = (1,1,0)^T.$$

Since the calculated syndrome is equal to the 2nd column of $\mathbf{H}$*, decoded word is determined as*

$$\widetilde{\mathbf{u}} = \mathbf{u}' + \mathbf{i}_2 = (0,1,0,0,0,1,1) + (0,0,1,0,0,0,0) = (0,1,1,0,0,1,1) = \mathbf{u}.$$

4.3 Odd-weight column (OWC) SEC-DED code

4.3.1 Definition

OWC code is a liner code over GF(2) having minimum distance $d_{\min} = 4$, and thus this code can be used as either single-bit error correcting - double-bit error detecting (SEC-DED) code or triple-bit error detecting (TED) code. The code length n of the OWC code is upper bounded by $n \le 2^{r-1}$, where r is the number of check bits. Table 8 presents the maximum code length and information length of the OWC SEC-DED code for $3 \le r \le 11$.

Parity-check matrix of this code is generated from odd-weight column vectors. Systematic parity-check matrix of $(n, n-r)$ OWC code is expressed as $\mathbf{H} = [\,\mathbf{Q}_O | \mathbf{I}_r\,]$, where $\mathbf{Q}_O$ is an $r \times (n-r)$ matrix whose column vectors have odd Hamming weight $w \ge 3$, and $\mathbf{I}_r$ is the $r \times r$ identity matrix. Generator matrix of the code is given as $\mathbf{G} = [\,\mathbf{I}_k | \mathbf{Q}_O^T\,]$.

Example 18. *The following shows the parity-check and generator matrices of* $(8,4)$ *OWC code:*

$$\mathbf{H} = [\,\mathbf{Q}_O \,|\, \mathbf{I}_4\,] = \left[\begin{array}{cccc|cccc} 0&1&1&1&1&0&0&0 \\ 1&0&1&1&0&1&0&0 \\ 1&1&0&1&0&0&1&0 \\ 1&1&1&0&0&0&0&1 \end{array}\right] \quad \textit{and} \quad \mathbf{G} = [\,\mathbf{I}_4 \,|\, \mathbf{Q}_O^T\,] = \left[\begin{array}{cccc|cccc} 1&0&0&0&0&1&1&1 \\ 0&1&0&0&1&0&1&1 \\ 0&0&1&0&1&1&0&1 \\ 0&0&0&1&1&1&1&0 \end{array}\right].$$

m		3	4	5	6	7	8	9	10
n		7	15	31	63	127	255	511	1023
	$(t=1)$	4	11	26	57	120	247	502	1013
	$(t=2)$	-	7	21	51	113	239	493	1003
k	$(t=3)$	-	5	16	45	106	231	484	993
	$(t=4)$	-	-	11	39	99	223	475	983
	$(t=5)$	-	-	6	36	92	215	466	973

Table 9. Maximum code length n and information length k of t-bit error correcting BCH code.

4.3.2 Encoding

Information word $\mathbf{d} = (d_0, d_1, \ldots, d_{k-1})$ is encoded by either generator matrix $\mathbf{G}$ or systematic parity-check matrix $\mathbf{H} = \left[\mathbf{Q}_O \middle| \mathbf{I}_r\right]$ in the same way as the Hamming SEC code.

Example 19. *Information word* $\mathbf{d} = (0,1,0,1)$ *is encoded by the generator matrix* $\mathbf{G}$ *of Example 18 as*

$$\mathbf{u} = \mathbf{dG} = (0,1,0,1)\left[\begin{array}{cccc|cccc} 1&0&0&0&0&1&1&1 \\ 0&1&0&0&1&0&1&1 \\ 0&0&1&0&1&1&0&1 \\ 0&0&0&1&1&1&1&0 \end{array}\right] = (0,1,0,1,0,1,0,1).$$

4.3.3 Decoding

Decoding is based on the Hamming weight of syndrome $\mathbf{s} = \mathbf{Hu}'^T = \mathbf{He}'^T$. That is, since every column vector of $\mathbf{H}$ has an odd Hamming weight, syndrome $\mathbf{s}$ of a single-bit error has an odd weight, while that of a double-bit error has an even weight $w \geq 2$. This means that the syndromes of double-bit errors are distinct from those of single-bit errors. Hence, the OWC SEC-DED code can be decoded in the same way as Hamming code shown in **4.2.3**.

Example 20. *Let* $\mathbf{u} = (0,1,0,1,0,1,0,1)$ *be the codeword generated in Example 19, and let* $\mathbf{e} = (0,1,0,0,0,0,1,0)$ *be the error vector. Received word is given as*

$$\mathbf{u}' = \mathbf{u} + \mathbf{e} = (0,1,0,1,0,1,0,1) + (0,1,0,0,0,0,1,0) = (0,0,0,1,0,1,1,1).$$

The syndrome of $\mathbf{u}'$ *is calculated as*

$$\mathbf{s} = \mathbf{Hu}'^T = \left[\begin{array}{cccc|cccc} 0&1&1&1&1&0&0&0 \\ 1&0&1&1&0&1&0&0 \\ 1&1&0&1&0&0&1&0 \\ 1&1&1&0&0&0&0&1 \end{array}\right](0,0,0,1,0,1,1,1)^T = (1,0,0,1)^T.$$

Since the calculated syndrome has even Hamming weight $w(\mathbf{s}) = 2$, *the syndrome is not equal to any column vector of* $\mathbf{H}$. *Hence, the decoding algorithm indicates that* $\mathbf{u}'$ *has uncorrectable errors.*

4.4 BCH code

4.4.1 Definition

Binary primitive BCH code is a t-bit error correcting cyclic code of length $n = 2^m - 1$ with $r \leq mt$ check bits, where $t \geq 1$ and $m \geq 2$. In most cases, $r = mt$ holds, and thus information length is $k = 2^m - 1 - mt$. Table 9 presents the maximum code length n and information length k of the BCH code for $3 \leq m \leq 10$ and $1 \leq t \leq 5$ (Lin & Costello, 2004).

Let α be a primitive element of GF(2^m). The parity-check matrix of t-bit error correcting BCH code is defined as

$$\mathbf{H} = \begin{bmatrix} 1 & \alpha^1 & \alpha^2 & \alpha^3 & \cdots & \alpha^i & \cdots & \alpha^{n-1} \\ 1 & \alpha^3 & (\alpha^3)^2 & (\alpha^3)^3 & \cdots & (\alpha^3)^i & \cdots & (\alpha^3)^{n-1} \\ 1 & \alpha^5 & (\alpha^5)^2 & (\alpha^5)^3 & \cdots & (\alpha^5)^i & \cdots & (\alpha^5)^{n-1} \\ \vdots & \vdots & \vdots & \vdots & & \vdots & & \vdots \\ 1 & \alpha^{2t-1} & (\alpha^{2t-1})^2 & (\alpha^{2t-1})^3 & \cdots & (\alpha^{2t-1})^i & \cdots & (\alpha^{2t-1})^{n-1} \end{bmatrix},$$

where α^i is expressed as a column vector of length m.
Generator matrix of the binary primitive BCH code is derived from the generator polynomial as follows. Let $\mathrm{cnj}_m(i)$ be a set of exponents of *conjugates* of $\alpha^i \in$ GF(2^m), defined as follows:

$$\mathrm{cnj}_m(i) = \{\, i \cdot 2^j \bmod (2^m - 1) \mid j \in \{0, 1, 2, \dots\} \,\}.$$

Minimal polynomial of $\alpha^i \in$ GF(2^m) is defined as

$$\phi_i(x) = \prod_{j \in \mathrm{cnj}_m(i)} (x - \alpha^j).$$

The generator polynomial of t-bit error correcting BCH code is given as

$$\mathbf{g}(x) = g_0 + g_1 x + g_2 x^2 + \cdots + g_r x^r = \mathrm{LCM}\{\phi_1(x), \phi_3(x), \dots, \phi_{2t-1}(x)\},$$

where LCM is the least common multiple of polynomials, and $g_i \in$ GF(2). Then, generator matrix is determined as

$$\mathbf{G} = \begin{bmatrix} g_0 & g_1 & g_2 & \cdots\cdots & g_r & 0 & \cdots\cdots & 0 \\ 0 & g_0 & g_1 & g_2 & \cdots\cdots & g_r & 0 & \cdots & 0 \\ 0 & 0 & g_0 & g_1 & g_2 & \cdots\cdots & g_r & 0 \cdots & 0 \\ & & & & \vdots & & & & \\ 0 & \cdots\cdots & 0 & g_0 & g_1 & g_2 & \cdots\cdots & & g_r \end{bmatrix}.$$

4.4.2 Encoding/decoding

Information word is encoded using either generator matrix $\mathbf{G}$ or generator polynomial $\mathbf{g}(x)$ as described in **3.4.2**. From the definition of generator polynomial $\mathbf{g}(x)$, a codeword polynomial $\mathbf{u}(x) = u_0 + u_1 x + u_2 x^2 + \cdots + u_{n-1} x^{n-1}$ has $2t$ consecutive roots, $\alpha^1, \alpha^2, \dots, \alpha^{2t}$, that is $\mathbf{u}(\alpha^i) = 0$ for $i \in \{1, 2, \dots, 2t\}$. Using this relation, a received word $\mathbf{u}'(x) = u'_0 + u'_1 x + u'_2 x^2 + \cdots + u'_{n-1} x^{n-1}$ is decoded as follows.

1. *Syndrome calculation:* Syndrome $\mathbf{s}$ is determined as $\mathbf{s} = (s_1, s_2, \dots, s_{2t})$, where $s_i = \mathbf{u}'(\alpha^i)$. If $\mathbf{s} = (0, 0, \dots, 0)$, then $\mathbf{u}'(x)$ is assumed to have no error.
2. *Generation of error-location polynomial $\sigma(x)$:* Error-location polynomial

$$\sigma(x) = \sigma_0 + \sigma_1 x + \cdots + \sigma_{t'} x^{t'}$$

is calculated from the syndrome $\mathbf{s}$. This polynomial has t' roots, $\alpha^{-j_1}, \alpha^{-j_2}, \dots, \alpha^{-j_{t'}}$, where $t' \le t$ is the number of errors in $\mathbf{u}'(x)$, and $j_i \in \{0, 1, \dots, n-1\}$ is the location of i-th error. The following shows Berlekamp's algorithm to derive $\sigma(x)$ from $\mathbf{s}$.

(Berlekamp's algorithm) Error-location polynomial $\sigma(x)$ is derived using Table 10, where the rows of $\mu = -1$ and $\mu = 0$ are given initial values. In the following, μ is referred to as the

μ	ρ_μ	$\sigma^\mu(x)$	l_μ	$\mu - l_\mu$	d_μ
-1	-	1	0	-1	1
0	-	1	0	0	S_1
$\vdots$					
$2t$					

Table 10. Berlekamp's algorithm.

row number. Values in the rows from $\mu = 1$ to $\mu = 2t$ are determined as follows:
Step 1 Current row number is set as $\mu = 0$.
Step 2 If $d_\mu \neq 0$, $\rho_{\mu+1}$ is determined as

$$\rho_{\mu+1} = \arg \max_{\substack{-1 \leq \mu' < \mu \\ d_{\mu'} \neq 0}} (\mu' - l_{\mu'}).$$

That is, $\rho_{\mu+1}$ is a row number μ' which is prior to the current row μ, where $d_{\mu'} \neq 0$, and $\mu' - l_{\mu'}$ has the largest value among the prior rows.
Step 3 Polynomial $\sigma^{\mu+1}(x)$ is determined as follows:

$$\sigma^{\mu+1}(x) = \begin{cases} \sigma^\mu(x) & (d_\mu = 0) \\ \sigma^\mu(x) + d_\mu d_\rho^{-1} x^{\mu-\rho} \sigma^\rho(x) & (d_\mu \neq 0) \end{cases},$$

where ρ is $\rho_{\mu+1}$ determined in **Step 2**.
Step 4 If $\mu = 2t - 1$, then $\sigma^{\mu+1}(x) = \sigma^{2t}(x)$ gives the error-location polynomial.
Step 5 $l_{\mu+1}$ is determined as the degree of $\sigma^{\mu+1}(x)$.
Step 6 $d_{\mu+1}$ is determined as follows:

$$d_{\mu+1} = S_{\mu+2} + \sigma_1^{\mu+1} S_{\mu+1} + \sigma_2^{\mu+1} S_\mu + \cdots + \sigma_{l_{\mu+1}}^{\mu+1} S_{\mu+2-l_{\mu+1}},$$

where $\sigma_i^{\mu+1}$ is the coefficient of degree-i term of $\sigma^{\mu+1}(x)$.
Step 7 The current row number is incremented as $\mu = \mu + 1$, and go to **Step 2**.

3. *Search of the roots of $\sigma(x)$:* The roots of the error-location polynomial $\sigma(x)$ are determined by *Chien search*, which finds a set of integers, $\{l'_1, l'_2, \ldots, l'_\tau\}$, satisfying $\sigma(\alpha^{l'_i}) = 0$, where $0 \leq l'_i \leq n - 1$.
4. *Error correction:* Error pattern is determined as $\mathbf{e}(x) = x^{l_1} + x^{l_2} + \cdots + x^{l_\tau}$, where $l_i = (n - l'_i) \bmod n$ for $1 \leq i \leq \tau$. Finally, errors in $\mathbf{u}'(x)$ are corrected as $\tilde{\mathbf{u}}(x) = \mathbf{u}'(x) + \mathbf{e}(x)$.

4.5 Reed-Solomon code

RS code is a linear cyclic code over GF(q) of length $n = q - 1$ with r check symbols, where the minimum distance is $d_{\min} = r + 1$. Practically, q is a power of 2, such as $q = 2^8$, and thus the following considers the RS codes over GF(2^m). Let α be a primitive element of GF(2^m). The parity-check matrix of RS code over GF(2^m) is given as

$$\mathbf{H} = \begin{bmatrix} 1 & \alpha^1 & \alpha^2 & \ldots & \alpha^{n-2} & \alpha^{n-1} \\ 1 & \alpha^2 & \alpha^4 & \ldots & \alpha^{2(n-2)} & \alpha^{2(n-1)} \\ \vdots & \vdots & \vdots & & \vdots & \vdots \\ 1 & \alpha^{r-1} & \alpha^{(r-1)2} & \ldots & \alpha^{(r-1)(n-2)} & \alpha^{(r-1)(n-1)} \\ 1 & \alpha^r & \alpha^{r \cdot 2} & \ldots & \alpha^{r(n-2)} & \alpha^{r(n-1)} \end{bmatrix},$$

and the generator polynomial of RS code is defined as $\mathbf{g}(x) = (x - \alpha)(x - \alpha^2)\ldots(x - \alpha^r)$.

$$\mathbf{H}=\begin{bmatrix}1&0&0&1&0&0&1&0&0&1&0&0\\0&1&0&0&1&0&0&1&0&1&0&0\\0&0&1&0&0&1&0&0&1&1&0&0\\1&0&0&0&1&0&0&0&1&0&1&0\\0&1&0&0&0&1&1&0&0&0&1&0\\0&0&1&1&0&0&0&1&0&0&1&0\\1&0&0&0&0&1&0&1&0&0&0&1\\0&1&0&1&0&0&0&0&1&0&0&1\\0&0&1&0&1&0&1&0&0&0&0&1\end{bmatrix}$$

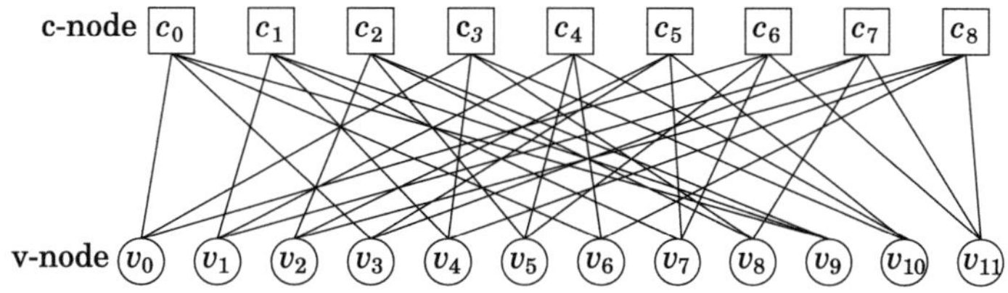

Fig. 8. Example of Tanner graph.

5. Low-Density Parity-Check (LDPC) code

LDPC code is a linear block code defined by a sparse parity-check matrix (Gallager, 1962), that is, the number of non-zero element in an $m \times n$ parity-check matrix is $O(n)$. The LDPC codes are employed in recent high-speed communication systems because appropriately designed LDPC codes have high error correction capability. The LDPC codes will be applicable to high-density MLC flash memory suffering from high BER.

5.1 Tanner graph

An LDPC matrix $\mathbf{H} = [h_{i,j}]_{m \times n}$ is expressed by a *Tanner graph*, which is a bipartite graph $\mathcal{G} = (\mathcal{V}, \mathcal{E})$, where $\mathcal{V} = V \cup C$ is a set of nodes, and $\mathcal{E}$ is a set of edges. Here, $V = \{v_0, v_1, \ldots, v_{n-1}\}$ is a set of variable-nodes (v-nodes) corresponding to column vectors of $\mathbf{H}$, and $C = \{c_0, c_1, \ldots, c_{m-1}\}$ is a set of check-nodes (c-nodes) corresponding to row vectors of $\mathbf{H}$. The edge set is defined as $\mathcal{E} = \{(c_i, v_j) | h_{i,j} \neq 0\}$. That is, c-node c_i and v-node v_j are connected by an edge (c_i, v_j) if and only if $h_{i,j} \neq 0$. *Girth* of $\mathcal{G}$ is defined as the length of shortest cycle in $\mathcal{G}$. The girth affects the error correction capability of LDPC code, that is, a code with a small girth l, e.g., $l = 4$, will have poor error correction capability compared to codes with a large girth.

Example 21. *Figure 8 presents a parity-check matrix* $\mathbf{H}$ *and corresponding Tanner graph* $\mathcal{G}$.

5.2 Regular/irregular LDPC code

5.2.1 Regular LDPC code

Regular LDPC code is defined by a parity-check matrix whose columns have a constant weight $\lambda \ll m$ and rows have almost constant weight. More precisely, Hamming weight $w_c(\mathbf{H}_{*,j})$ of the j-th column in $\mathbf{H}$ satisfies $w_c(\mathbf{H}_{*,j}) = \lambda$ for $0 \leq j \leq n-1$, and Hamming weight $w_r(\mathbf{H}_{i,*})$ of the i-th row in $\mathbf{H}$ satisfies $\lfloor n\lambda/m \rfloor \leq w_c(\mathbf{H}_{i,*}) \leq \lceil n\lambda/m \rceil$ for $0 \leq i \leq m-1$. Note that the total number of nonzero elements in $\mathbf{H}$ is $n\lambda$. The regular LDPC matrix is constructed as follows (Lin & Costello, 2004; Moreira & Farrell, 2006).

- *Random construction:* LDPC matrix $\mathbf{H}$ is randomly generated by computer search under the following constraints:
  - Every column of $\mathbf{H}$ has a constant weight λ.
  - Every row of $\mathbf{H}$ has weight either $\lfloor n\lambda/m \rfloor$ or $\lceil n\lambda/m \rceil$.
  - Overlapping of nonzero element in every pair of columns in $\mathbf{H}$ is at most one.

  The last constraint guarantees that the girth of generated $\mathbf{H}$ is at least six.
- *Geometric construction:* LDPC matrix can be constructed using geometric structure, such as, Euclidean geometry and projective geometry.

5.2.2 Irregular LDPC code

Irregular LDPC code is defined by an LDPC matrix having unequal column weight. The codes with appropriate column weight distribution have higher error correction capability compared to the regular LDPC codes (Richardson et al., 2001).

Column no.	0	1	2	3	4	5	6	7	8	9	10	11	12	13	14
Locations	0	32	64	8	31	63	14	30	17	28	22	27	7	19	6
of 1s.	1	34	70	18	42	76	45	47	62	48	60	49	53	44	46
(Row no.)	4	39	78	95	54	91	94	83	80	82	81	84	77	85	75

Table 11. Position of 1s in the base matrix $\mathbf{H}_0$ of IEEE 802.15.3c.

5.3 Example

5.3.1 WLAN (IEEE 802.11n, 2009)

(1296,1080) LDPC code is defined by the following parity-check matrix:

$$\mathbf{H} = \begin{bmatrix} 48 & 29 & 37 & 52 & 2 & 16 & 6 & 14 & 53 & 31 & 34 & 5 & 18 & 42 & 53 & 31 & 45 & - & 46 & 52 & 1 & 0 & - & - \\ 17 & 4 & 30 & 7 & 43 & 11 & 24 & 6 & 14 & 21 & 6 & 39 & 17 & 40 & 47 & 7 & 15 & 41 & 19 & - & - & 0 & 0 & - \\ 7 & 2 & 51 & 31 & 46 & 23 & 16 & 11 & 53 & 40 & 10 & 7 & 46 & 53 & 33 & 35 & - & 25 & 35 & 38 & 0 & - & 0 & 0 \\ 19 & 48 & 41 & 1 & 10 & 7 & 36 & 47 & 5 & 29 & 52 & 52 & 31 & 10 & 26 & 6 & 3 & 2 & - & 51 & 1 & - & - & 0 \end{bmatrix},$$

where "$-$" indicates the 54×54 zero matrix, and integer i indicates a 54×54 matrix generated from the 54×54 identity matrix by cyclically shifting the columns to the right by i elements.

5.3.2 WiMAX (IEEE 802.16e, 2009)

(1248,1040) LDPC code is defined by the following parity-check matrix:

$$\mathbf{H} = \begin{bmatrix} 0 & 13 & 29 & - & 25 & 2 & - & 49 & 45 & 4 & 46 & 28 & 44 & 17 & 2 & 0 & 19 & 10 & 2 & 41 & 43 & 0 & - & - \\ - & 3 & - & 19 & 21 & 25 & 6 & 42 & 25 & - & 22 & 11 & 6 & 38 & 7 & 39 & 0 & 23 & 26 & 0 & 0 & 0 & 0 & - \\ 27 & 43 & 44 & 2 & 36 & - & 11 & - & 16 & 13 & 49 & 33 & 43 & 4 & 46 & 42 & 32 & 47 & 36 & 8 & - & - & 0 & 0 \\ 36 & - & 27 & 8 & - & 19 & 7 & 5 & 5 & 10 & 28 & 48 & 15 & 49 & 30 & 16 & 45 & 49 & 5 & 35 & 43 & - & - & 0 \end{bmatrix},$$

where "$-$" indicates the 52×52 zero matrix, and integer i indicates a 52×52 matrix generated from the 52×52 identity matrix by cyclically shifting the columns to the right by i elements.

5.3.3 WPAN (IEEE 802.15.3c, 2009)

Let $\mathbf{H}_0$ be a 96×15 matrix whose elements are all-zero expect the elements listed in Table 11. (1440,1344) Quasi-cyclic LDPC code is defined by the following parity-check matrix:

$$\mathbf{H} = \left[\, \mathbf{H}_0 \middle| \mathbf{H}_1 \middle| \mathbf{H}_2 \middle| \ldots \middle| \mathbf{H}_{94} \middle| \mathbf{H}_{95} \,\right],$$

where $\mathbf{H}_i$ is obtained by cyclically i-row upward shifting of the base matrix $\mathbf{H}_0$.

5.4 Soft input decoding algorithm of binary LDPC code

Let $\mathbf{u} = (u_0, u_1, \ldots, u_{n-1})$ be a codeword of binary LDPC code defined by an $m \times n$ LDPC matrix $\mathbf{H}$. To retrieve a codeword $\mathbf{u}$ stored in the flash memory, the posteriori probability $f_i(x)$ is determined from readout values $(v_0, v_1, \ldots, v_{n-1})$, where $f_i(x)$ denotes the probability that the value of i-th bit of the codeword is $x \in \{0,1\}$. For example, if a binary input asymmetric channel with channel matrix $\mathbf{P} = [p_{i,j}]_{2\times 2}$ is assumed, then the posteriori probability is given as $f_i(x) = p_{x,v_i}/(p_{0,v_i} + p_{1,v_i})$, where it is assumed that $\Pr(u_i = 0) = \Pr(u_i = 1) = 1/2$. The sum-product algorithm (SPA) determines a decoded word $\widetilde{\mathbf{u}} = (\widetilde{u}_0, \widetilde{u}_1, \ldots, \widetilde{u}_{n-1})$ from the posteriori probabilities $(f_0(x), f_1(x), \ldots, f_{n-1}(x))$. The SPA is an iterative belief propagation algorithm performed on the Tanner graph $\mathcal{G} = (\mathcal{V}, \mathcal{E})$, where each edge $e_{i,j} = (c_i, v_j) \in \mathcal{E}$ is assigned two probabilities $Q_{i,j}(x)$ and $R_{i,j}(x)$, where $x \in \{0,1\}$. The following notations are used in the SPA.

- $d_i^c = |\{j \mid e_{i,j} \in \mathcal{E}\}|$: degree of c-node c_i.

- $\{J_0^{i,j}, J_1^{i,j}, \ldots, J_{d_i^c-2}^{i,j}\} = \{\, J \mid e_{i,J} \in \mathcal{E}, J \neq j\}$: set of indices of v-nodes adjacent to c-node c_i excluding v_j.

Sum-product algorithm

1. Initialize $R_{i,j}(x)$ as $R_{i,j}(0) = R_{i,j}(1) = 1/2$ for each $e_{i,j} \in \mathcal{E}$.
2. Calculate $Q_{i,j}(x)$ for each $e_{i,j} \in \mathcal{E}$:

$$Q_{i,j}(x) = \eta \times f_j(x) \times \prod_{I \in \{I \mid e_{I,j} \in \mathcal{E}\} \setminus \{i\}} R_{I,j}(x),$$

   where $x \in \{0,1\}$ and η is determined such that $Q_{i,j}(0) + Q_{i,j}(1) = 1$.
3. Calculate $R_{i,j}(x)$ for each $e_{i,j} \in \mathcal{E}$:

$$R_{i,j}(0) = \sum_{(x_0,\ldots,x_{d_i^c-2}) \in X_{d_i^c-1}} \left(\prod_{k=0}^{d_i^c-2} Q_{i,J_k^{i,j}}(x_k) \right), \quad R_{i,j}(1) = 1 - R_{i,j}(0),$$

   where $X_l = \left\{ (x_0, \ldots, x_{l-1}) \,\middle|\, \sum_{i=0}^{l-1} x_i = 0 \right\}$.
4. Generate a temporary decoded word $\widetilde{\mathbf{u}} = (\widetilde{u}_0, \widetilde{u}_1, \ldots, \widetilde{u}_{n-1})$ from

$$Q_j(x) = f_j(x) \times \prod_{I \in \{I \mid e_{I,j} \in \mathcal{E}\}} R_{I,j}(x),$$

   where $x \in \{0,1\}$ and

$$\widetilde{u}_j = \begin{cases} 0 & (Q_j(0) > Q_j(1)) \\ 1 & (\text{otherwise}) \end{cases}.$$

5. Calculate syndrome $\mathbf{s} = \mathbf{H}\widetilde{\mathbf{u}}^T$. If $\mathbf{s} = \mathbf{o}$, then output $\widetilde{\mathbf{u}}$ as a decoded word, and terminate.
6. If the number of iterations is greater than a predetermined threshold, then terminate with uncorrectable error detection; otherwise go to step 2.

There exist variations of the SPA, such as Log domain SPA and log-likelihood ratio (LLR) SPA. Also, there are some reduced-complexity decoding algorithms, such as bit-flipping decoding algorithm and min-sum algorithm (Lin & Costello, 2004).

5.5 Nonbinary LDPC code

5.5.1 Construction

Nonbinary LDPC code is a linear block code over GF(q) defined by an LDPC matrix $\mathbf{H} = [h_{i,j}]_{m \times n}$, where $h_{i,j} \in \mathrm{GF}(q)$. The nonbinary LDPC codes generally have higher error correction capability compared to the binary codes (Davey & MacKay, 1998). Several construction methods of the nonbinary LDPC matrix have been proposed. For example, high performance quasi-cyclic LDPC codes are constructed using Euclidean geometry (Zhou et al., 2009). It is shown in (Li et al., 2009) that, under a Gaussian approximation of the probability density, optimum column weight of $\mathbf{H}$ over GF(q) decreases and converges to two with increasing q. For example, the optimum column weight of rate-1/2 LDPC code on the AWGN channel is 2.6 for $q = 2$, while that is 2.1 for $q = 64$.

5.5.2 Decoding

The SPA for the binary LDPC code can be extended to the one for nonbinary codes straightforwardly, in which probabilities $Q_{i,j}(x)$ and $R_{i,j}(x)$ are iteratively calculated for $x \in \mathrm{GF}(q)$. However, the computational complexity of $R_{i,j}(x)$ is $O(q^2)$, and thus the SPA is impractical for a large q. For practical cases of $q = 2^b$, a reduced complexity SPA for nonbinary LDPC code has been proposed using the fast Fourier transform (FFT) (Song & Cruz, 2003).

Definition 2. *Let* $(X(0), X(\alpha^0), X(\alpha^1), \ldots, X(\alpha^{q-2}))$ *be a vector of real numbers of length* $q = 2^p$*, where* α *is a primitive element of* $\mathrm{GF}(q)$*. Function* f_k *is defined as follows:*

$$f_k(X(0), X(\alpha^0), X(\alpha^1), \ldots, X(\alpha^{q-2})) = (Y(0), Y(\alpha^0), Y(\alpha^1), \ldots, Y(\alpha^{q-2})),$$

where

$$Y(\beta_0) = \frac{1}{\sqrt{2}}(X(\beta_0) + X(\beta_1)) \text{ and } Y(\beta_1) = \frac{1}{\sqrt{2}}(X(\beta_0) - X(\beta_1)).$$

Here, $\beta_0 \in \mathrm{GF}(2^p)$ *and* $\beta_1 \in \mathrm{GF}(2^p)$ *are expressed as*

$$\mathrm{vec}(\beta_0) = (i_{p-1}, i_{p-2}, \ldots, i_{k+1}, 0, i_{k-1}, \ldots, i_0) \text{ and}$$
$$\mathrm{vec}(\beta_1) = (i_{p-1}, i_{p-2}, \ldots, i_{k+1}, 1, i_{k-1}, \ldots, i_0).$$

The FFT of $(X(0), X(\alpha^0), \ldots, X(\alpha^{q-2}))$ *is defined as*

$$\mathcal{F}(X(0), X(\alpha^0), \ldots, X(\alpha^{q-2})) = f_{p-1}(f_{p-2}(\cdots f_1(f_0(X(0), X(\alpha^0), \ldots, X(\alpha^{q-2})))\ldots)).$$

Let $\mathcal{G} = (\mathcal{V}, \mathcal{E})$ be the Tanner graph of LDPC matrix $\mathbf{H} = [h_{i,j}]_{m \times n}$ over $\mathrm{GF}(q)$, where each edge $e_{i,j} \in \mathcal{E}$ is assigned a nonzero value $h_{i,j} \in \mathrm{GF}(q)$. The following shows the outline of the FFT-based SPA for given posteriori probability $f_j(x)$, that is, the probability of the i-th symbol being x, where $x \in \mathrm{GF}(q)$ and $0 \le i \le n-1$.

FFT-based Sum-product algorithm for nonbinary LDPC code

1. Initialize $R_{i,j}(x)$ as $R_{i,j}(x) = 1/q$ for each $e_{i,j} \in \mathcal{E}$ and $x \in \mathrm{GF}(q)$.
2. Calculate $Q_{i,j}(x)$ for each $e_{i,j} \in \mathcal{E}$ and $x \in \mathrm{GF}(q)$:

$$Q_{i,j}(x) = \eta \times f_j(x) \times \prod_{I \in \{I | e_{I,j} \in \mathcal{E}\} \setminus \{i\}} R_{I,j}(x),$$

   where η is determined such that $\sum_{x \in \mathrm{GF}(q)} Q_{i,j}(x) = 1$.

3. Calculate $R_{i,j}(x)$ for each $e_{i,j} \in \mathcal{E}$ and $x \in \mathrm{GF}(q)$ as follows:
   (a) Generate the probability distribution permuted by $h_{i,j}$, that is, $Q'_{i,j}(x \cdot h_{i,j}) = Q_{i,j}(x)$.
   (b) Apply the FFT to $Q'_{i,j}(x)$ as

$$(\widetilde{Q}_{i,j}(0), \widetilde{Q}_{i,j}(\alpha^0), \ldots, \widetilde{Q}_{i,j}(\alpha^{q-2})) = \mathcal{F}(Q'_{i,j}(0), Q'_{i,j}(\alpha^0), \ldots, Q'_{i,j}(\alpha^{q-2})).$$

   (c) Calculate the product of $\widetilde{Q}_{i,j}(x)$ for each $e_{i,j} \in \mathcal{E}$ as $\widetilde{R}_{i,j}(x) = \prod_{k=0}^{d_i^c - 2} \widetilde{Q}_{i,j_k^{i,j}}(x)$.
   (d) Apply the FFT to $\widetilde{R}_{i,j}(x)$ as

$$(R'_{i,j}(0), R'_{i,j}(\alpha^0), \ldots, R'_{i,j}(\alpha^{q-2})) = \mathcal{F}(\widetilde{R}_{i,j}(0), \widetilde{R}_{i,j}(\alpha^0), \ldots, \widetilde{R}_{i,j}(\alpha^{q-2})).$$

   (e) Generate the probability distribution permuted by $h_{i,j}^{-1}$, that is, $R_{i,j}(x) = R'_{i,j}(x \cdot h_{i,j})$.

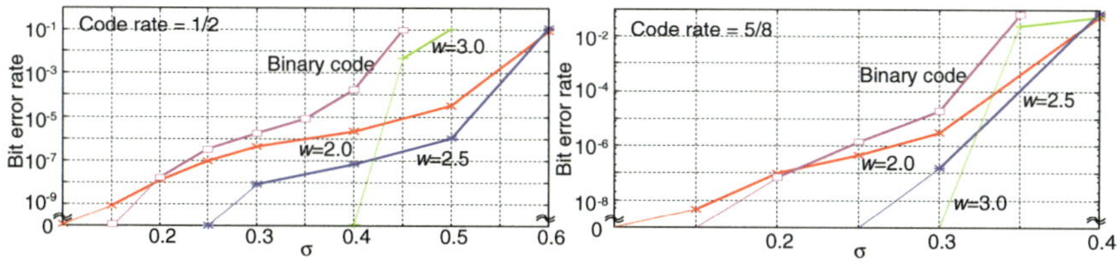

Fig. 9. Decoded BER of LDPC code over GF(8).

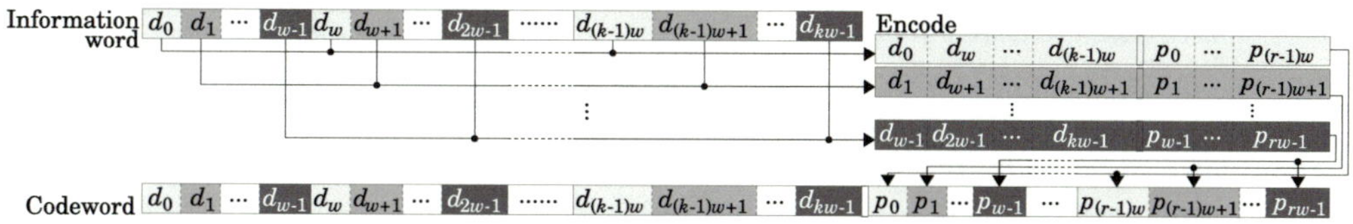

Fig. 10. w-Way interleave of $(k+r, k)$ systematic code.

4. Generate a temporary decoded word $\widetilde{\mathbf{u}} = (\widetilde{u}_0, \widetilde{u}_1, \ldots, \widetilde{u}_{n-1})$ using

$$Q_j(x) = f_j^x \times \prod_{I \in \{I | e_{I,j} \in \mathcal{E}\}} R_{I,j}(x) ,$$

where $x \in \text{GF}(q)$ and $\widetilde{u}_j = \arg\max_{x \in \text{GF}(q)} Q_j(x)$.

5. Calculate syndrome $\mathbf{s} = \mathbf{H}\widetilde{\mathbf{u}}^T$. If $\mathbf{s} = \mathbf{o}$, then output $\widetilde{\mathbf{u}}$ as a decoded word, and terminate.
6. If the number of iterations is greater than a predetermined threshold, then terminate with uncorrectable error detection; otherwise go to step 2.

5.6 Nonbinary LDPC code for flash memory

The following evaluates the decoded BER of the nonbinary LDPC codes for a channel model of 8-level cell flash memory (Maeda & Kaneko, 2009), where the threshold voltages are hypothesized as $\mu_0 = -3.0000, \mu_1 = -2.0945, \mu_2 = -1.2795, \mu_3 = -0.4645, \mu_4 = 0.3505, \mu_5 = 1.1655, \mu_6 = 1.9805$, and $\mu_7 = 3.0000$. These threshold voltages are determined to minimize the raw BER under the condition that $\mu_0 = -3.0000$, $\mu_{Q-1} = 3.0000$, and the standard deviation σ_i of $P_i(v)$ is given as $\sigma_i = \sigma$ for $i \in \{1, 2, \ldots, Q-2\}$, $\sigma_0 = 1.2\sigma$, and $\sigma_{Q-1} = 1.5\sigma$.
The decoded BER is calculated by decoding 100,000 words, where the maximum number of iterations in the SPA is 200. Figure 9 illustrates the relation between the standard deviation σ and the decoded BER of nonbinary LDPC codes over GF(8) having code rates $1/2$ and $5/8$. The decoded BER is evaluated for the code length 8000, where the column weights of the parity-check matrix are 2, 3, and 2.5. This figure also shows the decoded BER of binary irregular LDPC code. This figure says that the nonbinary LDPC codes have lower BER than binary irregular LDPC codes, and the nonbinary codes with column weight $w = 2.5$ give the lowest BER in many cases.

6. Combination of error control codes

6.1 Fundamental techniques

Interleaving: Interleaving is an effective technique to correct burst errors. Figure 10 illustrates the w-way interleave of a $(k+r, k)$ systematic code. Here, information word of length wk is interleaved to generate w information subwords of length k, which are

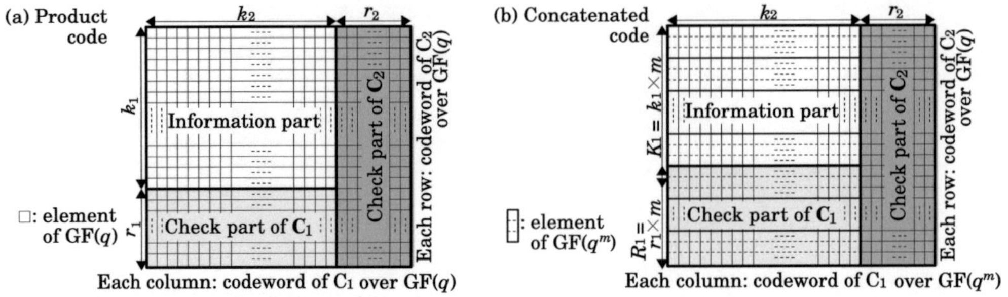

Fig. 11. Product/concatenated code using systematic block codes.

independently encoded by the $(k+r,k)$ systematic code. Then, the generated check bits are interleaved and appended to the information word. If the $(k+r,k)$ code can correct burst l-bit errors, then the interleaved code can correct burst wl-bit errors.

Product code: Product code is defined using two block codes over GF(q), that is, $(k_1 + r_1, k_1)$ code $\mathbf{C}_1$ and $(k_2 + r_2, k_2)$ code $\mathbf{C}_2$, as illustrated in Fig. 11(a). Information part is expressed as a $k_1 \times k_2$ matrix over GF(q). Each column of the information part is encoded by $\mathbf{C}_1$, and then each row of the obtained $(k_1 + r_1) \times k_2$ matrix is encoded by $\mathbf{C}_2$. The minimum distance of the product code is $d = d_1 \times d_2$, where d_1 and d_2 are the minimum distances of $\mathbf{C}_1$ and $\mathbf{C}_2$, respectively.

Concatenated code: Concatenated code is defined using two block codes $\mathbf{C}_1$ and $\mathbf{C}_2$, where $\mathbf{C}_1$ is a $(k_1 + r_1, k_1)$ code over GF(q^m), and $\mathbf{C}_2$ is a $(k_2 + r_2, k_2)$ code over GF(q), as shown in Fig. 11(b). Information part is expressed as a $K_1 \times k_2$ matrix, where $K_1 = k_1 \times m$. Each column of the information part, which is regarded as a vector of length k_1 over GF(q^m), is encoded by $\mathbf{C}_1$, and then each row of the obtained $(K_1 + R_1) \times k_2$ matrix over GF(q) is encoded by $\mathbf{C}_2$, where $R_1 = r_1 \times m$. For example, we can construct the concatenated code using a RS code over GF(2^8) as $\mathbf{C}_1$ and a binary LDPC code as $\mathbf{C}_2$, by which bursty decoding failure of the LDPC code $\mathbf{C}_2$ can be corrected using the RS code $\mathbf{C}_1$.

6.2 Three-level coding for solid-state drive

The following outlines a three-level error control coding suitable for the SSD (Kaneko et al., 2008), where the SSD is assumed to have N memory chips accessed in parallel. A *cluster* is defined as a group of N pages stored in the N memory chips, where the pages have same memory address, and is read or stored simultaneously. Let $(\mathbf{D}_0, \mathbf{D}_1, \ldots, \mathbf{D}_{N-2})$ be the information word, where $\mathbf{D}_i$ is a binary $k \times b$ matrix. This information word is encoded as follows.

1. *First level coding:* Generate a parity-check segment as $\mathbf{P} = \mathbf{D}_0 \oplus \mathbf{D}_1 \oplus \cdots \oplus \mathbf{D}_{N-2}$, where $\mathbf{P}$ is a binary $k \times b$ matrix and $\oplus$ denotes matrix addition over GF(2).
2. *Second level coding:* Let $\mathbf{d} = (\mathbf{d}_0, \mathbf{d}_1, \ldots, \mathbf{d}_{N-2}, \mathbf{p})$ be a binary row vector with length kN, where $\mathbf{d}_i = (\mathbf{d}_{i,0} \oplus \mathbf{d}_{i,1} \oplus \cdots \oplus \mathbf{d}_{i,b-1})^T$ and $\mathbf{p} = (\mathbf{p}_0 \oplus \mathbf{p}_1 \oplus \cdots \oplus \mathbf{p}_{b-1})^T$. Encode $\mathbf{d}$ by the code $C_{\rm CL}$ to generate the shared-check segment $\mathbf{Q} = (\mathbf{Q}_0, \mathbf{Q}_1, \ldots, \mathbf{Q}_{N-1})$ having $r_0 bN$ bits, where $\mathbf{Q}_i = [\ \mathbf{q}_{i,0}\mathbf{q}_{i,1} \cdots \mathbf{q}_{i,b-1}\ ]$ is a binary $r_0 \times b$ matrix for $i \in \{0, 1, \ldots, N-1\}$. Here, the check bits of $C_{\rm CL}$ are expressed as a row vector with length $r_0 bN$ bits, that is, $(\mathbf{q}_{0,0}^T, \mathbf{q}_{0,1}^T, \ldots, \mathbf{q}_{0,b-1}^T, \mathbf{q}_{1,0}^T, \ldots, \mathbf{q}_{N-1,b-1}^T)$. Then, for $i \in \{0, 1, \ldots, N-2\}$, append $\mathbf{Q}_i$ to the bottom of $\mathbf{D}_i$, and also append $\mathbf{Q}_{N-1}$ to the bottom of $\mathbf{P}$.

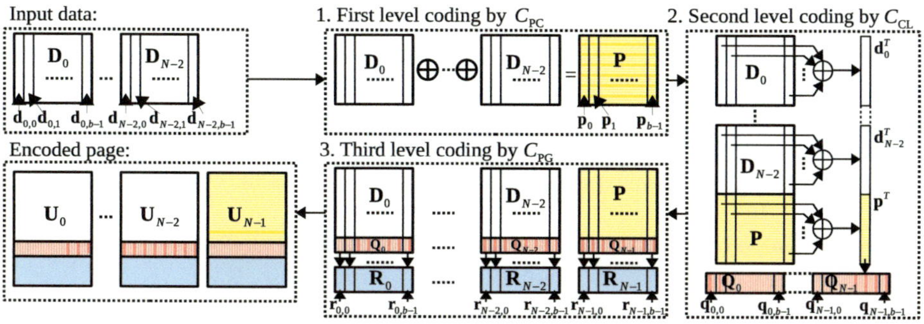

Fig. 12. Encoding process of three level ECC for SSD.

3. *Third level coding:* For $i \in \{0, 1, \ldots, N-2\}$ and $j \in \{0, 1, \ldots, b-1\}$, encode $\begin{pmatrix} \mathbf{d}_{i,j} \\ \mathbf{q}_{i,j} \end{pmatrix}$ by code C_{PG} to generate check bits $\mathbf{r}_{i,j}$, where $\mathbf{d}_{i,j}$, $\mathbf{q}_{i,j}$, and $\mathbf{r}_{i,j}$ are binary column vectors with lengths k, r_0, and r_1, respectively. Similarly, for $j \in \{0, 1, \ldots, b-1\}$, encode $\begin{pmatrix} \mathbf{p}_{j} \\ \mathbf{q}_{N-1,j} \end{pmatrix}$ by the code C_{PG} to generate check bits $\mathbf{r}_{N-1,j}$, where $\mathbf{p}_j$, $\mathbf{q}_{N-1,j}$, and $\mathbf{r}_{N-1,j}$ are binary column vectors with lengths k, r_0, and r_1, respectively.

The above encoding process generates encoded page $\mathbf{U}_i$ as shown in Fig. 12.

7. References

Lin, S. & Costello, D. J. Jr. (2004). *Error Control Coding*, Pearson Prentice Hall, 0-13-042672-5, New Jersey.

Fujiwara, E. (2006). *Code Design for Dependable Systems –Theory and Practical Applications–*, Wiley-Interscience, 0-471-75618-0, New Jersey.

Muroke, P. (2006). Flash Memory Field Failure Mechanisms, *Proc. 44th Annual International Reliability Physics Symposium*, pp. 313–316, San Jose, March 2006, IEEE, New Jersey.

Mohammad, M. G.; Saluja, K. K. & Yap, A. S. (2001). Fault Models and Test Procedures for Flash Memory Disturbances, *Journal of Electronic Testing: Theory and Applications*, Vol. 17, pp. 495–508, 2001.

Mielke, N.; Marquart, T.; Wu, N.; Kessenich, J.; Belgal, H.; Schares, E.; Trivedi, F.; Goodness, E. & Nevill, L. R. (2008). Bit Error Rate in NAND Flash Memories, *Proc. 46th Annual International Reliability Physics Symposium*, pp. 9–19, Phenix, 2008, IEEE, New Jersey.

Ielmini, D.; Spinelli, A. S. & Lacaita, A. L. (2005). Recent Developments on Flash Memory Reliability, *Microelectronic Engineering*, Vol. 80, pp. 321–328, 2005.

Chimenton, A.; Pellati, P. & Olivo, P. (2003). Overerase Phenomena: An Insight Into Flash Memory Reliability, *Proceedings of the IEEE*, Vol. 91, no. 4, pp. 617–626, April 2003.

Claeys, C.; Ohyama, H.; Simoen, E.; Nakabayashi, M. and Kobayashi, K, (2002). Radiation Damage in Flash Memory Cells, *Nuclear Instruments and Methods in Physics Research B*, Vol. 186, pp. 392–400, Jan. 2002.

Oldham, T. R.; Friendlich, M.; Howard, Jr., J. W.; Berg, M. D.; Kim, H. S.; Irwin, T. L. & LaBel, K. A. (2007). TID and SER Response of an Advanced Samsung 4Gb NAND Flash Memory, *Proc. IEEE Radiation Effects Data Workshop on Nuclear and Space Radiation Effect Conf*, pp. 221–225, July 2007.

Bagatin, M.; Cellere, G.; Gerardin, S.; Paccagnella, A.; Visconti, A. & Beltrami, S. (2009). TID Sensitivity of NAND Flash Memory Building Blocks, *IEEE Trans. Nuclear Science*, Vol. 56, No. 4, pp. 1909–1913, Aug. 2009.

Witzke, K. A. & Leung, C. (1985). A Comparison of Some Error Detecting CRC Code Standards, *IEEE Trans. Communications*, Vol. 33, No. 9, pp. 996–998, Sept. 1985.

Gallager, R. G (1962). Low Density Parity Check Codes, *IRE Trans. Information Theory*, Vol. 8, pp. 21–28, Jan. 1962.

Moreira, J. C. & Farrell, P. G. (2006). *Essentials of Error-Control Coding*, Wiley, 0-470-02920-X, West Sussex.

Richardson, T. J.; Shokrollahi, M. A. & Urbanke, R. L. (2001). Design of Capacity-Approaching Irregular Low-Density Parity-Check Codes, *IEEE Trans. Information Theory*, Vol. 47, No. 2, pp.619–637, Feb. 2001.

IEEE Std 802.11n-2009, Oct. 2009.

IEEE Std 802.16-2009, May 2009.

IEEE Std 802.15.3c-2009, Oct. 2009.

Davey, M. C. & MacKay, D. (1998). Low-Density Parity-Check Codes over GF(q), *IEEE Communications Letters*, Vol. 2, No. 6, pp. 165–167, June 1998.

Zhou, B.; Kang, J.; Tai, Y. Y.; Lin, S. & Ding, Z. (2009) High Performance Non-Binary Quasi-Cyclic LDPC Codes on Euclidean Geometry, *IEEE Trans. Communications*, Vol. 57, No. 5, pp. 1298–1311, May 2009.

Li, G.; Fair, I, J. & Krzymien, W. A. (2009). Density Evolution for Nonbinary LDPC Codes Under Gaussian Approximation, *IEEE Trans. Information Theory*, Vol. 55, No. 3, pp. 997–1015, March 2009.

Song, H. & Cruz, J. R. (2003). Reduced-Complexity Decoding of Q-Ary LDPC codes for Magnetic Decoding, *IEEE Trans. Magnetics*, Vol. 39, No. 3, pp. 1081–1087, March 2003.

Maeda, Y. & Kaneko, H. (2009). Error Control Coding for Multilevel Cell Flash Memories Using Nonbinary Low-Density Parity-Check Codes, *Proc. IEEE Int. Symp. Defect and Fault Tolerance in VLSI Systems*, pp. 367–375, Oct. 2009.

Kaneko, H.; Matsuzaka, T. & Fujiwara, E. (2008). Three-Level Error Control Coding for Dependable Solid-State Drives. *Proc. IEEE Pacific Rim International Symposium on Dependable Computing*, pp. 281–288, Dec. 2008.

3

Error Correction Codes and Signal Processing in Flash Memory

Xueqiang Wang[1], Guiqiang Dong[2], Liyang Pan[1] and Runde Zhou[1]
[1]*Tsinghua University,*
[2]*Rensselaer Polytechnic Institute,*
[1]*China*
[2]*USA*

1. Introduction

This chapter is to introduce NAND flash channel model, error correction codes (ECC) and signal processing techniques in flash memory.

There are several kinds of noise sources in flash memory, such as random-telegraph noise, retention process, inter-cell interference, background pattern noise, and read/program disturb, etc. Such noise sources reduce the storage reliability of flash memory significantly. The continuous bit cost reduction of flash memory devices mainly relies on aggressive technology scaling and multi-level per cell technique. These techniques, however, further deteriorate the storage reliability of flash memory. The typical storage reliability requirement is that non-recoverable bit error rate (BER) must be below 10^{-15}. Such stringent BER requirement makes ECC techniques mandatory to guarantee storage reliability. There are specific requirements on ECC scheme in NOR and NAND flash memory. Since NOR flash is usually used as execute in place (XIP) memory where CPU fetches instructions directly from, the primary concern of ECC application in NOR flash is the decoding latency of ECC decoder, while code rate and error-correcting capability is more concerned in NAND flash. As a result, different ECC techniques are required in different types of flash memory.

In this chapter, NAND flash channel is introduced first, and then application of ECC is discussed. Signal processing techniques for cancelling cell-to-cell interference in NAND flash are finally presented.

2. NAND flash channel model

There are many noise sources existing in NAND flash, such as cell-to-cell interference, random-telegraph noise, background-pattern noise, read/program disturb, charge leakage and trapping generation, etc. It would be of great help to have a NAND flash channel model that emulates the process of operations on flash as well as influence of various program/erase (PE) cycling and retention period.

2.1 NAND flash memory structure

NAND flash memory cells are organized in an array->block->page hierarchy, as illustrated in Fig. 1., where one NAND flash memory array is partitioned into many blocks, and each block contains a certain number of pages. Within one block, each memory cell string typically contains 16 to 64 memory cells.

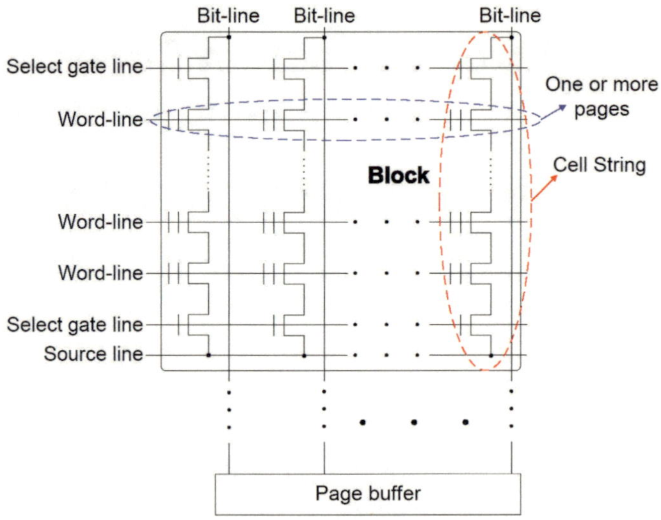

Fig. 1. Illustration of NAND flash memory structure.

All the memory cells within the same block must be erased at the same time and data are programmed and fetched in the unit of page, where the page size ranges from 512-byte to 8K-byte user data in current design practice. All the memory cell blocks share the bit-lines and an on-chip page buffer that holds the data being programmed or fetched. Modern NAND flash memories use either even/odd bit-line structure, or all-bit-line structure. In even/odd bit-line structure, even and odd bit-lines are interleaved along each word-line and are alternatively accessed. Hence, each pair of even and odd bit-lines can share peripheral circuits such as sense amplifier and buffer, leading to less silicon cost of peripheral circuits. In all-bit-line structure, all the bit-lines are accessed at the same time, which aims to trade peripheral circuits silicon cost for better immunity to cell-to-cell interference. Moreover, relatively simple voltage sensing scheme can be used in even/odd bit-line structure, while current sensing scheme must be used in all-bit-line structure. For MLC NAND flash memory, all the bits stored in one cell belong to different pages, which can be either simultaneously programmed at the same time, referred to as full-sequence programming, or sequentially programmed at different time, referred to as multi-page programming.

2.2 NAND flash memory erase and program operation model

Before a flash memory cell is programmed, it must be erased, i.e., remove all the charges from the floating gate to set its threshold voltage to the lowest voltage window. It is well known that the threshold voltage of erased memory cells tends to have a wide Gaussian-like distribution. Hence, we can approximately model the threshold voltage distribution of erased state as

$$p_e(x) = \frac{1}{\sigma_e\sqrt{2\pi}} e^{-\frac{(x-\mu_e)^2}{2\sigma_e^2}} \tag{1}$$

where μ_e and δ_e are the mean and standard deviation of the erased state.

Regarding memory programming, a tight threshold voltage control is typically realized by using incremental step pulse program (ISPP), i.e., memory cells on the same word-line are recursively programmed using a program-and-verify approach with a stair case program word-line voltage V_{pp}, as shown in Fig.2.

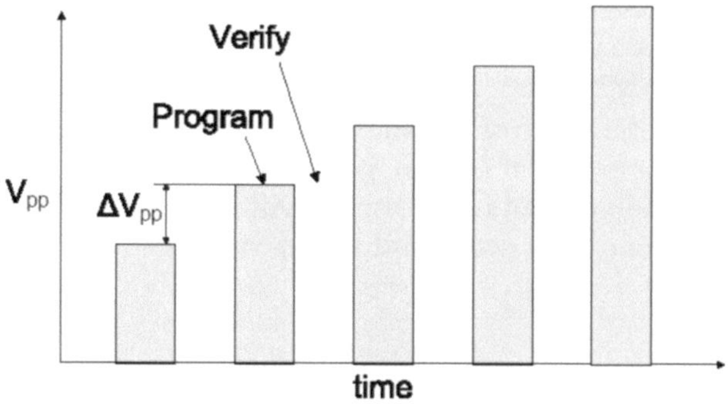

Fig. 2. Control-gate voltage pulses in program-and-verify operations.

Under such a program-and-verify strategy, each programmed state (except the erased state) associates with a verify voltage that is used in the verify operations and sets the target position of each programmed state threshold voltage window. Denote the verify voltage of the target programmed state as V_p, and program step voltage as ΔV_{pp}. The threshold voltage of the programmed state tends to have a uniform distribution over $[V_p, V_p + \Delta V_{pp}]$. Denote V_p and $V_p + \Delta V_{pp}$ for the *k*-th programmed state as V_l^k and V_r^k. We can model the ideal threshold voltage distribution of the *k*-th programmed state as:

$$p_p^{(k)}(x) = \begin{cases} \frac{1}{\Delta V_{pp}}, & \text{if } V_l^{(k)} \leq x \leq V_r^{(k)} \\ 0, & \text{else} \end{cases} \quad (2)$$

The above *ideal* memory cell threshold voltage distribution can be (significantly) distorted in practice, mainly due to PE cycling effect and cell-to-cell interference, which will be discussed in the following.

2.3 Effects of program/erase cycling

Flash memory PE cycling causes damage to the tunnel oxide of floating gate transistors in the form of charge trapping in the oxide and interface states, which directly results in threshold voltage shift and fluctuation and hence gradually degrades memory device noise margin. Major distortion sources include

1. Electrons capture and emission events at charge trap sites near the interface developed over PE cycling directly result in memory cell threshold voltage fluctuation, which is referred to as random telegraph noise (RTN);
2. Interface trap recovery and electron detrapping gradually reduce memory cell threshold voltage, leading to the data retention limitation.

RTN causes random fluctuation of memory cell threshold voltage, where the fluctuation magnitude is subject to exponential decay. Hence, we can model the probability density function $p_r(x)$ of RTN-induced threshold voltage fluctuation as a symmetric exponential function:

$$p_r(x) = \frac{1}{2\lambda_r} e^{-\frac{|x|}{\lambda_r}} \tag{3}$$

Let N denote the PE cycling number, λ_r scales with N in an approximate power-law fashion, i.e., λ_r is approximately proportional to N_a.
Threshold voltage reduction due to interface trap recovery and electron detrapping can be approximately modeled as a Gaussian distribution $\mathcal{N}(\mu_d, \delta_d^2)$. Both μ_d and δ_d^2 scale with N in an approximate power-law fashion, and scale with the retention time t in a logarithmic fashion. Moreover, the significance of threshold voltage reduction induced by interface trap recovery and electron detrapping is also proportional to the initial threshold voltage magnitude, i.e., the higher the initial threshold voltage is, the faster the interface trap recovery and electron detrapping occur and hence the larger threshold voltage reduction will be.

2.4 Cell-to-cell interference

In NAND flash memory, the threshold voltage shift of one floating gate transistor can influence the threshold voltage of its adjacent floating gate transistors through parasitic capacitance-coupling effect, i.e. one float-gate voltage is coupled by the floating gate changes of the adjacent cells via parasitic capacitors. This is referred to as cell-to-cell interference. As technology scales down, this has been well recognized as one of major noise sources in NAND flash memory. Threshold voltage shift of a victim cell caused by cell-to-cell interference can be estimated as

$$F = \sum_k (\Delta V_t^{(k)} \cdot \gamma^{(k)}) \tag{4}$$

where $\Delta V_t^{(k)}$ represents the threshold voltage shift of one interfering cell which is programmed after the victim cell, and the coupling ratio is defined as

$$\gamma^{(k)} = \frac{C^{(k)}}{C_{total}} \tag{5}$$

where $C^{(k)}$ is the parasitic capacitance between the interfering cell and the victim cell, and C_{total} is the total capacitance of the victim cell. Cell-to-cell interference significance is affected by NAND flash memory bit-line structure. In current design practice, there are two different bit-line structures, including conventional even/odd bit-line structure and emerging all-bit-line structure. In even/odd bit-line structure, memory cells on one word-line are alternatively connected to even and odd bit-lines and even cells are programmed ahead of odd cells in the same wordline. Therefore, an even cell is mainly interfered by five neighboring cells and an odd cell is interfered by only three neighboring cells, as shown in Fig. 3. Therefore, even cells and odd cells experience largely different amount of cell-to-cell interference. Cells in all-bit-line structure suffers less cell-to-cell inference than even cells in odd/even structure, and the all-bit-line structure can effectively support high-speed current sensing to improve the memory read and verify speed. Therefore, throughout the remainder of this paper, we mainly consider NAND flash memory with the all-bit-line structure. Finally, we note that the design methods presented in this work are also applicable when odd/even structure is being used.

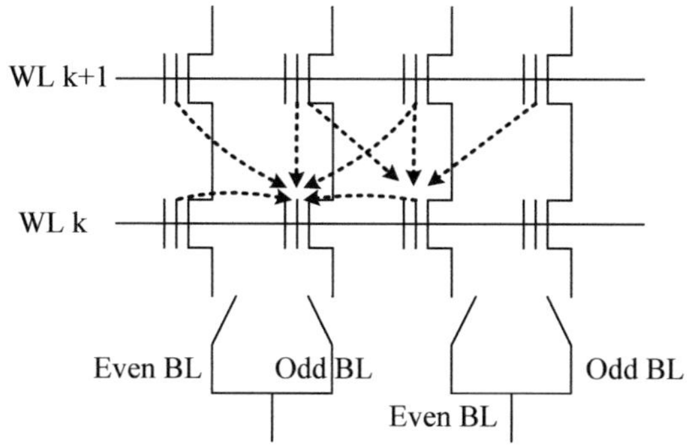

Fig. 3. Illustration of cell-to-cell interference in even/odd structure: even cells are interfered by two direct neighboring cells on the same wordline and three neighboring cells on the next wordline, while odd cells are interfered by three neighboring cells on the next wordline.

2.5 NAND flash memory channel model

Based on the above discussions, we can approximately model NAND flash memory device characteristics as shown in Fig. 4, using which we can simulate memory cell threshold voltage distribution and hence obtain memory cell raw storage reliability.

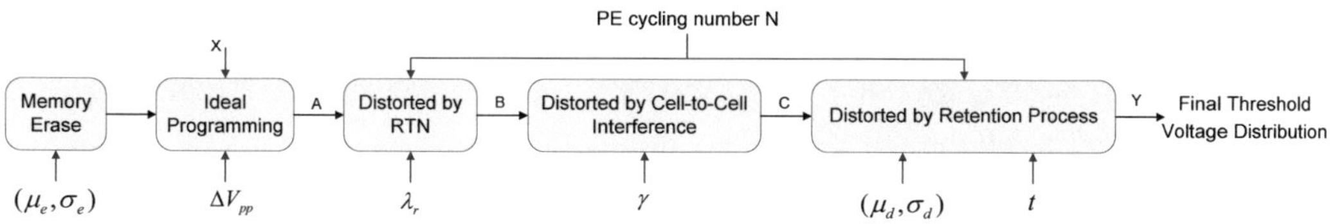

Fig. 4. Illustration of the approximate NAND flash memory device model to incorporate major threshold voltage distortion sources.

Based upon the model of erase state and ideal programming, we can obtain the threshold voltage distribution function $p_p(x)$ right after ideal programming operation. Recall that $p_{pr}(x)$ denotes the RTN distribution function, and let $p_{ar}(x)$ denote the threshold voltage distribution after incorporating RTN, which is obtained by convoluting $p_p(x)$ and $p_r(x)$, i.e.,

$$p_{ar}(x) = p_p(x) \bigotimes p_r(x) \tag{6}$$

The cell-to-cell interference is further incorporated based on the model of cell-to-cell interference. To capture inevitable process variability, we set both the vertical coupling ratio and diagonal coupling ratio as random variables with tailed truncated Gaussian distribution:

$$p_c(x) = \begin{cases} \frac{c_c}{\sigma_c\sqrt{2\pi}} \cdot e^{-\frac{(x-\mu_c)^2}{2\sigma_c^2}}, & \text{if } |x-\mu_c| \leq w_c \\ 0, & \text{else} \end{cases} \tag{7}$$

where μ_c and δ_c are the mean and standard deviation, and C_C is chosen to ensure the integration of this tail truncated Gaussian distribution equals to 1. In all the simulations in this section, we set $w_c = 0.1\mu_c$ and $\delta_c = 0.4\mu_c$.

Let $p_{ac}(x)$ denote the threshold voltage distribution after incorporating cell-to-cell interference. Denote the retention noise distribution as $p_t(x)$. The final threshold voltage distribution $p_f(x)$ is obtained as

$$p_f(x) = p_{ac}(x) \bigotimes p_t(x) \tag{8}$$

The above presented approximate mathematical channel model for simulating NAND flash memory cell threshold voltage is further demonstrated using the following example.

Example 1: Let us consider 2bits/cell NAND flash memory. Normalized μ_e and σ_e of the erased state are set as 1.4 and 0.35, respectively. For the three programmed states, the normalized program step voltage ΔV_{pp} is 0.2, and the normalized verify voltages V_p are 2.6, 3.2 and 3.93, respectively. For the RTN distribution function, we set the parameter $\lambda_r = K_r N^{0.5}$, where K_r equals to 0.00025. Regarding to cell-to-cell interference, we set the ratio between the means of γ_y and γ_{xy} as 0.08 and 0.0048, respectively. For the function $\mathcal{N}(\mu_d, \sigma_d^2)$ to capture trap recovery and electron detrapping during retention, we set that μ_d scales with $N^{0.5}$ and σ_d^2 scales with $N^{0.6}$, and both scale with $\ln(1 + t/t_0)$, where t denotes the memory retention time and t_0 is an initial time and can be set as 1 hour. In addition, as pointed out earlier, both μ_d and σ_d also depend on the initial threshold voltage. Hence we set that both approximately scale $K_s(x - x_0)$, where x is the initial threshold voltage, and x_0 and K_s are constants. Therefore, we have

$$\begin{cases} \mu_d = K_s(x - x_0)K_d N^{0.5} \ln(1 + t/t_0) \\ \sigma_d^2 = K_s(x - x_0)K_m N^{0.6} \ln(1 + t/t_0) \end{cases} \tag{9}$$

where we set $K_s = 0.38$, $x_0 = 1.4$, $K_d = 4 \times 10^{-4}$, and$K_m = 4 \times 10^{-6}$. Accordingly, we carry out Monte Carlo simulations to obtain

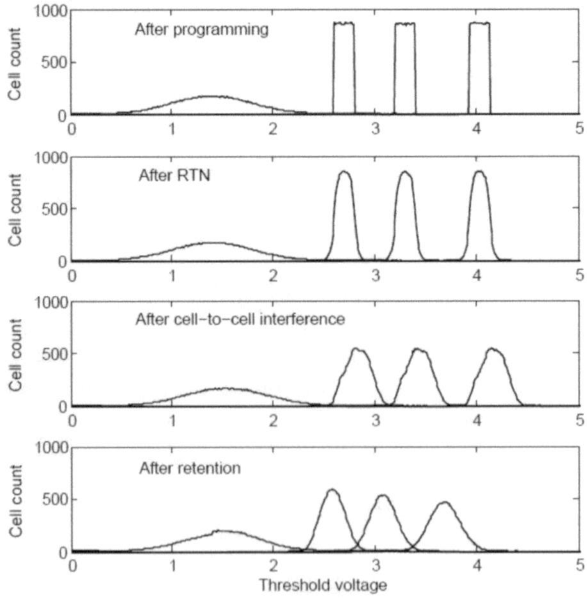

Fig. 5. Simulated results to show the effects of RTN, cell-to-cell interference, and retention on memory cell threshold voltage distribution after 10K PE cycling and 10-year retention.

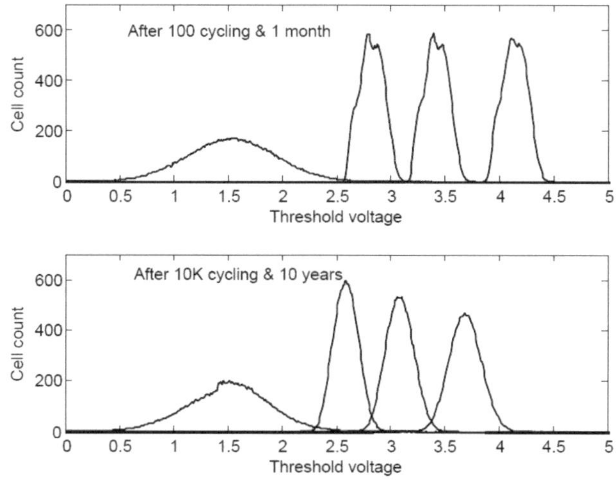

Fig. 6. Simulated threshold voltage distribution after 100 PE cycling and 1-month retention and after 10K PE cycling and 10-year retention, which clearly shows the dynamics inherent in NAND flash memory characteristics.

Fig. 5 shows the cell threshold voltage distribution at different stages under 10K PE cycling and with 10-year storage period. The final threshold voltage distributions after 100 PE cycling and 1 month storage and after 10K PE cycling and 10 years storage are shown in Fig. 6. Fig. 7 presents the evolution of simulated raw BER with program/erase cycling.

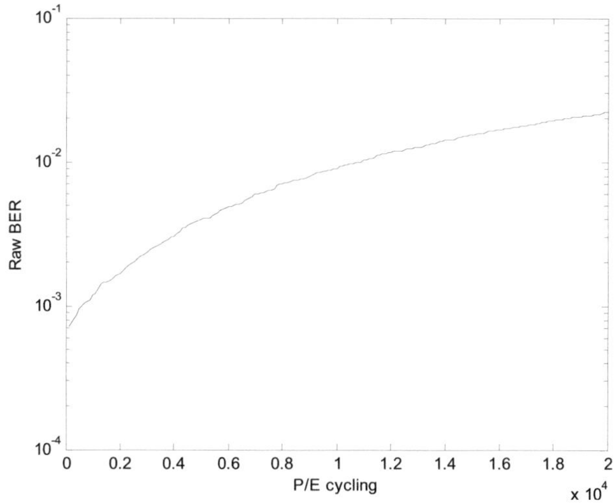

Fig. 7. The evolution of raw BER with program/erase cycling under 10-year storage period.

3. Basics of error correction codes

In the past decades, error correction codes (ECC) have been widely adapted in various communication systems, magnetic recording, compact discs and so on. The basic scheme of ECC theory is to add some redundancy for protection. Error correction codes are usually divided into two categories: block codes and convolution codes. Hamming codes, Bose-Chaudur-Hocquenghem(BCH) codes, Reed-Solomon(RS) codes, and Low-density parity-check (LDPC) codes are most notable block codes and have been widely used in communication, optical, and other systems.

The encoding/decoding scheme of a block code in a memory is shown in Fig. 8. When any k-bit information data is written to flash memory, an encoder circuit generates the parity bits, adds these parity bits to the k-bit information data and creates a n-bit codeword. Then the whole codeword is written in and stored on a page of the memory array. During the reading operation, a decoder circuit searches errors in a codeword, and corrects the erroneous bits within its error capability, thereby recovering the codeword.

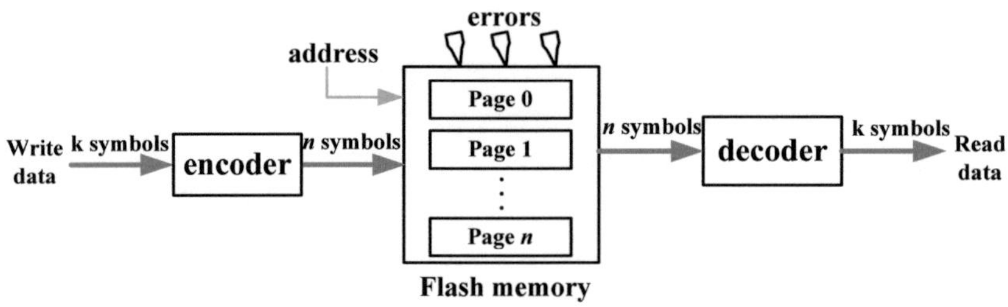

Fig. 8. ECC encoding and decoding system in a flash memory

Current NOR flash memory products use Hamming code with only 1-bit error correction. However, as raw BER increases, 2-bit error corretion BCH code becomes a desired ECC. Besides, in current 2b/cell NAND flash memory. BCH codes are widely employed to achieve required storage reliability. As raw BER soars in future 3b/cell NAND flash memory, BCH codes are not sufficient anymore, and LDPC codes become more and more necessary for future NAND flash memory products.

3.1 Basics of BCH codes

BCH codes were invented through independent researches by Hocquenghen in 1959 and by Bose and Ray-Chauduri in 1960. Flash memory uses binary primitive BCH code which is constructed over the Galois fields $GF(2^m)$. Galois field is a finite field in the coding theory and was first discovered by Evariste Galois. In the following, we will recall some algebraic notions of $GF(2^m)$.

Definition 3.1 Let α be an element of $GF(2^m)$, α is called primitive element if the smallest natural number n that satisfies $\alpha^n=1$ equals 2^m -1, that is, $n=2^m$ -1.

Theorem 3.1 Every none null element of $GF(2^m)$ can be expressed as power of primitive element α, that is, the multiplicative group $GF(2^m)$ is cyclic.

Definition 3.2 $GF(2^m)[x]$ is indicated as the set of polynomials of any degree with coefficients in $GF(2^m)$. An irreducible polynomial $p(x)$ in $GF(2^m)[x]$ of degree m is called primitive if the smallest natural number n, such that $x^n–1$ is a multiple of $p(x)$, is $n=2^m–1$.

In fact, if $p(x)=x^m+a_{m-1}x^{m-1}+\ldots+a_1x+a_0$ is a primitive polynomial in $GF(p)[x]$ and α is one of its roots, then we have

$$a^m = a_0 + a_1\alpha + a_2\alpha^2 + \cdots + a_{m-1}\alpha^{m-1} \tag{10}$$

Equation (10) indicates that each power of α with degree larger than m can be converted to a polynomial with degree m-1 at most. As an example, some elements in the field GF(2^4), their binary representation, and according poly representation forms are shown in Table 1.

Element	Binary representation	Polynomial representation
0	0000	0
α^0	1000	1
α^1	0100	α
α^3	0001	α^3
α^4	1100	$1+\alpha$
α^5	0110	$\alpha+\alpha^2$
α^6	0011	$\alpha^2+\alpha^3$

Table 1. Different representations of elements over GF(2^4)

Based on the Galois fields GF(2^m), the BCH(n, k) code is defined as
Codeword length: $n = 2^m-1$
Information data length: $k \geq 2^m-mt$
In a BCH code, every codeword polynomial $c(x)$ can be expressed as $c(x)=m(x)g(x)$, where $g(x)$ is the generator polynomial and $m(x)$ is the information polynomial.
Definition 3.3 Let α be the primitive element of GF(2^m). Let t be the error correction capability of BCH code. The generator polynomial $g(x)$ of a primitive BCH code is the minimal degree polynomial with root: $\alpha, \alpha^2, \ldots \alpha^t$. g(x) is given by

$$g(x) = LCM\{\psi_0(x), \psi_1(x), \cdots \psi_{d-2}(x)\} \tag{11}$$

Where Ψ_i is the minimal polynomial of α^i.
Generally, the BCH decoding is much more complicated than the encoding. A typical architecture of BCH code application in a flash memory is presented in Fig. 9.

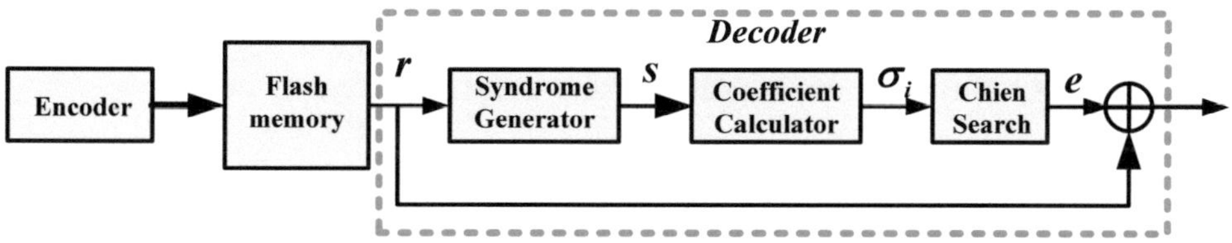

Fig. 9. Architecture of BCH code application in a flash memory

3.1.1 BCH encoding

For a BCH(n,k) code, assuming its generator polynomial is $g(x)$, and the polynomial of the information to be encoded is $m(x)$ with degree of k-1. The encoding process is as follows: First, the message $m(x)$ is multiplied by x^{n-k}, and then divided by $g(x)$, thereby obtaing a quotient $q(x)$ and a remainder $r(x)$ according to equation (12). The remainder $r(x)$ is the polynomial of the parity information; hence the desired parity bits can be obtained.

$$\frac{m(x)\cdot x^{n-k}}{g(x)}=q(x)+\frac{r(x)}{g(x)} \tag{12}$$

As mentioned above, any codeword of BCH code is a multiple of the generator polynomial. Therefore, an encoded codeword $c(x)$ can be expressed as:

$$c(x)=m(x)\cdot x^{n-k}+r(x) \tag{13}$$

3.1.2 BCH decoding

Generally the decoding procedure for binary BCH codes includes three major steps, which is shown in Fig. 9.

- Step 1: Calculating the syndrome S.
- Step 2: Determining the coefficients of the error-location polynomial.
- Step 3: Finding the error location using Chien Search and correcting the errors.

During the period of data storage in flash memory, the repeated program/erase (P/E) cycles may damage the stored information; thereby some errors occur in the read operation. The received codeword can be expressed as $r(x) = c(x) + e(x)$ with the error polynomial representation $e(x) = e_0 + e_1x + \dots e_{n-1}x^{n-1}$

The first step in the BCH decoding is to calculate $2t$ syndromes with the received r(x). The computation is given by

$$\frac{r(x)}{\psi_i(x)}=Q_i(x)+\frac{S_i(x)}{\psi_i(x)} \quad for \ \ 1\le i\le 2t \tag{14}$$

Where Ψ_i is the minimal polynomial of element α^i, t is the error numbers in codeword. $S_i(x)$ is called syndrome. Since $\Psi_i(a^i)$=0, the syndrome can also be obtained as $S_i(\alpha^i) = r(\alpha^i)$.

$$S_i(a^i) = r(a^i) \tag{15}$$

From equation (14), it can be seen that the syndrome calculation in the BCH decoding is similar to the encoding process in equation (12). Hence, they both employ the linear feedback shift register (LFSR) circuit structure.

The next step is to compute the coefficients of the error-location polynomial using the obtained syndrome values. The error-location polynomial is defined as

$$\sigma(x)=1+\sigma_1x+\sigma_2x^2+\cdots\sigma_tx^t \tag{16}$$

Where and σ_i ($1\le i \le t$) is the required coefficient.

There are two main methods to compute the coefficients, one is Peterson method and the other is Berlekamp-Massey algorithm. In the following sections, we will discuss and employ both methods for error correction in different types of flash memory.

The last step of BCH decoding is Chien search. Chien search is employed to search for the roots of the error locator polynomial. If the roots are found $\sigma(\alpha^i)$ =0 for $0\le i \le n$-1, then the error location is n-1-i in the codeword. It should be noted that the three modules of a BCH decoder is commonly designed with three pipeline stages, leading to high throughput of the BCH decoding.

3.2 LDPC code

Low-density parity-check (LDPC) codes can provide near-capacity performance. It was invented by Gallager in 1960, but due to the high complexity in its implementation, LDPC codes had been forgotten for decades, until Mackey rediscovered LDPC codes in the 1990s. Since then LDPC codes have attracted much attention.

A LDPC code is given by the null space of a sparse mxn 'low-density' parity-check matrix H. Regular LDPC codes have identical column weight and identical row weight. Each row of H represents one parity check. Define each row of H as check node (CN), and each column of H as variable node (VN). A LDPC code can be represented by Tanner graph, which is a bipartite graph and includes two types of nodes: n variable nodes and m check nodes. In Tanner graph, the i-th CN is connected to j-th VN, if $h_{i,j}$=1.

Consider a (6, 3) linear block code with H matrix as

$$H = \begin{bmatrix} 1 & 1 & 1 & 0 & 1 & 0 \\ 1 & 1 & 0 & 1 & 0 & 1 \\ 1 & 0 & 1 & 1 & 1 & 1 \end{bmatrix}$$

The corresponding Tanner graph is shown in Fig. 10.

The performance of LDPC code depends heavily on parity-check matrix H. Generally speaking, LDPC code with larger block length, larger column weight and larger girth trends to have better performance. In Tanner graph, a cycle is defined as a sequential of edges that form a closed path. Short cycles degrade the performance of LDPC codes, and length of the shortest cycle in Tanner graph is named as girth.

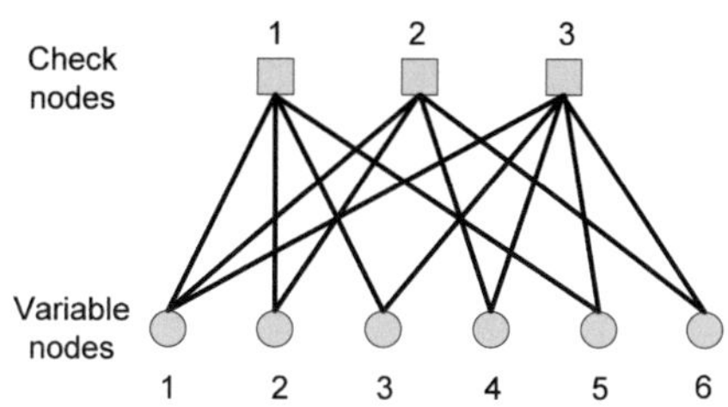

Fig. 10. The Tanner graph for the given (6, 3) linear block code.

There have been lots of methods to construct parity-check matrix. To reduce the hardware complexity of LDPC encoder and decoder, quasi-cyclic (QC) LDPC code was proposed and has widely found its application in wireless communication, satellite communicate and hard-disk drive.

As for LDPC decoding, there are several iterative decoding algorithms for LDPC codes, including bit-flipping (BF) like decoding algorithms and soft-decision message-passing decoding algorithms. Among all BF-like decoding, BF and candidate bit based bit-flipping (CBBF) can work with only hard-decision information. Other BF-like decoding require soft-decision information, which incurs large sensing latency penalty in flash memory devices as discussed later, though they may increase the performance a little bit.

Soft-decision message passing algorithm, such as Sum-product algorithm (SPA), could provide much better performance than BF-like decoding, upon soft-decision information. However, the complexity of SPA decoding is very high. To reduce the decoding complexity, min-sum decoding was proposed, with tolerable performance loss. Readers can refer to "Channel Codes: Classical and Modern" by Willian E. Ryan and Shu Lin.

4. BCH in NOR flash memory

Usually NOR flash is used for code storage and acts as execute in place (XIP) memory where CPU fetches instructions directly from memory. The code storage requires a high-reliable NOR flash memory since any code error will cause a system fault. In addition, NOR flash memory has fast read access with access time up to 70ns. During read operation, an entire page, typical of 256 bits, is read out from memory array, and the ECC decoder is inserted in the critical data path between sense amplifiers and the page latch. The fast read access imposes a stringent requirement on the latency of the ECC decoder (required <10% overhead), and the ECC decoder has to be designed in combinational logic. As a result, decoding latency becomes the primary concern for ECC in NOR Flash memory.

Traditionally, hamming code with single-error-correction (SEC) is applied to NOR flash memory since it has simple decoding algorithm, small circuit area, and short-latency decoding. However, in new-generation 3xnm MLC NOR flash memory, the raw BER will increase up to 10^{-6} while application requires the post-ECC BER be reduced to 10^{-12} below. From Fig. 11, it is clear that hamming code with t=1 is not sufficient anymore, and double-error-correction (DEC) BCH code gains more attraction in future MLC NOR flash memory. However, the primary issue with DEC BCH code applied in NOR flash is the decoding latency. In the following, a fast and adaptive DEC BCH decoding algorithm is proposed and a high-speed BCH(274,256,2) decoder is designed for NOR flash memory.

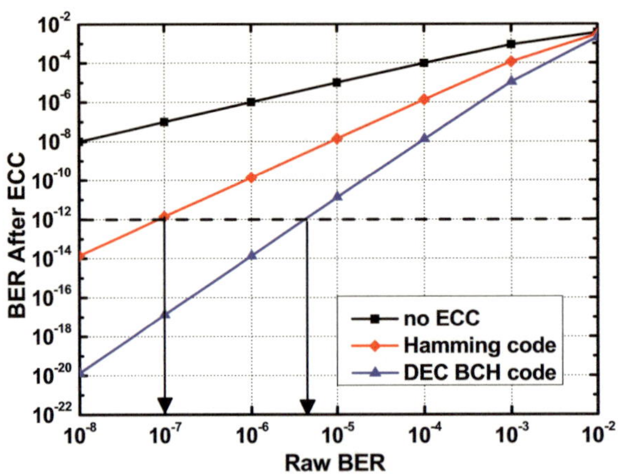

Fig. 11. BER curves of different ECC in NOR flash memory with 256-bit page size

4.1 High-speed DEC BCH decoding algorithm

First we employ equation equation (15) for high-speed syndrome computation. The entire expression of syndromes is

$$(S_1, S_2, \cdots S_{2t}) = r \cdot H^T = (r_0, r_1 \ . \ . \ . \ r_n) \cdot \begin{pmatrix} 1 & 1 & . & 1 \\ (\alpha) & (\alpha^2) & . & (\alpha^{2t}) \\ . & . & . & . \\ (\alpha)^{n-1} & (\alpha^2)^{n-1} & . & (\alpha^{2t})^{n-1} \end{pmatrix} \quad (17)$$

Here $\boldsymbol{r}$ is the received codeword and $\boldsymbol{H}$ is defined as the parity matrix

Each element of GF(2^m) α^i can be represented by a m-tuples binary vector, hence each element in the vector can be obtained using mod-2 addition operation, and all the syndromes can be obtained with the XOR-tree circuit structure. Furthermore, for binary BCH codes in flash memory, even-indexed syndromes equal the squares of the other one, i.e., $S_{2i}=S_i^2$, therefore, only odd-indexed syndromes (S_1, S_3 ...S_{2t-1}) are needed to compute.

Then we propose a fast and adaptive decoding algorithm for error location. A direct solving method based on the Peterson equation is designed to calculate the coefficients of the error-location polynomial. Peterson equation is show as follows

$$\begin{bmatrix} S_{t+1} \\ S_{t+2} \\ \cdot \\ \cdot \\ S_{2t} \end{bmatrix} = \begin{bmatrix} S_1 & S_2 & \cdots & S_t \\ S_2 & S_3 & \cdots & S_{t+1} \\ \cdot & \cdot & & \cdot \\ \cdot & \cdot & & \cdot \\ S_t & S_{t+1} & \cdots & S_{2t-1} \end{bmatrix} \begin{bmatrix} \sigma_t \\ \sigma_{t-1} \\ \cdot \\ \cdot \\ \sigma_1 \end{bmatrix} \tag{18}$$

For DEC BCH code t=2, with the even-indexed syndrome S_1, S_3, the coefficient σ_1, σ_2 can be obtained by direct solving the above matrix as

$$\sigma_1 = S_1,\ \sigma_2 = S_1^2 + S_3 / S_1 \tag{19}$$

Hence, the error-locator polynomial is given by

$$\sigma(x) = 1 + \sigma_1 x + \sigma_2 x^2 = 1 + S_1 x + (S_1^2 + \frac{S_3}{S_1})x^2 \tag{20}$$

To eliminate the complicate division operation in above equation, a division-free transform is performed by multiplying both sides by S_1 and the new polynomial is rewritten as (21). Since it always has $S_1 \neq 0$ when any error exists in the codeword, this transform has no influence of error location in Chien search where roots are found in $\sigma(x)$ =0, that is also $\sigma'(x)$ =0.

$$\sigma'(x) = \sigma_0' + \sigma_1' x + \sigma_2' x^2 = S_1 + S_1^2 x + (S_1^3 + S_3)x^2 \tag{21}$$

The final effort to reduce complexity is to transform the multiplications in the coefficients of equation (21) to simple modulo-2 operations. As mentioned above, over the field GF(2^m), each syndrome vector ($S[0]$, $S[1]$, $\cdots$ $S[m\text{-}1]$) has a corresponding polynomial $S(x) = S[0] + S[1]x + \cdots + S[m\text{-}1]x^{m-1}$. According to the closure axiom over GF(2^m), each component of the coefficient σ_1' and σ_2' is obtained as

$$\begin{aligned} \sigma_1'[i] &= \sum S_1[j] \text{ for } 0 \le i, j \le m-1 \\ \sigma_2'[i] &= S_3[i] + \sum S_1[j] \bullet S_1[k] \text{ for } 0 \le i, j, k \le m-1 \end{aligned} \tag{22}$$

It can be seen that only modulo-2 additions and modulo-2 multiplications are needed to calculate above equation, which can be realized by XOR and AND logic operations, respectively. Hardware implementation of the two coefficients in BCH(274, 256, 2) code is shown in Fig. 12. It can be seen that coefficient σ_1' is implemented with only six 2-input XOR gates and coefficient σ_2' can be realized by regular XOR-tree circuit structure. As a result, the direct solving method is very effective to simplify the decoding algorithm, thereby reduce the decoding latency significantly.

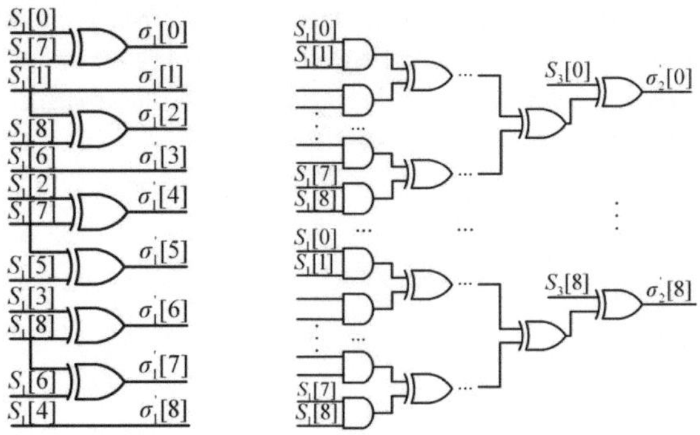

Fig. 12. Implementation of the two coefficient in BCH(274,256,2)

Further, an adaptive decoding architecture is proposed with the reliability feature of flash memory. As mentioned above, flash memory reliability is decreased as memory is used. For the worst case of multi-bit errors in flash memory, 1-bit error is more likely happened in the whole life of flash memory (R. Micheloni, R. Ravasio & A. Marelli, 2006). Therefore, the best-effort is to design a self-adaptive DEC BCH decoding which is able to dynamically perform error correction according to the number of errors. Average decoding latency and power consumption can be reduced.

The first step to perform self-adaptive decoding is to detect the weight-of-error pattern in the codeword, which can be obtained with Massey syndrome matrix.

$$L_j = \begin{bmatrix} S_1 & 1 & 0 & \cdots & 0 \\ S_3 & S_2 & S_1 & \cdots & 0 \\ S_{2j-1} & S_{2j-2} & S_{2j-1} & \cdots & S_j \end{bmatrix} \quad (23)$$

where S_j denotes each syndrome value ($1 \le j \le 2t-1$).

With this syndrome matrix, the weight-of-error pattern can be bounded by the expression of $\det(L_1)$, $\det(L_2)$, …, $\det(L_t)$. For a DEC BCH code in NOR flash memory, the weight-of-error pattern is illustrated as follows

- If there is no error, then det(L1) = 0, det(L2) = 0, that is,

$$S_1 = 0,\ S_1^3 + S_3 = 0 \quad (24)$$

- If there are 1-bit errors, then $\det(L_1) \neq 0$, $\det(L_2) = 0$, that is

$$S_1 \neq 0,\ S_1^3 + S_3 = 0 \quad (25)$$

- If there are 2-bit errors, then $\det(L_1) \neq 0$, $\det(L_2) \neq 0$, that is

$$S_1 \neq 0,\ S_1^3 + S_3 \neq 0 \quad (26)$$

Let define $\boldsymbol{R} = S_1^3 + S_3$. It is obvious that variable R determines the number of errors in the codeword. On the basis of this observation, the Chien search expression partition is presented in the following:

- Chien search expression for SEC

$$\Lambda_{SEC}(\alpha^i) = S_1 + S_1^2(\alpha^i) \qquad \text{for } 2^m - n \le i \le 2^m - 1 \tag{27}$$

- Chien search expression for DEC

$$\Lambda_{DEC}(\alpha^i) = \Lambda_{SEC}(\alpha^i) + R(\alpha^i)^2 \qquad \text{for } 2^m - n \le i \le 2^m - 1 \tag{28}$$

Though above equations are mathematically equivalent to original expression in equation (21), this reformulation make the Chien search for SEC able to be launched once the syndrome S_1 is calculated. Therefore, a short-path implementation is achieved for SEC decoding in a DEC BCH code. In addition, expression (27) is included in expression (28), hence, no extra arithmetic operation is required for the faster SEC decoding within the DEC BCH decoding. Since variable R indicates the number of errors, it is served as the internal selection signal of SEC decoding or DEC decoding. As a result, self-adaptive decoding is achieved with above proposed BCH decoding algorithm reformulation.

To meet the decoding latency requirement, bit-parallel Chien search has to be adopted. Bit-parallel Chien search performs all the substitutions of (28) of n elements in a parallel way, and each substitution has m sub-elements over GF(2^m). Obviously, this will increase the complexity drasmatically. For BCH(274, 256, 2) code, the Chien search module has 2466 expression, each can be implemented with a XOR-tree. In (X. Wang, D. Wu & C. Hu, 2009), an optimization method based on common subexpression elimination (CSE) is employed to optimize and reduce the logic complexity.

4.2 High-speed BCH decoder implementation

Based on the proposed algorithm, a high-speed self-adaptive DEC BCH decoder is design and its architecture is depicted in Fig. 13. Once the input codeword is received from NOR flash memory array, the two syndromes S_1, S_3 are firstly obtained by 18 parallel XOR-trees. Then, the proposed fast-decoding algorithm is employed to calculate the coefficients of error location polynomial in the R calculator module. Meanwhile, a short-path is implemented for SEC decoding once the syndrome value S_1 is obtained. Finally, variable R determines whether SEC decoding or DEC decoding should be performed and selects the according data path at the output.

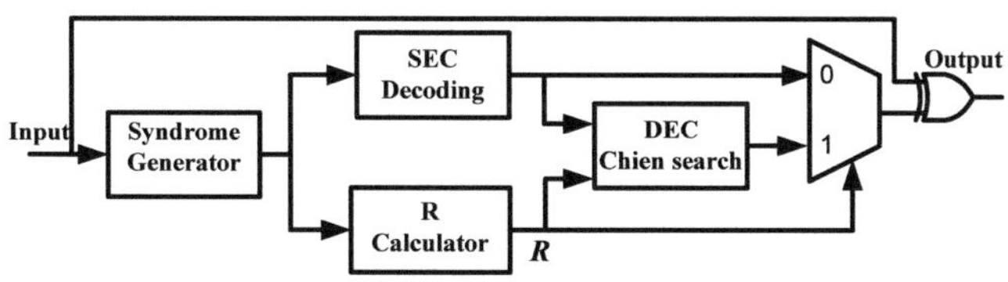

Fig. 13. Block diagram of the proposed DEC BCH decoder.

The performance of an embedded BCH (274,256,2) decoder in NOR flash memory is summarized in Table 2. The decoder is synthesized with Design Compiler and implemented in 180nm CMOS process. It has 2-bit error correction capability and achieves decoding latency of 4.60ns. In addition, it can be seen that the self-adaptive decoding is very effective to speed up the decoding and reduce the power consumption for 1-bit error correction. The DEC BCH decoder satisfies the short latency and high reliability requirement of NOR flash memory.

Code Parameter	BCH(274, 256) codes	
Information data	256 bits	
Parity bits	18 bits	
Syndrome time	1.66ns	
Data output time	1-bit error	3.53ns
	2-bit errors	4.60ns
Power consumption (Vdd=1.8V, T=70ns)	1-bit error	0.51mW
	2-bit error	1.25mW
Cell area	0.251 mm2	

Table 2. Performance of a high-speed and self-adaptive DEC BCH decoder

5. LDPC ECC in NAND flash memory

As raw BER in NAND flash increases to close to 10^{-2} at its life end, hard-decision ECC, such as BCH code, is not sufficient any more, and such more powerful soft-decision ECC as LDPC code becomes necessary. The outstanding performance of LDPC code is based on soft-decision information.

5.1 Soft-decision log-likelihood information from NAND flash

Denote the sensed threshold voltage of a cell as V_{th}, the distribution of erase state as $p_0(x)$, the distribution of programmed states as $p_k(x)$, where k is the index of programmed state. Denote S_i as the set of the states whose i-th bit is 0. Thus, given the V_{th}, the LLR of i-th code bit in one cell is:

$$L(b_i) = \log \frac{\sum_{k \in S_i} p^{(k)}(V_{th})}{\sum_k p^{(k)}(V_{th}) - \sum_{k \in S_i} p^{(k)}(V_{th})} \tag{29}$$

Clearly, LLR calculation demands the knowledge of the probability density functions of all the states, and threshold voltage of concerned cells.

There exist many kinds of noises, such as cell-to-cell interference, random-telegraph noise, retention process and so on, therefore it would be unfeasible to derive the closed-form distribution of each state, given the NAND flash channel model that captures all those noise sources. We can rely on Monte Carlo simulation with random input to get the distribution of all states after being interrupted by several noise sources in NAND flash channel. With random data to be programmed into NAND flash cells, we run a large amount of simulation on the NAND flash channel model to get the distribution of all states, and the obtained threshold voltage distribution would be very close to real distribution under a large amount of simulation. In practice, the distribution of V_{th} can be obtained through fine-grained sensing on large amount of blocks.

In sensing flash cell, a number of reference voltages are serially applied to the corresponding control gate to see if the sensed cell conduct, thus the sensing result is not the exact target threshold voltage but a range which covers the concerned threshold voltage. Denote the sensed range as $[R_l, R_r)$ (R_l and R_r are two adjacent reference voltages). There is be $R_l \leq V_{th} < R_r$.

Example 2: Let's consider a 2-bit-per-cell flash cell with threshold voltage of 1.3V. Suppose the reference voltage starts from 0V, with incremental step of 0.3V. The reference voltages applied to the flash cell is: 0, 0.3V, 0.6V, 0.9V, 1.2V, 1.5V ... This cell will not be open until the reference voltage of 1.5V is applied, so the sensing result is that the threshold voltage of this cell stays among (1.2, 1.5].

The corresponding LLR of i-th bit in one cell is then calculated as

$$L(b_i) = \log \frac{\int_{R_l}^{R_r} \sum_{k\in\mathcal{S}_i} p^{(k)}(x)dx}{\int_{R_l}^{R_r} \sum_k p^{(k)}(x)dx - \int_{R_l}^{R_r} \sum_{k\in\mathcal{S}_i} p^{(k)}(x)dx} \tag{30}$$

5.2 Performance of LDPC code in NAND flash

With the NAND flash model presented in section 2 and the same parameters as those in Example 1, the performances of (34520, 32794, 107) BCH code and (34520, 32794) QC-LDPC codes with column weight 4 are presented in Fig. 14, where floating point sensing is assumed on NAND flash cells. The performance advantage of LDPC code is obvious.

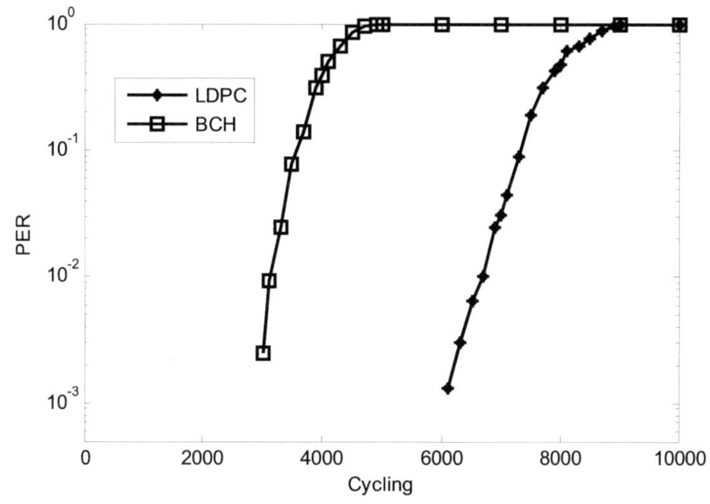

Fig. 14. Page error rate performances of LDPC and BCH codes with the same coding rate under various program/erase cycling.

5.3 Non-uniform sensing in NAND flash for soft-decision information

As mentioned above, sensing flash cell is performed through applying different reference voltages to check if the cell can open, so the sensing latency directly depends on the number of applied sensing levels. To provide soft-decision information, considerable amount of sensing levels are necessary, thus the sensing latency is very high compared to hard-decision sensing.

Soft-decision sensing increases not only the sensing latency, but also the data transfer latency from page buffer to flash controller, since these data is transferred in serial.

Example 3: Let's consider a 2-bit-per-cell flash cell with threshold voltage of 1.3V. Suppose the hard reference voltages as 0, 0.6V and 1.2V respectively. Suppose sensing one reference voltage takes 8us. The page size is 2K bytes and I/O bus works as 100M Hz with 8-bit width. For hard-decision sensing, we need to apply all three hard reference voltages to sense it out, resulting in sensing latency of 24us. To sense a page for soft-decision information with 5-bit precision, we need $2^5 * 8 = 256$ us, more than ten times the hard-decision sensing latency. With 5-bit soft-decision information per cell, the total amount of data is increased by 2.5 times, thus the data transfer latency is increased by 2.5 times, from 20.48 us to 51.2us. The overall sensing and transfer latency jumps to 51.2+256=307.2 us from 20.48+24=44.48 us.

Based on above discussion, it is highly desirable to reduce the amount of soft-decision sensing levels for the implementation of soft-decision ECC. Conventional design practice tends to simply use a uniform fine-grained soft-decision memory sensing strategy as illustrated in Fig. 15, where soft-decision reference voltages are uniformly distributed between two adjacent hard-decision reference voltages.

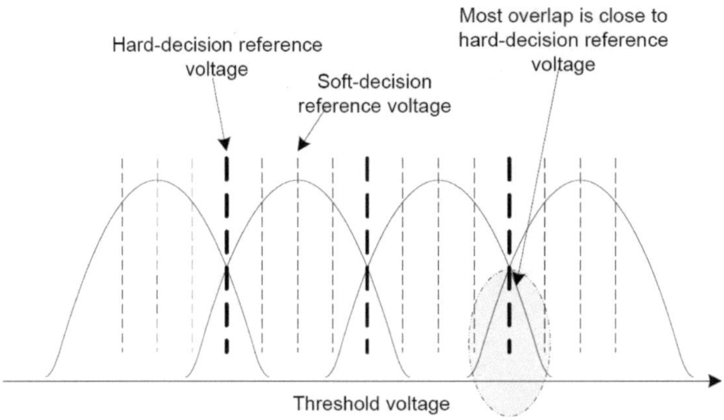

Fig. 15. Illustration of the straightforward uniform soft-decision memory sensing. Note that soft-decision reference voltages are uniformly distributed between any two adjacent hard-decision reference voltages.

Intuitively, since most overlap between two adjacent states occurs around the corresponding hard-decision reference voltage (i.e., the boundary of two adjacent states) as illustrated in Fig. 15, it should be desirable to sense such region with a higher precision and leave the remainder region with less sensing precision or even no sensing. This is a non-uniform or non-linear memory sensing strategy, through which the same amount of sensing voltages is expected to provide more information.

Given a sensed threshold voltage V_{th}, its entropy can be obtained as

$$H(V_{th}) = \sum_k P(\text{state} = k|V_{th}) \log \frac{1}{P(\text{state} = k|V_{th})} \quad (31)$$

Where

$$P(\text{state} = k|V_{th}) = \frac{p^{(k)}(V_{th})}{\sum_v p^{(v)}(V_{th})} \tag{32}$$

For one given programmed flash memory cell, there are always just one or two items being dominating among all the $P(\text{state} = k|V_{th})$ items for the calculation of $H(V_{th})$. Outside of the dominating overlap region, there is only one dominating item very close to 1 while all the other items being almost 0, so the entropy will be very small. On the other hand, within the dominating overlap region, there are two relatively dominating items among all the $P(\text{state} = k|V_{th})$ items, and both of them are close to 0.5 if V_{th} locates close to the hard-decision reference voltage, i.e., the boundary of two adjacent states, which will result in a relatively large entropy value $H(V_{th})$. Clearly the region with large entropy tends to demand a higher sensing precision. So, it is intuitive to apply a non-uniform memory sensing strategy as illustrated in Fig. 16. Associated with each hard-decision reference voltage at the boundary of two adjacent states, a so-called *dominating overlap region* is defined and uniform memory sensing is executed only within each dominating overlap region.
Given the sensed V_{th} of a memory cell, the value of entropy $H(V_{th})$ is mainly determined by two largest probability items, and this translates into the ratio between the two largest probability items. Therefore, such a design trade-off can be adjusted by a probability ratio R, i.e., let $[B_l^{(k)}, B_r^{(k)}]$ denote the dominating overlap region between two adjacent states, we can determine the border $B_l^{(k)}$ and $B_r^{(k)}$ by solving

$$\frac{p^{(k)}(B_l^{(k)})}{p^{(k+1)}(B_l^{(k)})} = \frac{p^{(k+1)}(B_r^{(k)})}{p^{(k)}(B_r^{(k)})} = R \tag{33}$$

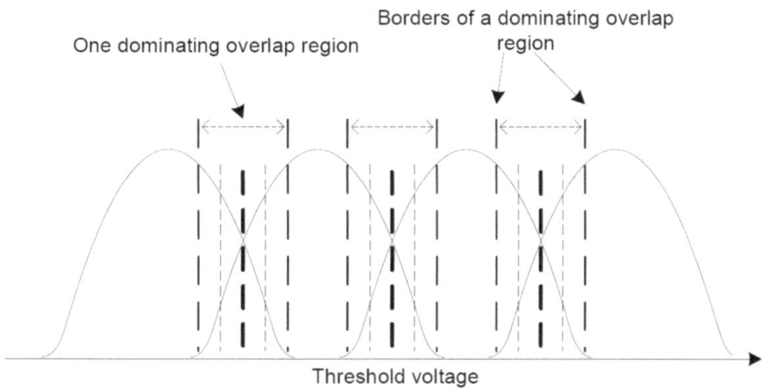

Fig. 16 Illustration of the proposed non-uniform sensing strategy. Dominating overlap region is around hard-decision reference voltage, and all the sensing reference voltages only distribute within those dominating overlap regions.

Since each dominating overlap region contains one hard-decision reference voltage and two borders, at least $3(K-1)$ sensing levels should be used in non-uniform sensing. Simulation results on BER performance of rate-19/20 (34520, 32794) LDPC codes in uniform and non-uniform sensing under various cell-to-cell interference strengths for 2 bits/cell NAND flash are presented in Fig. 17. Note that at least 9 non-uniform sensing levels is required for non-uniform sensing for 2 bits/cell flash. The probability ratio R is set as 512. Observe that

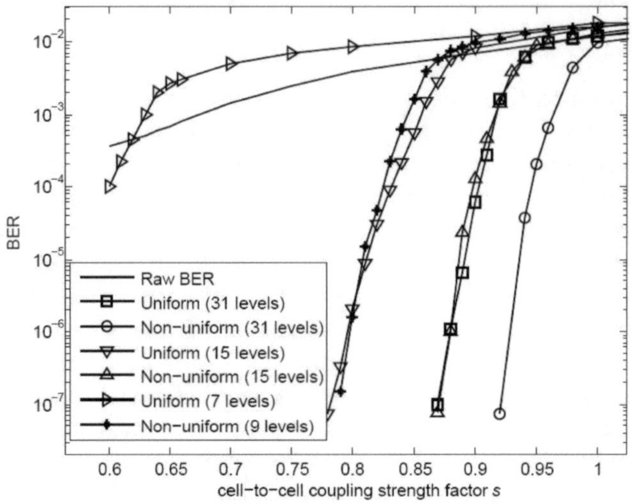

Fig. 17. Performance of LDPC code when using the non-uniform and uniform sensing schemes with various sensing level configurations.

15-level non-uniform sensing provides almost the same performance as 31-level uniform sensing, corresponding to about 50% sensing latency reduction. 9-level non-uniform sensing performs very closely to 15-level uniform sensing, corresponding to about 40% sensing latency reduction.

6. Signal processing for NAND flash memory

As discussed above, as technology continues to scale down and hence adjacent cells become closer, parasitic coupling capacitance between adjacent cells continues to increase and results in increasingly severe cell-to-cell interference. Some study has clearly identified cell-to-cell interference as the major challenge for future NAND flash memory scaling. So it is of paramount importance to develop techniques that can either minimize or tolerate cell-to-cell interference. Lots of prior work has been focusing on how to minimize cell-to-cell interference through device/circuit techniques such as word-line and/or bit-line shielding. This section presents to employ signal processing techniques to tolerate cell-to-cell interference.

According to the formation of cell-to-cell interference, it is essentially the same as inter-symbol interference encountered in many communication channels. This directly enables the feasibility of applying the basic concepts of post-compensation, a well known signal processing techniques being widely used to handle inter-symbol interference in communication channel, to tolerate cell-to-cell interference.

6.1 Technique I: Post-compensation

It is clear that, if we know the threshold voltage shift of interfering cells, we can estimate the corresponding cell-to-cell interference strength and subsequently subtract it from the sensed threshold voltage of victim cells. Let $\tilde{V}_t^{(k)}$ denote the sensed threshold voltage of the k-th interfering cell and $\bar{V}_e$ denote the mean of erased state, we can estimate the threshold voltage shift $\Delta\tilde{V}_t^{(k)}$ of each interfering cell as $(\tilde{V}_t^{(k)} - \bar{V}_e)$. Let $\bar{\gamma}^{(k)}$ denote the mean of the corresponding coupling ratio, we can estimate the strength of cell-to-cell interference as

$$\tilde{F} = \sum_k \left((\tilde{V}_t^{(k)} - \bar{V}_e) \cdot \bar{\gamma}^{(k)}\right) \tag{34}$$

Therefore, we can post-compensate cell-to-cell interference by subtracting estimated $\tilde{F}$ from the sensed threshold voltage of victim cells. In [Dong, Li & Zhang, 2010], the authors presents simulation result of post-compensation on one initial NAND flash channel with the odd/even structure. Fig. 18 shows the threshold voltage distribution before and after post-compensation. It's obvious that post-compensation technique can effectively cancel interference.

Note that the sensing quantization precision directly determines the trade-off between the cell-to-cell interference compensation effectiveness and induced overhead. Fig. 19 and Fig. 20 show the simulated BER vs. cell-to-cell coupling strength factor s for even and odd pages, where 32-level and 16-level uniform sensing quantization schemes are considered. Simulation results clearly show the impact of sensing precision on the BER performance. Under 32-level sensing, post-compensation could provide large BER performance improvement, while 16-level sensing degrades the odd cells' performance when cell-to-cell interference strength is low.

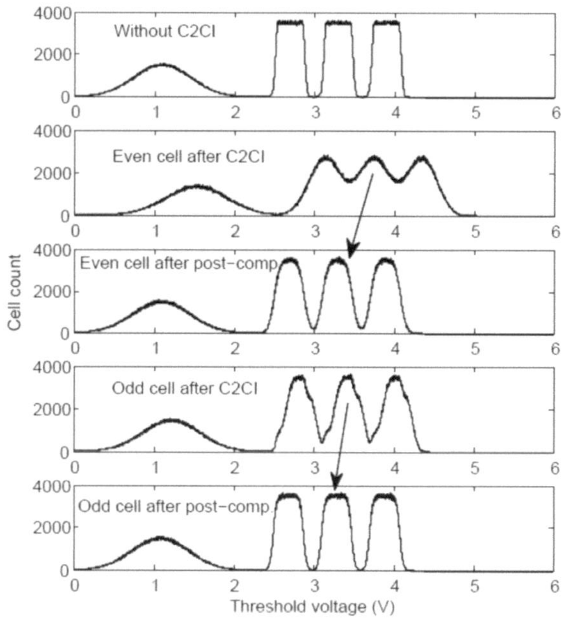

Fig. 18. Simulated victim cell threshold voltage distribution before and after post-compensation.

Reverse Programming for Reading Consecutive Pages

To execute post-compensation for concerned page, we need the threshold voltage information of its interfering page. When consecutive pages are to be read, information on the interfering pages become inherently available, hence we can capture the approximate threshold voltage shift and estimate the corresponding cell-to-cell interference on the fly during the read operations for compensation.

Since sensing operation takes considerable latency, it would be feasible to run ECC decoding on the concerned page first, and sensing the interfering page will not be started until that ECC decoding fails, or will be started while ECC decoding is running.

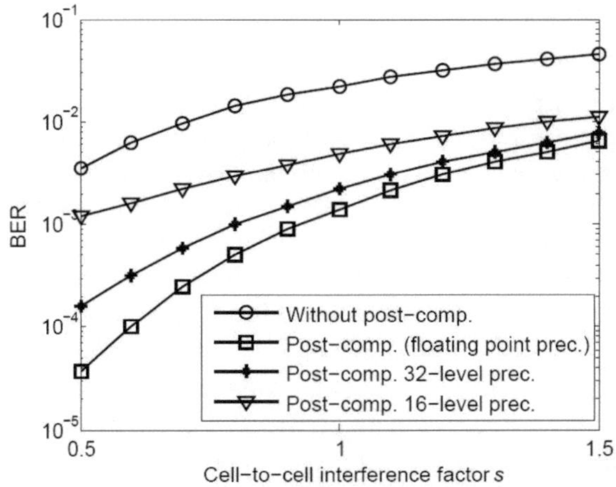

Fig. 19. Simulated BER performance of even cells when post-compensation is used.

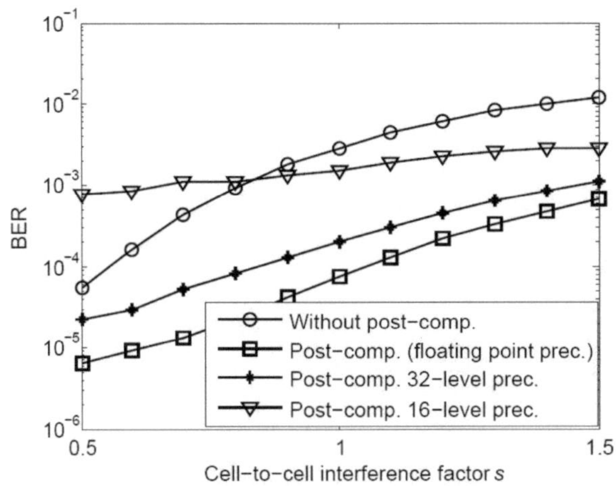

Fig. 20. Simulated BER performance of odd cells when post-compensation is used.

Note that pages are generally programmed and read both in the same order, i.e. page with lower index is programmed and read prior to page with higher index in consecutive case. Since later programmed page imposes interference on previously programmed neighbor page, as a result, one victim page is read before its interfering page is read in reading consecutive pages, hence extra read latency is needed to wait for reading interfering page of each concerned page. In the case of consecutive pages reading, all consecutive pages are concerned pages, and each page acts as the interfering page to the previous page and meanwhile is the victim page of the next page. Intuitively, reversing the order of programming pages to be descending order, i.e., pages with lower index are programmed latter, meanwhile reading pages in the ascending order can eliminate this extra read latency in reading consecutive pages. This is named as *reverse programming* scheme.

In this case, when we read those consecutive pages, after one page is read, it can naturally serve to compensate cell-to-cell interference for the page being read later. Therefore the extra sensing latency on waiting for sensing interfering page is naturally eliminated. Note that this reverse programming does not influence the sensing latency of reading individual pages.

6.2 Technique II: Pre-distortion

Pre-distortion or pre-coding technique widely used in communication system can also be used in NAND flash: Before a page is programmed, if its interfering pages are also known, we can predict the threshold voltage shift induced by cell-to-cell interference for each victim cell, and then correspondingly pre-distort the victim cell target programming voltage. Hence, after its interfering pages are programmed, the pre-distorted victim cell threshold voltages is expected to shift to its desired location by cell-to-cell interference.

Let $\bar{V}_t^{(k)}$ denote the expected threshold voltage of the k-th interfering cell after programming and $\bar{V}_e$ denote the mean of erased state, we can predict the cell-to-cell interference experienced by the victim cell as

$$\hat{F} = \sum_k \left((\bar{V}_t^{(k)} - \bar{V}_e) \cdot \bar{\gamma}^{(k)} \right) \tag{35}$$

Let V_p denote the target verify voltage of the victim cell in programming operation, we can pre-distort the victim cell by shifting the verify voltage from V_p to $V_p - \hat{F}$. The threshold voltage of the victim cell will be shifted towards its desired location after the occurrence of cell-to-cell interference. It should be emphasized that, since we cannot change the threshold voltage if the victim cell should stay at the erased state, this pre-distortion scheme can only handle cell-to-cell interference for those programmed states but is not effective for erased state. Fig. 21 illustrates the process of pre-distortion, where the verify voltage V_p is assumed to be able to be adjusted with a floating-point precision. Clearly, this technique can be considered as a counterpart of the post-compensation technique.

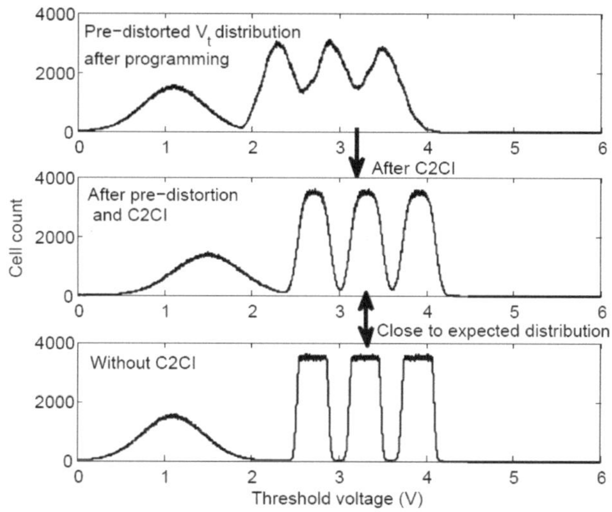

Fig. 21. Illustration of threshold voltage distribution of victim even cells in even/odd structure when data pre-distortion is being used.

Fig.22 shows the cell threshold distribution with the cell-to-cell interference strength factor $s = 0.8$ under the same initial NAND flash channel model as in above subsection, where the pre-distortion is assumed to be able to be adjusted with a floating-point precision.

Fig. 23 shows the simulated BER of even cells over a range of cell-to-cell interference strength factor s. Besides the ideal floating point precision, pre-distortion with finite precision is also shown, where the range of pre-distorted V_p is quantized into either 16 or 32 levels. Clearly, as the finite quantization precision of pre-distorted V_p increases, it can achieve a better tolerance to cell-to-cell interference, at the cost of increased programming latency, a larger page buffer to hold the data and higher chip-to-chip communication load.

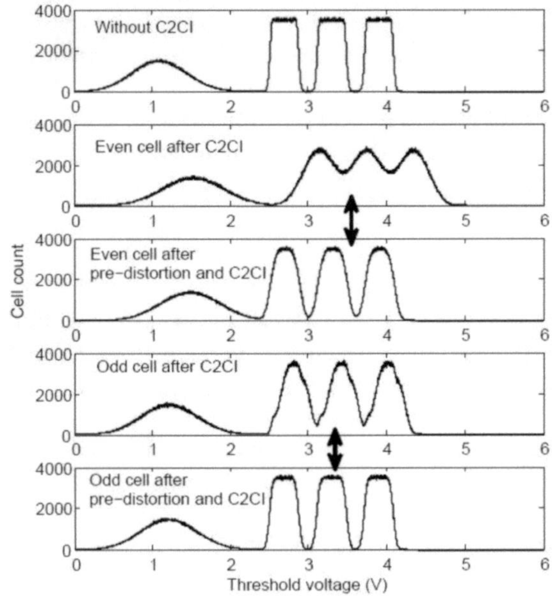

Fig. 22. Simulated threshold voltage distribution when using pre-distortion.

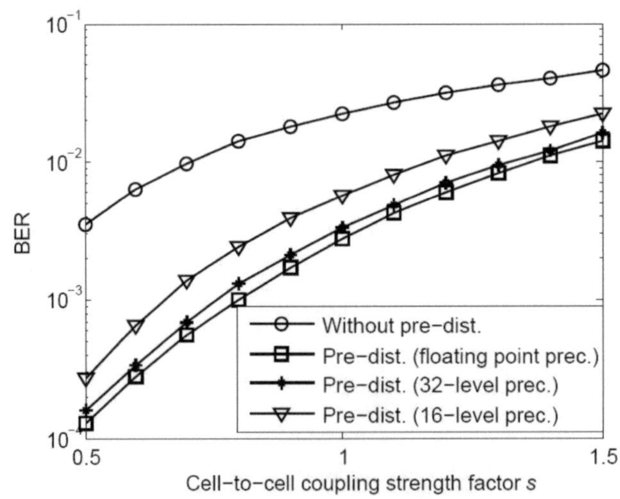

Fig. 23. The simulated BER of even cells with pre-distortion under various cell-to-cell strength factor.

7. Reference

K. Kim et.al, "Future memory technology: Challenges and opportunities," in *Proc. of International Symposium on VLSI Technology, Systems and Applications*, Apr. 2008, pp. 5–9.

G. Dong, S. Li, and T. Zhang, "Using Data Post-compensation and Pre-distortion to Tolerat Cell-to-Cell Interference in MLC NAND Flash Memory", *IEEE Transactions on Circuits and Systems I*, vol. 57, issue 10, pp. 2718-2728, 2010

Y. Li and Y. Fong, "Compensating for coupling based on sensing a neighbor using coupling," *United States Patent* 7,522,454, Apr. 2009.

G. Dong, N. Xie, and T. Zhang, "On the Use of Soft-Decision Error Correction Codes in NAND Flash Memory", *IEEE Transactions on Circuits and Systems I*, vol. 58, issue 2, pp. 429-439, 2011

E. Gal and S. Toledo, "Algorithms and data structures for flash memories," *ACM Computing Surveys*, vol. 37, pp. 138–163, June 2005.

Y. Pan, G. Dong, and T. Zhang, "Exploiting Memory Device Wear-Out Dynamics to Improve NAND Flash Memory System Performance", *USENIX Conference on File and Storage Technologies (FAST)*, Feb. 2011

G. Dong, N. Xie, and T. Zhang, "Techniques for Embracing Intra-Cell Unbalanced Bit Error Characteristics in MLC NAND Flash Memory", *Workshop on Application of Communication Theory to Emerging Memory Technologies* (in conjection with IEEE Globecom), Dec. 2010

N. Mielke et al., "Bit error rate in NAND flash memories," in *Proc. of IEEE International Reliability Physics Symposium*, 2008, pp. 9–19.

K. Kanda et al., "A 120mm2 16Gb 4-MLC NAND flash memory with 43nm CMOS technology," in *Proc. of IEEE International Solid-State Circuits Conference (ISSCC)*, 2008, pp. 430–431,625.

Y. Li et al., "A 16 Gb 3-bit per cell (X3) NAND flash memory on 56 nm technology with 8 MB/s write rate," *IEEE Journal of Solid-State Circuits*, vol. 44, pp. 195–207, Jan. 2009.

S.-H. Chang et al., "A 48nm 32Gb 8-level NAND flash memory with 5.5MB/s program throughput," in *Proc. of IEEE International Solid-State Circuits Conference*, Feb. 2009, pp. 240–241.

N. Shibata et al., "A 70nm 16Gb 16-level-cell NAND flash memory," *IEEE J. Solid-State Circuits*, vol. 43, pp. 929–937, Apr. 2008.

C. Trinh et al., "A 5.6MB/s 64Gb 4b/cell NAND flash memory in 43nm CMOS," in *Proc. of IEEE International Solid-State Circuits Conference*, Feb. 2009, pp. 246–247.

K. Takeuchi et al., "A 56-nm CMOS 99-mm2 8-Gb multi-level NAND flash memory with 10-mb/s program throughput," *IEEE Journal of Solid-State Circuits*, vol. 42, pp. 219–232, Jan. 2007.

G. Matamis et al., "Bitline direction shielding to avoid cross coupling between adjacent cells for NAND flash memory," *United States Patent* 7,221,008, May. 2007.

J. W. Lutze and N. Mokhlesi, "Shield plate for limiting cross coupling between floating gates," *United States Patent* 7,335,237, Apr. 2008.

H. Chien and Y. Fong, "Deep wordline trench to shield cross coupling between adjacent cells for scaled NAND," *United States Patent* 7,170,786, Jan. 2007.

S. Li and T. Zhang, "Improving multi-level NAND flash memory storage reliability using concatenated BCH-TCM coding," *IEEE Transactions on Circuits and Systems-I: Regular Papers*, vol. PP, pp. 1–1, 2009.

K. Prall, "Scaling non-volatile memory below 30 nm," in *IEEE 2nd Non-Volatile Semiconductor Memory Workshop*, Aug. 2007, pp. 5–10.

H. Liu, S. Groothuis, C. Mouli, J. Li, K. Parat, and T. Krishnamohan, "3D simulation study of cell-cell interference in advanced NAND flash memory," in *Proc. of IEEEWorkshop on Microelectronics and Electron Devices*, Apr. 2009.

K.-T. Park et al., "A zeroing cell-to-cell interference page architecture with temporary LSB storing and parallel MSB program scheme for MLC NAND flash memories," *IEEE J. Solid-State Circuits*, vol. 40, pp. 919–928, Apr. 2008.

K. Takeuchi, T. Tanaka, and H. Nakamura, "A double-level-Vth select gate array architecture for multilevel NAND flash memories," *IEEE J. Solid-State Circuits*, vol. 31, pp. 602–609, Apr. 1996.

K.-D. Suh et al., "A 3.3 V 32 Mb NAND flash memory with incremental step pulse programming scheme," *IEEE J. Solid-State Circuits*, vol. 30, pp. 1149–1156, Nov. 1995.

C. M. Compagnoni et al., "Random telegraph noise effect on the programmed threshold-voltage distribution of flash memories," *IEEE Electron Device Letters*, vol. 30, 2009.

A. Ghetti, et al., "Scaling trends for random telegraph noise in deca-nanometer flash memories," *in IEEE International Electron Devices Meeting*, 2008, 2008, pp. 1–4.

J.-D. Lee, S.-H. Hur, and J.-D. Choi, "Effects of floating-gate interference on NAND flash memory cell operation," *IEEE Electron. Device Letters*, vol. 23, pp. 264–266, May 2002.

K. Takeuchi et al., "A 56-nm CMOS 8-Gb multi-level NAND flash memory with 10-MB/s program throughput," *IEEE Journal of Solid-State Circuits*, vol. 42, pp. 219–232, Jan. 2007.

Y. Li et al., "A 16 Gb 3 b/cell NAND flash memory in 56 nm with 8 MB/s write rate," in *Proc. of IEEE International Solid-State Circuits Conference (ISSCC)*, Feb. 2008, pp. 506–632.

R.-A. Cernea et al., "A 34 MB/s MLC write throughput 16 Gb NAND with all bit line architecture on 56 nm technology," *IEEE Journal of Solid-State Circuits*, vol. 44, pp. 186–194, Jan. 2009.

N. Shibata et al., "A 70 nm 16 Gb 16-level-cell NAND flash memory," *IEEE J. Solid-State Circuits*, vol. 43, pp. 929–937, Apr. 2008.

H. Zhong and T. Zhang, "Block-LDPC: A practical LDPC coding system design approach," *IEEE Transactions on Circuits and Systems-I: Regular Papers*, vol. 52, no. 4, pp. 766–775, 2005.

I. Alrod and M. Lasser, "Fast, low-power reading of data in a flash memory," in *United States Patent* 20090319872A1, 2009.

Y. Kou, S. Lin, and M. Fossorier, "Low-density parity-check codes based on finite geometries: a rediscovery and new results", *IEEE Trans. Inf. Theory*, vol. 47, pp. 2711-2736, Nov. 2001.

R. G. Gallager, "Low density parity check codes", *IRE Trans. Inf. Theory*, vol. 8, pp. 21-28, Jan. 1962.

G. Dong, Y. Li, N. Xie, T. Zhang and H. Liu, "Candidate bit based bit-flipping decoding algorithm for LDPC codes", *IEEE ISIT* 2009, pp. 2166-2168, 2009

J. Zhang and M. P. C. Fossorier, "A modified weighted bit-flipping decoding of low-density parity-check codes", *IEEE Commun. Lett.*, vol. 8, pp. 165-167, Mar. 2004.

F. Guo and L. Hanzo, "Reliability ratio based weighted bit-flipping decoding for low-density parity-check codes", *Electron. Lett.*, vol. 40, pp. 1356-1358, Oct. 2004.

C.-H. Lee and W. Wolf, "Implementation-efficient reliability ratio based weighted bit-flipping decoding for LDPC codes", *Electron. Lett.*, vol. 41, pp. 755-757, Jun. 2005.

D. J. C. MacKay and R. M. Neal, "Near Shannon limit performance of low density parity check codes", *Electron. Lett.*, vol. 32, pp. 1645–1646, Aug. 1997.

X. Wang, L. Pan, D. Wu et al., "A High-Speed Two-Cell BCH Decoder for Error Correcting in MLC NOR Flash Memories", *IEEE Trans. on Circuits and Systems II*, vol.56, no.11, pp.865-869, Nov. 2009.

X. Wang, D. Wu, C. Hu, et al., "Embedded High-Speed BCH Decoder for New Generation NOR Flash Memories" *Proc. IEEE CICC 2009*, pp. 195-198, 2009.

R. Micheloni, R. Ravasio, A. Marelli, et al., "A 4Gb 2b/cell NAND flash memory with embedded 5b BCH ECC for 36MB/s system read throughput", *Proc. IEEE ISSCC*, pp. 497-506, Feb. 2006.

4

Block Cleaning Process in Flash Memory

Amir Rizaan Rahiman and Putra Sumari
Multimedia Research Group, School of Computer Sciences, University Sains Malaysia, Malaysia

1. Introduction

Flash memory is a non-volatile storage device that can retain its contents when the power is switched off. Generally, it is a form of an electrically erasable programmable read-only memory (EEPROM) that offers several excellent features such as less noise, solid-state reliability, lower power consumption, smaller size, light weight, and higher shock resistant [1 - 5]. Flash memory acts as a slim and compact storage device. It's main applications are such as compact flash (CF), secured digital (SD), and personal computer memory card international association (PCMCIA) cards, for storage and data transfer in most portable electronic gadgets such as mobile phones, digital cameras, personal digital assistants (PDAs), portable media players (PMPs), gobal positioning system receivers (GPS), just to name a few.

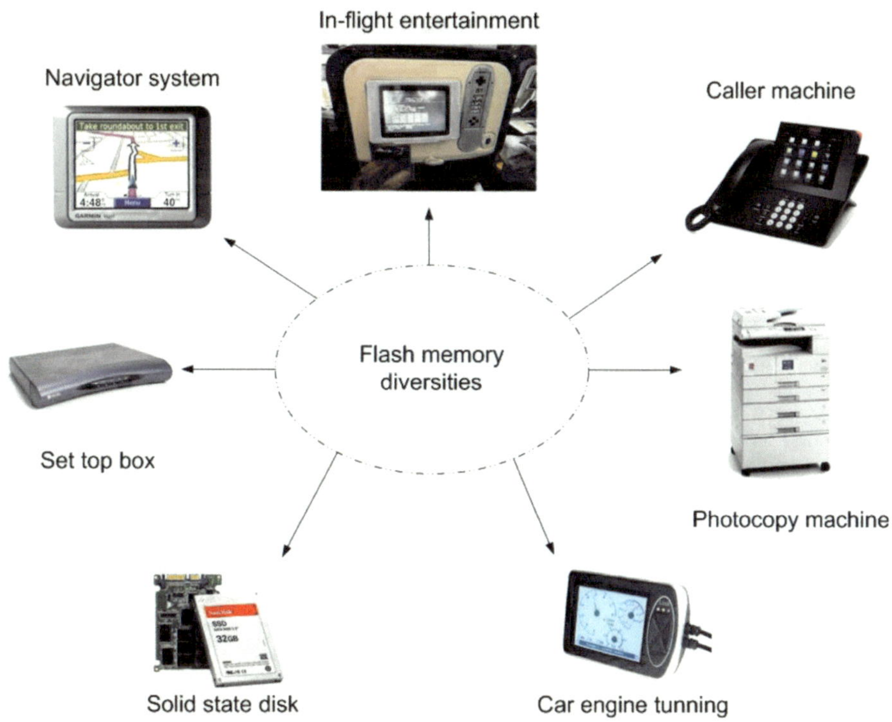

Fig. 1. Diverse applications of flash memory as embedded systems.

The demand for flash memory has reformed its usage to wide areas. For instance, as illustrated in Figure 1, flash memory is extensively used as embedded systems in several intelligent and novelty applications such as household appliances, telecommunication devices, computer applications, automotives and high technology machinery.

2. Flash memory architecture

As shown in Figure 2, flash memory is a block and page based storage device. The page unit is used to store data where a group of pages is referred to as a block. The page unit is partitioned into two areas, namely, 1) *Data* and 2) *Spare*. The data area is used to store the actual data while the spare area is used to store the supporting information for the data area (such as bad block identification, page and block data structures, error correction code (ECC), etc.). According to present production practices, the page size is fixed from 512 B to 4 KB, while the block size is between 4 KB and 128 KB [18]. Figure 3 shows the attributes of a 4 GB flash memory.

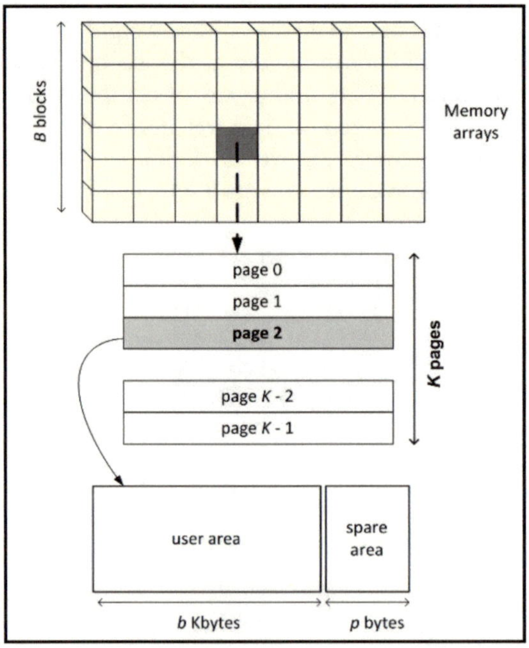

Fig. 2. Block and page layout in flash memory.

There are two different types of flash memory in the current market, namely, 1) *NOR-flash*, and 2) *NAND-flash* [2, 6]. The main distinction between both types is the I/O interface connection mechanism to the host system. The NOR-flash employs a memory mapped random access interface with a dedicated address and data lines that are similar to random access memory (RAM). Besides that, it is a byte-addressable data accessing device that permits random I/O access with higher performance in reading functionality. On the contrary, data access in NAND-flash is controlled and managed through two indirect I/O interface logic methods. They are the emulating block accessing method referred to as the flash translation layer (FTL) and native file system. The FTL allows physical accessing units

Symbol	Description	Value
-	Power consumption	2.70 – 3.60 V
-	Dimension (h x w x d) mm	12 x 20 x 1.2
R_t	Data read from a page into the data register	25 μs
W_t	Data write from a data register into memory page	200 μs
E_t	Block erasure access time	1.5 ms
S_t	Sequential access to the data register (bus data)	100 μs
V	Number of chips per device	2
B	Number of blocks per chip	8192
K	Number of pages per block	64
p	Page size	4 KB
b	Block size	256 KB
r_{data}	Data register	4 KB
D	Capacity per chip	2 GB
u_i	Block i utilization, $0 \leq i \leq B - 1$	[0, 1]
-	Program/Erase cycles	1,000,000

Fig. 3. Flash memory attributes and specifications.

(block and page) to be addressed as a set of different accessing units (such as 512 B, 2 KB, 4 KB, depending on the manufacturers). In the native file system, the device accessing unit can directly be accessed without the translation layer. An example of the native file system employed in NAND-flash is the journaling flash file system (JFFS) [7] and yet another flash filing system (YAFFS) [23]. For application purposes, the NOR-flash is used for small amounts of code storage while the NAND-flash is mostly used in data storage applications since its characteristic are more similar to disk storage.

3. Flash memory characteristics

The characteristics of the flash memory can be summarized as follows [8, 9]:

i. **Free accessing time penalties**: The flash memory is a semiconductor device which eliminates the use of mechanical components. This allows the time required to access data to be uniform, regardless of the data's location. For instance, let's say both data *a* and data *b*, which are 4 KB in size each, are randomly located in block *i* and *k* (see Figure 4). The total time required to retrieve data *a* is 0.088 *ms* and data *b* is retrieved directly after retrieving data *a*.

   Data accessing (retrieving and storing) in flash memory is carried out in three phases, 1) *Setup*, 2) *Busy*, and 3) *Data transfer* [24]. The accessing command is initialized in the setup phase. In the busy phase, the required data is temporarily loaded into the flash memory I/O buffer within a fixed accessing time. Then, the stored data in the I/O buffer is transferred sequentially to the host system at every fixed serial access time during the data transfer phase. Similarly, the storing/writing process also requires constant access time, wherever the location might be.

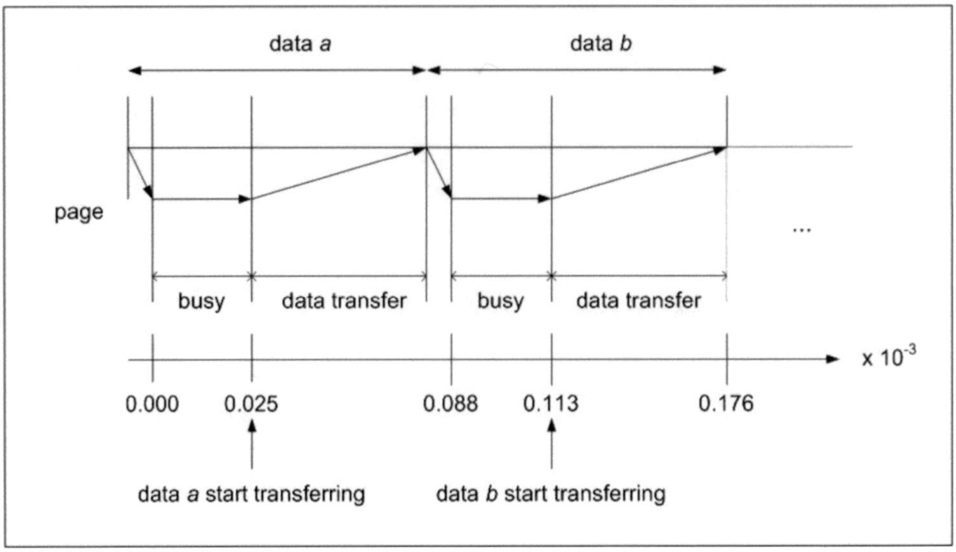

Fig. 4. Data accessing in flash memory array.

ii. **Out-place updating scheme**: Data updating in the flash memory is performed via an out-place scheme rather than an in-place scheme. Due to its EEPROM characteristic, if the in-place scheme is employed, the block where the updated data is located needs to be erased first before the data can be restored into the similar location. Furthermore, block erasure in flash memory is time consuming that can degrade I/O performance. Thus, the out-place scheme is employed where the updated data is stored into a new location while its original copy is set as garbage and will not be used any further [10 – 11] (see Figure 5). The main purpose of the out-place scheme is to avoid block erasure during every update process.

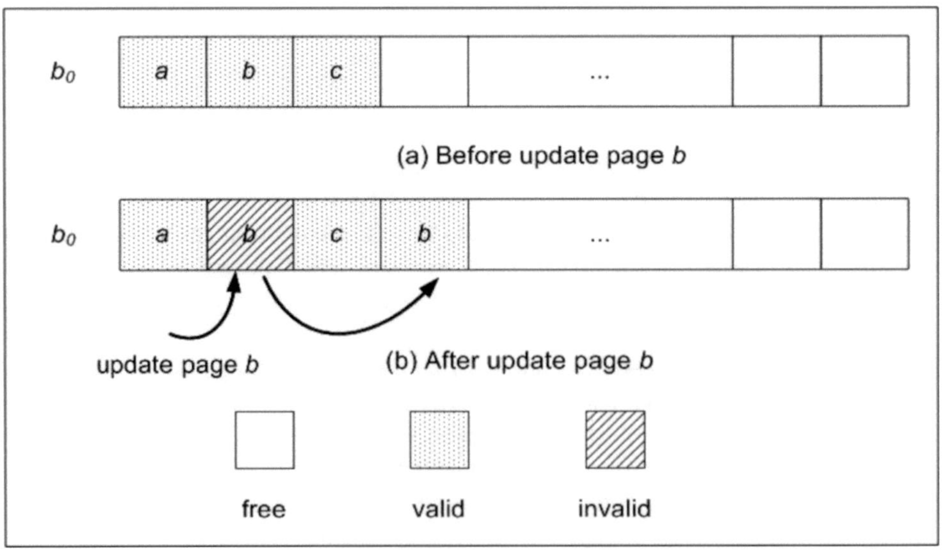

Fig. 5. The out-place updating scheme in the flash memory.

Due to the out-place scheme, the page in flash memory falls into three states, namely, 1) *Free*, 2) *Valid*, and 3) *Invalid*. The free state is when a page contains no data and is ready for storing/writing a new or updated data. The valid state is a page that contains the current version of the data while the invalid state refers to a page that contains garbage. In addition, the block status can either be active or inactive [12 - 13] due to the page states.

iii. **Asymmetric accessing time and unit**: There are three types of access functions in flash memory. They are 1) *Read*, 2) *Write/program*, and 3) *Erase*. Each function is realized in an asymmetric accessing unit and time (see Figure 3). The write function takes an order of magnitude longer than the read function and both are carried out in page unit, while the erase function requires the longest access time which is performed in block unit. The read function fetches a valid data from a valid target page, while the write function stores data (either new or updated) into a free target page. On the contrary, the erase function is used to erase an active or an inactive block with free or invalid pages.

iv. **Bulk cleaning with limited block life cycle**: The cleaning process is essential in flash memory due to the employed out-place updating scheme. The cleaning process is carried out on block unit rather than page unit. The block may contain valid data, thus, before initiating the process, all valid data residing in the block must be copied out into available free spaces in other free blocks. However, each block could be tolerant with a limited number of erasure cycles, for example one million (10^6) cycles. Exceeding the erasure cycles will cause the block to become unreliable and spoiled, permanently. For example, a multi-level cell (MLC) block type typically supports 10,000 erasure cycles. If the same block is erased and then re-programmed every second, the block would exceed the 10,000 cycle limit in just three hours. Thus, wear-leveling policy that wears down all memory blocks as evenly as possible is necessary [14, 15].

4. Cleaning process in flash memory

The cleaning process in flash memory refers to the process of collecting the garbage scattered throughout the memory array and then reclaiming them back into free space due to the out-place updating scheme. It is an essential process to guarantee free space availability on the memory array to ensure new data can be continually stored. However, the cleaning process is carried out by the erase function and involves bulk size of data rather than specific locations. The valid data in the block must be copied into the other blocks (free cells) first, before the cleaning can be initiated. Besides, each flash memory block could tolerate with an individual erasure lifetime. Frequently erasing blocks causes the blocks to become unreliable and thus, reduces physical device capacity.

The effectiveness of the cleaning process is heavily dependent on the efficient cleaning algorithm as well as the data allocation scheme employed by the flash memory system. Moreover, the cleaning process and the block utilization level are key to the cleaning process performance and have substantial impact on the access performance, energy consumption and block endurance [1, 10, 14]. Block utilization is the ratio between valid cells and total cells and it is represented in percentage. Two categories of cleaning processes in flash memory are 1) *Automatic*, and 2) *Semi-automatic* [16]. Both processes are initiated routinely by the flash memory controller.

4.1 Automatic cleaning

The automatic cleaning process is automatically commenced when a particular block's state in the memory array turns from an active to an inactive (all pages in the block have turned into invalid state or mixing with several number of free pages). Since there is no valid data copying process required, the block can be erased in the background during execution of the current I/O operations (such as read or write) from/into the memory array. Accordingly, this process requires a constant erase accessing time (E_t) where the target block ID is given to the memory controller to erase. Moreover, only a single inactive block (also known as victim block) can be erased each time the automatic cleaning process is commenced. In addition, the automatic cleaning process is influence by an efficient data allocation scheme engaged by the flash memory. There are several data allocation schemes in flash memory that share identical queuing techniques with a CPU scheduling policy such as first come first serve (FCFS), first re-arrival first serve (FRFS), online first re-arrival first serve (OFRFS), and Best Matching (BestM) [12 - 13]. Unlike CPU scheduling policies, the main objective of the data allocation scheme in the flash memory is to minimize the amount of active blocks required. The scheme requires the lowest amount of active blocks to minimize the amount of blocks to be erased when the actual cleaning process is initiated due to the limitation of the out-place updating scheme.

For example, let's say file *A* has been partitioned evenly into five parts (denoted by *a, b, c, d,* and *e*). Assume the accessing pattern of the file is *a, b, c, d, a, b, b, a, c, d, a, b, c, d, a, b, d, a, c, c, d, a, b, c*. The snapshot of storing each of the accessed data into the flash memory consisting of 10 blocks with 4 pages (each, sequentially) is shown in Figure 6. Firstly, the first four accessed data are stored sequentially in block b_1. When storing the second accessed data *d* (the 10th appearance data in the access pattern) into the second free page in block b_3, block b_1

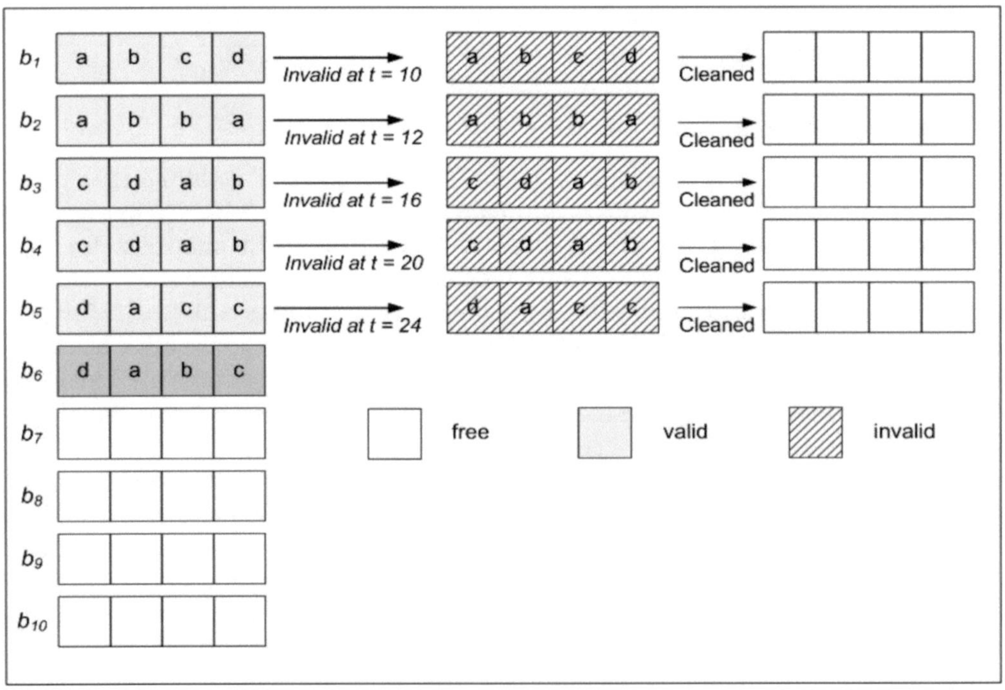

Fig. 6. Automatic cleaning process in sequential data allocation scheme.

turns into an inactive state and can be erased automatically. Then, block b_2 is erased when storing the last free page in block b_3 with data *b*. Block b_3 is erased when finish storing the 5th appearance of data *b* into the last free page of *b4*. At the end of the access pattern, only block b_6 is in the active state. When the inactive block is erased, all of its pages are changed into the free state and the block is ready for storing new or updated data.

4.2 Semi-automatic cleaning

Semi-automatic cleaning is commenced when the memory array free spaces reach a certain threshold, for instance, when the available free space is fewer than 20% - 35% of the total memory space. Two primary goals of the semi-automatic cleaning process are: 1) *Minimizing cleaning cost*, and 2) *Wearing blocks evenly*. Unlike the automatic cleaning process, single or multiple active block(s) can be cleaned simultaneously when the semi-automatic process has been initiated. Therefore, since the blocks to be cleaned contain valid data, the data needs to be migrated first before the cleaning process can be initiated and the current memory operations are temporarily halted. It is resumed when the process has ended. Besides, the cleaning cost required is inconsistent and it solely depends on the block utilization (u_i) level and the number of active blocks involved in the cleaning process. The cleaning cost is the total access time required to erase the victim blocks which includes several reads and writes accessing time (depending on the block utilization levels) plus the erasure time. In short, it can be simplified as in Equation 1 [17]. Block utilization is the ratio between valid pages and total pages.

$$T(b_i) = R_t + (W_t \times 10) + E_t \times 75 \quad (1)$$

In Equation 1, the write function is assumed to be 10 times slower than the read function while the erase function is 75 times slower than the read function. Figure 7 presents the cleaning cost required for cleaning a single victim block in the memory array. To illustrate this, assume a block containing 64 pages, and the block utilization level is between 0 and 100 %. The actual time for read, write and erase access functions were taken from Figure 3.

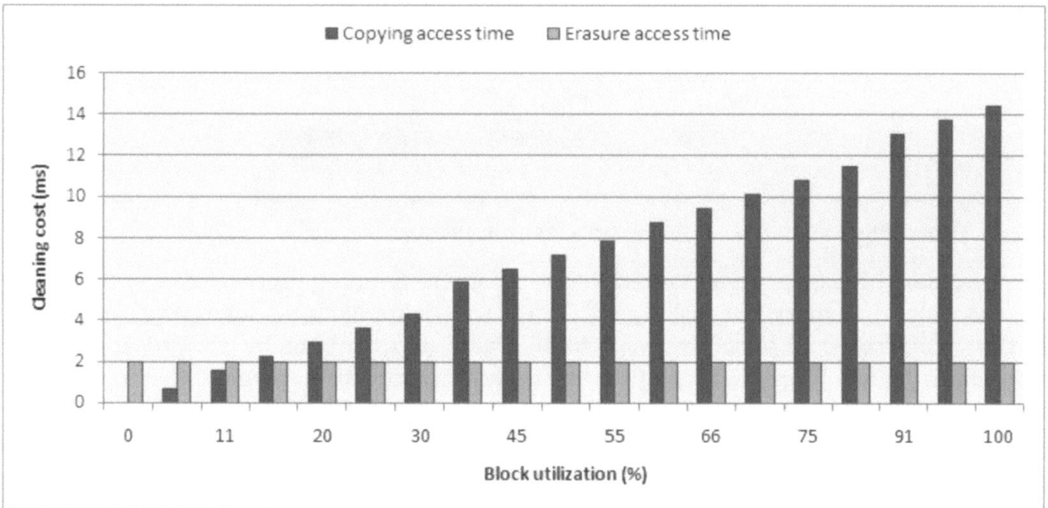

Fig. 7. The cleaning cost for single block.

As illustrated in Figure 8, the semi-automatic cleaning is undertaken in three stages. First, a victim block (b_1) to be cleaned is selected. Second, all valid pages residing in block b_1 are identified (e.g., *a, b, c,* and *d*) and copied/migrated into free pages in block b_3 (initially, b_3 is in an inactive state). In the last stage, block b_1 is erased when all the valid pages have been copied. Since multiple victim blocks can be erased simultaneously, the process could affect the current I/O operational functions. Therefore, the numbers of victim blocks becomes a crucial factor in the semi-automatic cleaning process. Unlike the automatic cleaning process, there are several important issues that need to be considered in semi-automatic cleaning. The four main issues in the semi-automatic cleaning process are 1) *Execution time,* 2) *Victim block selection procedure,* 3) *Victim block amount,* and 4) *Valid data re-organization* [18].

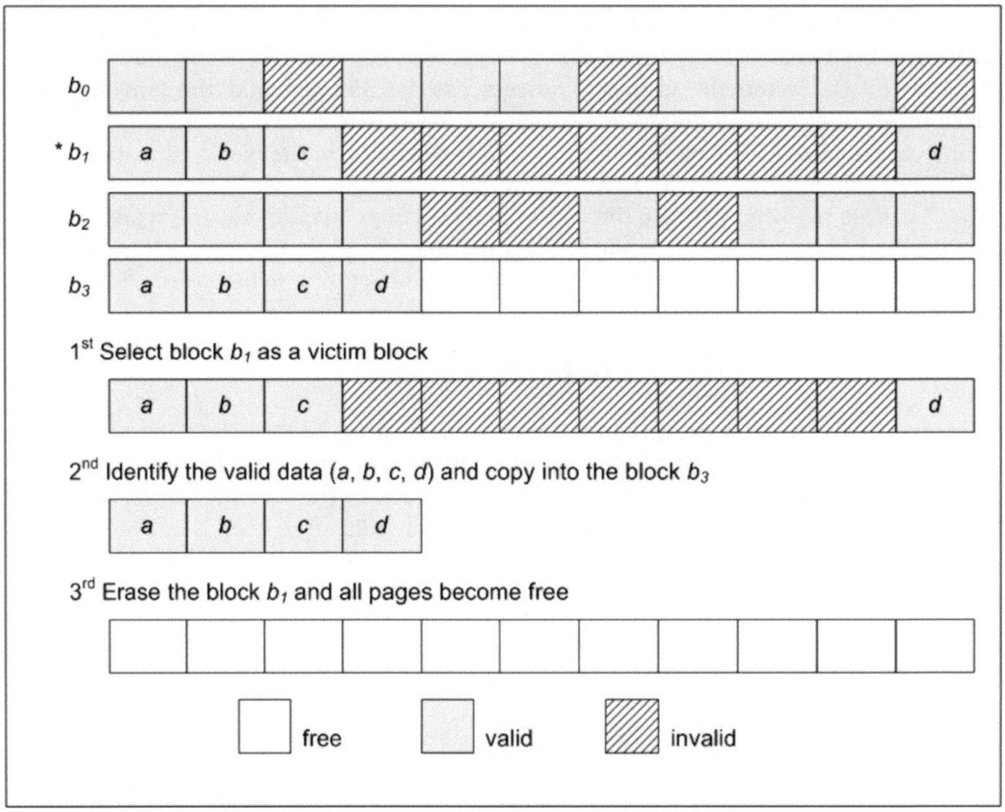

Fig. 8. Three stages in the semi-automatic cleaning process.

The execution time issue refers to the time to initiate the cleaning process, either periodically or according to memory free space availability. The victim block selection procedure refers to the method used to select the block to be erased and the straight forward approach is selecting a victim block that contains the largest amount of garbage. Other parameters include cost to erase, block lifespan, erasure count, and age of data [1, 10, 21, 22]. Again, the victim block amount issue in the semi-automatic cleaning enables single or multiple victim blocks to be erased simultaneously. On the other hand, both approaches have their own pros and cons. Cleaning a single block requires smaller access time but it also requires many erase operations. In contrast, erasing multiple blocks can distract the execution of normal

I/O operational system execution [18], but multiple victim blocks cleaning helps in reorganizing many valid data and can also help in reducing the number of blocks to be further erased. Then, the valid data re-organization issue refers to the process of copying the valid data in the victim block into a new free location in the available active blocks. The common approach is the valid data clustering technique, where valid data will be grouped into the similar block according to the data feature (such as regularly modified, irregularly modified, data time-stamp, and related data file). Thus, in order to improve the semi-automatic cleaning process performance, a number of studies that focuses on determining victim blocks have been proposed. The accompanying table shows the summary of the studies. In addition, the cleaning cost in the semi-automatic process depends on two important parameters, namely, 1) *Number of victim blocks* and 2) *Amount of valid data.* The cleaning cost will be extremely boosted when both parameters increase. However, the number of active blocks is not fixed and it is a controllable parameter. Due to this, by employing a proper allocation scheme, the amount could be minimized since the inactive block can be erased at the background.

Cleaning scheme	Victim block selection procedure/equation	Wear-leveling
Greedy (GR) [19]	$\cos t(B_i) = \frac{u_i}{1-u_i}$	No
Cost-benefit (CB) [20]	Block with maximum value from equation $a \times \frac{(1-u_i)}{2u_i}$	No
Cost age time (CAT) & Dynamic dAta clustering (DAC) [21]	Block with minimum value from equation $\left(\frac{u_i}{1-u_i}\right) \times \frac{1}{a} \times e$	Yes
Cost Age Time with Age Sort (CATA) [18]	Blocks those maximize equation $\left(\frac{1-u_i}{1+u_i}\right) \times a \times \frac{1}{e}$	Yes
S-Greedy (S-GR) [22]	Based on GR algorithm and focus on valid data distribution	Yes

u_i: block i utilization level. a: the last invalidation time in the block. e: block erasure count.

Table 1. A summary of previously proposed victim block selection algorithm.

5. Summary

Flash memory offers several superior features as a secondary storage and has recently been employed in many consumer electronic gadgets. However, due to the hardware operational characteristics, especially the out-place updating scheme, several challenges have emerged in terms of data management in designing and implementing an efficient data storage system. There are existing issues that influence flash memory performance, which are related to the cleaning process in order to allow data storage continuity. Both the automatic and the semi-automatic cleaning processes are two important issues in guaranteeing cleaning process performance in the flash memory. The automatic cleaning is directly related with the efficient data allocation schemes where the cleaning can be initiated without having to disturb the current operations in the flash memory. Although only single inactive blocks can be cleaned every time the process is initiated, when the amount of active-to-inactive state conversion increases, the cleaning performance of the flash memory is guaranteed since the inactive block can be erased automatically without having to disturb current I/O operations. Conversely, the semi-automatic cleaning process is initiated according to a memory array free space threshold or it can be initiated periodically. There are several parameters employed in establishing the victim block to be erased such as cleaning cost, erasure count, age of data, block utilization, etc. Although the cleaning can be initiated on multiple victim blocks, the process can impose a blocking time that would distract the normal I/O operation execution on the memory. On the other hand, the efficiency of re-organizing the valid data in the victim blocks could influence the cleaning process performance further. The well-organized valid data in the new active block will group the regular and irregular accessed data into different blocks and could further increase the amount of inactive blocks. The increase of inactive blocks in the memory array would increase the automatic cleaning process and guarantee flash memory performance. Thus, both cleaning processes are important in order to improve the cleaning process performance in flash memory as well as its endurance.

6. References

[1] Douglis, F., Kaashoek, F., Marsh, B., Caceres, R., Li, K. and Tauber, J. (1994) Storage alternatives for mobile computers. In: Proceedings of the 1st USENIX Conference on Operating Systems Design and Implementation (OSDI'94), Nov. 14-17, Monterey, California: ACM/IEEE. pp. 25 – 37.

[2] Chang, L.P. and Kuo, T.W. (2004) An efficient management scheme for large-scale flash memory storage systems. In: Proceedings of the 2004 ACM Symposium of Applied Computing (SAC'04), March 14-17, Nicosia, Cyprus: ACM. pp. 862 – 868.

[3] Lawton, G. (2006) Improved flash memory grows in popularity. IEEE Computer, 39(1), p. 16 – 18.

[4] Lim, S.H. and Park, K.H. (2006) An efficient NAND flash file system for flash memory storage. IEEE Transactions on Computers, 55(7), p. 906 – 912.

[5] Breeuwsma, M., Jongh, M.d., Klaver, C., Knijff, R.v.d. and Roeloffs, M. (2007) Forensic data recovery from flash memory. Small Scale Digital Device Forensic Journal, 1(1), p. 1 – 17.

[6] Hsieh, J.W., Tsai, Y.L., Kuo, T.W. and Lee, T.L. (2008) Configurable flash-memory management: Performance versus overheads. IEEE Transactions on Computer, 57(11), p. 1571 – 1583.

[7] Woodhouse, D. (2001) JFFS: The journaling flash file system. In: Proceedings of the 2001 Ottawa Linux Symposium, July 13-16, Ottawa, Canada.

[8] Barre, A.G. (1993) Flash memory magnetic disk replacement? IEEE Transactions on Magnetics, 29(6), p. 4104 – 4107.

[9] Sharma, A.K. (2003) Advanced semiconductor memories: Architecture, designs, and applications. Canada: WILEY-IEEE Press. P.4

[10] Kawaguchi, A., Nishioka, S. and Motada, H. (1995) Flash memory based file system. In: Proceedings of USENIX 95 Technical Conference, Jan. 16-20, New Orleans, Louisiana: USENIX. pp. 155 - 164.
[11] Wu, M. and Zwanepoel, W. (1994) eNVy: a non-volatile, main memory storage system. In: Proceedings of the 6th International Conference on Architectural Support for Programming language and Operating Systems (ASPLOS), Oct. 5-7, San Jose, California: ACM. pp. 86 - 97.
[12] Chou, L.F. and Liu, P. (2005) Efficient allocation algorithms for flash file systems. In: Proceedings of 11th International Conference on Parallel and Distribution Systems (ICPADS'05), July 20-22, Fukuoka, Japan: IEEE. pp. 634 - 641.
[13] Liu, P., Chuang, C.H. and Wu, J.J. (2007) Block-based allocation algorithms for flash memory in embedded systems. In: Proceedings of 9th International Conference on Parallel Computing Technologies (PaCT 2007), Sept. 3-7, Pereslavl-Zalessky, Russia: Springer. pp. 569 - 578.
[14] Kim, H. and Lee, S.G. (2002) An effective flash memory manager for reliable flash memory space management. IEICE Trans. Information and System, E85-D(6), p. 950 - 964.
[15] Chang, Y.H., Hsieh, J.W. and Kuo, T.W. (2007) Endurance enhancement of flash-memory storage systems: An efficient static wear leveling design. In: Proceedings of 44th ACM/IEEE Design Automation Conference (DAC 2007), June 4-8, San Diego, California: ACM. pp. 212 - 217.
[16] Rahiman, A.R. and Sumari, P. (2009). Probability based page data allocation scheme in flash memory. In: Proceedings of IEEE Pacific-Rim Conference on Multimedia (PCM 2009), Dec. 15-18, Bangkok, Thailand: IEEE. pp. 300 - 310.
[17] Ko, S., Jun, S., Kim, K., and Ryu, Y. (2008) Study on garbage collection schemes for flash based Linux swap system. In: International Conference on Advanced Software Engineering & Its Applications (ASEA 2008), Dec. 13-15, Hainan Island, China: IEEE. pp. 13 - 16.
[18] Han, L.Z., Rhu, Y., Chung, T.S., Lee, M. and Hong, S. (2006) An intelligent garbage collection algorithm for flash memory storages. In: Proceedings of International Conference on Computational Science and Its Applications (ICCSA 2006), May 8-11, Glasgow, UK: Springer. pp. 1019 - 1027.
[19] Rosenblum, M. and Ousterhout, J.K. (1992) The design and implementation of a log-structured file system. ACM Transactions on Computer Systems, 10(1), p. 26 - 52.
[20] Kawaguchi, A., Nishioka, S. and Motada, H. (1995) Flash memory based file system. In: Proceedings of USENIX 95 Technical Conference, Jan. 16-20, New Orleans, Louisiana: USENIX. pp. 155 - 164.
[21] Chiang, M.L., Lee, P.C.H, and Chang, R.C. (1999) Cleaning policies in mobile computers using flash memory. Journal of Systems and Software, 48(3), p. 213 - 231.
[22] Kwon, O., Ryu, Y. and Koh, K. (2007) An efficient garbage collection policy for flash memory based swap systems. In: Proceedings of International Conference on Computer Science and Applications (ICCSA 2007), Oct. 24-26, San Francisco, USA: IAENG. pp. 213 - 223.
[23] Yaffs (2006) How does YAFFS work? [Online], [Accessed 30th July, 2010], Available from World Wide Web: http://www.yaffs.net/yaffs-internals.

[24] Kang, J.U., Kim, J.S., Park, C., Park, H. and Lee, J. (2007) A multi-channel architecture for high-performance NAND flash-based storage system. Journal of Systems Architecture, 53(9), p. 644 - 658.

5

Behavioral Modeling of Flash Memories

Igor S. Stievano, Ivan A. Maio and Flavio G. Canavero
Diartimento di Elettronica, Politecnico di Torino,
Corso Duca degli Abruzzi, 24, 10129, Torino
Italy

1. Introduction

Over the past ten years, the interest in the development of accurate and efficient models of high-speed digital integrated circuits (ICs) has grown. The generation of IC models is of paramount importance for the simulation of many advanced electronic applications. IC models are used in system level simulation to predict the integrity of the signals flowing through the system interconnects and the switching noise generated by the current absorption of the circuits, that can interfere on the stable functioning of the entire system.
In this scenario, the common modeling resource is based on the detailed description of the IC functional behavior obtained from the information on the internal structure of devices and on the their physical governing equations. These models, however, are seldom available since they disclose proprietary information of silicon vendors. In addition they turn out to be extremely inefficient to handle the complexity of recent devices and demand for the availability of simplified models. Owing to this, the most promising strategy is the generation of the so-called behavioral models or macromodels, that mimic the external behavior of a device and that can be obtained from external simulations or measurements.
A typical example of devices that strongly demand for the availability of reliable behavioral models is represented by the class of digital memories, that are widely used in modern electronic equipments and that are often provided by external suppliers along with low-order or partial models only. The modeling of the power delivery network of ICs is addressed in (ICEM, 2001; Labussiere-Dorgan et al., 2008; Stievano et al., 2011b) and the modeling of I/O ports in (Stievano et al., 2004; Mutnury et. al., 2006; IBIS, 2008; Pulici et al., 2008; Cao and Zhang, 2009; Stievano et al., 2011a). In these contributions most of the efforts are made to define and improve the model structures and to provide general modeling guidelines for the computation of model parameters from both numerical simulations and real measurements.
The aim of this chapter is to provide a unified modeling framework for the combined application of state-of-the-art techniques to the generation of behavioral models of digital ICs from numerical simulation and real measured data. All the results presented in this study are based on a 512Mb NOR Flash memory in 90 nm technology produced by Numonyx, which is representative of a wide class of memory chips.

2. Macromodel description

This section focuses on the classification of the external ports of a Flash memory and on the available resources for the modeling of its external behavior.

2.1 Classification

The schematic of Fig. 1, represents the typical structure of packaged memory chips in stacked configuration. These devices are composed of a number of silicon dies encapsulated within the same package and connected through bonding wires to the package pads as shown in the example structure. For a single memory chip like the die #1 in the figure, the external pads allowing the chip to communicate to the external circuitry can be classified into three classes:

(*a*) the VDDn and VSSn pads, corresponding to the core power delivery network of the memory that carries the energy to the memory matrix, the digital circuitry and possible additional analog blocks within the die;

(*b*) the DQn pads, corresponding to the high-speed I/O buffers;

(*c*) the VDDQn and VSSQn pads, corresponding to a dedicated power structure, i.e., the so-called power rail, that consists of two on-chip traces connecting the supply pads and supplying the I/O buffers. A limited number of buffers (in general from one to four) is supplied by two adjacent VDDQn and VSSQn pads;

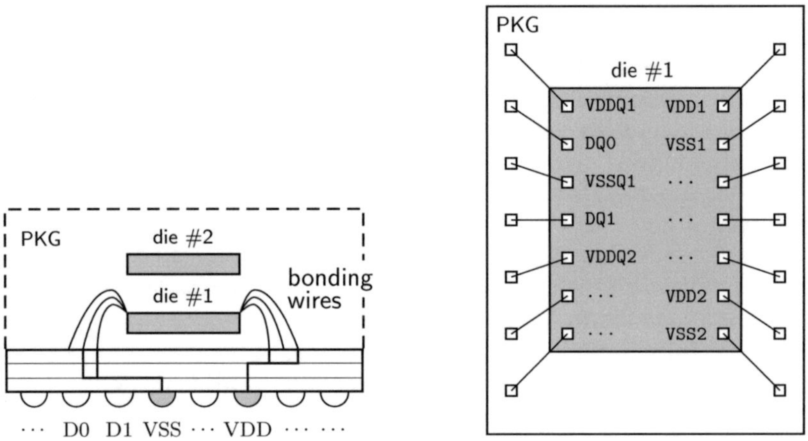

Fig. 1. Typical structure of a memory chip (i.e., the die #1) encapsulated in package. Left panel: side view; right panel; top view.

It is important to remark that the structure of Fig. 1 provides an exemplification aimed at classifying the ports and the behavior of a memory. Some minor differences might exist and depend on the specific device at hand. However, possible differences do not change the above classification and the proposed modeling methodology.

Based on the previous classification, a memory macromodel is a multiport equivalent describing the port behavior of the electrical voltage and current signals at die pads. Also, due to the inherent internal structure of this class of devices, the macromodel can be decomposed into the following submodels.

(*a*) a dynamical model for the **core power delivery network** that reproduces the port constitutive relation of the multi-terminal circuit element defined by the VDDn and VSSn pads.

(*b*) a set of dynamical models for the **I/O buffers** that include the effect of their dedicated power supply structure and that describe the port constitutive relations of the three terminal circuit elements defined by the DQn, VDDQn and VSSQn pads.

(c) a dynamical model for the VDDQn and VSSQn **power rail** network.

It is worth noticing that in many practical cases, the above submodels can be assumed independent one to each other since the possible coupling among the three physical structures turns out to be extremely low and can be neglected. As an example, this has been verified by a set of on-chip measurements carried out on the same memory IC considered in this study (see Fig. 2).

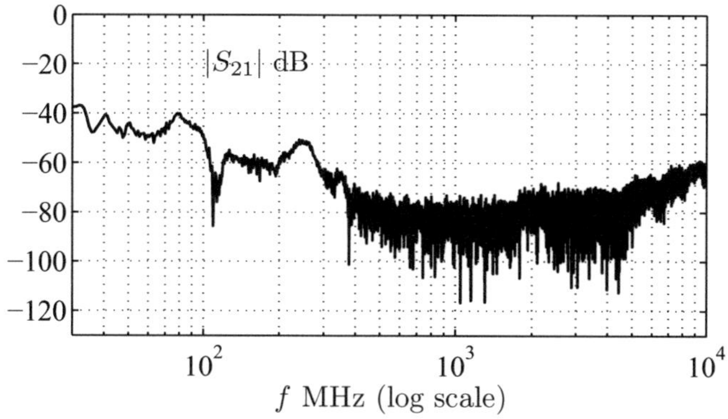

Fig. 2. On-chip measurement of the S21 scattering parameter carried out between two heterogeneous pairs of VDDn-VSSn and VDDQn-VSSQn supply pads. The measurement highlights the low coupling between the core and the buffer power delivery networks for the example test chip considered in the study.

2.2 Core power delivery network

According to (Stievano et al., 2011a;b), the model for the core power supply of ICs is defined by a simplified - physically inspired - circuit equivalent that attempts to describe the different blocks involved in the power delivery network of a digital IC. A common assumption in these approaches is the description of the core power delivery network of the IC by means of a Norton equivalent like the one of Fig. 3a, where the short-circuit current generator $A(s)$ accounts for the internal switching activity of the device and the equivalent impedance $Z_e(s)$ accounts for the passive interconnect structure and body diodes. This assumption holds when the physical dimension of the silicon die and the frequency bandwidth of interest are compatible with lumped modeling. When these conditions are met, this simplification is the best solution to estimate the model parameters from external measurements. In the state-of-the art modeling resources, the simple Norton equivalent of Fig. 3a can be complemented by possible additional passive circuit elements guessed from some information on the internal structure of the IC.

The estimation of the model parameters of the Norton equivalent amounts to computing the short-circuit current source via the transient measurement or simulation of the current drawn by the IC core during normal operation and the short-circuit admittance via frequency-domain measurements (e.g., via the scattering parameter responses of the VDD-VSS structure). It goes without saying that the frequency-domain measurements do not directly provide a computational model that can be directly used in a simulation environment like SPICE. Experience, supported also by the evidence that the die is electrically small, teaches us that the interpretation of $Z_e(s)$ and its conversion into an equivalent circuit is rather straightforward.

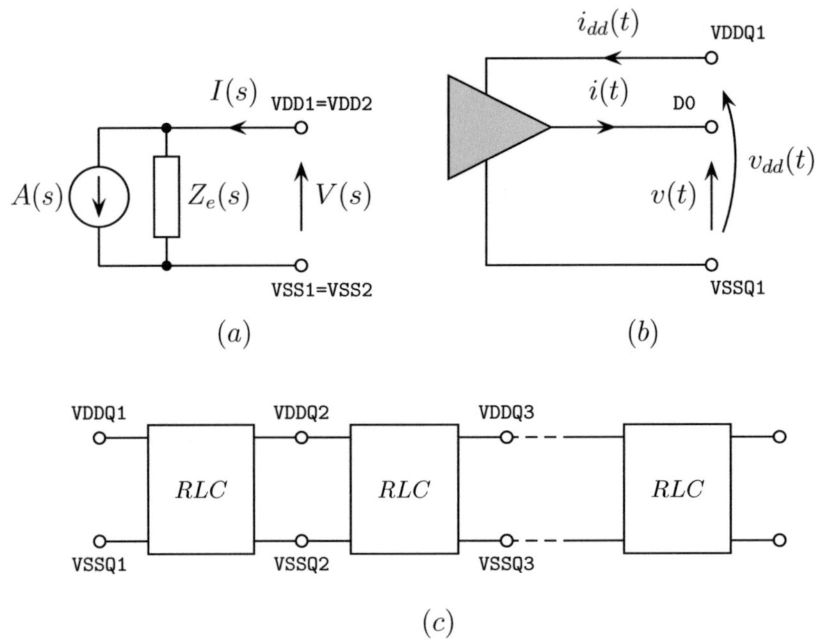

Fig. 3. Model structures: (*a*) Norton equivalent for the VDD-VSS core power delivery network; (*b*) nonlinear dynamical model for the I/O buffers (e.g., the DQ0 pad of Fig. 1); (*b*) cascade lumped equivalent of the power rail.

2.3 I/O buffers

Different approaches are used to obtain behavioral models of the I/O ports of a digital IC. The most common approach is based on simplified equivalent circuits derived from the internal structure of the modeled devices. This approach leads to the I/O Buffer Information Specification (IBIS, 2008; Pulici et al., 2008), which is widely supported by electronic design automation tools and dominates modeling applications. However, the growing complexity of recent devices and their enhanced features like pre-emphasis and specific control circuit, demand for refinements of the basic equivalent circuits. In order to facilitate the modeling of these features, alternate methodologies based on the estimation of suitable parametric relations have been proposed (Stievano et al., 2004; Mutnury et. al., 2006). These methodologies are aimed at reproducing the electrical behavior of device ports (see Fig. 3*b*), without any use of physical insights and of equivalent circuit representations. The advantage of these approaches relies in the flexibility of the mathematical description of models with respect to the circuit representation and on the computation of model parameters from the responses recorded at the device ports only. Furthermore, the parametric approaches offer simple and well-established procedures for the estimation of model parameters from real measured data.

For the case of output buffers, the common assumption in the current state-of-the-art solutions is the description of the port electrical behavior of the circuit via the following two-piece relation:

$$\begin{aligned} i(t) = {} & w_H(t)i_H(v(t), v_{dd}(t), \tfrac{d}{dt}v(t), \tfrac{d}{dt}v_{dd}(t), \tfrac{d^2}{dt^2}\ldots) + \\ & w_L(t)i_L(v(t), v_{dd}(t), \tfrac{d}{dt}v(t), \tfrac{d}{dt}v_{dd}(t), \tfrac{d^2}{dt^2}\ldots) \end{aligned} \tag{1}$$

where v, v_{dd} and i are the buffer output and power supply port voltage and current variables, with associated reference directions, w_H and w_L are switching signals accounting for the device state transitions and i_H and i_L are nonlinear dynamical relations accounting for the device behavior in the fixed high and low logic states, respectively. A similar relation holds for the power supply current and a simplified model structure, that can be considered as a subclass of eq. (1), can be adopted for the alternate case of input ports. The readers should refer to (Stievano et al., 2004) for additional details.
The estimation of model (1) amounts to computing the parameters of submodels i_H and i_L and the weighting signals w_H and w_L from suitable port transient responses.

2.4 Power rail

As outlined in the introduction, the power rail supplying the I/O buffers consists of two on-chip coplanar metallic traces connecting the VDDQn the and VSSQn pads, that have a non negligible size and that are regularly distributed along the rail (see Fig. 1). Owing to this, a simple transmission line model for coplanar structures can be hardly used. Instead, a model structure like the one of Fig. 3c, that consists of the cascade connection of lumped blocks, is more suitable for the description of the rail and allows the computation of model parameters from external measurements and simulations.

3. Model estimation by simulation

This section briefly outlines the resources for the generation of a memory macromodel from the simulation of detailed numerical models of devices.
When simulation models based on the governing equations describing the behavior of a memory are available, the estimation of the parameters of the submodels of Fig. 3 is a standard procedure. State-of-the-art techniques are ready to be used for the computation of model parameters.
For the core power delivery network, transient and frequency-domain simulations can be processed for the computation of the short-circuit current and of the equivalent impedance of the Norton equivalent of Fig. 3. Readers are referred to (ICEM, 2001) for additional details. It is also important to remark that when the structure of a device is known, even possible different model structures can be effectively used.
Similar comments apply to the power rail structure. Also for this case, frequency-domain 3D EM simulations of the power structure can be used for the fitting of the parameter of a circuit equivalent, like the one of Fig. 3c.
On the other hand, I/O buffer models, either defined by simplified equivalent circuits or by black-box mathematical relations, can be obtained via the procedure suggested by IBIS (IBIS, 2008) and collected in (Stievano et al., 2004; Mutnury et. al., 2006), respectively .

4. Model estimation by measurements

This section summarizes the procedure for the estimation of the models shown in Fig. 3 from measurements. In this work a special emphasis is given on the model generation from measured data since this procedure is less established and possible difficulties in the computation of model parameters from experimental data worth to be highlighted and discussed.

4.1 Core power delivery network

The generation of the Norton equivalent of the core power delivery network requires the estimation of the equivalent impedance and of the short-circuit current source of Fig. 3*a*.

Short-circuit current source. The computation of the current source is the most critical step of the modeling process and special care must be taken in collecting, interpreting and processing the measured data. From a theoretical point of view, the determination of the A term would require the measurement of the current flowing through ideal short-circuits terminating the core power supply pads on the right panel of Fig. 1 (i.e., the VDD*n* and VSS*n* pads). However, in practice, the pads cannot be shortened and the circuit operation of the die must be assessed with the device encapsulated in a package and mounted on a board. Figure 4 shows the equivalent circuit, in the Laplace domain, of the setup for the external measurement of the switching current I_{SS}.

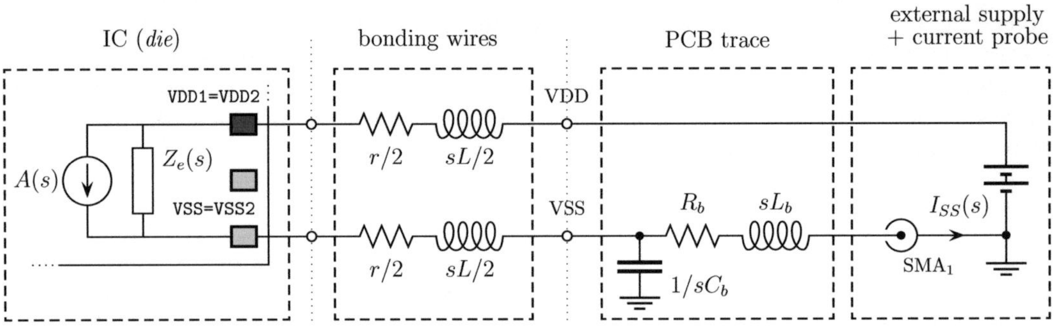

Fig. 4. Simplified equivalent of the setup used for the measurement of the equivalent impedance of the core power delivery network and the short-circuit switching current of a digital IC.

In the scheme of Fig. 4 the external power supply provided by a voltage regulator and a possible shunt capacitance is simply represented by an ideal battery connected to the VDD ball. The VSS ball is connected to a SMA connector via an on-board trace, that is represented by a lumped equivalent in Fig. 4. The transient current $i_{ss}(t)$ is obtained via an indirect measurement of the voltage drop across a R=1 Ω resistor mounted on the connector SMA_1. This method, following the standard for the measurement of the conducted emission of ICs in the range from dc to 1GHz (IEC61967, 2006), has been selected among a limited number of possible alternative techniques, since it is simple to implement and has proved to demonstrate accurate results in practical applications (Fiori & Musolino, 2003).

Once the switching activity current $i_{SS}(t)$ is recorded, the measured waveform needs to be suitably processed for de-embedding the effects of the measurement setup. The readers should refer to (Stievano et al., 2011a) for additional details and a more comprehensive discussion of the post-processing for the same example test chip of this work.

Equivalent impedance. The estimation of the equivalent impedance $Z_e(s)$ is obtained from the scattering frequency-domain measurements of the core-power delivery structure of Fig. 1. This can be done by using the same setup of Fig. 4 from the S_{11} measurements of the scattering parameter response of the structure seen from the connector SMA_1 with and without the IC mounted on it. The measured data is converted into the impedance representation

$$Z_{11} = R_0 \frac{(1 + S_{11})}{(1 - S_{11})} \tag{2}$$

where $R_0 = 50\,\Omega$ is the reference impedance of the VNA. The values of the circuit equivalent of Fig. 4 are then estimated via simple fitting from Z_{11}. Briefly speaking, the above fitting is achieved by means of the following two step procedure:

- Measurement of S_{11} without the IC mounted on the board and computation of the values of the R_b, L_b and C_b elements;
- Measurement of S_{11} with the IC mounted on the board and computation of the remaining parameters values r, L and network response $Z_e(s)$.

Test board. Figure 5 shows the board designed for the measurement required by the proposed modeling methodology. The board implements the basic features required by the ideal setup of Fig. 4. It is composed of a general purpose control circuitry for the operation of the device under test, and of a measurement board holding the IC under test and the measurement fixture. The measurement board is connected to the control board via a pair of 40-pin QTE connectors, and can be replaced to test different ICs. The memory controller, implemented in a FPGA, has been designed to allow the memory to operate at 66MHz and perform repeatedly the basic cycles (*program, erase, read*).

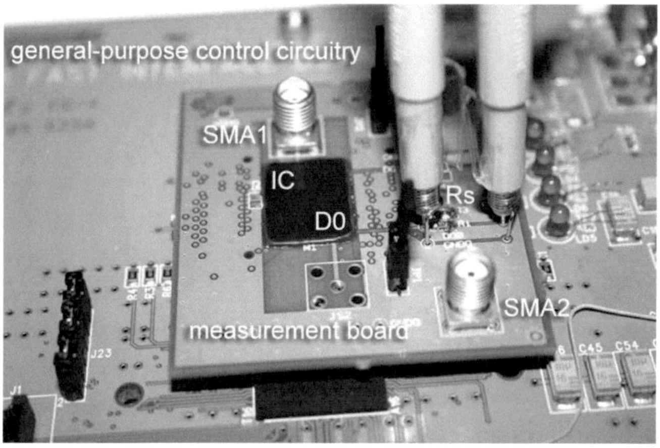

Fig. 5. Measurement board for recording the core switching activity current for the example IC.

The indirect measurement of the transient current via the voltage drop on series resistors mounted on the connector $SMA_1$was carried out with a LeCroy WavePro 7300A scope (3 GHz bandwidth, 10 GS/s). To reduce the effects of the measurement noise, the memory buffers have been forced to produce a periodic bit pattern and the averaging feature of the scope has been set (16 waveforms were considered for the average). As an example, Figure 6 shows a slice of the measured transient current $i_{ss}(t)$ observed during a complete operation phase.
The frequency domain scattering measurements for the computation of the Norton equivalent impedance has been carried out via a Agilent Vector Network Analyzer (VNA) E5071B (300 kHz to 8.5 GHz). As an example, Fig. 7 shows the impedance seen by the connector that has been recorded with and without the IC mounted on the board. This Figure also compares the measurements with the responses of the lumped simplified equivalent circuits of Fig. 4 that has been estimated via simple fitting. The measured transfer functions in Fig. 7 shows some spurious resonances in a frequency region above 200 MHz that does not need to

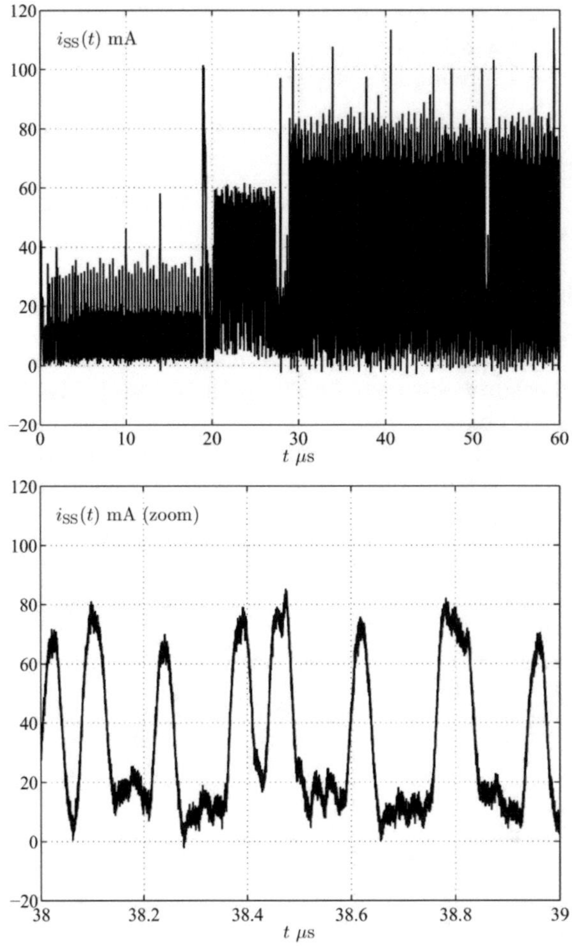

Fig. 6. Measured transient current $i_{SS}(t)$ carried out on the example commercial memory chip.

be modeled by a lumped equivalent accounting for the behavior of the IC. These effects are determined by the test fixture and by the package, and do not belong to the supply structure of the silicon device, that is generally dominated by a smooth capacitive behavior.

It is worth noticing that the on-chip probing, when available, is a good alternative option to collect measured data that can be readily converted into the admittance representation (an example of such test strategy is available in (Stievano et. al., 2009), where partial results are available for the same test vehicle considered in this study). In this work, the measurements have been carried out by means of a CascadeMicrotech probing station and a Agilent vector network analyzer. The two-port responses are obtained via Signal-Ground (SG) probes, with the G contact connected to the reference pad of the port. The power supply is provided to some die pads via DC and RF probes to mimic the actual biasing conditions. An example of the measurement setup is shown in Fig. 8.

Figure 9 shows a selection of two-port measured scattering responses of the VDD-VSS network of Figure 1 compared to the responses of a simple lumped equivalent $Z_e = 1/sC$.

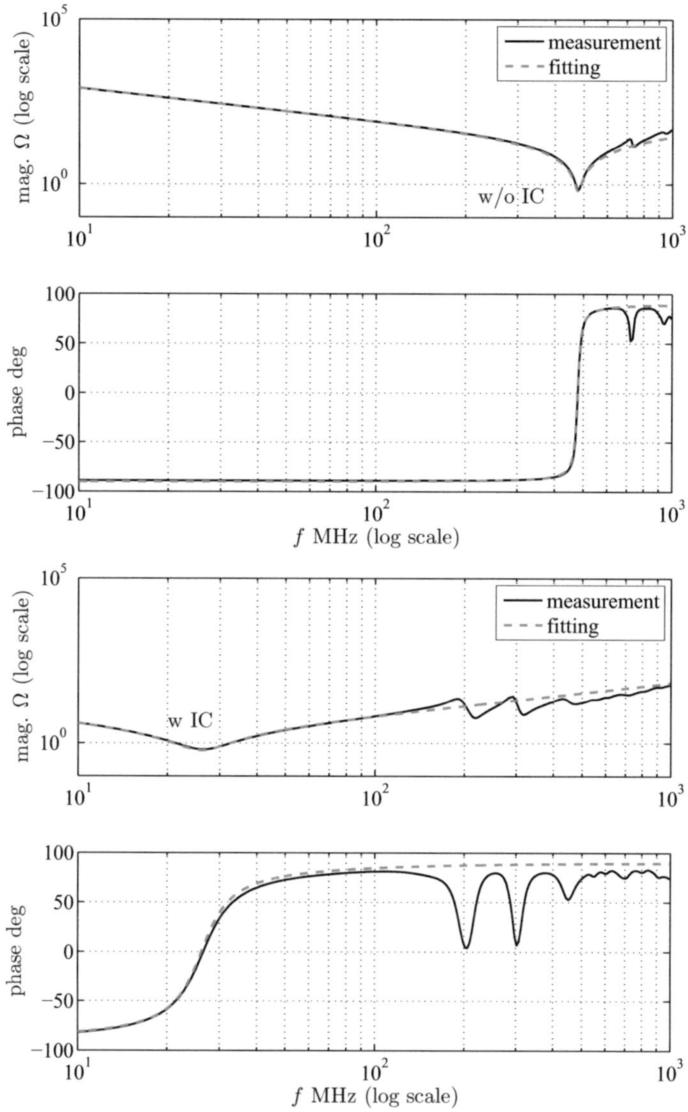

Fig. 7. Impedance seen from the terminals of the resistor of Fig. 4 without and with the IC mounted on it. Solid lines: real measurement carried out on the test board of Fig. 5; dashed lines: prediction obtained via the equivalent of Fig. 4 ($L = 5\,\text{nH}$, $L_b = 5.8\,\text{nH}$ $C_b = 19.15\,\text{pF}$ $r = 01.\,\Omega$, $R_b = 0.6\,\Omega$ and $Z_e(s) \approx 1/sC$, with $C = 3.45\,\text{nF}$.

Figure 9 confirms the dominant capacitive behavior of the core power network already observe in the curves of Fig. 7.

If needed, the accuracy of the fitting can be improved by considering the inherent multiport nature of the die and a two-pole equivalent (e.g., see (Stievano et al., 2011b) for additional details). Briefly speaking, this extension is achieved by considering a multiport Norton equivalent that replaces the model of Fig. 3*a* and a modified version of the test setup of Fig. 4.

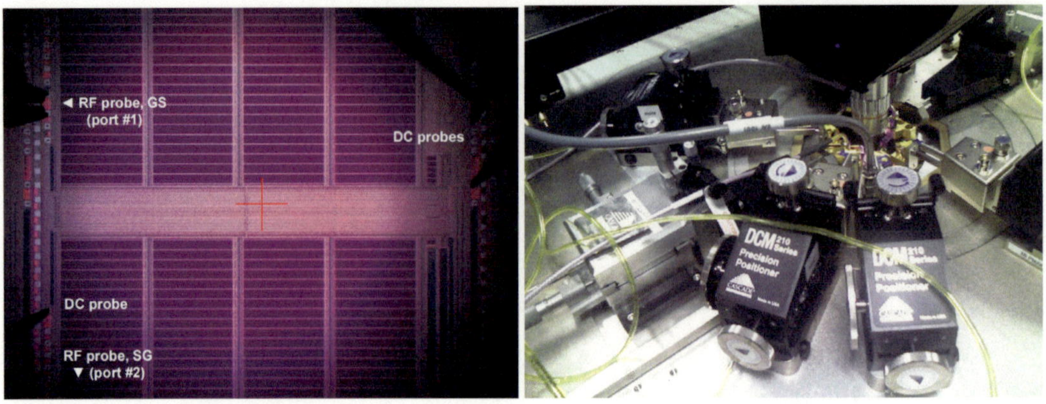

(a) Memory die (b) RF and DC probes

Fig. 8. On-wafer measurement setup used for the estimation of the equivalent impedance of the core power delivery network.

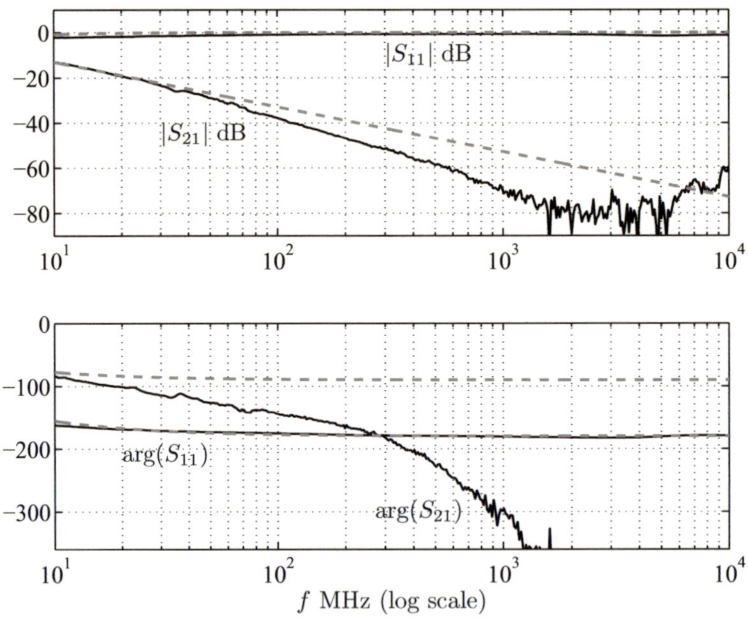

Fig. 9. Selection of the scattering responses of the VDD-VSS structure. Solid lines: reference measured responses; dashed lines: responses of lumped capacitor $Z_e(s) = 1/sC$.

4.2 I/O buffers

This section outlines the step-by-step modeling procedure for the generation of IC output port behavioral models. As discussed in Sec. 2.3, a behavioral model of an input port can be considered as a special case only (see (Stievano et al., 2004; 2011a) for additional details).

In order to devise a robust modeling procedure from real measurements carried out on a test board, the general two-piece model structure defined by (1) is particularized as follows.

$$\begin{cases} i(t) & = w_H(t)[i_{sH}(v_{dd}-v)+i_{dH}(v_{dd}-v,\frac{d}{dt}\ldots)] + \\ & \quad w_L(t)[i_{sL}(v)+i_{dL}(v,d/dt)] \\ i_{dd}(t) & = w_H(t)i_{sH}(v_{dd}-v)+i_{dH}(v_{dd}-v,\frac{d}{dt}\ldots) \end{cases} \tag{3}$$

In the above equation, the output port current is a weighted combination of two submodels accounting for the buffer behavior in the fixed high and low logic states (i.e., $i_{H,L}$ of (1)) that are split into the sum of a static $i_{sH,L}$ and of a dynamic $i_{dH,L}$ contributions to facilitate model estimation and to make the modeling procedure more robust. Also, the specific choice of the variables in (3) as well as the model structure for the description of the power supply current have been adopted to facilitate the parameter estimation from measurements by incorporating in the model equations the typical operation of CMOS output buffers. Specifically, the main contribution of the power supply current i_{dd} of a CMOS buffer is the one drawn during the driver operation in the high output state and therefore provided by the corresponding contibution of the output port current model in the high state.

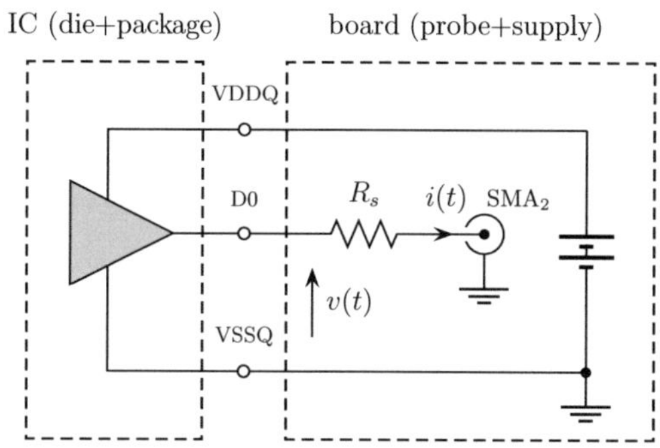

Fig. 10. Simplified equivalent of the setup used for the measurement of the port transient voltage and current of the I/O buffer of a digital IC. Current is indirectly measured through the voltage drop on the series resistor R_S (e.g., Rs=47 Ω).

Once the model structure (3) is assumed, the model parameters can be obtained via the following procedure that is based on the ideal setup shown in Fig. 10.

1. *Estimation of the buffer static characteristics.* In principle, the estimation of the device static characteristics $i_{sH,L}$ can be done by collecting a number of voltage-current pairs $\{v,i\}$ that are observed while an ideal voltage source is applied to the output port of the buffer and the source produces a DC sweep (this is also suggested by the IBIS specification (IBIS, 2008)). However, to simplify the modeling setup and to avoid dedicated test fixtures for the extraction of the static curves only, a different solution has been proposed: the buffer under modeling is driven to produce a periodic "01" bit pattern on a transmission line load that is plugged into the SMA$_2$ connector of Fig. 10. A transmission line load forces the port voltage and current waveforms to produce a stepped response. Hence, the static values of the buffer characteristics are extracted from the flat parts of the responses as described in (Stievano et. al., 2008; Stievano et al., 2011a).

   It is worth noticing that the number of static points used to approximate the static characteristics of the buffer is defined by the number of steps that are in general $3 \div 5$ for typical buffer circuits loading 50 Ω distributed interconnects. Also, no specific care must be paid in designing the distributed load. A simple 50 Ω coaxial cable or the shunt connection of two cables are sufficient to generate a set of responses with some steps. The only design parameter is the line length, that decides the timing of reflections and the duration of the flat responses, and that must be chosen on the basis of the device transition times. Roughly speaking, a device with 300 ps rise time would require a $1.5 \div 3$ m long transmission line.

2. *Estimation of the dynamical submodels.* The dynamical models used for i_{dH} and i_{dL} in (3) can be either defined by lumped circuit element (IBIS assumes a capacitor (IBIS, 2008)) or discrete-time parametric representations, whose parameters can be estimated by standard algorithms as in (Stievano et. al., 2008). For the latter case, the device responses used to feed the estimation algorithm are the slices of the voltage and current responses of the buffer on a distributed load recorded while the device is in the high (low) logic state.
3. *Computation of weighting coefficients.* The weighting signals w_H and w_L are computed after the estimation of the submodels $i_{sH,L}$ and $i_{dH,L}$ from the portion of the port responses occurring during state switching, as discussed in (Stievano et. al., 2008; Stievano et al., 2011a). In our problem, this amounts to solving the single linear equation (3) of the output current where v and i are the advocated voltage and current responses recorded during a single transition event and w_L is assumed to be $w_L = (1 - w_H)$. In principle, such an assumption can be removed and two sets of port responses can be used to compute two independent w_H and w_L signals. However, the latter simplification benefits the quality of the complete model since it reduces possible ill-conditioning or inaccuracies of the solution of the linear problem arising from noisy measured data or from the approximated responses of the static and the dynamic submodels in (3).
4. *Model implementation.* Finally, the last step of the modeling process amounts to translating the model equations in a simulation environment. This can be done by representing the equation (3) in terms of an equivalent circuit and then implementing such circuit as a SPICE-like subcircuit. The circuit interpretation of model equations is a standard procedure that is based on the use of controlled-current sources for the static contributions, and on resistors, capacitors, and controlled source elements for the dynamic parts (Stievano et al., 2004). As an alternative, model (3) can be directly plugged into a mixed-signal simulation environment by describing model equations via metalanguages like Verilog-AMS or VHDL-AMS. In this work, the obtained models have been implemented in SPICE.

It is worth noting that the ideal setup of Fig. 10 assumes that the series resistor R_S will be mounted as close as possible to the IC in order to neglect the possible effects of the board trace connecting the D0 ball to the SMD component.

The waveforms corresponding to the validation of the model for the D0 buffer of the example memory chip built in this way are shown in Fig. 11. The validation test consists of the the D0 buffer producing a periodic "01" switching on a 4m long RG58 coaxial cable plugged into the SMA_2 connector of Fig. 5 terminated by a 82 pF capacitor. Figure 11 collects the measured response, the reference response of the high-order transistor-level model of the buffer provided by the foundry and the responses of two models estimated from simulation (see the top panel (a)) and from measurements (see the bottom panel (b)). The very good agreement among the curves of Fig. 11 confirms the strengths of the proposed methodology in generating accurate models from measured and simulated responses. Such models can be easily obtained by the proposed procedure and can effectively replace the hardly available and less efficient transistor-level models of ICs.

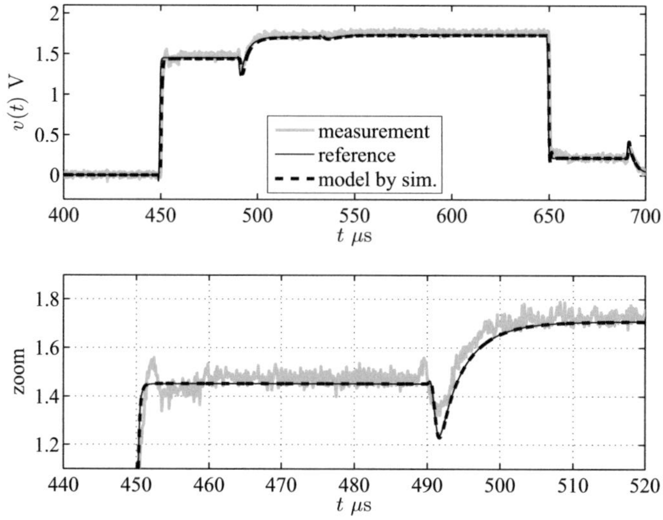

(a) Model by simulation via the procedure in Stievano et al. (2004).

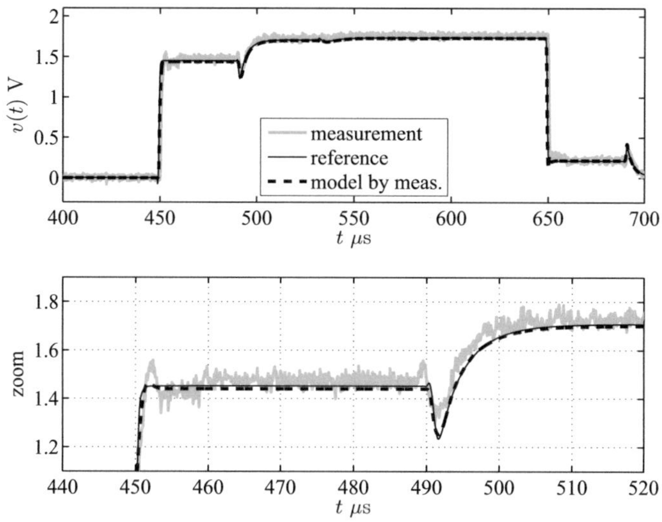

(b) Model by measurement.

Fig. 11. Port voltage responses of the D0 buffer for the validation tests considered in this study (see text for details). Top panel (a) compares measured responses with the reference responses of a transistor-level model and of a model generated from simulation; bottom panel (b) compares measured responses with the reference responses of a transistor-level model and of a model generated from measured data.

4.3 Power rail

The most suitable solution for the estimation of the lumped elements defining the model of the IC power rail structures (see Fig. 3c) is based on on-chip probing since the possible alternative on-board measurements are troublesome and would limit the possibility of

parameters estimation. The main reason is twofold: (*i*) the values of the *RLC* elements of the blocks of Fig. 3*c* are much lower than those of the corresponding parasitic elements of the package and test fixture and (*ii*) a custom package needs to be used since the VDDQ*n* and VSSQ*n* pads must be kept floating to avoid the undesired grounding effects of the bonding wires distributed along the rail. If the latter option is the only possible solution, a clever de-embedding strategy and parameters estimation procedure must be devised and adopted.
In this study, as already done for the core power delivery network, a VNA and two RF probes can be used to carry out the on-chip scattering responses of the power rail network. The probes are connected to the first and last pairs of VDDQ/VSSQ pads. Once the measurements are recorded, the parameters of the lumped models of Fig. 3*c* are obtained by least squares fitting. Figure 12 shows an example of the fitting, thus demonstrating the accuracy of the assumption of a model defined by the cascade connection of lumped blocks.
It is relevant to remark that the measurements carried out on the example memory chip include the mainly capacitive effects of the active devices, i.e., of the I/O buffers. Due to the typical large value of the buffers capacitance, the *C* value of the lumped *RLC* blocks of Fig. 3*c* can be hardly obtained from measurements and can be neglected.

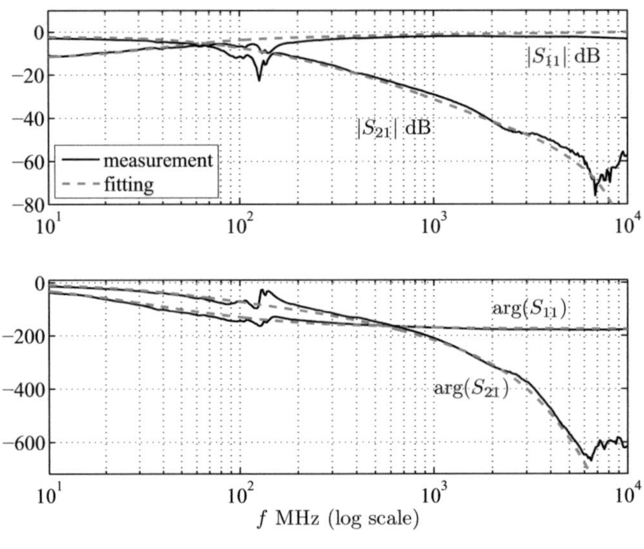

Fig. 12. Selection of the scattering responses of the power rail structure carried out between the first and the last pair of VDDQ-VSSQ pads, for the example test-case. Solid line: on-chip measurements; dashed line: responses by means of the simplified equivalent of Fig. 3*c*.

5. Conclusions

In this Chapter, the generation of a behavioral model of a memory IC is thoroughly discussed. Based on the physical structure of this class of devices, the proposed strategy amounts to defining three different classes of submodels for the description of the core and buffer power delivery network and of the I/O buffers of a memory device. State-of-the-art methodologies are used to generate models from both simulations and real measurements carried out on a board. Specific emphasis was given on model generation from real measured data with the aim of highlighting possible difficulties and inherent limitation in the generation of the responses required by the modeling process. The feasibility of the modeling approach was demonstrated on a commercial IC Flash memory from measurements carried out on a specifically designed test board.

6. Acknowledgments

This chapter provides a systematic and unified interpretation of several activities carried out under the MOCHA (MOdeling and CHAracterization for SiP - Signal and Power Integrity Analysis) grant no. 216732 of the European Community's Seventh Framework Programme. A. Girardi, R. Izzi, A. Vigilante and F. Vitale (Numonyx, Italy) are gratefully acknowledged for providing the example test chip and the general-purpose control board of Fig. 5 used in this study. Luca Rigazio, Politecnico di Torino, Italy, is also acknowledged for the design of the measurement board of Fig. 5 and for his support during the measurement activities.

7. References

ICEM (2001). "Integrated Circuits Electrical Model (ICEM)", International Electro-technical Commission (IEC) 61967.

IEC61967 (2006). "International Electro-technical Commission, IEC 61967 Part 4: Measurement of conducted emission - 1 Ω/150 Ω direct coupling method".

F. Fiori, F. Musolino. (2004). "Comparison of IC Conducted Emission Measurement Methods," *IEEE Trans. on Instrumentation and Measurement*, **Vol. 52** (No. 3), pp. 839–845.

I. S. Stievano, I. A. Maio, F. G. Canavero. (2004). "Mπlog, Macromodeling via Parametric Identification of Logic Gates," *IEEE Transactions on Advanced Packaging*, **Vol. 27** (No. 1), pp. 15–23.

B. Mutnury, M. Swaminathan, J. P. Libous. (2006). "Macromodeling of nonlinear digital I/O drivers," *IEEE Transactions on Advanced Packaging*, **Vol. 29**, (No. 1), pp. 102–113.

C. Labussiere-Dorgan, S. Bendhia, E. Sicard, J.Tao, H. J. Quaresma, C. Lochot, B. Vrignon. (2008). "Modeling the electromagnetic emission of a microcontroller using a single model," *IEEE Transactions on EMC*, **Vol. 50** (No. 1).

IBIS (2008). "I/O Buffer Information Specification (IBIS) Ver. 5.0," **URL:** http://www.eigroup.org/ibis/ibis.htm.

I. S. Stievano, I. A. Maio, F. G. Canavero. (2008). "Behavioral models of IC output buffers from on-the-fly measurements," *IEEE Transactions on Instrumentation and Measurement*, **Vol. 57** (No. 4), pp. 850–855.

P. Pulici, A. Girardi, G. P. Vanalli, R. Izzi, G. Bernardi, G. Ripamonti, A. G. M. Strollo, G. Campardo. (2008). "A Modified IBIS Model Aimed at Signal Integrity Analysis of Systems in Package," *IEEE Trans. On Circuits and Systems*, **Vol. 55** (No. 7).

I.S. Stievano et Al. (2009). "Characterization and modeling of the power delivery networks of memory chips," Proc. of *13-th IEEE Workshop on SPI*, Strasbourg, F, May. 12–15.

Yi Cao, Qi-Jun Zhang. (2009) "A New Training Approach for Robust Recurrent Neural-Network Modeling of Nonlinear Circuits," *IEEE Transactions on Microwave Theory and Techniques*, **Vol. 57** (No. 6), pp. 1539–1553.

I. S. Stievano, L. Rigazio, F. G. Canavero, T. R. Cunha, J. C. Pedro, H. M. Teixeira, A. Girardi, R. Izzi, F. Vitale. (2011a). "Behavioral modeling of IC memories from measured data," *IEEE Transactions on Instrumentation and Measurement* [in print].

I.S. Stievano, L. Rigazio, I.A. Maio, F.G. Canavero. (2011b). "Behavioral modeling of IC core power-delivery networks from measured data," *IEEE Transactions on Components, Packaging, and Manufacturing Technology,* **Vol. 1** (No. 3), pp. 367–373.

Part 2

Applications

6

Survey of the State-of-the-Art in Flash-Based Sensor Nodes

Soledad Escolar Díaz, Jesús Carretero Pérez
and Javier Fernández Muñoz
Computer Science and Engineering Department.
University Carlos III de Madrid, Madrid
Spain

1. Introduction

A wireless sensor network (WSN) is a distributed system composed of many battery-powered devices, which operate with no human intervention for long periods of time. These devices are called sensor nodes or *motes*.

Motes present features of both embedded and general-purpose systems (Han et al., 2005). Their tiny size, scarce resources, and their autonomous nature lead to strong restrictions of computation, communication, power, and storage. Typically, they are deployed in an *ad-hoc* fashion over a geographical area (e.g. a volcano, a glacier, an office), which is to be monitored. This means that —depending on the environment where they are installed— it could result very difficult to perform activities of maintenance such as the replacement of the node's batteries. Software built for the sensor nodes must be reliable and robust due to the difficulty for accessing sensor nodes, and sensor nodes must operate in an autonomous way even in presence of failures.

Motes are interconnected through wireless links and they execute a simple, small application, which is developed using a sensor node-specific operating system. Typically, sensor network applications consist of sensing the environment through different type of sensors (e.g. temperature, humidity, GPS, imagers), transforming analogical data into digital data in the node itself, and forwarding the data to the network. Data is forwarded through a multi-hop protocol to a special node denominated *gateway*, which is intended to redirect all data from the wireless network to a *base station* (e.g. PC, laptop), where the data will be permanently stored in order to allow data post-processing and analysis. Figure 1 shows the three elements previously described: sensor nodes, gateway, base station.

1.1 Data classification in a WSN

WSNs generate larger data sets as sampling frequency increase. Sensor nodes must manage data proceeding from different sources: *internal* data produced by the sensor node itself (e.g. sensor measurements, application data, logs), and *external* data transmitted by other nodes in the network (e.g. protocol messages, data packets, commands). Since the data

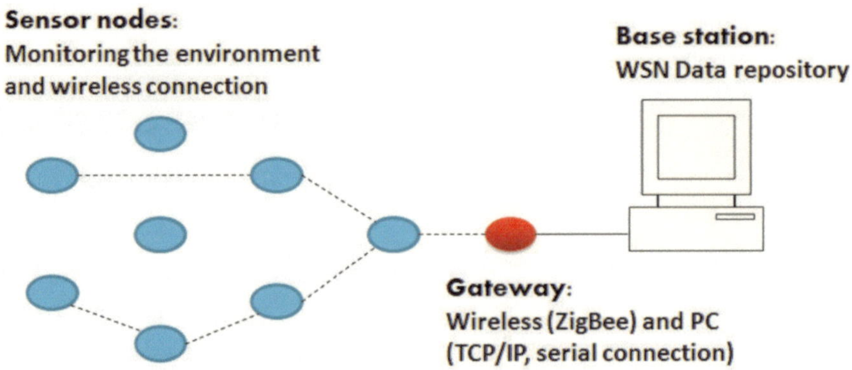

Fig. 1. A wireless sensor network: it is composed of a set of sensor nodes or motes, a communication gateway, and a base station.

memory[1] of a sensor node is a very scarce resource (typically 4 KB of RAM), nodes are forced to use other available devices to save data (such as the flash memory chip located outside the microcontroller) or to send data out of the node to prevent local storage. However, as explained below, the radio is the main consumer of energy in the sensor node and for this reason in many cases data are stored rather sent out. Subsequently, a tradeoff between the flash and radio power consumption is currently an important line of research (Diao et al., 2007) (Balani et al., 2005) (Shenker et al., 2003).

Other classification of data depends on the time when they were captured. In this sense, data may be *live* or *historical*. The first one corresponds to data acquired within a window of time and they are useful to detect meaningful events in quasi-real time (e.g. fire, earthquake). Moreover, in general, users do not want to renounce to the knowledge provided by the whole set of data, for example to identify trends or patterns and, therefore, historical data cannot be discarded. In this sense, flash memories can provide support for such an amount of data.

1.2 Importance of the flash memory chip in a sensor node

Flash memories have been embedded into sensor nodes from their earlier designs to nowadays. Along this time, these physical memories have suffered continuous updating, in order to be adapted to the specific features of sensor nodes. Specifically, they must be energy-efficient, since the energy is doubtless the most valuable and restricted resource. Many WSN applications found in the flash memory chip the only device that allow them satisfying their requirements, since it represents the device with the bigger capacity for permanent storage of application data in the sensor node.

There exist an increasing number of applications requiring the usage of non-volatile storage. Storing local and distributed data into sensor nodes has also promoted a set of high-level applications, which manage the network as a large database. Flash memories not just allow to store data when the RAM memory capabilities are near to be exceeded, but also they have made possible several relevant applications for sensor networks such as remote reprogramming of sensor nodes. Frequently, a WSN application could need both code

[1] The microcontroller of motes employ the Harvard Architecture which separates data and program into dedicated memories.

updates —for modifying the value of some variable— and important changes —as replacing the complete application's image. However, the unattended nature of sensor nodes, their ubiquity, and the inhospitable environments where they are deployed could difficult or even make impossible a manual installation of nodes. As an example, consider the extreme scenario where a sensor network has been affected by a virus disseminated from the base station. Another example more realistic is the necessity of degrading the application behaviour when the node's batteries are near to deplete, in order to increase the network lifetime. In both examples there is a necessity of reprogramming the network. Therefore, remote programming of sensor nodes is a fundamental task for ensuring the consistency of sensor network applications.

Consequently, flash memory chips, such as Atmel AT45DB, have become key devices that make possible a set of applications that currently are considered critical for wireless sensor networks.

This chapter presents a survey of the state-of-the-art in flash memories which are embedded into sensor nodes as external devices of general purpose. Along the chapter, we refer "flash memories" specifically to the flash memories which are external to microcontroller. At the beginning of the chapter we have presented a description of the technology of these flash memories, highlighting the more relevant features in the context of WSN, and their integration with other physical components hold into the sensor node. In the next section we describe the abstractions provided by several WSN-specific operating systems in order to manage the flash device. Then, we discuss the related work on flash-based sensor network applications, such as sensor nodes reprogramming and file systems. To conclude this chapter we provide our conclusions about this work.

2. Hardware technology

The hardware technology employed in sensor nodes manufacturing is an active research line that is carried out by both universities and by private companies around the world. The possibilities in this field are enormous because of the increasing need to look for new sensors for potential applications, advances in miniaturization, and the appearance of components to be integrated (e.g. GPS, scavengers). Since the sensor nodes are battery-powered devices, it is the most importance the looking for strategies at the hardware level that make an energy-efficient management of the devices.

The typical architecture of a *mote* presents the block diagram shown in Figure 2. It is composed of a set of hardware components which are described as follows:

- A microcontroller of low capacity which usually operates at very low frequencies (e.g. 7 MHz) and has an architecture ranging from 4-bit to 32-bit. It also integrates RAM and ROM memories, an Analogical-Digital Converter (ADC) and several *clocks* that enable local synchronizing. Some examples of microcontrollers are Atmega128L (Atmel, 2011) from ATMEL and MSP430 (Instrument, 2008) from Texas Instruments.
- The radio device provides wireless communication to the sensor node, and supports the WSN specific communication properties such as low energy, low data rate, and short distances. Some radio devices for motes are CC1000 (*CC1000 Single Chip Very Low Power RF Transceiver,* 2002) and CC2400 (*CC2400 2.4GHz Low-Power RF Transceiver,* 2003) from Chipcon, and

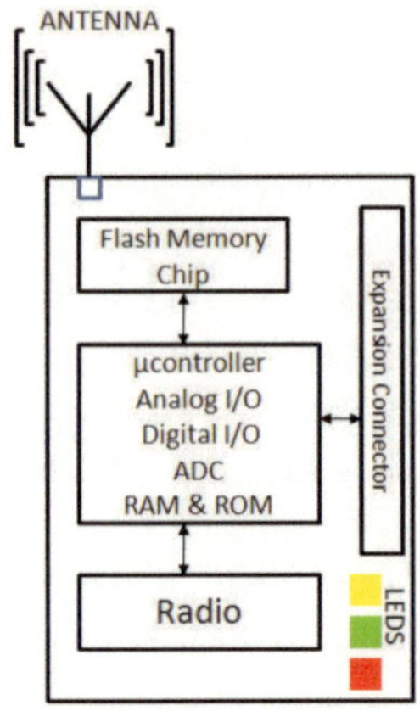

Fig. 2. Block diagram of a sensor node. It includes several interconnected physical devices such as the radio, the microcontroller and the flash memory chip.

nRF2401 (*nRF2401 Radio Transceiver Data Sheet*, 2003) radio transceiver from Nordic Semiconductors.

- The battery provides energy to the sensor node (e.g. alkaline batteries). Motes usually hold two conventional batteries as power supplier. Numerous research projects focus on alternatives for energy harvesting, which are typically based on solar cells.
- Several LEDs (Light-Emitting Diode) are attached to the mote board with the main purpose of helping to debug. Typically, there are three LEDs integrated into a sensor node (red, green and yellow) although in some motes, an additional blue LED has been added.
- A *sensor board* usually contains several sensors and actuators, which are able to sense the environment. When the sensor board is present, the *expansion connector* acts as a bridge between the sensor board and the mote microcontroller.
- Several *I/O buses* transfer internal data between physical components (microcontroller, radio, and memory) in accordance with a specific I/O protocol. Different interfaces coexist in a sensor node (e.g. Serial Peripheral Interface (SPI), Inter Integrated Circuit (I^2C) and Universal Asynchronous Receiver/Transmitter (UART)).
- Finally, an external *flash memory* with longer capacities than the internal memories (RAM and ROM), in order to temporally store data provided by different sources (sensors, network, or logs). Some of the most popular flash memory chips integrated into sensor nodes are Atmel AT45DB (*Atmel AT45DB011 Serial DataFlash*, 2001) and ST M25P40 (*M25P40 Serial Flash Memory*, 2002).

In the next subsection we will focus on describing the hardware technology for these flash memories embedded in sensor nodes.

2.1 Flash memory technology

Flash memory chips embedded within sensor nodes provide an additional and auxiliary storage space for general purpose usages. Flash memory is a specific type of EEPROM (Electrically Erasable Programmable Read-Only Memory) that enables the access to n-bytes blocks in a single operation —instead of one operation per byte like EEPROM memories— thus increasing the speed of the operations. This memory is non-volatile, which means that energy is not needed to maintain the information stored in the chip. For these reasons the usage of such a type of memory has been extended to many others digital devices like cameras, mobile phones, and MP3 players.

Physically, a flash memory chip consists of an array of memory cells which are manufactured using transistors. Every one of these cells is able to store one single bit (0 or 1) —in traditional chips— or a set of bits —in modern chips. Depending on the type of logical gate employed two underlying technologies can be distinguished:

- NOR flash is manufactured using NOR gates. Every cell in its default state is logically equivalent to the binary "1" value. This is interpreted as presence of voltage in the cell. NOR flash was first introduced by Intel in 1988.
- NAND flash uses NAND gates. In this case, every cell is in its default state set to the equivalent binary "0" value, which means that there is no voltage measured in that cell. NAND flash was introduced by Toshiba in 1989.

There is also a third type of technology used in the manufacturing of flash memory chips: the CMOS technology. CMOS enables to build logical gates in different way than NOR and NAND flash through a specific type of transistors: p-type and n-type *metaloxidesemiconductor* field-effect transistors.

Regardless of the underlying technology used, there exist two basic low-level operations that operate on a cell-basis: 1) the programming operation, which consists of inverting the default state of a cell; and 2) the erasing operation, which consists of resetting its default state. From these two operations most of high-level operations over the flash memory can be constructed.

2.2 Flash memory architecture

NOR flash memory architecture is organized in segments also called blocks or sectors. The operation of erasing is block-oriented since the minimum unit to be erased is a block. It means that all cells in this block must be erased together. The operation of programming can be generally performed on a per-byte basis, but it requires that the block to be modified be previously erased before of writing on it. Another feature is that it enables the random access for readings. Typical block sizes are 64, 128, or 256 KB. One example of NOR flash memory chip is the ST M25P40 (*M25P40 Serial Flash Memory*, 2002) which is hold into TelosB and Eyes sensor node platforms. This device has a capacity of 4 Mbit and it is organized into 8 sectors. Another example is Intel Strataflash (*Intel Strataflash*, 2002) which is integrated into Intel Mote2 sensor node. It is the lowest cost-per-bit NOR memory chip, with a capacity of 32 megabytes, which are divided into 128 KB sectors.

On the other hand, NAND flash memory is organized in blocks and pages. Each block is divided into a fixed number of pages and each page has n-bytes of extension where m bytes ($m < n$) are usually reserved for storing the metadata related to the data in that page (e.g. an error correcting code (ECC)). Typical page sizes are 512, 2048, or 4096 bytes, but in devices such as motes this length is even smaller. The high-level operations in a NAND flash —readings and writings— are typically performed on a per-page basis while the operation of erasing is performed on the whole block. The access in NAND memories differs from the random access in NOR memories. NAND memories enable direct access to the block level but only sequential access is allowed inside a block. A representative example is Samsung K9K1G08R0B (SAMSUNG, 2003) with a capacity of 128 MB, a length of page of 528 bytes (for programming) and a block size of 16 KB (for erasing).

The most notable example of flash chip using CMOS technology is the Atmel AT45DB041 (*Atmel AT45DB011 Serial DataFlash*, 2001) chip, which is integrated into Mica family and TelosA motes. The total capacity for this chip is 512 KB and it is divided into four sectors of 128 KB. Every sector is also divided into pages, each page is 264 bytes long (256 bytes for data and 8 bytes for metadata). The pages can only be written or erased as a whole and in order to maintain the consistency, pages should be erased before being written.

Unlike conventional flash memories, that enable random access to the data, this memory chip uses a serial interface to enable sequential access. The memory uses two intermediate page long RAM buffers to transfer data between the serial interface and main memory. Every buffer is identified by a code which specifies what buffer is being used. These buffers perform a read-modify-write operation to effectively change the contents of flash. Figure 3 shows the block diagram for AT45DB041.

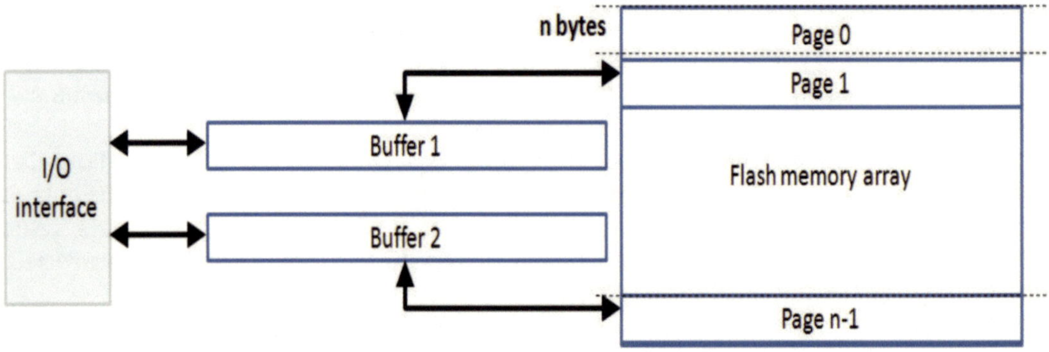

Fig. 3. Block diagram for AT45DB041 memory chip. It uses two page long RAM buffers to perform the operations on the memory.

Table 1 summarizes the features of the three technologies described above.

Feature	NOR flash	AT45DB	NAND flash
Erase	Slow (seconds)	Fast (ms)	Fast (ms)
Erase unit	Large (64KB-128KB)	Small (256B)	Medium (8KB-32KB)
Writes	Slow (100s KB/s)	Slow (60KB/s)	Fast (MBs/s)
Write unit	1 bit	256B	100's of bytes
Bit-errors	Low	Low	High (requires ECC, bad-block mapping)
Read	Bus limited	Slow+Bus limited	Bus limited
Erase cycles	10^4 - 10^5	10^4	$10^5 - 10^7$
Intended use	Code storage	Data storage	Data storage
Energy/byte	1uJ	1uJ	.01uJ

Table 1. Features for different flash memory technologies: in the first column NOR technology (e.g ST M25P40 and Intel PXA27x), in the second column the AT45DB041 memory chip (CMOS technology), and finally in third column NAND technology (e.g. Samsung K9K1G08R0B).

2.3 Limitations of flash memory

One of the main limitations of the flash memory is that there exists a limit on the number of times a page can be written, typically around 10000 times. This feature makes necessary a mechanism which ensures a uniform distribution of writes over all the pages of a flash. This technique is called wear levelling. Wear levelling techniques should be implemented for preventing the usage of a page for the maximum number of times. Subsequently, an efficient management of the flash should have into account this feature.
Another aspect to be considered is the access time, which is comparable with the disk access time (in the order of milliseconds). However, flash write operations consume more time and energy than read operations, since they require to erase the page before being written. This feature has forced to develop different high-level techniques intended to minimize the number of times that one page goes to be written —which impacts also in those previously described related to wear levelling—. For example, a simple technique consists of managing a page long buffer with the data to be written and transfer it to the flash only when the buffer is complete. SENFIS file system which is described later employes this approach. When the buffer contents are downloaded to the flash memory, the buffer must be cleared in order to be used again.

2.4 Specific issues to sensor nodes

Since motes are battery-powered devices, an efficient power consumption policy is of critical importance in order to increase their lifetime. The motes typically operate in cycles of snoozing (low power mode), processing, and transmitting. Radio transmitting is the operation that consumes most energy. In fact, transmitting one bit consumes about as much power as executing 800-1000 instructions (Hill et al., 2000). The total energy consumption of a node is computed as the addition of the energy spent by each physical component: radio, sensors, leds, CPU, and flash memory. It is important to point out that, in order to perform efficiently their tasks, every physical component in the sensor node might stay in different states for a time, and each state has a specific current draw, which is generally supplied by the manufacturer. Therefore, the consumption due to a physical component, for instance the radio, is the sum of the current draws corresponding to each one of the states.
Flash memory chips distinguish several states for representing the activity to perform. For example AT45DB041 presents the following four states: standby, read, write, and load. The first one and the last one are the lowest consumption states —here the devices act as if disconnected and no operation can be performed in these states— while the other two indicate reading and writing respectively. The current draws for every state expressed in milliamperes (mA) are 2×10^{-3}, 4, 15, and 2×10^{-3} respectively. Subsequently, if the application access pattern to flash memory is known, in particular the time spent in every flash state, it is possible to compute easily the energy model for the node's flash as:

$$E_{flash} = E_{standby} * T_{standby} + E_{read} * T_{read} + E_{write} * T_{write} + E_{load} * T_{load}$$

where T_i corresponds to the time spent in `i` state and E_i corresponds to the current draw in `i` state.

3. Operating system support

Operating systems (OSes) specifically designed to meet the WSN applications requirements and the sensor nodes restrictions constitute the backbone of the software architecture. The main challenge of the WSN operating systems is to manage the scarce hardware resources of the sensor nodes in an efficient and energy-aware way. OSes use the low-level interface (from HAL or hardware layer) to compose bigger grained operations, which are exported to the upper levels through a well-defined interface. Thus, OS abstractions are intended to mask the complexity of the hardware levels and facilitate the programming. High-level applications will use these abstractions that the OS provides to access the hardware resources in a transparent, simple way. Figure 4 depicts the software architecture of a sensor node.

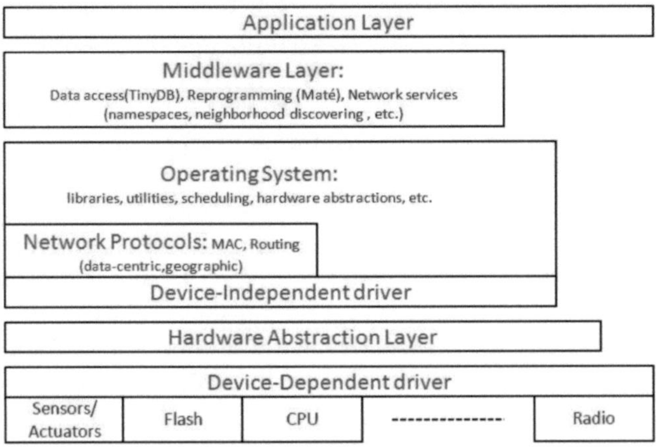

Fig. 4. A multi-layer software architecture for sensor nodes.

WSN OSes are very heterogeneous. They present one of the two following execution models: event- and thread-based. This is a relevant feature because it determines the programming model used and, subsequently, the interface provided by every OS is strongly coupled to its execution model. In this section we review the abstractions provided by a set of representative, popular operating systems in order to enable the flash memory access.

3.1 TinyOS 1.x

TinyOS (Hill et al., 2000) is the *de facto* standard for WSN operating systems, multi-platform, and open-source. Its execution model is event-based, but it presents some differences with regard to the pure model; in particular it distinguishes two scheduling levels: events and tasks. Events are preemptive and, therefore, they can be viewed as highest priority functions. On the other hand, there exists a second scheduling level, the tasks that can be viewed as non-preemptive functions (of lower priority) that run to completion. Tasks can only be interrupted by events, but not by other tasks.

TinyOS is written in nesC (Gay et al., 2003), a component-based programming language based on C that allows programming interfaces and components. The components in nesC communicate between each other through bi-directional interfaces. A nesC application is built through a configuration component, which declares the components and their connecting interfaces. A TinyOS application can be viewed as a combination of configuration and implementation components, whose behaviour and state is distributed through several interconnected components. Using this paradigm, TinyOS provides the implementation of hardware- and OS-level components as well as flexible abstractions to be used by the application level. Figure 5 shows an example of TinyOS application.

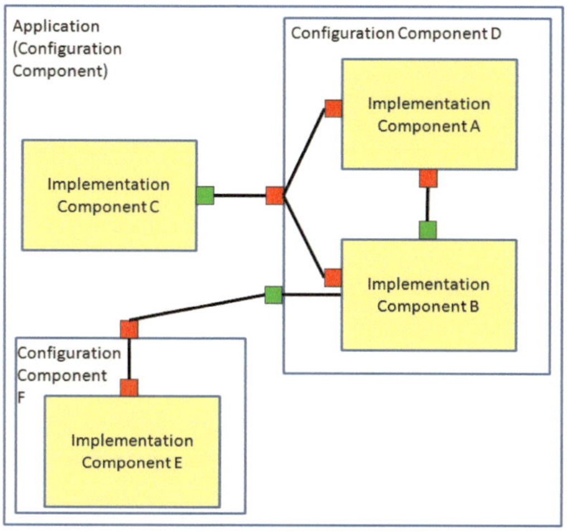

Fig. 5. A simple TinyOS application. It is composed of a set of components interconnected through interfaces, where one component provides the interface's implementation and the other one uses it. Configuration components allow encapsulate several components within it to build high-level components.

There exist two versions of TinyOS with substantial differences. We focus on describing the specific differences related to the flash memory management that they do. The first version of TinyOS provided three different interfaces to access data stored in the flash memory chip, every one of them located at different abstraction levels, from the lowest to the highest level:

1. A low-level implementation, based on pages (PageEEPROM).
2. A high-level memory-like interface, based on bytes (ByteeEEPROM).
3. A simple, basic file system (Matchbox).

3.1.1 The low-level implementation

The lowest level abstraction provides flash memory access on a per-page basis and it gives direct access to per-page read, write, and erase operations. The implementation is composed of several files:

- An interface file that includes the prototype of a set of commands (or functions) and events. Commands in TinyOS are functions that are implemented by the same or other component. For example, read and write operations over the flash memory take in TinyOS the shape of commands. On the other hand, in an event-based system events are signalled when an occurrence of some action takes place. Specifically, for the operations with high hardware latencies —which means that the operation response will be available only a time later— TinyOS requires declaring the corresponding event in the interface. When the response is obtained, the event is signalled from the hardware level to upper levels including also the

Commands
result_t write(eeprompage_t page, eeprompageoffset_t offset, void *data, eeprompageoffset_t n)
result_t erase(eeprompage_t page, uint8_t eraseKind)
result_t sync(eeprompage_t page)
result_t syncAll(void)
result_t flush(eeprompage_t page)
result_t flushAll(void)
result_t read(eeprompage_t page, eeprompageoffset_t offset, void *data, eeprompageoffset_t n)
result_t computeCrc(eeprompage_t page, eeprompageoffset_t offset, eeprompageoffset_t n)
Events
result_t writeDone(result_t result)
result_t eraseDone(result_t result)
result_t syncDone(result_t result)
result_t flushDone(result_t result)
result_t readDone(result_t result)
result_t computeCrcDone(result_t result, uint16_t crc)

Table 2. Low-level interface for flash memory access provided by TinyOS 1.x.

operation result. Note that in this latter case, another high-level component should provide one implementation for each event. Table 2 shows the API provided at this abstraction level. It includes a very reduced set of basic operations for reading, writing, and erasing; additionally it allows to compute the CRC for a memory page.

- A set of TinyOS components that provides the implementation for the API shown in Table 2. This implementation must invoke the hardware-level drivers which carry out the operations at the physical level. Several issues are left to the application level: firstly, flash memory must be accessed with mutual exclusion and therefore two operations over flash cannot be issued at the same time; secondly, the application must implement the event handlers corresponding to the commands that it invokes; thirdly, the high-level application must specify as arguments low-level details, such as the number of page to be read or written as well as the offset within the page. For instance, if the memory has a capacity of 512 KB —like AT45DB041 memory flash— there exists 2048 pages every one of them with 264 bytes to be read or written; both data must be specified for each operation on the flash.

3.1.2 High-level implementation

This interface provides read, write, and logging operations. The implementation operates on a per-byte basis and thus the operations must specify what is the position or offset in bytes from which data go to be read or written. This offset is expressed as an absolute value with regard to the total capacity of the flash memory. For instance, if the memory has a capacity of 512 KB the offset should ranges between 0x000000 and 0x07FFFF. In this sense, the abstraction level is still very low because it forces to the programmer to manage hardware details in order to invoke the operations. Table 3 shows the interface provided for this approach.

3.1.3 Matchbox

The idea of providing the file abstraction to access the data stored is a very useful approach typically performed at the operating system level. This approach is very attractive for users because it prevents them of managing hardware-level information such as offsets or number of pages. Matchbox (Gay, 2003) is the first file system developed for sensor nodes and it was

Commands
command result_t read(uint32_t offset, uint8_t* buffer, uint32_t numBytesRead);
command result_t write(uint32_t offset, uint8_t *data, uint32_t numBytesWrite);
command result_t erase();
command result_t append(uint8_t* data, uint32_t numBytes);
command uint32_t currentOffset();
command result_t request(uint32_t numBytesReq);
command result_t sync();
command result_t requestAddr(uint32_t byteAddr, uint32_t numBytesReq);
Events
event result_t readDone(uint8_t* buffer, uint32_t numBytesRead, result_t success);
event result_t writeDone(uint8_t *data, uint32_t numBytesWrite, result_t success);
event result_t eraseDone(result_t success);
event result_t appendDone(uint8_t* data, uint32_t numBytes, result_t success);
event result_t syncDone(result_t success);
event result_t requestProcessed(result_t success);

Table 3. High-level interface for flash memory provided by TinyOS 1.x.

included into the first version of TinyOS. The major goals of Matchbox are reliability (detection of data corruption) and low resource consumption. Matchbox offers operations for directories and files. Files are unstructured and are represented simply as a sequence of bytes. Matchbox allows the applications to open two files simultaneously, but it supports only sequential reads and appending writes and it does not allow random access to files. It also provides a simple wear levelling policy. The Matchbox code size is small, around 10 KB. The minimum footprint is 362 bytes and it increases when the number of files grows. For each flash memory page an 8-byte CRC is used to verify the integrity of the file during recovery from a system crash.
Table 4 shows the complete interface provided by the Matchbox file system. As shown, it is composed of a reduced number of primitives to manage the data stored in the flash using the file abstraction. In this sense, a file is a stream flow that can be read and updated. Additional operations on a file are renaming and deleting a file. Note that the writing operation only enables adding data at the end of the file. The advantages of this approach is that the user manages entities that are identified through file names in order to access data; subsequently, users do not need to be conscious about low-level details such as the number of the page to be read or written.

3.2 TinyOS 2.x

The second version of TinyOS focuses on designing high-level portable interfaces while the implementation is leaved up to the manufacturers. This approach satisfies the design principles of TinyOS 2.x (Handziski et al., 2005), where a layered design of the software architecture is proposed with the final goal of achieving portability. Subsequently, the abstractions provided by TinyOS 2.x are high-level and platform-independent interfaces, while their low level implementation is platform-specific. This represents an important difference with regard to the previous version of TinyOS, where both the interface and the implementation are specific-device. TinyOS 2.x proposes four non-volatile storage entities, every one of them is intended for store data with different nature and requirements:

- Volumes are fixed-size units in which the flash memory is organized for general purposes.

Commands
command result_t delete(const char *filename);
command result_t start();
command result_t readNext();
command uint32_t freeBytes();
command result_t open(const char *filename);
command result_t close();
command result_t read(void *buffer, filesize_t n);
command result_t getRemaining();
command result_t rename(const char *oldName, const char *newName);
command result_t append(void *buffer, filesize_t n);
command result_t reserve(filesize_t newSize);
command result_t sync();
Events
event result_t deleted(fileresult_t result);
event result_t ready();
event result_t nextFile(const char *filename, fileresult_t result);
event result_t opened(fileresult_t result);
event result_t closed(fileresult_t result);
event result_t readDone(void *buffer, filesize_t nRead, fileresult_t result);
event result_t remaining(filesize_t n, fileresult_t result);
event result_t renamed(fileresult_t result);
event result_t appended(void *buffer, filesize_t nWritten, fileresult_t result);
event result_t reserved(filesize_t reservedSize, fileresult_t result);
event result_t synced(fileresult_t result);

Table 4. Matchbox interface provided by TinyOS 1.x.

- Large objects that may occupy an undetermined space and they are intended to store a great amount of data, for instance a binary image that is received from the radio device.
- Loggers are intended to store records of fixed size, such as results and events.
- Small objects (of a few hundred bytes) with a transactional behaviour.

3.2.1 Volumes

Flash chip is divided in several volumes whose size must be specified at compilation time. The properties of the volumes are specified using an XML file where three data are specified per each volume: name, size, and base (optional). Note that such description is platform-independent. As an example consider the next XML file where four volumes of 65536 bytes are defined:

```
<volume_table>
    <volume name="DELUGE" size="65536" />
    <volume name="CONFIGLOG" size="65536" />
    <volume name="DATALOG" size="65536" />
    <volume name="GOLDENIMAGE" size="65536" base="983040" />
</volume_table>
```

When the application that defines the volumes configuration is compiled, the chip-specific implementation translates such configuration to the equivalent nesC code that must allocate the space for every volume. There is no restriction about how this translation should be done. Applications can simply use every one of the volumes previously defined instantiating the

Commands
command error_t read(storage_addr_t addr, void* buf, storage_len_t len);
command error_t computeCrc(storage_addr_t addr, storage_len_t len, uint16_t crc);
command storage_len_t getSize();
command error_t write(storage_addr_t addr, void* buf, storage_len_t len);
command error_t erase();
command error_t sync();
Events
event void readDone(storage_addr_t addr, void* buf, storage_len_t len, error_t error);
event void computeCrcDone(storage_addr_t addr, storage_len_t len, uint16_t crc, error_t error);
event void writeDone(storage_addr_t addr, void* buf, storage_len_t len, error_t error);
event void eraseDone(error_t error);
event void syncDone(error_t error);

Table 5. Interface for volumes and large objects provided by TinyOS 2.x.

generic component `BlockStorageC` which receives as argument the name of the volume to be used. Data stored in the volume can be read, written, and erased. Table 5 shows the interface to be used in order to access volumes. Note that the application specifies the relative address to the volume on which the operation is done.

3.2.2 Large objects

Large objects are a specific type of data with an interesting semantic: each byte in the object is written at most once. These data are written once and rarely it goes to be overwritten. In the WSN field, there are several examples of this type of data: considers for example binary files for network reprogramming or reliable packet whose contents must keep invariable. TinyOS 2.x provides the same interface for large objects than for volumes (see Table 5). In the same way, an instance of the generic component `BlockStorageC` must be created in order to access the large object.

3.2.3 Loggers

Storing the internal data generated in the sensor node itself is a common requirement for many WSN applications. Consider for example the need of scientists to know with a certain accuracy the value of the sensor readings in order to extract patterns that can help to predict some event. Such a logging should be reliable since data should not be lost and they should survive to a crash or reboot. Logs can be defined as linear —data are written sequentially from the beginning at the end of the log— or circular —if the log is full the data overwritten the beginning of the log—. Loggers access —both linear and circular— is always sequential. Loggers work on a per-record basis, where one record is the logic data structure to be read or written in every operation. The commit operation ensures that the data committed are successfully stored in flash and that they can be therefore recovered. Data not committed do not ensure this feature. Table 6 depicts the interface for loggers provided by TinyOS 2.x. In order to access logs the application instantiates the `LogStorageC` component, which takes two input arguments: a volume identifier and a boolean argument specifying whether the log is circular or not.

Commands
command error_t read(void* buf, storage_len_t len);
command storage_cookie_t currentOffset();
command error_t seek(storage_cookie_t offset);
command storage_len_t getSize();
command error_t append(void* buf, storage_len_t len);
command error_t erase();
command error_t sync();
Events
event void readDone(,void* buf, storage_len_t len, error_t error);
event void seekDone(error_t error);
event void appendDone(void* buf, storage_len_t len, bool recordsLost, error_t error);
event void eraseDone(error_t error);
event void syncDone(error_t error);

Table 6. Interface for loggers provided by TinyOS 2.x.

Commands
command error_t read(storage_addr_t addr, void* buf, storage_len_t len);
command error_t write(storage_addr_t addr, void* buf, storage_len_t len);
command error_t commit();
command storage_len_t getSize();
command bool valid();
command error_t mount();
Events
event void readDone(storage_addr_t addr, void* buf, storage_len_t len, error_t error);
event void writeDone(storage_addr_t addr, void* buf, storage_len_t len, error_t error);
event void commitDone(error_t error);
event void mountDone(error_t error);

Table 7. Interface for small objects provided by TinyOS 2.x.

3.2.4 Small objects

Some sensor network applications need to store their configuration. This configuration includes the initial data to be assigned to the application variables such as the mote identity, sampling rates, or thresholds. These critical data must be stored in a non-volatile support in order to be sure that on sensor failures —reboot or crash— the configuration can be recovered. A characteristic of this type of data is its small size, frequently of a few hundred bytes. Another interesting feature is the transactional behaviour of the operations performed on this type of data: each read is a separate transaction, all writes up to a commit defines a single transaction. Table 7 presents the interface provided by TinyOS 2.x for small objects. The application must instantiate the generic component `ConfigStorageC` previously to the data access. As shown, the operation must specify the address to be read or written.

3.3 Contiki

Contiki (Dunkels et al., 2004) is an operating system designed for networked and memory constrained systems, developed in the Swedish Institute of Computer Science (SICS) by Adam Dunkels as the leader of the project in 2003. Contiki is open source and it was written in the C programming language. The typical size of Contiki applications is around kilobytes, which means a bigger footprint than the applications developed in TinyOS. In spite of this, it could be considered the second most extended operating system for programming sensor nodes. At the

Functions	Description
int cfs_open (const char *name, int flags);	Open a file
void cfs_close (int fd);	Close an open file
int cfs_read (int fd, void *buf, unsigned int len);	Read data from an open file
int cfs_write (int fd, const void *buf, unsigned int len);	Write data to an open file
cfs_offset_t cfs_seek (int fd, cfs_offset_t offset, int whence);	Seek to a specified position in an open file
int cfs_remove (const char *name);	Remove a file
int cfs_opendir (struct cfs_dir *dirp, const char *name);	Open a directory for reading directory entries
int cfs_readdir (struct cfs_dir *dirp, struct cfs_dirent *dirent);	Read a directory entry
void cfs_closedir (struct cfs_dir *dirp);	Close a directory opened with cfs_opendir()

Table 8. Coffee file system interface.

operating system level Contiki provides an only way for accessing data: a file system. This file system is called Coffee (Contiki's Flash File System (Coffee)) (Tsiftes et al., 2009). Coffee is a flash-based file system, designed as a combination of extents and *micro log* files. The concept of micro log files is introduced to record file modifications without requiring a high consumption of memory space. In fact, every open file uses a small and constant memory footprint. Coffee provides POSIX-style primitives to manage both files and directories (see Table 8). Other outstanding features of Coffee are garbage collection, wear levelling techniques in order to avoid memory corruption, and fault recovery.

3.4 LiteOS

LiteOS (Cao et al., 2008) is a UNIX-like multi-threaded operating system with object-oriented programming support for wireless sensor networks. It includes several features of the Unix systems (e.g. a shell or the programming environment), which increase its footprint leaving it too far from operating systems such as TinyOS. LiteOS includes a built-in hierarchical file system called LiteFS (Cao & Abdelzaher, 2006). LiteFS supports both file and directory operations, and opened files are kept in RAM. Directory information is stored in the EEPROM while the serial flash stores file metadata. LiteFS implements two wear levelling techniques, one for the EEPROM chip and the other one for the serial flash. LiteOS provides also a UNIX-like shell that facilitates the interaction of the user with the file system by using UNIX-based commands (e.g. ls, cd, cp, mv, rm). The complete set of LiteFS primitives is presented in Table 9. As shown, there are basic primitives for managing files and directories (e.g. open, close, read, and write) as well as for administrating the sensor node (e.g. checking and formatting the EEPROM and flash memories).

3.5 Comparison

The three implementations provided by TinyOS 1.x are AT45DB-specific and subsequently in this first approach the portability was sacrificed. In general, the abstraction level offered by the OS is very low even when bigger grained entities such as files are managed. The applications are forced to be worried about hardware details (number of the page, offset), which makes programming complex and error-prone. Clearly the advantage of this approach is that it prevents the overload imposed by the management at the OS level. In TinyOS 2.x the major goal was increasing the portability though richer interfaces that are platform-independent. TinyOS 2.x renounces to offer a general implementation at the OS level due to the heterogeneity of the different flash devices. The interfaces provided are recommended for a particular type of data: small objects, volumes, loggers and large object.

Functions	Description
FILE* fopen(const char *pathname, const char *mode);	Open file
int fclose(FILE *fp);	Close file
int fseek (FILE *fp, int offset, int position);	Seek file
int fexist(char *pathname);	Test file/directory
int fcreatedir(char *pathname);	Create directory file
int fdelete(char *pathname);	Delete file/directory
int fread(FILE *fp, void *buffer, int nBytes);	Read from file
int fwrite(FILE *fp, void *buffer, int nBytes);	Write to file
int fmove(char *source, char *target);	Move file/directory
int fcopy(char *source, char *target);	Copy file/directory
void formatSystem();	Format file system
void fchangedir(char *path);	Change current directory
void fcurrentdir(char *buffer, int size);	Get current directory
int fcheckEEPROM();	Check EEPROM Usage
int fcheckFlash();	Check Flash Usage
void fsearch(char *addrlist, int *size, char *string);	Search by name
void finfonode(char *buffer, int addr);	Get file/directory info

Table 9. LiteFS file system interface.

However, as deduced from their interfaces the abstraction level of the application is low since they must specify again hardware details for accessing data.

TinyOS 1.x and other operating systems as Contiki and LiteOS provide abstractions in the shape of file systems to data access. The advantages of this approach is that the user manages entities that are identified through file names in order to access data; subsequently, users do not need to be conscious about low-level details such as the number of the page to be read or written. It definitively facilitates the programming and prevents errors. Table 10 shows a brief comparison among the file systems studied in this section and in the following section.

	ELF	Matchbox	LiteFS	SENFIS
1	TinyOS	TinyOS	LiteOS	TinyOS
2	Mica2	Mica Family Motes	MicaZ	Mica Family Motes
3	Dynamic	Static	Dynamic	Dynamic
4	RAM, EEPROM, Flash	Flash	RAM, EEPROM, Flash	RAM, EEPROM, Flash
5	14 bytes (per flash page)	8 bytes (per flash ge)	8 bytes (per flash page)	8 bytes (per flash page)
	14 bytes		168 bytes RAM	1062 bytes flash
	14 bytes per i-node (RAM)		2080 bytes ROM	208 bytes RAM/EEPROM
6	Unlimited	2 (Read/Write)	8	64
7	Sensor Data	Data files	Data	Data stream
	Configuration Data		Binary applications	Binary applications
	Binary program Image		Device Drivers	

Table 10. Comparison among different file systems for sensor nodes. Features: 1:Operating system; 2:Sensor platforms; 3:Memory allocation; 4:Memory chips used; 5:Metadata size; 6:Number of files opened; 7:Types of files.

4. Taxonomy of applications

Wireless sensor network applications are often multi-disciplinary and obey many types of requirements. Several authors have classified WSN applications according to their application domain (Akyildiz et al., 2002; Xu, 2002). In this section we will focus on those WSN applications that use the flash memory chip to carry out their operations. Thus, we distinguish three main type of applications: 1) file systems to store both internal and external data; 2) data-centric middlewares that provide an abstraction of the sensors network as a long database; and 3) applications for network reprogramming. These three types of applications use the flash memory chip as data storing support. Note that in a four category should appear the applications that use the flash for specific purposes. Figure 6 shows this classification. In following subsections we review some relevant examples in each category.

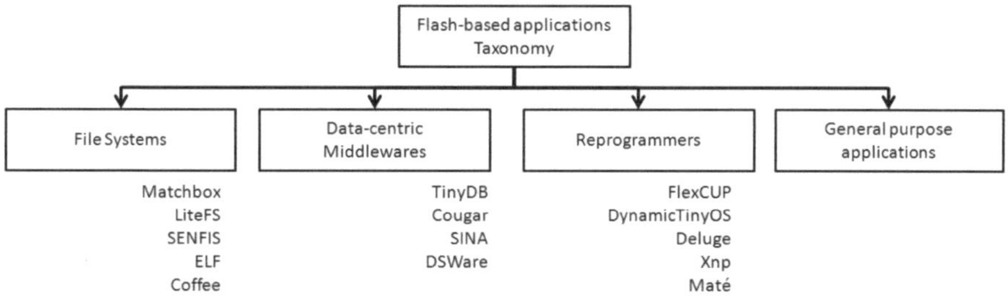

Fig. 6. A classification of applications that use the flash memory chip.

4.1 File systems

In addition to the OS-specific file systems presented in the previous section, we review here two file systems that were designed with no regard to be OS-independent: ELF and SENFIS. The usage of file systems is justified: the continuous data production through a wide set of versatile applications drives researchers to think about different methods of data storing and recovering, which can provide an efficient abstraction to give persistent support to the data generated into the sensor node.

4.1.1 ELF

ELF (Dai et al., 2004) is a file system for WSNs based on the log file system paradigm (Kawaguchi et al., 1995). The major goals of ELF are memory efficiency, low power operation, and support for common file operations (such as reading and appending data to a file). The data to be stored in files are classified into three categories: data collected from sensors, configuration data, and binary program images. The access patterns and reliability requirements of these categories of data are different. Typically, the reliability of sensor data is verified through the CRC checksum mechanism. For binary images a greater reliability may be desirable, such as recovery after a crash. Typically, traditional log-structured file systems group log entries for each write operation into a sequential log. ELF keeps each log entry in a separate log page due to the fact that, if multiple log entries are stored on the same page, an error on this page will destroy all the history saved until that moment. ELF also provides a simple garbage collection mechanism and crash recovery support.

4.1.2 SENFIS

SENFIS (Escolar et al., 2008; 2010) is a file system designed for Mica family motes and intended to be used in two scenarios: firstly, it can transparently be employed as a permanent storage for distributed TinyDB queries (see next subsection), in order to increase their reliability and scalability; secondly, it can be directly used by a WSN application for

Primitive Prototype	Description
int8_t open (char *filename, uint8_t mode)	Open a file
result_t close (uint8_t fd)	Close a file
int8_t write (uint8_t fd, char *buffer, int8_t length)	Append data to a file
int8_t read (uint8_t fd, char *buffer, int8_t length)	Read from a file
result_t rename(char *oldname, char *newname)	Rename a file
result_t lseek (uint8_t fd, uint32_t ptr)	Update the offset of a file
result_t stat(uint8_t fd, struct inode *inode)	Obtain metadata of a file
result_t delete (uint8_t fd)	Delete a file

Table 11. Basic high-level interface for SENFIS.

permanent storage of data on the motes. SENFIS uses the flash for persistent storage and RAM as a volatile memory. The flash chip is divided into blocks called segments, whose pages are accessed in a circular way, guaranteeing an optimal intra-segment wear levelling. The global wear-levelling is a best-effort algorithm: a newly created file is always assigned the lowest used segment.

In SENFIS, the flash is organized in segments. For instance, for AT45DB041 the flash may consist of 64 segments of 32 pages each. Each segment may be assigned to at most one file but a file can use an arbitrary number of segments. A segment is written always sequentially in a circular way. For implementing this behaviour a pointer to the last written page is kept in the segment metadata structure which is stored in a *segment table*. Every segment in this table records a pointer to the first page of the segment, a pointer to the next segment as well as a counter indicating the number of times the pages of this segment have been written. To minimize the number of times that a page flash is accessed the reading and writing operations use an intermediate cache such as shown in Figure 7. SENFIS provides a POSIX-style interface which is shown in Table 11.

SENFIS uses a writing buffer to reduce the number of times that a page is accessed. Figure 7 shows graphically this behaviour.

4.2 Data-centric middlewares

The most common approach to bridge the gap between the applications and low-level software, has been to develop a middleware layer mapping one level into the other. A survey of middleware is given in (Marrón, 2005) where a taxonomy of middlewares is discussed. In particular, authors identify data-centric middlewares as those ones that operate the sensor network as a database abstraction. Most of them rely on some form of SQL-like language in order to recover the data stored in different memories within the sensor node (RAM, EEPROM, and external flash). There exist different data-centric middlewares such as Cougar (Fung et al., 2002), TinyBD (Madden et al., 2005), DSWare (Li et al., 2003) and SINA (Jaikaeo et al., 2000)); some of them are summarized in the following paragraphs.

4.2.1 TinyDB

TinyDB (Madden et al., 2005) focuses on acquisitional query processing techniques which differ from other database query techniques for WSN in that it does not simply postulate the a priori existence of data, but it focuses also on location and cost of acquiring data. The acquisitional techniques have been shown to reduce the power consumption in several orders of magnitude and to increase the accuracy of query results. A typical query of TinyDB is active

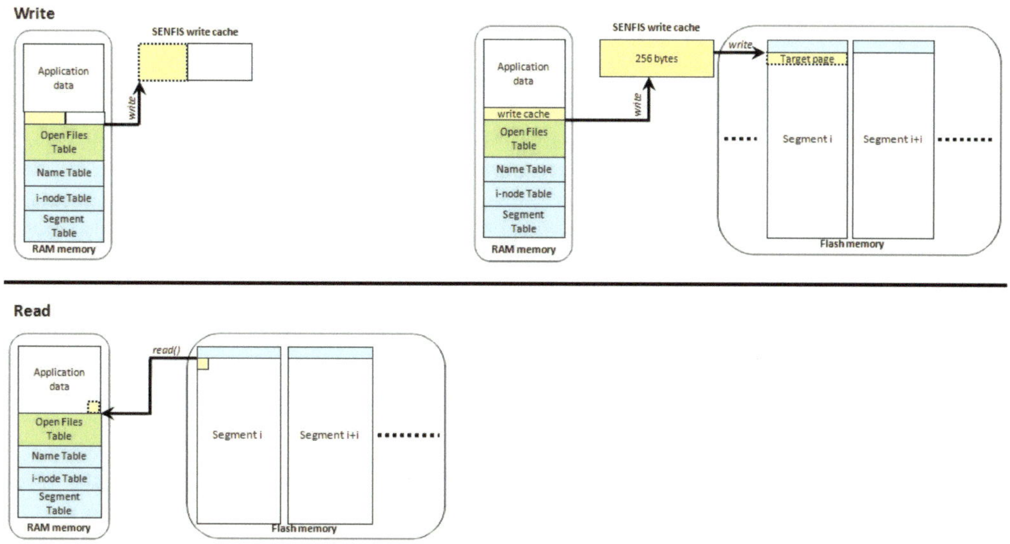

Fig. 7. Writing and reading operations in SENFIS: 1) Above, the writing operation which appends data to the end of a file. The modification is done in a small buffer cache in RAM and it is committed to the flash either when a page is completely written or when the RAM is full. The first case tries to avoid that a page is committed to flash several times for small writes; 2) below, the reading operation which get the data from the flash to an application buffer. If the data is already in the small buffer cache, it is copied to the application buffer from there.

in a mote for a specified time frame and is data intensive. The results of a query may produce communication or be temporarily stored in the RAM memory. In TinyDB the sampled values of the various sensor attributes (e.g. temperature, light) are stored in a table called sensors. The columns of the table represent the sensor attributes and the rows the instant of time when the measure was taken. Projections and transformations of sensor table are stored in materialization points. A materialization point is a type of temporal table that can be used in subsequent select operations. Materialization points are declared by the users and correspond to files in our system. TinyDB query syntax is similar to SQL SELECT-FROM-WHERE-GROUPBY clause, supporting selection, join, projection and aggregation. In addition TinyDB provides SAMPLE PERIOD clause defining the overall time of the sampling called epoch and the period between consecutive samples. The materialization points are created by CREATE STORAGE POINT clause, associated with a SELECT clause, which selects data either from the sensor table or from a different materialization point.

4.2.2 Cougar

Cougar (Fung et al., 2002) is another data-centric middleware approach intended to address the goals of scalability and flexibility in monitoring the physical world. In Cougar system sensor nodes are organized in clusters and they can assume two roles: cluster leader or signal processing nodes. The leaders receive the queries and plan how they must be executed within of a cluster; in particular, they must decide what nodes the query should be sent to, and keep waiting for the response. On the other hand, signal processing nodes generate data from their sensor readings. Signal processing functions are modelled by using Abstract Data Type (ADT). Like TinyDB, Cougar uses a SQL-like language to implement queries.

4.3 Network reprogramming applications

Code dissemination for network reprogramming is nowadays one of the important issues in the WSN field. WSN applications are conceived to execute for the maximum period of time. However, during their lifetime is very probable that the application needs to be total or partially updated. There are several reasons for it as to meet new requirements or to correct errors detected at execution time. There exist in the literature a large set of applications that enables this feature. Despite every particular implementation, a common characteristic of all of them is the employment of the flash memory to store the updates that are received from the network. In fact, there is no other choice due to the limited capacity of the node RAM memory. According to (Munawar et al., 2010) applications for remote reprogramming can be classified in four main categories:

- Full-image replacement: the first approach for network reprogramming operated disseminating in the network a new image to replace the current application running in the nodes. Examples of this type of reprogrammers are Deluge and XNP, which are both TinyOS 1.x specific. In a first step, the image was received from the network and locally stored in the node flash. Once the packet reception was completed, the sensor node reboots which makes a copy of the binary stored in the flash into the microcontroller. The main disadvantage of this approach is that even for small updates the transmission of the full image should be done, which impacts negatively on the waste of energy in the sensor node.
- Virtual machines: with the goal of reducing the energy consumption in which the previous approach incurs, there exist different works that propose disseminating virtual machine code (byte-code) instead of native code, since the first is in general more compact than the second one. The most relevant example is Mate (Levis & Culler, 2002). Maté disseminates to the network packets denominated capsules which contain the binary to be installed. In the sensor nodes the byte-code is interpreted and installed in the sensor node. The advantage of this approach is that reduces significantly the program size that travels through the network, which decreases the energy consumption due to the communication as well as the storing cost.
- Dynamic operating systems: there exists WSN operating systems that include support for the dynamic reprogramming of sensor nodes. For example, in Contiki applications can be more easily updated, due to the fact that Contiki supports load dynamic of programs on the top of the operating system kernel. In this way, code updates can be remotely downloaded into the network. There are, however, certain restrictions to perform this since only application components can be modified. LiteOS (Cao et al., 2008) is another example of this type of OSes. LiteOS provides dynamic reprogramming at the application level which means that the operating system image can not be updated. To do this it manages the modified HEX files instead using ELF files —as Contiki— in order to store relocation information.
- Partial-image replacement approach is based on disseminate only the changes between the current executable installed in the network and the new version of the same application. This is the most efficient solution since only is sent the piece of code that

needs to be updated. There are in the literature several works using this approach. Zephyr (Panta et al., 2009) compares the two binary images at the byte-level and send only a small delta, reducing the size of data to be sent. FlexCup (Marrón et al., 2006) is an efficient code update mechanism that allows the replacement of TinyOS binary components. FlexCup is specific for TinyOS 1.x and does not include the new extensions of nesC. Dynamic TinyOS (Munawar et al., 2010) preserves the modularity of TinyOS which is lost during the compilation process and enables the composition of the application at execution time.

5. Conclusions

Through this chapter we have analyzed the main features of the flash memory chip as well as their main applications within the wireless sensor networks field. We have described the different technologies employed in the manufacturing of flash memory given specific examples used by the sensor nodes. The sensor node architecture has been presented while the flash memory has been introduced as an important component that possibilities a great amount of usages which would not be possible without its presence.

We have described some relevant WSN operating systems highlighting the different abstractions that they provide at the application level in order to access the data stored in the flash. As discussed, in general the portability has been sacrificed and the implementation is typically device-specific. The abstraction level provided by the OSes is very low since the application must manage hardware level details such as the number of the page to be read or written and the offset within the page, which make complex the applications programming. To alleviate this problem, the operating systems can supply a basic implementation of a file system to facilitate the data access. Here, the users manipulate abstract entities called file descriptors which allow to uncouple the data from its physical location. Subsequently, file systems simplify the data access but in general they do not completely address the issues regarding to the flash memory such as the implementation of wear levelling techniques to prevent reaching the maximum number of times that a page can be written. For this reason, the literature presents some other file systems that has been proposed in order to improve the features or the performance of the existing files systems included into the operating systems.

Recently, the attention paid to the flash memory chip trends to grow due to the appearance of new applications that will use the flash memory to perform their tasks. Since the flash chip represents the device with the bigger capacity for permanent storage of application data in the sensor node, there exist an increasing number of applications that require its usage to be able to satisfy their requirements, for example, applications for dynamic reprogramming.

Finally in this chapter, we have identified a taxonomy of WSN applications that uses the flash memory providing specific examples of applications in each category of the taxonomy. We will envision that the number of emerging applications that will use the flash memory as basis for their operations will continue increasing.

6. Acknowledgements

This work has been partially funded by the Spanish Ministry of Science and Innovation under the grand TIN2010-16497.

7. References

Akyildiz, I. F., Su, W., Sankarasubramaniam, Y. & Cayirci, E. (2002). Wireless sensor networks: a survey., *Computer Networks* 38(4): 393–422.

Atmel (2011). Atmel 8-bit AVR microcontroller Datasheet, *Available in:* URL: *http://www.atmel.com/dyn/resources/prod_documents/doc2467.pdf* .

Atmel AT45DB011 Serial DataFlash (2001). URL: *http://www.datasheetcatalog.com/datasheets_pdf/A/T/4/5/AT45DB.shtml.*

Balani, R., chieh Han, C., Raghunathan, V. & Srivastava, M. (2005). Remote storage for sensor networks.

Cao, Q. & Abdelzaher, T. (2006). LiteOS: a lightweight operating system for C++ software development in sensor networks, *SenSys '06: Proceedings of the 4th international conference on Embedded networked sensor systems*, ACM, New York, NY, USA, pp. 361–362.

Cao, Q., Stankovic, J. A., Abdelzaher, T. F. & He, T. (2008). LiteOS, A Unix-like operating system and programming platform for wireless sensor networks, *Information Processing in Sensor Networks(IPSN/SPOTS)*, St. Loius, MO, USA.

CC1000 Single Chip Very Low Power RF Transceiver (2002). URL: *http://focus.ti.com/lit/ds/symlink/cc1000.pdf.*

CC2400 2.4GHz Low-Power RF Transceiver (2003). URL: *http://focus.ti.com/lit/ds/symlink/cc2400.pdf.*

Dai, H., Neufeld, M. & Han, R. (2004). Elf: an efficient log-structured flash file system for micro sensor nodes, *SenSys '04: Proceedings of the 2nd international conference on Embedded networked sensor systems*, ACM, New York, NY, USA, pp. 176–187.

Diao, Y., Ganesan, D., Mathur, G. & Shenoy, P. (2007). Rethinking data management for storage-centric sensor networks.

Dunkels, A., Gronvall, B. & Voigt, T. (2004). Contiki - a lightweight and flexible operating system for tiny networked sensors, *Proceedings of the 29th Annual IEEE International Conference on Local Computer Networks*, LCN '04, IEEE Computer Society, Washington, DC, USA, pp. 455–462. URL: *http://dx.doi.org/10.1109/LCN.2004.38*

Escolar, S., Carretero, J., Isaila, F. & Lama, S. (2008). A lightweight storage system for sensor nodes, *in* H. R. Arabnia & Y. Mun (eds), *PDPTA*, CSREA Press, pp. 638–644.

Escolar, S., Isaila, F., Calderón, A., Sánchez, L. M. & Singh, D. E. (2010). Senfis: a sensor node file system for increasing the scalability and reliability of wireless sensor networks applications, *The Journal of Supercomputing* 51(1): 76–93.

Fung, W. F., Sun, D. & Gehrke, J. (2002). Cougar: the network is the database, *Proceedings of the 2002 ACM SIGMOD international conference on Management of data*, SIGMOD '02, ACM, New York, NY, USA, pp. 621–621. URL: *http://doi.acm.org/10.1145/564691.564775*

Gay, D. (2003). The Matchbox File System, URL: *http://webs.cs.berkeley.edu/tos/tinyos-1.x/doc/matchbox-design.pdf.*

Gay, D., Levis, P., von Behren, R., Welsh, M., Brewer, E. & Culler, D. (2003). The nesc language: A holistic approach to networked embedded systems, *PLDI '03: Proceedings of the ACM SIGPLAN 2003 conference on Programming language design and implementation*, ACM, New York, NY, USA, pp. 1–11.

Han, C.-C., Kumar, R., Shea, R., Kohler, E. & Srivastava, M. (2005). A dynamic operating system for sensor nodes, *Proceedings of the 3rd international conference on Mobile systems, applications, and services*, MobiSys '05, ACM, New York, NY, USA, pp. 163–176.
URL: *http://doi.acm.org/10.1145/1067170.1067188*

Handziski, V., Polastrey, J., Hauer, J.-H., Sharpy, C., Wolisz, A. & Culler, D. (2005). Flexible Hardware Abstraction for Wireless Sensor Networks, *2nd European Workshop on Wireless Sensor Networks (EWSN 2005)*, Istanbul, Turkey.

Hill, J., Szewczyk, R., Woo, A., Hollar, S., Culler, D. & Pister, K. (2000). System architecture directions for networked sensors, *SIGPLAN Not.* 35: 93–104.
URL: *http://doi.acm.org/10.1145/356989.356998*

Instrument, T. (2008). Msp430x1xx 8mhz datasheet, *Available in:* URL: *http://www.ti.com/lit/gpn/msp430c1101* .

Intel Strataflash (2002).
URL: *http://www-mtl.mit.edu/Courses/6.111/labkit/datasheets/28F128J3A.pdf.*

Jaikaeo, C., Srisathapornphat, C. & chung Shen, C. (2000). Querying and tasking in sensor networks.

Kawaguchi, A., Nishioka, S. & Motoda, H. (1995). A flash-memory based file system, *USENIX Winter*, pp. 155–164.
URL: *citeseer.ist.psu.edu/kawaguchi95flashmemory.html*

Levis, P. & Culler, D. (2002). Mate: a tiny virtual machine for sensor networks, *ASPLOS-X: Proceedings of the 10th international conference on Architectural support for programming languages and operating systems*, ACM, New York, NY, USA, pp. 85–95.

Li, S., Lin, Y., Son, S. H., Stankovic, J. A. & Wei, Y. (2003). Event detection services using data service middleware in distributed sensor networks.

M25P40 Serial Flash Memory (2002).
URL: *http://www.datasheetcatalog.org/datasheet/stmicroelectronics/7737.pdf*.

Madden, S. R., Franklin, M. J., Hellerstein, J. M. & Hong, W. (2005). TinyDB: an acquisitional query processing system for sensor networks, *ACM Trans. Database Syst.* 30(1): 122–173.

Marrón, P. J. (2005). Middleware approaches for sensor networks. University of Stuttgart, Summer School on WSNs and Smart Objects. Schloss Dagstuhl, Aug. Germany. URL: *http://www.vs.inf.ethz.ch/events/dag2005/program/lectures/marron-2.pdf.*

Marrón, P. J., Gauger, M., Lachenmann, A., Minder, D., Saukh, O. & Rothermel, K. (2006). Flexcup: A flexible and efficient code update mechanism for sensor networks.
URL: *http://citeseerx.ist.psu.edu/viewdoc/summary?doi=10.1.1.71.8622*

Munawar, W., Alizai, M. H., L, O. & Wehrle, K. (2010). Dynamic tinyos: Modular and transparent incremental code-updates for sensor networks.

nRF2401 Radio Transceiver Data Sheet (2003). URL: *http://www.nvlsi.no/.*

Panta, R. K., Bagchi, S. & Midkiff, S. P. (2009). Zephyr: efficient incremental reprogramming of sensor nodes using function call indirections and difference computation, *Proceedings of the 2009 conference on USENIX Annual technical conference*, USENIX'09, USENIX Association, Berkeley, CA, USA, pp. 32–32.
URL: *http://portal.acm.org/citation.cfm?id=1855807.1855839*

SAMSUNG (2003). Samsung K9K1G08R0B, 128M x 8 bit NAND Flash Memory.

Shenker, S., Ratnasamy, S., Karp, B., Govindan, R. & Estrin, D. (2003). Data-centric storage in sensornets, *SIGCOMM Comput. Commun. Rev.* 33(1): 137–142.

Tsiftes, N., Dunkels, A., He, Z. & Voigt, T. (2009). Enabling Large-Scale Storage in Sensor Networks with the Coffee File System, *Proceedings of the 8th ACM/IEEE International Conference on Information Processing in Sensor Networks (IPSN 2009)*, San Francisco, USA.
URL: *http://www.sics.se/ adam/tsiftes09enabling.pdf*

Xu, N. (2002). A survey of sensor network applications, *IEEE Communications Magazine* 40.

Adaptively Reconfigurable Controller for the Flash Memory

Ming Liu[1,2], Zhonghai Lu[2], Wolfgang Kuehn[1] and Axel Jantsch[2]
[1]*Justus-Liebig-University Giessen*
[2]*Royal Institute of Technology*
[1]*Germany*
[2]*Sweden*

1. Introduction

As the continuous development on the capacity and work frequency, Programmable Logic Devices (PLD) especially Field-Programmable Gate Arrays (FPGA) are playing an increasingly important role in embedded systems designs. The FPGA market has hit about 3 and 4 billion US dollars respectively in 2009 and 2010, and is expected by Xilinx CEO Moshe Gavrielov to grow steadily to 4.5 billion by the end of 2012 and 6 billion by the end of 2015. The application fields of FPGAs and other PLDs range from bulky industrial and military facilities to portable computer devices or communication terminals. Figure 1 demonstrates the market statistics of some most significant fields in the third quarter of 2009.

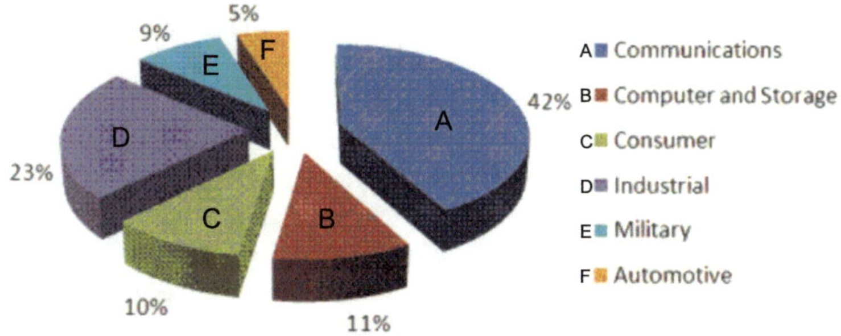

Fig. 1. PLD market by end applications in the third quarter of 2009 (Dillien, 2009)

FPGAs were originally used as programmable glue logic in the early period after its birth. Due to the capacity and clock frequency constraints at that time, they typically worked to bridge Application-Specific Integrated Circuit (ASIC) chips by adapting signal formats or conducting simple logic calculation. However at present, modern FPGAs have obtained enormous capacity and many advanced computation/communication features from the semiconductor process development; they can accommodate complete computer systems consisting of hardcore or softcore microprocessors, memory controllers, customized hardware accelerators, as well as peripherals, etc. Taking advantage of design IP cores and interconnection architecture, it has become a reality to easily implement System-on-Programmable-Chip (SoPC) or system-on-an-FPGA.

In spite of large advances, the chip area utilization efficiency as well as the clock speed of FPGAs is still very low in comparison with ASICs. One of the reasons is that FPGA employs Look-Up Table (LUT) to construct combinational logic, rather than primary gates as in ASICs. In (Kuon & Rose, 2006), the authors have measured FPGAs to be 35X larger in area and 3X slower in speed than a standard cell ASIC flow, both using 90-nm technology; In (Lu et al., 2008), a 12 year old *Pentium*® design was ported on a Xilinx Virtex-4 FPGA. A 3X slower system speed (25 MHz vs. 75 MHz) is still observed, although the FPGA uses a recent 90-nm technology while the original ASICs were 600-nm. The speed and area utilization gap between FPGAs and ASICs has been additionally quantified in (Zuchowski et al., 2002) and (Wilton et al., 2005) for various designs. Therefore we understand that FPGA programmable resources are still comparatively expensive. Efficient resource management and utilization remain to be a challenge especially for those applications with simultaneous high performance and low cost requirements.

Flash memory is often used to store nonvolatile data in embedded systems. Due to its intrinsic access mode, normally it does not feature as high speed read and write operations as volatile memories such as Dynamic Random Access Memory (DRAM) or Static Random Access Memory (SRAM). In many applications, flash memory is only used to hold data or programs which are expected to be retrievable after each time power off. It is only addressed very occasionally or even never during the system run-time, when those data or programs have already been loaded in the main memory of the system. For example, an embedded Operating System (OS) kernel may be loaded from the flash into DDR for fast execution in case of system power-on. Afterwards, the flash memory will never be addressed in systems operation unless the OS kernel is scheduled to be updated. Because of the occasionality of flash accesses, it generates resource utilization inefficiency if the flash memory controller is statically mapped on the FPGA design but does not operate frequently.

In the recent years, an advanced FPGA technology called Dynamic Partial Reconfiguration (DPR or PR) has emerged and become gradually mature for practical designs. It offers the capability to dynamically change part of the design without disturbing the remaining system. Based on the FPGA PR technology, which enables more efficient run-time resource management, we present a peripheral controller reconfigurable system design in this chapter: A NOR flash memory controller can be multiplexed with other peripheral components (in the case study an SRAM controller), time-sharing the same hardware resources with all the required system functionalities realized. We will elaborate the design in the following sections.

2. Conventional static design on FPGAs

2.1 Static design approach

A peripheral controller is the design component which interfaces to the peripheral device and interprets or responds to access instructions from the CPU or other master devices. So a flash memory controller is the design by which CPU addresses external flash chips. Figure 2 shows the top-level block diagram of a flash memory controller for the Processor Local Bus

(PLB) (IBM, 2007) connection. It receives control commands from the PLB to read from and write to external memory devices. The controller design provides basic read/write control signals, as well as the ability to configure the access time for read, write, and recovery time when switching between read and write operations. In addition, the memory data width and the bus data width are parameterizable. They can be automatically matched by performing multiple memory cycles when the memory data width is less than PLB. This design structure is capable of realizing both synchronous and asynchronous device access. It may also support other parallel memory accesses with small modification effort, such as SRAM.

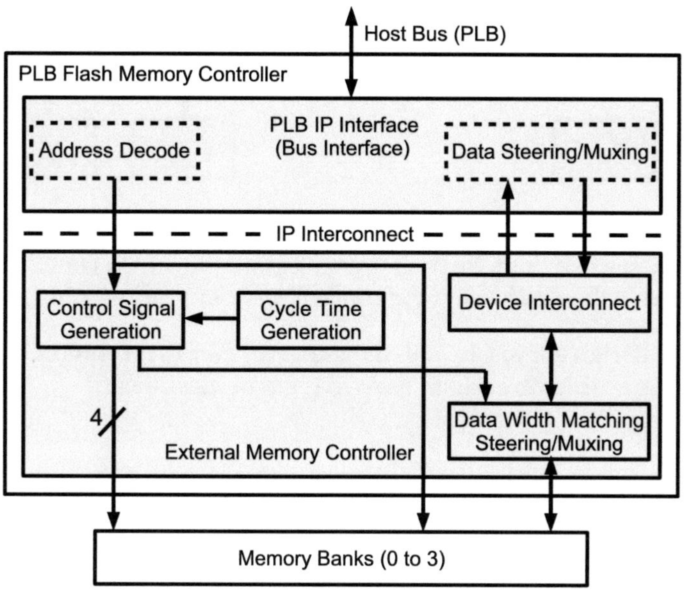

Fig. 2. Top-level block diagram of the PLB flash memory controller (Xilinx, 2006)

Figure 3 demonstrates a typical system-on-an-FPGA design for embedded applications. As an example, we adopt the Xilinx Virtex-4 FX FPGA for the implementation. We observe that all components are interconnected by the PLB, including the microprocessor, memory controllers, the application-specific algorithm accelerator as well as peripheral devices. In case of system power-on, the FPGA firmware bitstream is firstly downloaded to configure the FPGA via a special configuration interface (Dunlap & Fischaber, 2010). Afterwards an embedded Linux OS kernel is loaded by a bootloader program into the main memory of DDR for fast execution. In the design, a NOR flash memory stores nonvolatile data necessary for system startup in the field, including both the bitstream file and the OS kernel.

Suppose we are constructing a system aiming at memory bandwidth hungry computation for certain applications. Hence a Zero-Bus Turnaround (ZBT) SRAM is integrated in the system in addition to the main DDR memory. The SRAM is utilized as a Look-Up Table (LUT) component by the algorithm accelerator to carry out application-specific computation. It features higher data bandwidth and more efficient data movement than DDR. With the

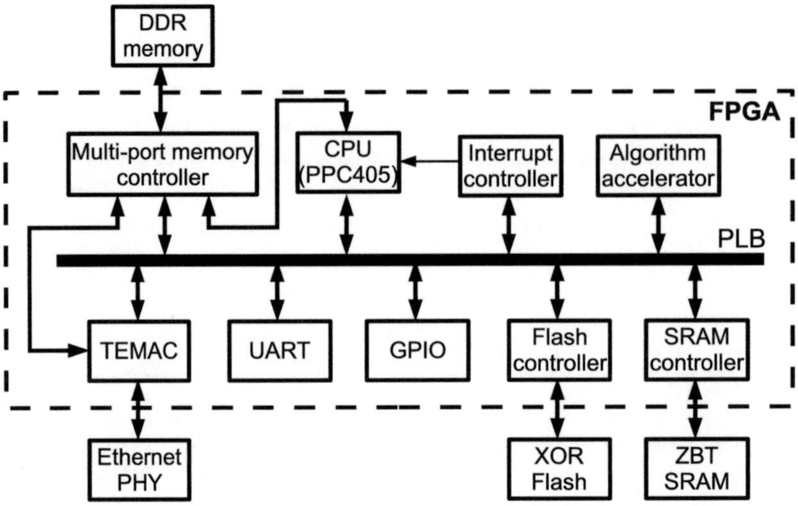

Fig. 3. Static design on an FPGA. The system is bus-based and all components are connected to the PLB. We may see that both the flash controller and the SRAM controller are concurrently placed in the design with the conventional static approach.

conventional static design approach, both the flash and the SRAM controller are concurrently placed on the FPGA in order to address the two types of memories.

2.2 Motivation

The flash memory is used to hold nonvolatile data for in-field system startup. It will be rarely addressed during the system operation unless external management commands require the bitstream or the OS kernel to be updated. On the other hand, application-specific computation starts only after the FPGA firmware is configured and the OS is successfully booted. Therefore on account of the occasionality of flash access as well as the operation exclusiveness between flash and SRAM, it generates resource utilization inefficiency if the flash controller is permanently mapped on the FPGA design but does not function frequently. Hence we consider to make the flash memory controller dynamically changeable and time-share the same on-chip resources with the SRAM controller.

3. FPGA partial reconfiguration technology

Modern FPGAs (e.g. Xilinx Virtex-4, 5, and 6, Altera Stratix 5 FPGAs) offer the partial reconfiguration capability to dynamically change part of the design without disturbing the remaining system. This feature enables alternate utilization of on-FPGA programmable resources, therefore resulting in large benefits such as more efficient resource utilization and less static power dissipation (Kao, 2005). Figure 4 illustrates a reconfigurable design example on Xilinx FPGAs: In the design process, one Partially Reconfigurable Region (PRR) A is reserved in the overall design layout mapped on the FPGA. On the early-stage dynamically reconfigurable FPGAs (e.g. Xilinx Virtex-II and Virtex-II Pro), PRR reservation must run through a complete slice column, because a slice column is the smallest load unit of a configuration bitstream frame (Hubner et al., 2006; Xilinx, 2004). With respect to the latest FPGA generations (e.g. Xilinx Virtex-4, 5, and 6), PRRs can be the combination of slice squares. Various functional Partially Reconfigurable Modules (PRM) are individually implemented within the PR region in the implementation process, and their respective partial bitstreams are generated and collectively initialized in a design database residing in a memory device in the system. During the system run-time, various bitstreams can be dynamically loaded into the FPGA configuration memory by its controller named Internal Configuration Access Port (ICAP). With a new module bitstream overwriting the original one in the FPGA configuration memory, the PRR is loaded with the new module and the circuit functions according to its concrete design. In the dynamic reconfiguration process, the PRR has to stop working for a short time (reconfiguration overhead) until the new module is completely loaded. The static portion of the system will not be interfered at all.

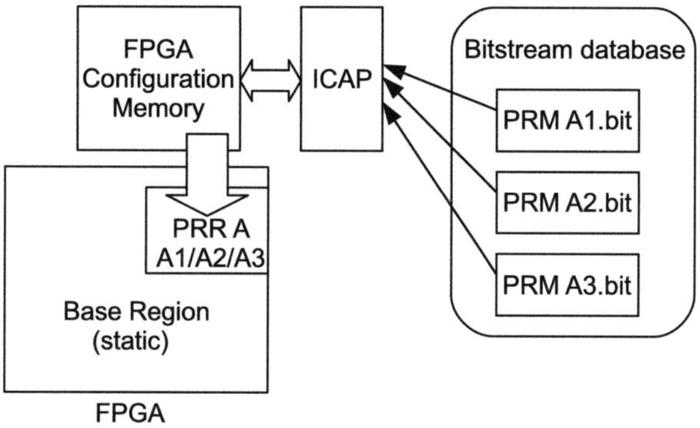

Fig. 4. Partially reconfigurable design on Xilinx FPGAs

The ICAP primitive is the hardwired FPGA logic by which the bitstream can be downloaded into the configuration memory. As shown in Figure 5, ICAP interfaces to the configuration memory and provides parallel access ports to the circuit design based on programmable resources. During the system run-time, a master device (typically an embedded microprocessor or Direct Memory Access (DMA)) may transfer partial reconfiguration bitstreams from the storage device to ICAP to accomplish dynamic reconfiguration. The complete ICAP design, in which the ICAP primitive is instantiated, interfaces to the system interconnection fabric to communicate with the processor and memories. In (Liu, Kuehn, Lu & Jantsch, 2009), (Delorme et al., 2009) and (Liu, Pittman & Forin, 2009), the authors explore the design space of ICAP IP module and present optimized designs. Through using either DDR or SRAM memories to hold partial bitstreams, these designs may achieve a run-time reconfiguration throughput of about 235 MB/s or close to 400 MB/s. The reconfiguration time overhead is linearly proportional to the size of partial bitstreams. Thus, a typical modular design of several tens or hundreds of KiloBytes in the partial bitstream requires several tens up to hundreds of microseconds (μs) for run-time reconfiguration.
The PR technology is coupled very closely to the underlying framework of the FPGA chip itself. We use the Xilinx FPGAs to explain the PR design flow as illustrated in Figure 6: The design begins from partitioning the system between the static base design and the reconfigurable part. Usually basic hardware infrastructures that expect continuous work

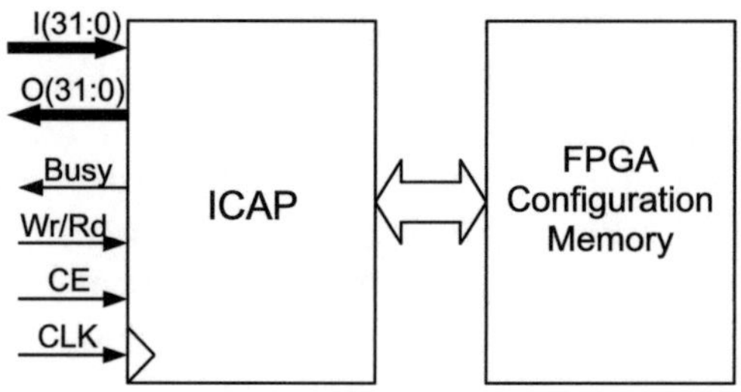

Fig. 5. The ICAP primitive on Xilinx FPGAs

and do not want to be unloaded or replaced during the operation are classfied into the static category, such as the system processor or the main memory controller. The partially reconfigurable part delegates those modules with dynamically swapping needs in the PR region. All the modular designs including PRMs are assembled to form an entire system. After synthesis, netlist files are generated for all the modules as well as the top-level system. The netlists serve as input files to the FPGA implementation. Before implementation, the Area Group (AG) constraints must be defined to prevent the logics in PRMs from being merged with the ones in the base design. Each PRR will be only restricted in the area defined by the RANGE constraints. Then after the following independent implementation of the base design and PR modules, the final step in the design flow is to merge them and create both the complete bitstream (with default PR modules equipped) and partial bitstreams for respective PR modules. Hence, the run-time reconfiguration process is initiated when one partial bitstream is loaded into the FPGA configuration memory and overwrites the corresponding segment.

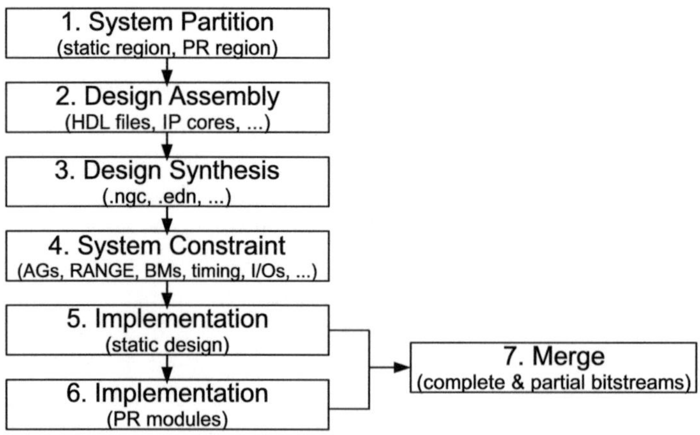

Fig. 6. Xilinx PR design flow

4. Design framework of adaptively reconfigurable peripherals

The modular design concept popularly adopted in static systems applies also to run-time reconfigurable designs on FPGAs. As we discussed in the previous section, the entire system is partitioned and different tasks are individually implemented as functional modules in dynamically reconfigurable designs. Analogous to software processes running on top of OSes and competing for the CPU time, each functional module can be regarded as a *hardware process* which is to be loaded into reconfigurable slots (i.e. PRRs) on the FPGA rather than General-Purpose microprocessors (GPCPU). Multiple hardware processes share the programmable resources and are scheduled to work according to certain types of disciplines on the awareness of computation requirements. Context switching happens when the current hardware process in charge of one task is leaving the reconfigurable slot (being overwritten) and another new task is to be loaded to start working. All these key issues in the adaptive computing framework are classified into and addressed within certain layers in hardware or software. Figure 7 demonstrates the layered hardware/software architecture and details in different aspects will be presented in the following subsections respectively.

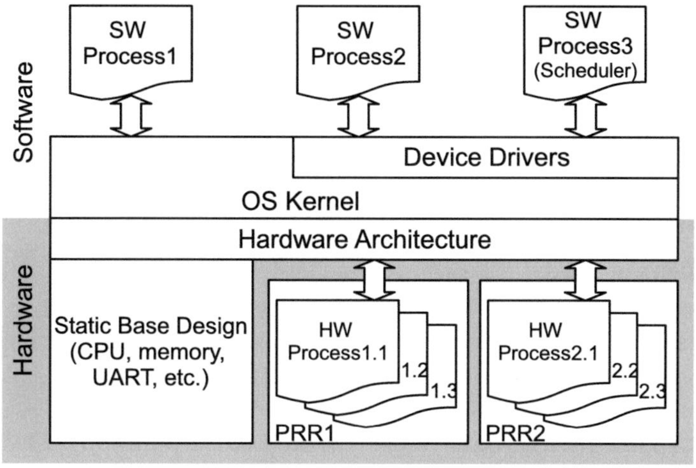

Fig. 7. Hardware/software layers of the adaptive reconfigurable system

4.1 Hardware structure

A dynamically reconfigurable platform may contain a general-purpose host computer system and application-specific functional modules. Figure 8 shows a system on a Xilinx Virtex-4 FPGA. Existing commercial IP cores can be exploited to quickly construct the general computer design, consisting of the processor core, the main DDR memory controller, peripherals, and the interconnection infrastructure using the PLB bus. In addition to the fundamental host computer system, run-time reconfigurable slots are reserved for being dynamically equipped with different functional modules. In the figure we show only one PRR to explain the principle. When incorporated in the PRR, PR modules communicate with the static base design, specifically the PLB bus for receiving controls from the processor and I/O buffers to external devices. Noting that the output signals of a PR module may unpredictably toggle during active reconfiguration, "disconnect" logic (illustrated in the callout frame in Figure 8) is required to be inserted to disable PRM outputs and isolate the unsteady signal state for the base design from being interfered. Furthermore, a dedicated "reset" signal aims to solely reset the newly loaded module after each partial reconfiguration. Both the "disconnect" and the separate "reset" signal can be driven by software-accessible General-Purpose I/Os (GPIO).

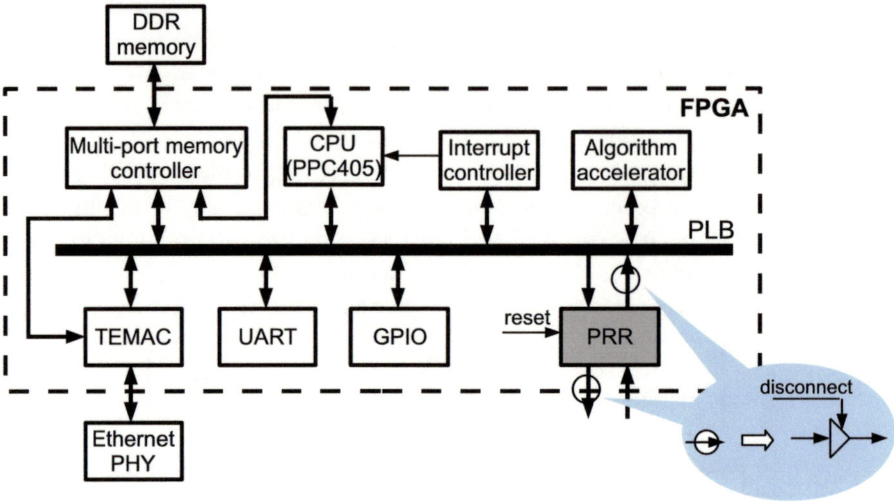

Fig. 8. The hardware infrastructure of the PR system

In the previous Xilinx Partial Reconfiguration Early Access design flow (Xilinx, 2008), a special type of component called Bus Macro (BM) must be instantiated to straddle the PR region and the static design, in order to lock the implementation routing between them. This is the particular treatment on the communication channels between the static and the dynamically reconfigurable regions. The BM components have been removed in the new PR design flow (Xilinx, 2010). They are no longer needed and the partition I/Os are automatically managed by the development software tool.

One significant advantage of this hardware structure, is that it conforms to the modular design appraoch: Different functional tasks are respectively implemented into IP cores. They are wrapped by the PLB interface and integrated in the bus-based system design. Normal static designs can be easily converted into a PR system by attentively treating the connection interface and mapping various functional modules in the same time-shared PR region. Little special consideration is needed to construct a PR system on the basis of conventional static designs.

4.2 OS and device drivers

As in conventional static designs, all hardware modules sharing a same reconfigurable slot can be managed by the host processor with or without OS support. In a standalone mode without OS, the processor addresses device components with low-level register accesses in application programs. While in OSes, device drivers are expected to be customized. In a Unix-like OS, common file operations are programmed to access devices (Corbet et al., 2005), including *"open"*, *"close"*, *"read"*, *"write"*, *"ioctl"*, etc. Interrupt handlers should also be implemented if the hardware provides interrupt services.

Different device components multiplexed in a same PR region are allowed to share the same physical address space for system bus addressing, due to their operation exclusiveness on the time axis. In order to match software operations with the equipped hardware component, two approaches can be adopted: Either a universal driver is customized for all the reconfigurable modules sharing a same PR region. Respective device operations are regulated and collected in the code. The ID number of PR modules is kept track of and passed to the driver, branching to the correct instructions according to the currently activated hardware module; or the drivers are separately compiled into software modules for different hardware components. The old driver is to be removed and the new one inserted, along with the presence of a newly loaded hardware device. Among these two approaches, the former one can avoid the driver module removing/inserting time overhead in the OS, while the latter one is more convenient for system upgrades when a new task is added to share a PR region.

Little special consideration or modification effort is required on the OS and device drivers for run-time reconfigurable systems in comparison with static designs. The most important thing to note, is to keep track of the presently activated module in the PRR and correctly match the driver software with the hardware. Otherwise the device module may suffer from misoperations.

4.3 Reconfiguration management

In dynamically reconfigurable designs, run-time module loading/unloading is managed by a scheduler. Analogous to the scheduler in an OS kernel which determines the active process for CPU execution, the scheduler in FPGA reconfigurable designs monitors trigger events and decides which functional module is to be configured next to utilize the reconfigurable slot. All hardware processes are preemptable and they must comply with the management from the scheduler. The scheduling policy may be implemented in hardware with Finit State Machines (FSM). However for more design convenience, it can be ported in the software application program running on the host processor with or without OS support. Distinguished from the kernel space scheduling in (So et al., 2006) and the management unit design in hardware in (Ito et al., 2006), the user space software scheduling possesses significant advantages of convenient portability to other platforms, avoidance of error-prone OS kernel modification, and flexibility to optimize scheduling disciplines. Scheduling policies are very flexible. But they have direct effect on the system performance and should be optimized according to concrete application requireiments, such as throughput or reaction latency. One general rule is to minimize the hardware context switching times, taking into account the dynamic reconfiguration time overhead and extra power dissipation needed during the reconfiguration process.

The scheduler program is only in charge of light-weight control work and usually does not feature intensive computation. In addition, the host CPU only initiates run-time reconfiguration by providing the bitstream storage address as well as the length, and it is actually the master block or the DMA component in the ICAP designs that transports the configuration data (Delorme et al., 2009; Liu, Kuehn, Lu & Jantsch, 2009; Liu, Pittman & Forin, 2009). Therefore dynamic reconfiguration scheduling does not typically take much CPU time, especially when the trigger events of module switching happen only infrequently and the scheduler is informed by CPU interrupts.

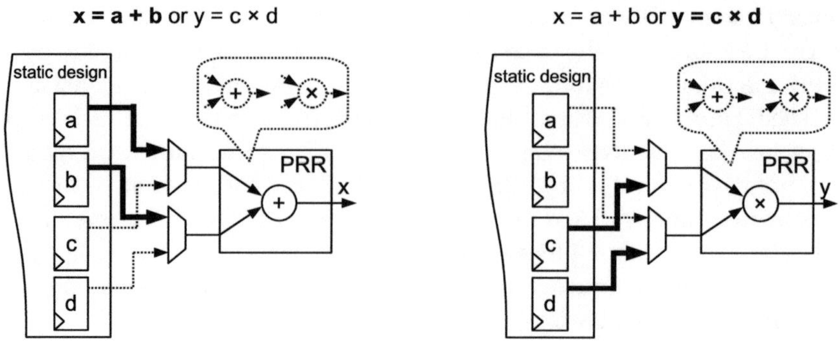

(a) x = a + b (b) y = c × d

Fig. 9. Contextless module switching in the reconfigurable design

4.4 Context switching

The context of hardware processes refers to the buffered incoming raw data, intermediate calculation results and control parameters in registers or on-chip memory blocks residing in the shared resources of PR regions or static interface blocks. In some applications, it becomes contextless when the buffered raw data are completely consumed and no intermediate state is needed to be recorded. Thus the scheduler may simply swap out an active PR module. After some time when it resumes, a module reset will be adequate to restore its operation. Otherwise, context saving and restoring must be accomplished. Figure 9 and 10 respectively demonstrate these two circumstances: In the design in Figure 9, two dynamically reconfigurable functional modules (adder and multiplier) do not share the interface registers and they both feature pure conbinational logic in using the PRR. Hence during each time when the PRR is reconfigured with an arithmetic operator, the register values in the interface block are not needed to be saved or restored in order to obtain correct results of *x* and *y*. By contrast in the design of Figure 10, the operand registers in the static interface are shared and the reconfigurable region also contains the context of one operand for the addition operation. Therefore in case of module switching, the operands of the former operation must be saved in the system memory, and the ones for the recently resumed operator are to be restored.
Generally speaking, two approaches can be employed to address the context saving and restoring issue: In case of small amounts of parameters or intermediate results, register accesses can efficiently read out the context into external memories and restore it when the corresponding hardware module resumes (Huang & Hsiung, 2008). When there are large quantities of data buffered in on-chip memory blocks, the ICAP interface can be utilized to read out the bitstream and extract the storage values for context saving (Kalte & Porrmann, 2005). In order to avoid the design effort and large time overhead in the latter case, an alternative solution is to intentionally generate some periodic "pause" states without any context for the data processing module. Context switching can be then delayed by the scheduler until meeting a pause state.

4.5 Inter-process communication

Reconfigurable modules (hardware processes) placed at run-time may need to exchange data among each other. With respect to those modules that are located in different PR regions,

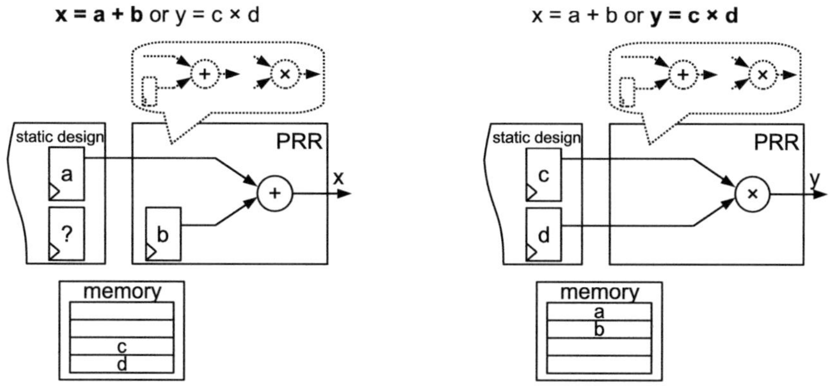

(a) x = a + b (b) y = c × d

Fig. 10. Context saving and restoring in the reconfigurable design

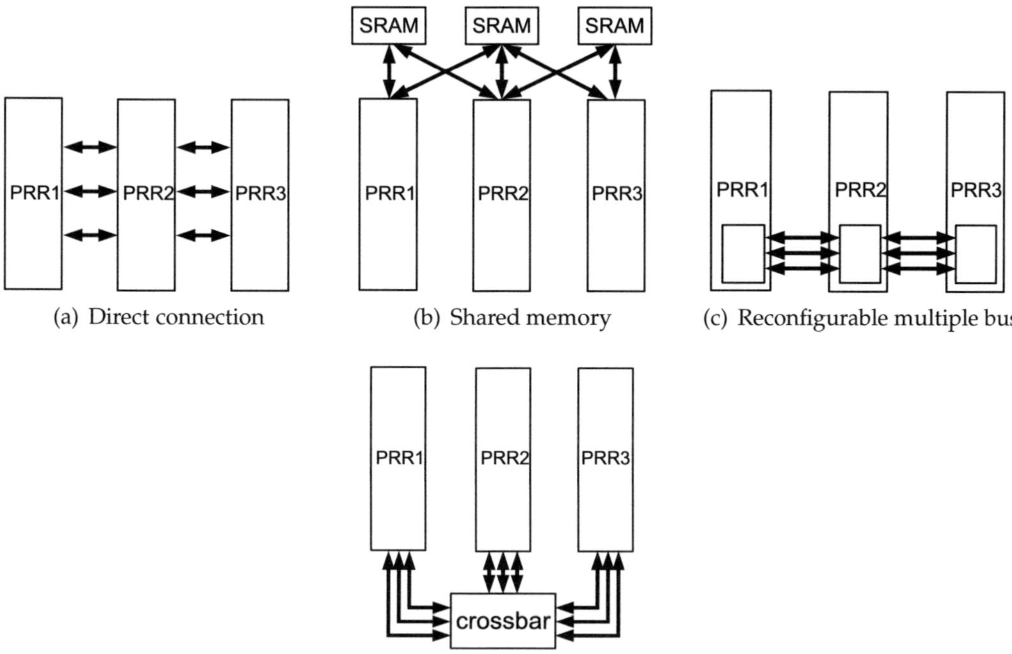

(a) Direct connection (b) Shared memory (c) Reconfigurable multiple bus

(d) Crossbar

Fig. 11. Inter-process communication approaches among PRRs (Majer et al., 2007)

they can communicate through canonical approaches as in static designs. For example Figure 11 demonstrates some general solutions for inter-PRR communications, including direct connection, shared memory, Reconfigurable Multiple Bus (RMB) (Ahmadinia et al., 2005; Elgindy et al., 1996), and crossbar. Detailed description on these approaches can be found in (Majer et al., 2007) and (Fekete et al., 2006), in which inter-module communications have been intensively investigated in dynamically reconfigurable designs.

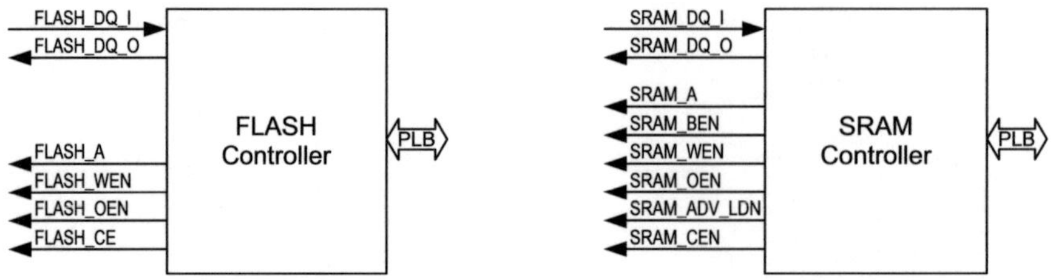

(a) Flash controller (b) SRAM controller

Fig. 12. Blackboxes of the flash controller and the SRAM controller

More generally, communications among PR modules that are time-multiplexed in the same reconfigurable slot may also exist and be required in the hardware implementation. In this circumstance, static buffer devices must be employed to hold the IPC information while the PRR is being dynamically reconfigured (Liu et al., 2010). As the producer module is active to work, the IPC information is injected into the buffer. Afterwards the consumer module may take the place of the producer in the reconfigurable slot and digest the IPC data destined to it. The buffer device can either directly interface to the PRR, or be located in the main memory and accessed via interconnection architectures such as the system bus. The concrete IPC using this approach for the reconfigurable controller design will be revisited in the next section.

5. Reconfigurable design of flash/SRAM controllers

5.1 Hardware/software design

Both the flash and the SRAM controllers are picked up from the Xilinx IP library. We do not concern their in-depth design details, but simply regard them as blackboxes instead with communication interfaces demonstrated in Figure 12. In the figure, the left side is the interface to external memory devices (Flash or SRAM) and the right side is to the system bus.

Figure 13 shows the hardware structure: An off-chip asynchronous NOR flash memory and a synchronous SRAM share the same data, address and control bus I/O pads of the FPGA. These two chips are exclusively selected by the "CE" signal. The flash and the SRAM controllers are both slave devices on the system bus. They are selectively activated in the reserved PRR by run-time partial reconfiguration. In order to isolate the unsteady output signals from the PRR during active reconfiguration, "disconnect" logic is inserted in both interfaces between the controllers and the PLB bus or external devices. Moreover, a dedicated "reset" signal takes charge of solely reseting the newly loaded module after each run-time reconfiguration. Both the "disconnect" and the separate "reset" signals are driven by a GPIO core under the control of the host processor.

An open-source Linux kernel runs on the host PowerPC 405 processor. To manage run-time operations in Linux, device drivers for hardware IP cores have been brought up to provide programming interfaces to application programs. We configure the open-source Memory Technology Device (MTD) driver (Woodhouse, 2005) to support NOR flash accesses in Linux. Other drivers are customized specifically for the LUT block in SRAM, PLB_GPIO and MST_HWICAP. With drivers loaded, device nodes will show up in the "/dev" directory of the Linux file system, and can be accessed by predefined file operations. The drivers are

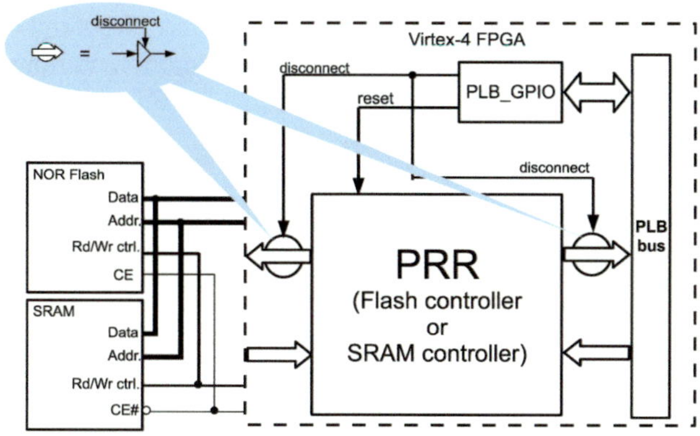

Fig. 13. Hardware structure of the flash/SRAM PR design

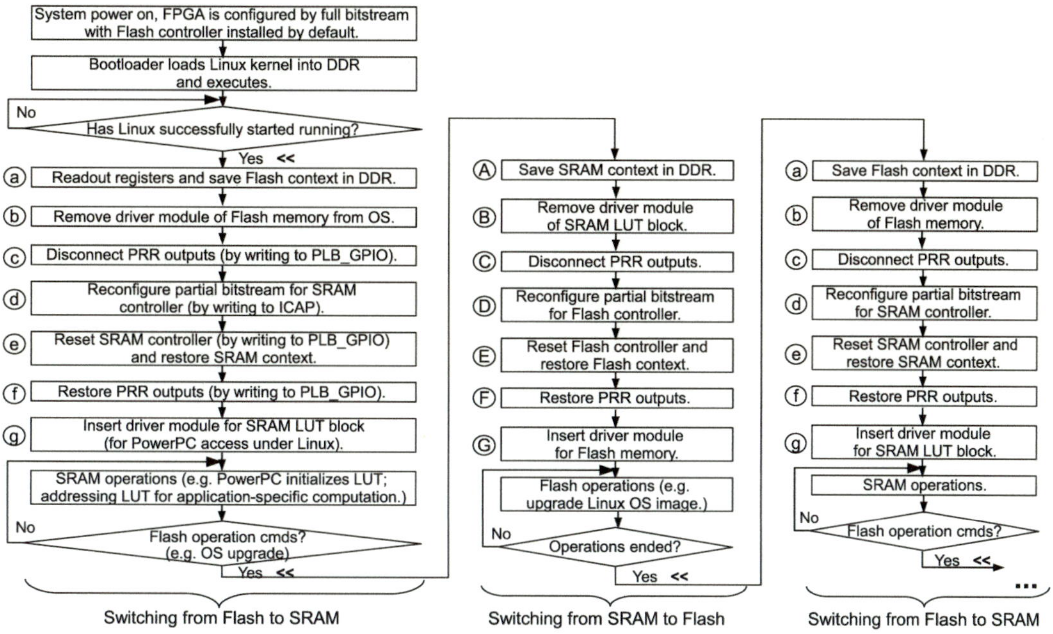

Fig. 14. Flow chart of multiplexing flash/SRAM in Linux

compiled into modules. They will be inserted into the OS kernel when the corresponding device hardware is configured, or removed when not needed any longer.

The hardware process scheduler is implemented in a C program. It detects the memory access requirements on flash or SRAM from either the system interior or external user commands, and meanwhile manages the work sequence of both types of memories. Figure 14 shows a flow chart, in which the scheduler alternately loads the flash and the SRAM controller with context awareness. During the device module reconfiguration, the Linux OS as well as the remaining hardware system keeps running without breaks. In this figure, steps labeled with "a - g" are used to dynamically configure the SRAM controller, and the ones labeled with

"A - G" are to load the flash controller. Events marked by the symbol "$\ll$" are detected by the scheduler to trigger hardware context switching. Main switching steps before device operations include:

1. To save the register context of the to-be-unloaded device in DDR variables if necessary.
2. To remove the driver module of the to-be-unloaded device from the OS.
3. To disconnect the PRR outputs for isolating its unsteady state during active reconfiguration from the static design.
4. To dynamically load the partial bitstream of the expected controller by initiating the MST_HWICAP core.
5. To solely reset the newly loaded device controller, and recover its register context if there exists.
6. To re-enable the PRR outputs, restoring the communication links from the PRR to the static design.
7. To insert the corresponding device driver in the OS, for the processor access with high-level application software.

After these steps, the recently equipped controller module becomes ready for memory accesses on the NOR flash or the SRAM.
In this design, IPC operations can be realized through the third-party shared memory such as DDR. For example when the system is just powered on, the SRAM LUT initialization data are retrieved from the nonvolatile flash and buffered in the system DDR memory. After the flash controller is unloaded and the SRAM controller is activated in the PRR by dynamic reconfiguration, the LUT data are then migrated into the SRAM chip for application-specific computation. The IPC data flow is illustrated in Figure 15.

5.2 Results

Through enabling either the flash controller or the SRAM controller with system self-awareness, multitasking has been accomplished within a single reconfigurable slot on the FPGA. Figure 16 demonstrates the rectangular shape of the reserved PR region on a Virtex-4 FX20 FPGA layout, as well as two controller implementations after place-and-route. The reconfigurable design results in a more efficient utilization of hardware resources, as listed in Table 1. We understand that both the flash memory controller and the SRAM controller must be concurrently placed in the static system design, implying a total resource consumption equivalent to the sum of both device modules. A PR region is reserved in the reconfigurable design, sufficiently large to accommodate all kinds of needed resources of both device modules. Moreover, a little more resource margin is added for the place-and-route convenience of the software tool. In contrast to the conventional static approach, we observe that the reconfigurable system saves 43.7% LUTs, 33.8% slice registers and 47.9% I/O pads, with both flash and SRAM services realized. The reduced resource requirement not only enables to fit a large system design on small FPGA chips for lower hardware cost, but also makes the I/O pads shared and simplifys the Printed Circuit Board (PCB) routing.

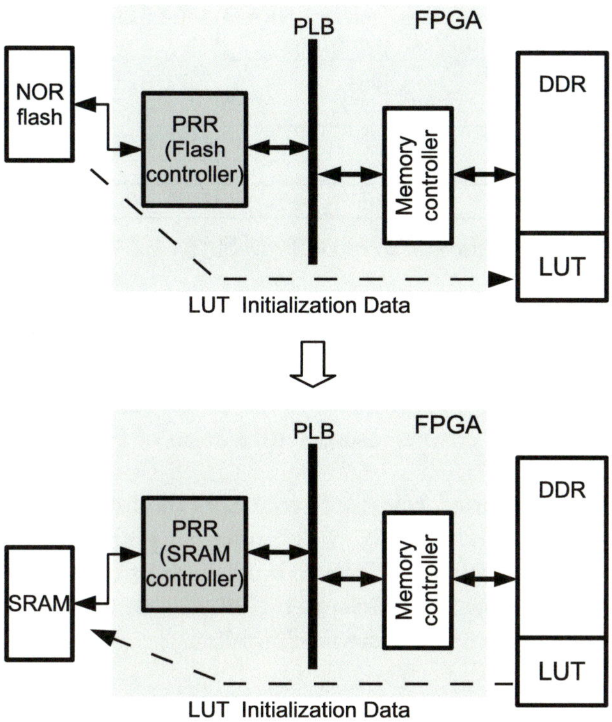

Fig. 15. Migrating LUT initialization data from the flash memory to the SRAM

(a) The flash implementation in PRR

(b) The SRAM implementation in PRR

Fig. 16. Implementation of the flash and the SRAM controller within the PRR on a Virtex-4 FX20 FPGA

6. Conclusion

Based on the FPGA run-time reconfigurability, we present a dynamically reconfigurable NOR flash controller for embedded designs. This technique is motivated by the operation occasionality of the flash memory and the resultant programmable resource waste on the FPGA, when adopting the conventional static development approach. We discuss the

Resources	Static flash controller	Static SRAM controller	Total	PRR	Resource saving
4-input LUTs	923	954	1877	1056	43.7%
Slice Flip-Flops	867	728	1595	1056	33.8%
I/O pads	56	61	117	61	47.9%

Table 1. Resource utilization of the static/reconfigurable flash/SRAM designs

design framework of adaptively reconfigurable peripherals in this chapter, concerning various aspects in hardware and software. In the practical experiment, a reserved reconfigurable slot is time-shared by the flash memory controller and an SRAM controller. Both system requirements of accessing the flash memory and the SRAM are equally accomplished in the reconfigurable design, with much less resource utilization of FPGA LUTs, slice registers as well as I/O pads.

This design technique is not limited to memory controller modules, but can apply to all kinds of modular devices operating exclusively. In addition, system functionalities can be later extended by adding more functional modules to time-share a same reconfigurable slot. It not only enhances the resource utilization efficiency on FPGAs, but also enables the possibility of future firmware upgrade without hardware modification.

7. Acknowledgment

This work was supported in part by BMBF under contract Nos. 06GI9107I and 06GI9108I, FZ-Jülich under contract No. COSY-099 41821475, HIC for FAIR, and WTZ: CHN 06/20. The authors also thank Xilinx Inc. for the software donation.

8. References

Ahmadinia, A., Bobda, C., Ding, J., Majer, M., Teich, J., Fekete, S. & van der Veen, J. (2005). A practical approach for circuit routing on dynamic reconfigurable devices, *Proceedings of the IEEE International Workshop on Rapid System Prototyping*, pp. 84–90.

Corbet, J., Rubini, A. & Kroah-Hartman, G. (2005). *Linux Device Drivers (Third Edition)*, O'REILLY & Associates, Inc.

Delorme, J., Nafkha, A., Leray, P. & Moy, C. (2009). New opbhwicap interface for realtime partial reconfiguration of fpga, *Proceedings of the International Conference on Reconfigurable Computing and FPGAs*, pp. 386–391.

Dillien, P. (2009). An overview of fpga market dynamics. SOCcentral webpage. URL: *http://www.soccentral.com*

Dunlap, C. & Fischaber, T. (2010). Partial reconfiguration user guide. UG702, Xilinx Inc.

Elgindy, H. A., Somani, A. K., Schroeder, H., Schmeck, H. & Spray, A. (1996). Rmb Íc a reconfigurable multiple bus network, *Proceedings of the International Symposium on High-Performance Computer Architecture*, pp. 108–117.

Fekete, S., van der Veen, J., Majer, M. & Teich, J. (2006). Minimizing communication cost for reconfigurable slot modules, *Proceedings of the International Conference on Field Programmable Logic and Applications*, pp. 1–6.

Huang, C. & Hsiung, P. (2008). Software-controlled dynamically swappable hardware design in partially reconfigurable systems, *EURASIP Journal on Embedded Systems* 2008: 1–11.

Hubner, M., Schuck, C. & Becker, J. (2006). Elementary block based 2-dimensional dynamic and partial reconfiguration for virtex-ii fpgas, *Proceedings of the International Parallel and Distributed Processing Symposium*.

IBM (2007). 128-bit processor local bus architecture specifications. Version 4.7, IBM Inc.

Ito, T., Mishou, K., Okuyama, Y. & Kuroda, K. (2006). A hardware resource management system for adaptive computing on dynamically reconfigurable devices, *Proceedings of the Japan-China Joint Workshop on Frontier of Computer Science and Technology*, pp. 196–202.

Kalte, H. & Porrmann, M. (2005). Context saving and restoring for multitasking in reconfigurable systems, *Proceedings of the International Conference on Field Programmable Logic and Applications*, pp. 223–228.

Kao, C. (2005). Benefits of partial reconfiguration, *Xcell Journal* Fourth Quarter: 65–67.

Kuon, I. & Rose, J. (2006). Measuring the gap between fpgas and asics, *Proceedings of the International Symposium on Field-Programmable Gate Arrays*, ACM Press, pp. 21–30.

Liu, M., Kuehn, W., Lu, Z. & Jantsch, A. (2009). Run-time partial reconfiguration speed investigation and architectural design space exploration, *Proceedings of the International Conference on Field Programmable Logic and Applications*, pp. 498–502.

Liu, M., Lu, Z., Kuehn, W. & Jantsch, A. (2010). Inter-process communications using pipes in fpga-based adaptive computing, *Proceedings of the IEEE Computer Society Annual Symposium on VLSI*, p. 80.

Liu, S., Pittman, R. N. & Forin, A. (2009). Minimizing partial reconfiguration overhead with fully streaming dma engines and intelligent icap controller, *Technical Report MSR-TR-2009-150*, Microsoft Research.

Lu, S., Yiannacouras, P., Suh, T., Kassa, R. & Konow, M. (2008). A desktop computer with a reconfigurable *pentium*®, *ACM Transactions on Reconfigurable Technology and Systems* 1(1): 1–15.

Majer, M., Teich, J., Ahmadinia, A. & Bobda, C. (2007). The erlangen slot machine: A dynamically reconfigurable fpga-based computer, *The Journal of VLSI Signal Processing* 47(1): 15–31.

So, H. K., Tkachenko, A. & Brodersen, R. (2006). A unified hardware/software runtime environment for fpga-based reconfigurable computers using borph, *Proceedings of the International Conference on Hardware/Software Codesign and System Synthesis*, pp. 259–264.

Wilton, S., Kafafi, N., Wu, J., Bozman, K., Aken'Ova, V. & Saleh, R. (2005). Design considerations for soft embedded programmable logic cores, *IEEE Journal of Solid-State Circuits* 40(2): 485–497.

Woodhouse, D. (2005). Memory technology device (mtd) subsystem for linux. MTD webpage. URL: *http://linux-mtd.infradead.org/archive/index.html*

Xilinx (2004). Two flows for partial reconfiguration: Module based or difference based. XAPP290, Xilinx Inc.

Xilinx (2006). Plb external memory controller (plb emc) (2.00a). DS418, Xilinx Inc.

Xilinx (2008). Early access partial reconfiguration user guide for ise 9.2.04i. UG208, Xilinx Inc.

Xilinx (2010). Partial reconfiguration user guide. UG702, Xilinx Inc.

Zuchowski, P., Reynolds, C., Grupp, R., Davis, S., Cremen, B. & Troxel, B. (2002). A hybrid asic and fpga architecture, *Proceedings of the International Conference on Computer-Aided Design*, pp. 187–194.

8

Programming Flash Memory in Freescale S08/S12/CordFire MCUs Family

Yihuai Wang and Jin Wu
Soochow University
China

1. Introduction

The features of Flash memory include electrically erasable, no back-up power to protect data, in-circuit programming, high-density memory, low-cost and so on, which rapidly increase the using of Flash memory in embedded system.

The programming methods of Flash memory include Programmer Mode and In-Circuit Programmer Mode. Programmer Mode means erasing/programming Flash by programming tool (programmer), with the purpose of writing programs into MCU[1]. In-Circuit Programmer Mode means erasing/programming some region of Flash by MCU's internal programs during run time, with the purpose of saving relevant data and preventing from lost after power off. Take AW60/XS128/MCF52233 in Freescale 8/16/32bits S08/S12/ColdFire serials' MCUs for example, we elaborate the In-Circuit Programming method of Flash memory in this chapter. The programming method of the other MCUs in the whole Freescale S08/S12/ColdFire MCU family is similar. Besides, we discuss the protection mechanisms and security operations for AW60/XS128/MCF52233 Flash memory. Some instances are also provided in this chapter.

1.1 Flash memory characteristics

The most perfect memory should be a high-speed, non-volatile, low-cost and high-density memory. But only one or several specialties are implemented in general memory. With the maturity of its technology, flash memory has become an ideal memory in recent years. It is endowed with characteristics such as electrical erasure, data preservation without power supply, in-system programming, high storage density, low power consumption and low cost. These are just what MCU are expecting, because MCU with internal flash memory introduced in earlier years has some shortages in reliability and stability. With the maturity of the Flash technology, now more and more above characteristics are integrated to MCU and become an important part of it. Hence flash memory makes MCU progress enormously.

Flash memory is really a high-density, high-performance reading/writing memory with non-volatility, low-power and high-reliability and has the following characteristics comparing with old solid state memory.

---

[1] MCU – Microcontroller Unit

1. Non-volatility: Flash memory protects data without power supply the same as magnetic storage.
2. Easy-updating: Comparing with old EPROM[2], the electrical erasure of flash memory shortens the programming cycle for developers and makes end users' updating memory become true.
3. Low-cost, high-density and reliability: The parameters are much better than EEPROM (or E2PROM).

1.2 Flash memory program concepts

In many embedded systems, the memory which can protect program parameters and important data without external power supply is necessary as EEPROM previously was. The ColdFire MCU family provides the function of in-system programming of flash memory in user mode instead of EEPROM, hence making the circuit design simpler and cost lower.
However, different from the reading/writing of generic RAM, flash memory operations need two special processes—Erase and Program. The former, which converts all bits to 1, consists of mass erase and page erase. The latter, which converts bit to 0, can program only one word at a time. During erasing and programming, voltage higher than the power is usually needed and it is generated by Coldfire MCU inner electric charge pump. Besides, before programming, it should be insured that the program field has not been written after last erasure. That is, the field is blank (the content is $FF). So generally, erase should be carried out before perform.

1.3 In-circuit programming concepts of flash memory

In-circuit programming of flash memory in user mode (U-ICP) is a technique by which user programs stored in flash memory can modify data or programs also stored in the flash memory during run time. The electrically erasable characteristics of flash memory allow such programs to execute erase or write functions. This important branch of computer technology, an outgrowth of embedded systems development, makes it possible to update embedded programs, provide power-off protection and the recovery of important parameters, and modify the static parameters of embedded applications. In addition, U-ICP improves the expansibility and upgradeability of embedded systems. Portions of flash memory can substitute for the traditional EEPROM functions mentioned above, increasing system stability. And make the circuit design simpler and cost lower.
U-ICP was introduced to MCU technology by the semiconductor department of Motorola (now called Freescale) in 2000, and has been widely applied and developed ever since. However, different from the reading/writing of generic RAM, flash memory operations need two special processes—Erase and Program. The former, which converts all bits to 1, consists of mass erase and page erase. The latter, which converts bit to 0, can program only one word at a time. During erasing and programming, voltage higher than the power is usually needed and it is generated by Freescale S08/S12/CordFire MCU inner electric charge pump. Besides, before programming, it should be insured that the program field has not been written after last erasure. That is, the field is blank (the content is $FF). So generally, erase should be carried out before perform.
U-ICP can erase and reprogram other regions of flash memory by executing internal flash functions, but these may also prove unstable at high voltage. This problem, which is indicated

[2] EEPROM—Electrically Programmable Read-Only-Memory

in the data sheet of the Freescale S08/S12/CordFire MCU family, has not yet been solved by hardware design. It can be solved on the software level, by proper design of the U-ICP bottom driver program. So we describe an embedded software engineering rule that should improve the stability of the general erase and write functions in U-ICP for any flash device.

2. Programming flash in freescale MC9S08AW60 MCU

The flash memory in-circuit programming implement for 8bit MC9S08AW60 MCU will be explained in this section, as follows:

2.1 How to operate MC9S08AW60 flash memory

2.1.1 MC9S08AW60 Flash memory-mapping

S08 serials MCUs' addressable address space is 64Kbyte, which ranges from \$0000 ~ \$FFFF. This addressing range is divided into different sectors. Each sector has different function. The memory map of AW60 MCU is shown in Fig.1, which includes the address distribution of 2KB RAM[3], 2 parts of Flash memory and some I/O image registers.

As can be seen from the Fig.1, the Flash memory of AW60 is divided into two parts in this 64K memory address space. These addresses range from \$0870~\$17FF(3984 bytes) and \$1860~\$FFFF(59296 bytes). Among \$1860~\$FFFF only the addresses range from \$1860~\$FFAF can be used to erase and program user program. The addresses range from \$FFB0~\$FFBF are the 16 bytes non-volatile registers region and the addresses range from \$FFC0~\$FFFF are the 64 bytes interrupt vector region.

Flash memory is organized by page and row in the chip. The size of each page is 512 bytes. And the size of each row is 64 bytes. There are about 60K bytes of Flash memory address space in AW60, the page addresses are rounding 512 in \$0000~\$FFFF. For example, the first page's address of Flash memory in the 3984bytes region (\$0870~\$17FF) is \$1000~\$11FF, instead of \$0870~\$0A6F.

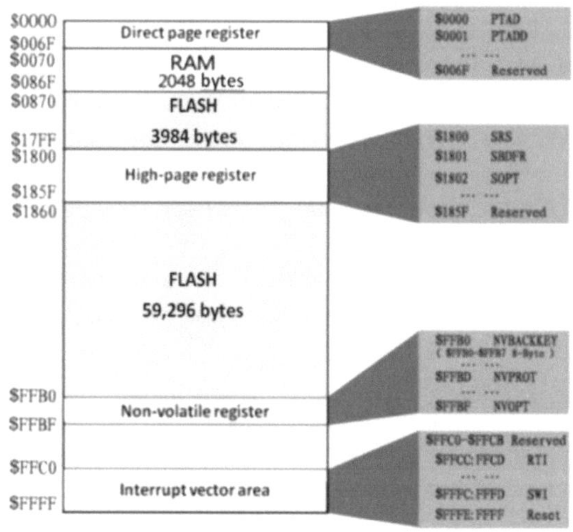

Fig. 1. The memory map of AW60 MCU

[3]RAM—Random Access Memory

For S08 serials MCU (AW60, etc.), we can do mass erasing operation for the Flash memory, or can erasing one page(512 bytes) from a certain start address. But we can't only erase a certain byte or some bytes which are less than 512 bytes. Noting this feature, it is important for the data arranging. The programming operation of AW60 is based on row (64 bytes). The data which can be programmed continuously at a time is only within one row. Certainly, the region that has not been erased can't be programmed.

As can be seen from the above, in order to program Flash memory, we should prepare a set of data and move them into RAM, then erase the corresponding region of Flash memory, so programming operation can be done. Because erasing /programming a certain byte of Flash memory will influence the follow-up one page, it is necessary to reasonably arrange the relevant data of erasing region before erasing/programming the Flash.

2.1.2 MC9S08AW60 FLASH registers and control bits

In AW60, Erasing and programming operations relate to registers such as FCDIV、FOPT、FCNFG、FPROT、FSTAT and FCMD. Their corresponding addresses are $1820、$1821、$1823、$1824、$1825 and $1826. For the detailed function and use of these registers, please refer to the Reference Manual "*MC9S08AW60 Data Sheet (HCS08 Microcontrollers)*"[1].

2.1.3 Flash programming procedure

1. The execution steps of Flash commands
   a. Write a data in an address of Flash. The address and data information will be locked into Flash interface. For blank check command, the data information is an arbitrary value; For page erase command, the address information is either one of the address in erase page (512 bytes) addresses; For blank check and mass erase commands, the address information is either one of the address in flash.
   b. Write the commands which are needed to be executed into FCMD.
   c. Execute commands. The FCBEF bit of FSTAT register is set, simultaneously execute the commands in the FCMD.
2. The flowcharts of the Flash programming

When programming flash, we need follow strict timing process. Fig.2 gives the programming flowchart with the other flash commands (not include the command "burst mode byte program"). Writing a byte with burst mode command is very different from the execution with other commands. Burst mode means a lot of continuous data need to be written into Flash. Each time a write command has been executed, the writing high voltage in flash will not be removed, which will speed up the write speed of data; But for other commands, the high voltage is given to ensure the command executing, and the high voltage is immediately removed when the command ended. The programming flowchart with burst mode command is shown in Fig.3.

3. Flash Memory Illegal Operations

   In the following processing, an error occurs, and the FACCERR bit is automatically set.
   a. Writing the flash memory before initializing FCDIV register.
   b. Writing the flash memory while FCBEF is not set.
   c. Writing the second command to the FCMD register before executing the previously written command。
   d. After write the flash memory, initializing the other flash control registers in addition to FCMD.

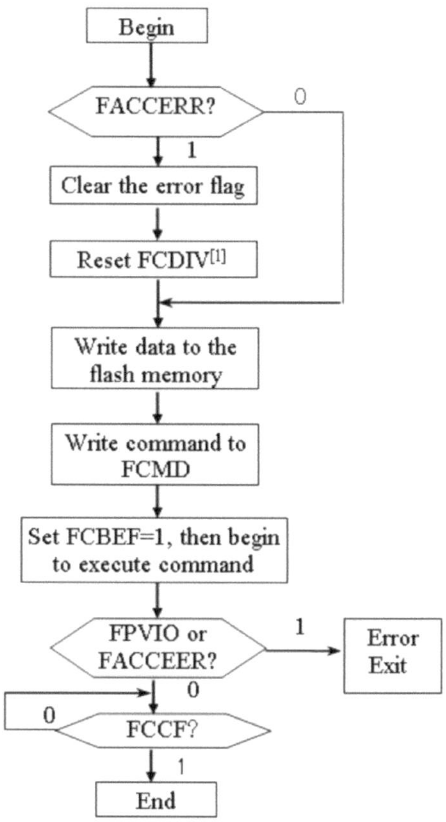

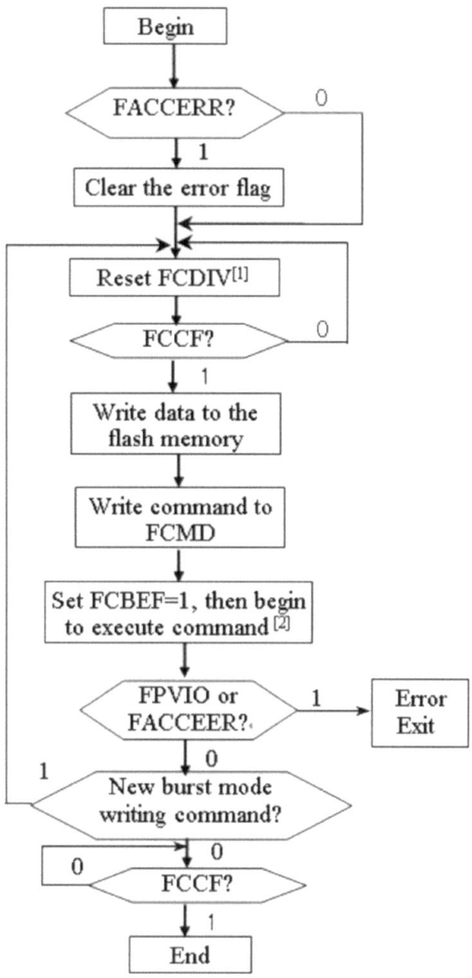

Note: [1]Write once after resetting.
[2]Wait at least 4 bus cycles before check FCBEF or FCCF.

Fig. 2. AW60 Flash programming flowchart

Fig. 3. AW60 Flash burst mode programming flowchart

e. Writing an invalid flash normal mode command to the FCMD register.
f. Try to operate the other registers in addition to FSTAT after finished writing command values to FCMD.
g. MCU enters into STOP mode when execute the command.
h. When MCU is in secure state, erase pages or write flash memory with background debug interface (If MCU is in encrypted state, we can only execute blank check or mass erase commands with background debug interface).
i. Aborting a command write sequence by writing 0 to the FCBEF flag.

2.2 MC9S08AW60 flash memory in-circuit programming instance

We first give the AW60's Flash programming subroutine in this section. Then put forward the Flash in-circuit programming instance in user mode. And verify the result by the serial communication mode with PC.

2.2.1 The erasing and programming c language subroutines of flash memory

For the Flash programming subroutines are not solidified in the internal monitoring ROM[4] of AW60, the initial loaded user program should contain the flash erasing and programming subroutines in order to do in-circuit programming for Flash. Because these subroutines resident in Flash, when running the erasing/programming subroutines, the whole Flash region will be added programming voltage that is higher than the normal operating voltage, which results in instable Flash region's reading, and may lead to program's error running. In order to make the erasing/programming subroutines running normally, these subroutines should be moved into RAM and run in RAM. Therefore, a buffer should be opened up in RAM to store these subroutines. The following sample program gives a convenient method to save the machine codes which are generated by erasing/programming subroutines in RAM. The machine codes include 57 bytes. Necessarily, you can directly call these codes to implement the Flash in-circuit erasing/programming. For the detailed Erasing and Programming subroutines, please refer to the program in our program directory "*..\Flash_Program\S08(AW60)-Flash*"[5]. These subroutines contain the following operations:

1. Some public operation of erasing/programming processing

For the codes of erasing/programming operation must run in RAM, so we write the C language program according to Fig.2. After being compiled, the corresponding machine code bytes are saved in the array PGM (volatile unsigned char PGM[57]). Therefore we need not copy the codes to RAM to realize the erasing/programming operations.

2. Page erasing subroutine (*Flash_PageErase*)

In this subroutine we should calculate the page's top address by the page number, and change the Flash command to erasing command 0x40, then call and execute the erasing codes.

3. Flash programming subroutine

In this subroutine we calculate the top programming address according to the page number and page offset, then change the Flash command to erasing command 0x20, and program flash one byte by one byte.

2.2.2 Programming essentials of erasing /programming subroutines

Using Flash in-circuit programming technology eliminates the need for external EEPROM, which not only simplify the circuit design, but also improve the stability of system. We compile the Flash programs and save them in Flash. When you need to use these codes, they will be copied to RAM. Just because of this special procedure, we put forward the following notes according to the experience which is accumulated in the actual programming and debugging, and project development process.

1. There are 57 bytes in RAM to store the erasing/programming machine codes, don't forget to calculate when using RAM.
2. The region that has been erased for one time and has not been programmed can be programmed by calling Flash programming subroutine again, but the region that has been programmed can't be programmed again if it hasn't been erased.

---

[4] ROM—Read Only Memory

[5] You can download the program directory "*Flash_Program*" in our website (http://sumcu.suda.edu.cn/flash.htm), which involves three Flash programming instances in three subdirectory ("*\S08(AW60)-Flash*", "\ S12X(XS128)-Flash" and "\ ColdFire(MCF52233)-Flash").

3. For we do erasing for one page (512 bytes) each time, so we should arrange the data reasonably to avoid wrong erasing.
4. The start address of the page should be defined according to the rules of the FPROT register.
5. It is invalid to do in-circuit programming for the protection block set in FPROT.

2.2.3 Validate flash memory implements

In order to more clearly understand the method of Flash memory in-circuit programming, we give a flash memory validating project. Its function is as the following: the MCU receives formatted data from PC[6] by SCI[7] tools and erases, programs or reads its flash memory. The PC software is any SCI testing tool.
Now, list some flash operating commands using the SCI debug (as shown in Table 1):

Commands	Functions
?	MCU sends some items to PC
E:8	Erase page 8
R:8:0:4	Read 4 bytes the word 0 of page 8
W:8:0:4:A,C,B,D	Write "ACBD" (4 bytes) to the word 0 of page 8
B:8,7,6,5,4,3,2,1	Set the Flash back door key, the password is "87654321"
M:8,7,6,5,4,3,2,1	Verify the Flash back door key, the password is "87654321"
D	Delete passwords
U	Encryption lift
P:8	Protect block, protect the addresses from 8 to 0xFFFF

Table 1. Flash operating commands using the SCI debug

Above examples only give the program data less than one page (512 bytes). Only slightly modify the program, you can program data that exceeds one page.

2.3 Protection mechanisms and security operations of MC9S08AW60 flash memory

2.3.1 Protection mechanisms

Being a non-volatile memory (NVM), flash memory may be used by programmers to store some important parameters and data. To prevent from erasing or programming these significant regions by accident, the MC9S08AW60 MCU supplies protection mechanisms for its flash memory. That's to say, it can't erase or program the protected region.
The Flash Protect Register (FPROT and NVPROT [1]) is interrelated with the protection mechanisms of S08 flash memory. And for the register's bit definition and programming method you can refer to the reference manual [1]. By setting this register, we can protect the Flash memory.

---

[6] PC—Personal Computer
[7] SCI—Serial Communication Interface

For the programming codes for setting block protection, please refer to the program in our program directory "..\ *Flash_Program\ S08(AW60)-Flash*"

2.3.2 Security operations

The debug module is added in the S08 series MCUs, which increased the practicality of the chip, and brought risks to the security of the chip. In order to ensure the safety of the chip, the security mechanisms are much more complex.

S08 series MCUs use hardware mechanisms to prevent unauthorized users trying to access the Flash and RAM memory data. Having been set security, Flash and RAM are all counted as secure resources. But the direct page register, high-end page register and background debugging module are all counted as unsecure resources. During executing process, we can access any memory data, but can't access secure sources by background debugging interface or unsafe method.

The security can be set by the nonvolatile data bit SEC01 ：SEC00 in FOPT. Table.2 gives the security state of MCU.

SEC01:SEC00	state
0:0	Secure
0:1	Secure
1:0	Unsecure
1:1	Secure

Table 2. Security state

1. Set MCU to Security Mode

To prevent the programs in the flash memory from being read out illegally, the MCU should be set in security mode. Two methods for locking the flash memory are shown in the following.

Method A. Lock the MCU by modifying the security configuration field in the file isr.c(that is, modify the values of the FOPT's address 0xFFBF and the key's address 0xFFB0~0xFFB7).

Method B. we can lock the flash memory by calling the custom subroutine Flash_Secure to modify relevant address matters when the program is running. By modify the content in the address of NVOPT, the value of this register are automatically loaded in FPOT while the system is set. For the detailed *Flash_secure* subroutine, please refer to the program in our program directory "..\ *Flash_Program\ S08(AW60)-Flash*"

2. Unlock from Security Mode

If we want to program locked S08 serials MCU again, we should unlock it. Here two methods are provided to unlock it.

Method A. Use the BDM interface of our writer, mass erase the locked MCU. (The writer is designed by our lab.)

Method B. Call the subroutine *Flash_KEY_Match* to erase password or flash by memory-resident program. For the detailed *Flash_KEY_Match* subroutine, please refer to the program in our program directory "..\ *Flash_Program\ S08(AW60)-Flash*"

3. Programming flash memory in freescale S12XS128

The flash memory in-circuit programming implement for 16bit S12XS128 MCU will be explained in this section, as follows:

3.1 How to operate S12XS128 flash memory

3.1.1 The paging mechanism and MMC module in XS128 flash

1. The paging mechanism of S12XS memory

Take XS128 of S12XS serials MCU for example, XS128 contains 8KB RAM, 8KB D-Flash and 128KB P-Flash. But the basic address line of S12XS serials MCUs is 16bits, which determine its addressing scope range from 0x0000~0xFFFF. So the size of addressing space is 2^{16}B=64KB. That is, in most case MCU can only "see" these 64KB memory space.

As shown in Fig.4, the 64KB address space in S12XS serials MCUs is divided into four parts: I/O register, data Flash memory (D-Flash, also called as EEPROM), RAM and program Flash memory (P-Flash, directly called as Flash). The I/O register region ranges from 0x0000~0x07FF (2KB). D-Flash region ranges from 0x0800~0x0FFF (2K). RAM region ranges from 0x1000~0x3FFF (12K). P-Flash region ranges from 0x4000~0xFFFF (48K).

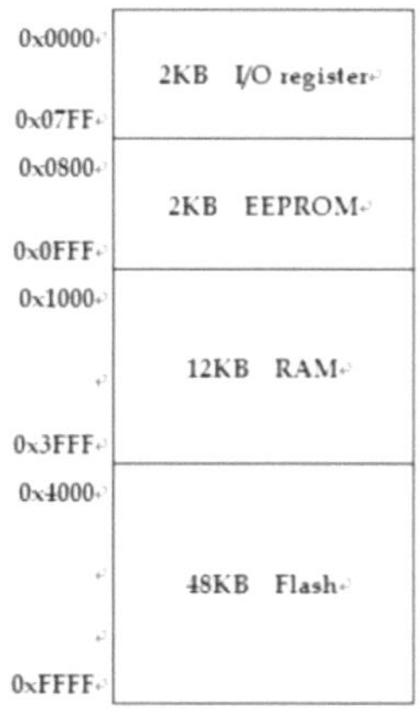

Fig. 4. S12XS's 64KB address space

In order to expand the memory space when using 16 bits address line, S12XS serials MCU integrates MMC (Memory Mapping Control) module, which expand the addressing space from 64KB (16bits) to 8MB (23bits) by using paging management mechanism.

Address analyzing and addressing are managed by the MMC module in XS128. The main functions of MMC module include address mapping, controlling the operation mode of MCU, multi-agent (MCU and BDM) priority addressing, choosing the internal resource and controlling internal bus (which include memory space and peripheral resources) etc.

When we provide a certain address, whether it is a local 16bits address or a global 23 bits address, it will be analysized by MMC and assigned automatically to PPAGE or EPAGE, then gain a remainning 16bits address so that 16bits machine can directly calculate the address space and addess. Without these registers, 16bits machine should calculate twice to deal with 23bits address. Using these registers can improve the addressing efficiency. The whole procedure is automatically completed by MMC without user's special care. Users only need to provide correct address.

There is a Global Page Index Register (GPAGE) in MMC. The highest bit of this register is fixed to 0, so GPAGE actually become a 7-bits register. MCU expands its 16 bits address to be 23 bits by means of GPAGE register. The 23 bits global address is composed of 7 bits GPAGE value [22:16] and CPU local address [15:0]. Meanwhile, specified 23 bits address read/write instructions are added in the instruction system of CPU. Only when CPU

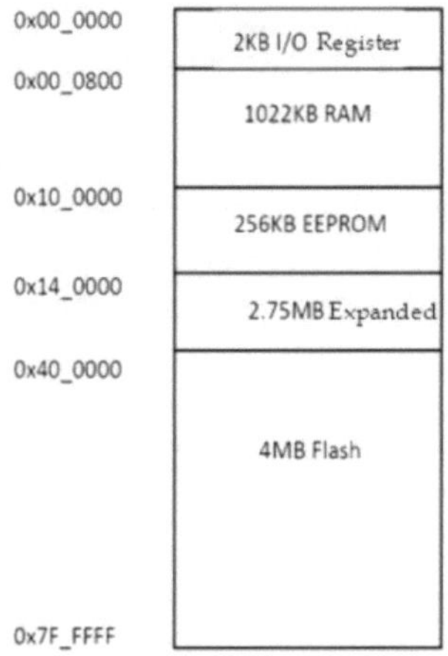

Fig. 5. S12XS's 8MB expanded address space

performs a global command GPAGE register is used. GPAGE provides a method to addressing 8MB space by using 23 bits global address. At this time the 8MB continuous addresses are distributed as Fig.5. The specific distribution is also shown as below:

0x00_0000~0x00_07FF	2KB I/O register address space
0x00_0800~0x0F_FFFF	64KB×16-2KB=1MB-2KB RAM space
0x10_0000~0x13_FFFF	64KB×4=256KB D-Flash space
0x14_0000~0x3F_FFFF	64KB×44=2816KB unused space
0x40_0000~0x7F_FFFF	64KB×64=4MB Flash space

Besides, in order to manage and use D-Flash, RAM and P-Flash, MMC adds three memory page registers: Data FLASH Page Index Register (EPAGE)[2], RAM Page Index Register (RPAGE)[2] and Program Page Index Register (PPAGE)[2], which are used to addressing corresponding expanded region. CPU opens up several windows in its 64KB addressing space. By using above page registers, CPU can map the memory space out of 64KB into these windows in 64KB space at any time. Meanwhile the window which is not used temporarily will be exchanged out. By using this method CPU can expand its addressing space. Besides, these page registers are also used to addressing the global address.

2. Paging memory mapping of XS128

For specific chip, not all the address spaces correspond to actual physical memory. For example, XS128 involves 8KB RAM, 8KB D-Flash and 128KB P-Flash. The address spaces used by these actual physical memories have been determined when chip is designed.

The global addresses of 8KB RAM in XS128 range from 0x0F_E000~0x0F_FFFF. RPAGE=0xFE~0xFF. When chip is reset, the default value in RPAGE is 0xFD, which is a invalid value. That is, addressing 0x1000~0x1FFF will make mistakes and produce illegal address interrupt. When MCU is initialized, we can initialize RPAGE to be 0xFE. So directly addressing 0x2000~0x2FFF will be same to addressing with global address 0x0F_E000~0x0F_EFFF. The global addresses of 8KB D-Flash range from 0x10_0000~0x10_1FFF, EPAGE=0x00~0x07. And the global addresses of 128KB P-Flash range from 0x7E_0000~0x7F_FFFF, PPAGE=0xF8~0xFF. Only these memory address resources mentioned above can be used in actual programming. The operation for the memory addresses outside of these addresses has no meaning.

3. The conversion of Local address, Logical address and Global address

Correctly comprehending the Local address, Logical address and Global address is the foundation to flexibly apply XS128 Flash module. In fact, for 16bits address line MCU, logical address is just the traditional 64Kb address space 0x0000~0xFFFF. Logical address is the expanded 24bits address. Its general format is 0xXX_XXXX. The two hexadecimal bits before "_" are the value of PPAGE or EPAGE (Page number). The other four hexadecimal bits behind "_" are the corresponding window address. For example, 0xFE_8000 is a logical address. 0xFE is P-Flash's page number, and 0x8000 is the P-Flash's corresponding window address in 64KB memory space. Global address is the physical space's address used to save data. The global address of XS128 has 23 bits. That is, range from 0x00_0000~0x7F_FFFF. For example, if PPAGE=0xFE, addressing any address in the local address space 0x8000~0xBFFF actually means addressing the logical address space 0xFE_8000~0xFE_BFFF, while the corresponding global address space is 0x7F_8000~0x7F_BFFF. These two addresses are equivalent, and they are only two kinds of index patterns.
The conversion of logical address and global address in P-Flash is shown as Fig.6

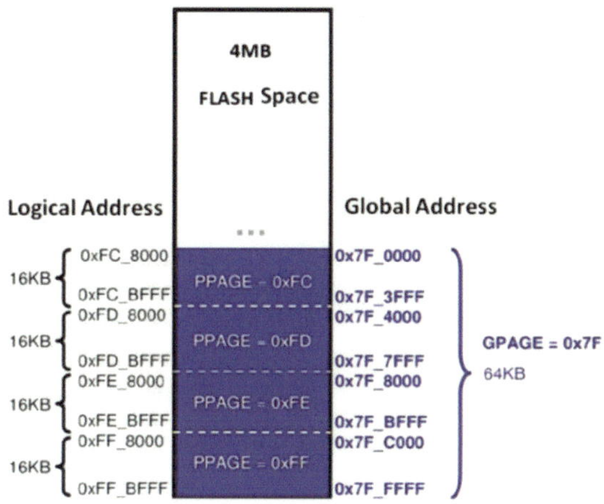

Fig. 6. The conversion of logical address and global address

As shown in Figure.6, the logical address ranges from 0xFC_8000~0xFC_BFFF. The corresponding value of PPAGE is 0xFC. When the logical address is converted into corresponding global address, the top bit [22] in the 23bits address is fixed to 1, the following 8bits [21:14] are the value of PPAGE, that is 0xFC. The lower 14bits are local address, which ranges from 0x0000~0x3FFF. So the corresponding global address ranges from 0x7F_0000~0x7F_3FFF.
On the contrary, the global address ranges from 0x7F_0000~0x7F_3FFF. The corresponding value of PPAGE is the value of [21:14] (0xFC). Bit [22]=1 means a P-Flash page's global address. The lower 16bits of logical address ranges from 0x8000~0xBFFF (P-Flash window address region). So the corresponding logical address ranges from 0xFC_8000~0xFC_BFFF.
Fig.7 provides the relation between local address and global address. The local address of P-Flash in XS128 ranges from 0x4000~0xFFFF. 0x8000~0xBFFF is P-Flash window address region. Its corresponding global address region is 0x7E_0000~0x7F_FFFF. 0x4000~0x7FFF and 0xC000~0xFFFF can directly addressing the global physical addresses (0x7F_4000~0x7F_7FFF and 0x7F_C000~0x7F_FFFF). The local address of D-Flash range from 0x0800~0x0FFF, which is used for EPAGE address mapping window. And the corresponding global address for this window range from 0x10_0000~0x10_1FFF.

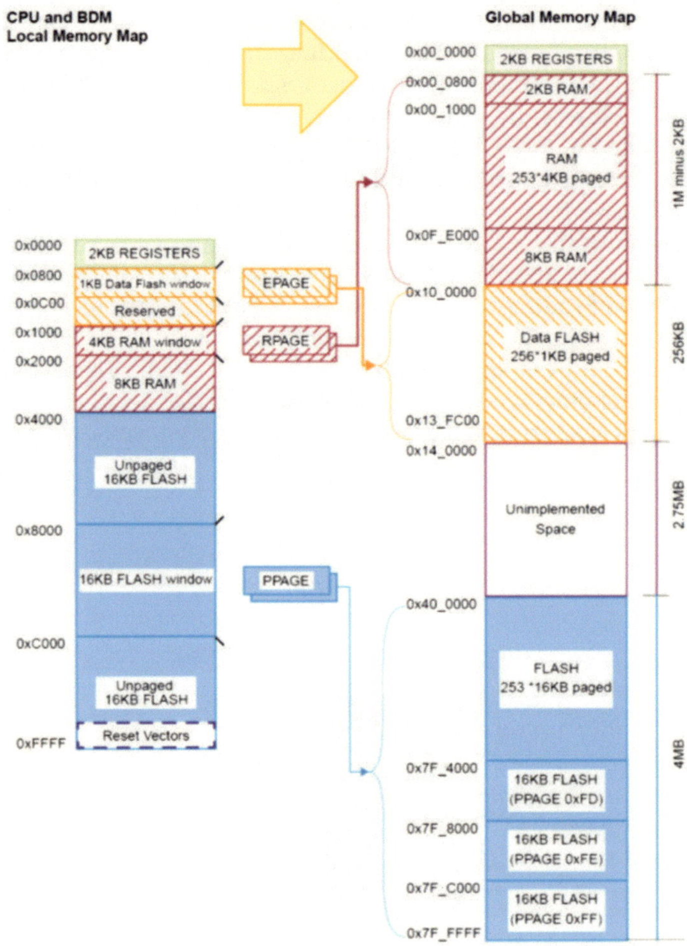

Fig. 7. The relation between the local address and global address in XS128

3.1.2 S12XS128 flash memory registers

In XS128 MCU, the relative registers for Flash programming include general registers and dedicated registers. Setting the general register can simultaneously set the characteristics of two Flash parts. While the dedicated register can only give service to a single Flash part at a certain time interval, the corresponding dedicated registers of the two Flash parts share the same address, so we should illustrate which Flash part is operated before using it.

There are 5 registers used in erasing and programming operation, which include FCLKDIV, FCNFG, FSTAT, FCCOBIX /FCCOB etc. FCLKDIV and FCNFG are general registers. FSTAT and FCCOBIX/FCCOB are dedicated registers. For the detailed function and use of these registers, please refer to the Reference Manual "*MC9S12XS256 Reference Manual*" [2].

3.1.3 XS128 special command mode NVM

For Loading of Flash commands, XS128 is different from the other Freescale MCUs (include DG128). The other MCUs mostly use a command register, which can be writen erasing/programming command codes directly. However, XS128 improve the previous mechanism. It loads the commands and parameters by using FCCOBIX register cooperate with FCCOB register.

The essence of NVM command mode is using the indexed FCCOB register to provide a command code and relevant parameter for memory controller. Users first according to need to set up all needed FCCOB registers domain, then initialize the execution of command by setting the CCIF bit in FSTAT register. When users clear the CCIF bit in FSTAT register, all the parameters in FCCOB register will be locked, which can't be modified before the completion of command execution. (When command finished, CCIF is set to be 1).

In NVM command mode, the general command formats of FCCOB are shown as Fig.8

CCOBIX[2:0]	Byte	FCCOB Parameter Fields (NVM Command Mode)
000	HI	FCMD[7:0] defining Flash command
	LO	0, Global address [22:16]
001	HI	Global address [15:8]
	LO	Global address [7:0]
010	HI	Data 0 [15:8]
	LO	Data 0 [7:0]
011	HI	Data 1 [15:8]
	LO	Data 1 [7:0]
100	HI	Data 2 [15:8]
	LO	Data 2 [7:0]
101	HI	Data 3 [15:8]
	LO	Data 3 [7:0]

Fig. 8. The general command formats of FCCOB

Users can load commands by assigning FCCOB and FCCOBIX register according to the specific command formats. For the detailed programming method, please refer to the follow-up section which gives specific erasing/programming subroutines.

3.1.4 Flash programming procedure

In general, the erasing/programming operation of Flash involves four steps as below.

1. Set FCLKDIV register

For the detailed setting, please refer to the introduction of FCLKDIV register in the above section.

Caution: If the frequency is less than 1MHz, the Flash erasing/programming operation will be unsuccessfully. Too high setting of FDIV may damage Flash memory module. But too low setting may lead to unsuccessfully erasing and incomplete programming for Flash memory units. So users should choice appropriate Clock Divider.

2. Set the corresponding commands and parameters for FCCOB and FCCOBIX registers as needed
3. Set the CCIF bit in FSTAT register
4. Judge whether errors occur during the running of commands

Fig.9 gives a general Flash programming flowchart. According to this flowchart we can erase/program Flash successfully. We only need to pay attention to that part of Flash codes for P-FLASH operation should be moved in RAM.

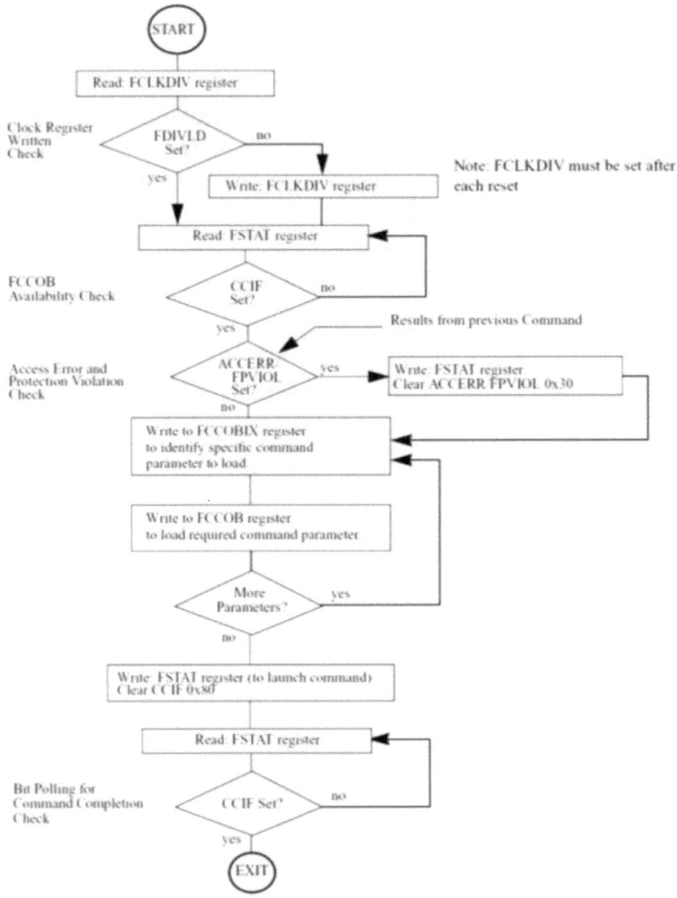

Fig. 9. A general Flash programming flowchart

3.2 XS128 D-FLASH in-circuit programming instance

We provide a D-FLASH In-circuit Programming Instance in our program directory "..*Flash_Program*\ *S12X(XS128)-Flash*", which contains the following parts:

3.2.1 Preparation for D-FLASH programming

XS128 contains 8Kb D-FLASH spaces, which is divided into 8 pages (1KB/page). The minimum erasable unit in programming is a sector, which is 256 bytes. There are 32 sectors in D-FLASH. For the detailed blocking codes, please refer to the head file *EEPROM.h* in our program directory "..*Flash_Program*\ *S12X(XS128)-Flash*".

3.2.2 Some common operation for erasing/programming procedure

The erasing/programming programs for D-FLASH need not run in RAM. For this kind of memory mode with multi paging mechanism, it is necessary to design a function which calculate the specific address with sector number and block number. Besides, we should set the FCLKDIV register before erasing/programming D-FLASH. And we also should detect the error flags to judge whether command run successfully.

3.2.3 Erasing subroutine

First we calculate the first address of erasing sector by sector number, load this first address and the D-FLASH sector erasing command CMD_D_ERASE_SECTOR (0x12) into FCCOB register by NVM command mode. Then execute the erasing command.

3.2.4 Programming subroutine

Calculate the first address of the programming sector by sector number and offset block number, load this first address and the D-FLASH sector programming command CMD_D_PROGRAM (0x11) into FCCOB register by NVM command mode. Then execute the programming command.

3.2.5 Reading/writing data

In regard to the reading/writing for content of Flash region, special additional remarks should be provided here.

The address space of Flash usually corresponds with multiple addresses. Here we elaborate the using method of these addresses, which apply some technique of C language.

Reading Flash can adopt the following 3 addressing patterns.

1. Addressing by Local Address. That is, addressing through 64KB address space. The addresses range from 0x0000~0xFFFF.
   For example: **Data= *(volatile uint8 *)0x0400;**
2. Addressing by Logical Address (Global Logical Address). The addresses cooperated by EPAGE range from 0x0800~0x0c00, which can be addressed by the format "__eptr". Caution: "__eptr" includes two underlines.
   For example: **Data= *(volatile uint8 * __eptr)0x00_0800;**
3. Addressing by Global address (Global Physical Address). According to the actual physical location of the whole memory, access the memory with the format "__far". Caution: "__far" includes two underlines.
   For example: **Data= *(volatile uint8 * __far)0x10_0000;**

Caution: A sector is the minimum unit to erase. For D-FLASH, the minimum size is 256 bytes.

3.3 XS128 P-FLASH in-circuit programming instance

XS128 contains 128Kb P-FLASH spaces, which is divided into 8 pages (16KB/page). The minimum erasable unit in programming is a sector, which is 1024 bytes. There are 128 sectors in P-FLASH. The programming procedure of P-FLASH is similar to that of D-FLASH. So we omit the detailed description for this P-FLASH programming instance. For the detailed program codes, please refer to the program in our program directory "*..\Flash_Program\ S12X(XS128)-Flash*".

3.4 Protection mechanisms and security operations Of XS128 flash memory

3.4.1 Protection mechanisms

The registers relate with XS128 Flash's protection mechanisms include FPROT (Flash Protection Register) and DFPROT (D-Flash Protection Register). After set the protection registers, the protected region can't be erased or programmed.

3.4.2 Security operations

The debugging module in XS128 improves the practical applicability of MCU, but simultaneously brings about hidden danger to the security of MCU. The common users may easily steal the programs from MCU by BDM. In order to prevent software piracy, XS128 brings in complex security mechanism to guarantee the security of MCU. When the MCU is encrypted, the common users can't read any content in memory by BDM[8] (Only messy codes can be read.) But the programs running in MCU can access arbitrary resources of MCU, and can decrypt MCU by using the back-door key access mechanism provided by MCU.

1. Set MCU to Security Mode

To prevent the programs in the flash memory from being read out illegally, the MCU should be set in security mode. The corresponding register is FSEC (Flash Security Register). If it is reset, FSEC register automatically load value from the configuration address 0x7F_FF0F. All bits of FSEC are related to the security of device, and these bits are read-only.

2. Unlock from Security Mode

a. Can't unlock by BDM

As manual states we can't unlock MCU by BDM with backdoor key access mechanism. Facts also show that we can't unlock MCU and obtain valid data by BDM. It is worth noting that we can entirely erase the locked MCU by BDM, while the flag bit FPVIOL of FSTAT register will be set. If we don't want to secure MCU now, we should program immediately by changing the later two bits of the byte in 0x7F_FF0F as the value 1:0. So after the next reset MCU will be in unlocked state.

b. The only way to unlock MCU—using backdoor key access mechanism.

Programs like buried treasure locked in chip. Treasure pretenders have tried every means to get it, but they are always blocked by an indestructible security door. Only intelligent master owns the key to open this security door. This is the so-called backdoor key access mechanisms.

How to start and use this kind of mechanism?

First, 8 bytes backdoor key together with the programs should be programmed into MCU. That is, 8 bytes key should be successively programmed into the addresses 0x7F_FF00~0x7F_FF07.

After that, the bits KEYEN[1:0] of FSEC register should be set as the value 10 to enable the backdoor key access mechanism.

Concerning how to unlock:

First, prepare to match the key. This step will use the FLASH backdoor key comparison command 0x0C. The backdoor key comparison command and 8 bytes key can be set to FCCOB. And setting flag bit CCIF can enable the comparison. If the comparison is successful, the security state will temporarily be unlocked. If the comparison is unsuccessful, the next comparison can be done only after reset, otherwise none operation can be done. Besides, if the comparison is successful, SEC[1:0] will be 10 which means unlocked state. If at this time users want to disable the encryption function, the bits KEY[1:0] should be set as disabled state to disable the backdoor key comparison function.

4. Programming flash in freescale MCF52233 flash

The flash memory in-circuit programming implement for 32bits MCF52233 MCU will be explained in this section, as follows:

[8] BDM-- Background Debug Monitor

4.1 How to operate coldfire flash memory

4.1.1 The basic concepts of MCF52233 flash memory

ColdFire Flash Module (CFM) is made up of 4 arrays, and each consists of 32K*16 bits, thus composing a flash memory space of 256 Kbytes, as is shown in Fig.10. Inner flash controller needs 2 cycles to access to the flash memory, but since across accessing enabled, it can read the flash consecutively with a higher frequency. Only one cycle is needed for reading each word.

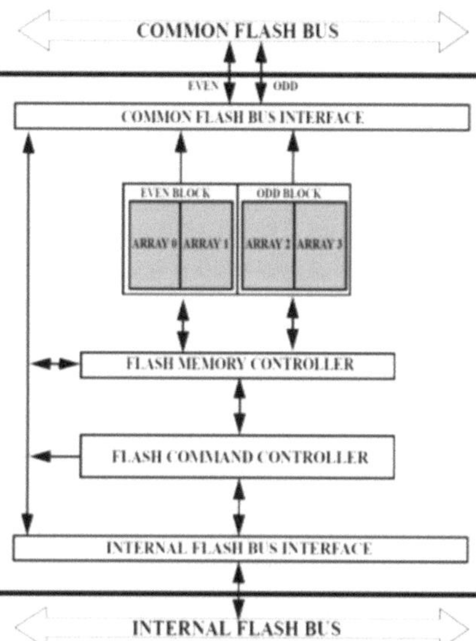

Fig. 10. CFM Block Diagram

In MCF52233, the 256KB flash memory space is divided into 32 8KB sectors. Each section has 4 pages and each page is of 2KB. When programming, note that the erase is carried out by page. That is to say, at least one page needs to be erased at a time. 2 words (4 bytes) are performed at a time.

The 32-bit MCF52233 has 32 address buses, and can address 4GB space. In principle, the initial address of MCF52233 is alterable. By setting the corresponding register, the 256KB 32-bit flash can be located to any continuous space. However, in practice its start address is set to 0x0000_0000. And it is suggested not to alter the address.

4.1.2 ColdFire flash memory registers

Erasing and programming relate to registers such as FLASHBAR, CFMCLKD, CFMMCR, CFMPROT, CFMSEC, CFMUSTAT and CFMCMD. For the detailed function and use of these registers, please refer to the Reference Manual "***MCF52235 ColdFire integrated** Microcontroller Reference Manual*" [3].

4.1.3 ColdFire flash memory erase and program implements

For ColdFire MCU, the entire flash memory or only one page (2KB) at the start address can be erased. That is, more than one byte or 2KB is erased at a time. To perform, a row of data should be prepared and put into the RAM first. Only after erasing the corresponding region in Flash memory can perform be carried out. Furthermore, the erasing or performing of any byte influences the page it is in, so before that it is necessary to arrange relevant data in the erasing region by linking files. In other words, the page which is being programmed cannot be erased. Below is a detailed procedure of Coldfire Flash memory erase and program. The corresponding sub-program instances are also provided in our program directory *"..\Flash_Program\ ColdFire(MCF52233)-Flash"*.

1. Common Operations for Erase and Program
   a. If the CFMCLKD register is written, the DIVLD bit is set automatically. If the DIVLD bit is 0, the CFMCLKD register has not been written since last reset. No command can be executed if the CFMCLKD register has not been written.
   b. Before starting a command write sequence, the ACCERR and PVIOL flags in the CFMUSTAT register must be cleared.
2. Erase

Step 1. set the clock frequency division by writing the CFMCLKD register. Clear error flags, and set the sector number. These operations take place at the beginning of all operations, and have been packaged into a subroutine which can be called directly.

Step 2. locate the sector to be erased. Write a value to any location in that sector.

Step 3. write 0x40 to command register CFMCMD (section 10.2.1 "CFM Registers").

Step 4. write a "1" to the command buffer empty interrupt flag (CBEIF) of register CFMUSTAT. This clears the flag and launches the flash command described in step three.

Step 5. wait for the command to be accomplished. This is indicated by the command complete interrupt flag (CCIF), which is also located in status register CFMUSTAT. This bit is set when the command is completed.

3. Program

If we need to write some words to a specific start address in flash memory (note: the address should be clean—non-written), detailed steps are as follows.

Step 1. is the same as in the erasing operation.

Step 2. set the start address. The process of writing words is then divided into sub-steps as follows:

- Step A. select a word (provide the source address and the target address).
- Step B. Step B, write 0x20 to command register CFMCMD (section 10.2.1 "CFM Registers").
- Step C. write a "1" to CBEIF in register CFMUSTAT, clearing the flag bit and executing the flash command.
- Step D. wait for the command to be accomplished (the CBEIF flag of register CFMUSTAT is 1), meanwhile the next command is receivable only.
- Step E. if data remain to be written, increase the source and target addresses then go to step B.

Notes: the register CFMCLKD is set only once anterior erase operation and in no any program case. Don't erase any region which stores codes.

4. Flash Memory Illegal Operations
   a. Writing to the flash memory before initializing CFMCLKD; Writing to the flash memory while CBEIF is not set; Writing to a flash block with a data size other than 32 bits; After writing to the even flash block, writing an additional word to the flash memory during the flash command write sequence other than the odd flash block; Writing an invalid flash normal mode command to the CFMCMD register (out of the 5 values); Writing to any CFM register other than CFMCMD after writing to the flash memory; Writing a second command to the CFMCMD register

before executing the previously written command;. Writing to any CFM register other than CFMUSTAT (to clear CBEIF) after writing to the command register, CFMCMD; entering stop mode with some commands uncompleted. Upon entering STOP mode, any active command is aborted; Aborting a command write sequence by writing a 0 to the CBEIF flag after writing to the flash memory or after writing a command to the CFMCMD register but before the command is launched.

b. The PVIOL flag is set during the command write sequence if any of the following illegal operations are performed, causing the command write sequence to immediately abort: Writing a program command if the address to program is in a protected flash logical sector; Writing a page erase command if the address to erase is in a protected flash logical sector; Writing a mass erase command while any protection is enabled. If a read operation is attempted on a flash logical block while a command is active on that logical block (CCIF=0), the read operation returns invalid data and the ACCERR flag in the CFMUSTAT register is not set.

For predigesting programming, various illegal operation types listed above are ignored in practice and are simply classified as: completed or aborted.

4.2 Validate ColdFire flash memory implements

The validate ColdFire flash memory application in our network site is as the following: the MCU receives formatted data from PC by SCI interface and erases, programs or reads its flash memory. The PC software is SCI debug or our testing tool. For the detailed codes and running windows, please refer to the program in our program directory
"..\Flash_Program\ ColdFire(MCF52233)-Flash".

Now, list some flash operating commands using the SCI debug:

Commands	**Functions**
?	**MCU sends some items to PC**
E:8	**Erase page 8**
R:8:0:4	**Read 4 bytes the word 0 of page 8**
W:8:0:4:A,C,B,D	**Write "ACBD" (4 bytes) to the word 0 of page 8**
P:8,7,6,5,4,3,2,1	**Encrypt Flash and the password is "87654321"**
D	**Delete passwords**

Above examples only give the program data less than one page (2048 bytes). Flash memory application for data that exceeds one page can been found in the aforesaid network site.

4.3 CFM protection mechanisms and security operations

4.3.1 CFM protection mechanisms

The CFMPROT register (refer to the reference manual[3]) is interrelated with the protection mechanisms of ColdFire flash memory which is divided to 32 sectors and each controlled by a flag of CFMPROT—the sector is presumed as in protected state while the corresponding flag is set to 1—there will be Illegal when erasing or programming the sector. Note to get it back to the protected state after erasing or programming the sector. In erase subroutine *Flash_Page_Erase* and program subroutine *Flash_Page_Write*, the Flash_Protect(page,FALSE) releases the sector from the protected state, but the MCF_CFM_CFMPROT = 0xffffffff reverses that.

4.3.2 CFM security operations

The ColdFire 0x0400~0x0417 is the flash configuration field whose security word is read automatically after each reset and is stored in the CFMSEC register. If the low 2 bytes of the

CFMSEC register offset (0x0414~0x0417) in the file vectors.s is equal to 0x4ac8, the MCU is in its security mode and programs in the flash memory can't be read, erased or programmed by 32-bit ColdFire programming writer in the BDM mode. Whereas it allows the password matching while the high 2 bytes is 0xc000. If the 32-bit ColdFire programming writer is set in JTAG mode, the password can be released by erasing the page 0 (the programs in the flash memory can't be used any longer), and then the flash memory can erase or program in the BDM mode again.

1. Set MCU to Security Mode

To prevent the programs in the flash memory from being read out illegally, the MCU should be set in security mode. Two methods for locking the flash memory are shown in the following.

Method A. Lock the MCU by modifying the security configuration field in the file vectors.s.

Method B. we can lock the flash memory by calling the custom subroutine Flash_Secure to modify relevant address matters when the program is running. For the locked subroutine, please refer to the program directory "*..\Flash_Program\ ColdFire(MCF52233)-Flash*".

2. Unlock from Security Mode

We must unlock the MCU first then can write into the program if it has been locked, because locked ColdFire family can't be mass erased by BDM. And here two methods are provided to unlock it.

First, after setting the writer into JTAG mode, mass erase the locked MCU. Refer to "32-bit ColdFire writer" in our network site (*http://sumcu.suda.edu.cn*) for details.

Second, call the subroutine Flash_Delete_Key to erase password or flash by memory-resident program. (the subroutine Flash_Delete_Key is shown in the program directory "*..\Flash_Program\ ColdFire(MCF52233)-Flash*")

5. Reference

[1] Freescale: MC9S08AW60 Data Sheet ,Rev.2,2006

[2] Freescale: MC9S12XS256 Reference Manual, Rev. 1.09, 2009

[3]Freescale: MCF52235 ColdFire integrated Microcontroller Reference Manual,Rev.4, 2007

[4] WANG Yi-huai, LIU Xiao-sheng, Embedded systems-design and application on HCS12 MCUs, Beihang, University Press, 2008

[5] Yihuai Wang ,Zhigui Lin. Stable In circuit Programming of Flash Memory in Freescale's MC9S12 MCU family. Proceedings–ICMTMA2010. Volume III:477-480 . IEEE Computer Society,2010

Part 3

Technology, Materials and Design Issues

9

Source and Drain Junction Engineering for Enhanced Non-Volatile Memory Performance

Sung-Jin Choi and Yang-Kyu Choi
Department of Electrical Engineering, KAIST
Republic of Korea

1. Introduction

There is strong demand to maintain the trend of increasing bit density and reducing bit cost in Flash memory technology. To this end, aggressive scaling of the device dimension and multi-level cell (MLC) or multi-bit cell (MBC) have been proposed in NAND and NOR Flash memory architectures. However, especially in NAND Flash memory, bit cost is expected to rise in the near future, because the process cost will increase more rapidly than the shrink rate. One solution to avoid such challenges is the use of three dimensionally stacked array structures, based on polycrystalline silicon (poly-Si). The utilization of poly-Si in the channel not only increases pass disturbs but also reduces the worst case string current. Indeed, for every doubling in density, the worst case string current halves. Since the channel of these devices is poly-Si and source/drain (S/D) regions are not formed (*i.e.*, a junction-free structure), the worst case string current (all cells in a string with high threshold voltage (V_T)) will quickly tend toward unreadably low values as density increases (Walker, 2009). Therefore, it is worthwhile to note that the impact on the S/D structures becomes important. Moreover, Fowler-Nordheim (FN) tunneling for programming is still very slow for certain applications that require high-speed operation.

In NOR Flash memory, channel length scaling has threatened continued scaling and approaching its end point. For uniform channel hot electron injection (CHEI) programming, a robust margin for punch-through is a pre-requisite for cell transistors. However, CHEI programming aggravates immunity against punch-through by increasing the drain voltage to a level that will trigger CHEI. It is clear that the drain voltage window to guarantee both programming speed and margin from drain disturbance is narrowed as the channel length scales down. Moreover, the low injection efficiency compromising from vertical and lateral fields and the high parasitic resistance at the S/D junctions also impose a constraint on scaling the cell size reduction. Consequently, the lower effective program voltage due to the high parasitic S/D resistance in an extremely scaled cell results in a small V_T window and thereafter retards the program speed.

Herein S/D engineering for enhanced performance of Flash memory for two novel structures is demonstrated: (i) a dopant-segregated Schottky-barrier device (DSSB), and (ii) a junctionless MOSFET. First, we utilized dopant-segregated metallic silicide S/D junctions on charge trapping memory cells. They boosted the program speed even at a low program bias with the aid of abrupt band bending at the edge of metal silicided junctions. Second, the structure of the junctionless transistor was examined from S/D junction engineering and cell size scaling points of view.

2. Schottky-Barrier (SB) MOSFET

SB-MOSFETs were initially proposed by Lepselter and Sze four decades ago (1968 - Bell Labs.), shortly after the invention of the current type of MOSFET by Kahng and Attala (1960 - Bell Labs.). Being different from the conventional MOSFET with doped/diffused S/D junctions, the SB-MOSFET has metallic silicided S/D junctions, realizing by employing a self-aligned silicide process, as shown in Fig. 2-1. The operating principle is based on gate induced electronic band bending to modulate the S/D thermionic and tunneling barrier (Larson et al., 2006). One remarkable advantage of the SB-MOSFETs is their low interface contact resistivity: $\rho_c \sim 10^{-9}\ \Omega\cdot cm^2$ for metallic S/D compared with $\rho_c \sim 10^{-7}\ \Omega\cdot cm^2$ in standard doped S/D junctions. Moreover, it is easier to control the abruptness/shallowness of the S/D junctions in metallic S/D junctions than in standard doped S/D junctions, and the solid solubility limitation associated with doping can also be resolved. From a fabrication viewpoint, the silicidation process is fully compatible with the standard CMOS technologies and does not require a high temperature annealing process; this prevents thermal degradation (in particular, for high-k gate dielectric layers and metal-gates) and reduces fabrication costs. However, for typical SB-MOSFETs, the on-state current is significantly limited by the existence of a SB height (SBH) at the S/D junctions; thus, the performance of SB-MOSFETs is still not comparable with that of conventional MOSFETs with highly doped S/D junctions. Therefore, it is necessary to find an appropriate material with a low SBH and develop a method to reduce the effective SBH, such as a dopant-segregation technique (Kinoshita et al., 2004), in order to enhance the performance of SB-MOSFETs.

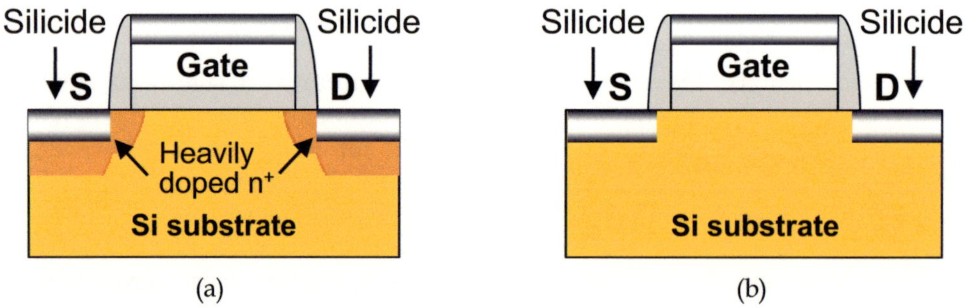

Fig. 2-1. Simplified schematic of (a) the conventional and (b) the SB devices

SB-MOSFETs are also interesting devices from a physics perspective. They can be used for high speed devices in highly scaled regimes because they have an abrupt energy band bending, which results from a large voltage drop at the source to the inversion channel. Importantly, a high lateral electric field exists around not the drain but the source edge. The carriers, *e.g.*, electrons for an n-channel SB-MOSFET, injected from the source thermally or via tunneling are accelerated by this electric field and become hot around the source edge. These properties are very useful and interesting for both logic and memory devices.

2.1 Operating principle of SB-MOSFETs

A band diagram schematically depicting the different operations of SB-MOSFETs is shown in Fig. 2-2. A small off-state current is possible at a gate voltage of 0 V as a result of the high effective barrier height for both electrons and holes. The effective barrier height for holes at a gate voltage of 0 V consists of two components: the intrinsic barrier for holes (Φ_{bp}) and the contact barrier ($\Phi_{contact}$). The contact potential results from the built-in potential energy (ψ_b) arising from the metal-semiconductor interface and the surface potential energy (ψ_s) resulting from the gate ($\Phi_{contact} = \psi_b + \psi_s$) (Fig. 2-2(a)). As a negative gate bias is applied, the effective barrier for holes is reduced to the intrinsic barrier height (Φ_{bp}) and the current increases as holes are ejected over the barrier primarily via thermionic emission (Fig. 2-2(b)). Note that when the effective barrier height ($\Phi_{effective} = \Phi_{bp} + \Phi_{contact}$) is the same as the intrinsic barrier height, the flat band source-to-body condition is formed (*i.e.*, $\Phi_{contact} \sim 0$ eV). For small gate voltage values, the drain voltage will mostly drop at the source, *i.e.*, the reverse bias contact, and current transport can be performed by the thermionic emission. This also holds in the subthreshold regime (small gate voltage). Further increases of the gate bias cause the bands to bend upwards and holes to tunnel through the barrier either directly or with thermal assistance (Fig. 2-2(c)). As noted above, the SBH limits the current flow in the subthreshold regime and becomes conductive in the on-state, where the channel resistance limits the current flow in an ideal case.

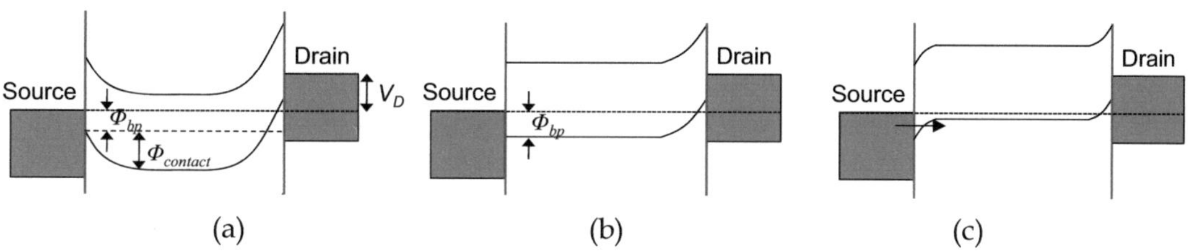

Fig. 2-2. Band diagrams of the different operating regimes of an SB-MOSFET: (a) off-state, (b) subthreshold regime, and (c) on-state.

2.2 Dopant-segregation technique

As mentioned earlier, the SB can limit the current drivability if an appropriate low SB material is not used. The dopant-segregation technique, an attractive technique to enhance the current density, has been introduced to SB-MOSFETs. If silicidation is performed on the doped silicon regions, the dopants can be redistributed at the interface between the silicide and silicon, which significantly affects the electrostatic properties of the SB junctions (Muraka, S. P. et al., 1087). The redistribution of dopants is determined by the diffusivity and solid solubility of dopants in the silicide and the presence of point defects at the interface between the silicide and silicon. Thermal annealing of silicide materials on ion implanted or doped (*i.e.*, activated or non-activated) silicon can induce redistribution of dopants during the silicidation process. In particular, dopants are segregated at the interface between the silicide and silicon as a result of the different solid solubility of these materials. Atoms of nickel (Ni), a candidate material in SB-MOSFETs, are the moving species, supplied by diffusion through the growing silicide layer to the silicide/Si interface. Subsequently, the covalent bonding of Si atoms is softened by the diffusion of Ni atoms. A significant change of volume occurs when the silicide is formed, which leads to high strain at the interface. As a result, point defects (self-interstitial or vacancies) can be generated to partially relieve the stress. Due to the formation of vacancies, the diffusivity of the arsenic in the silicon is enhanced and it is forced out of the silicon after the silicide is formed. The arsenic dopants move towards the interface where they accumulates at the moving interface between the silicide and silicon. Although the dopant concentrations are generally below the solid solubility limit in the silicides and silicon, the point defects induced by the high strain interface can lead to the increment of local dopant concentrations that are higher than the solid solubility. This segregation of dopants is possible with boron, antimony, sulfur, chlorine, etc. as well as arsenic. The segregated dopants form a thin layer with a high concentration, which causes strong upward or downward band bending depending on the type of dopants, as shown in Fig. 2-3. As a consequence, the tunneling probability of the carriers through the effectively lowered Schottky barrier increases significantly. Although dopant-segregation is performed at relatively low temperatures, a fraction of the dopants is located at substitution sites in the silicon lattice and is therefore activated. Therefore, owing to enhanced injection efficiency, dopant-segregated SB (DSSB) MOSFETs have attracted considerable attention as a candidate for a high performance devices in future ULSIs.

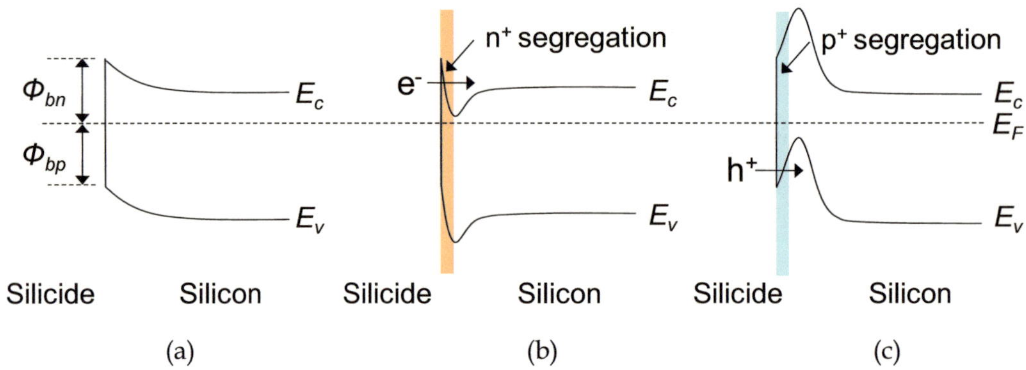

Fig. 2-3. Schematic band diagrams of (a) a mid-gap silicide with equal SB-heights for electrons and holes, (b) band bending induced by segregated n-type dopants, and (c) band bending induced by segregated p-type dopants.

2.3 Application to non-volatile memory devices

The metal-semiconductor SB diode is also known as a 'hot carrier diode'. The injected carriers from the semiconductor to the metal electrode, regardless of whether the injection mechanism is thermionic emission or tunneling, are forward biased Schottky barrier diodes, and they can obtain higher energies than the Fermi energies at the metal side. Moreover, the carriers injected from the metal to the semiconductor in the reverse biased junction can obtain higher energies than the Fermi energies in the semiconductor side, as shown in Fig. 2-4.

Both SB and DSSB MOSFETs at the on-state have an abrupt lateral voltage drop at the source end of the device due to the reverse biased source Schottky diode (Uchida et al., 2000, Kinoshita et al., 2006); therefore, a natural high electric field exists around the source edge. The carriers injected from the source electrode thermally or by tunneling will be accelerated by this electric field and will become hot around the source edge.

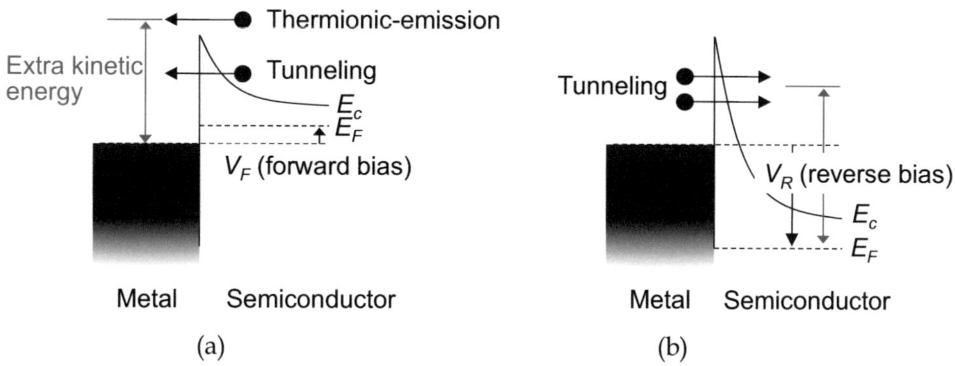

Fig. 2-4. (a) Conceptual explanation of hot carriers in (a) forward biased and (b) reverse biased in Schottky barrier diodes.

3. SB Flash memory

3.1 Hot-carrier program in double-gate DSSB FinFETs

Gate length scaling is the most critical limit in a NOR Flash memory cell, which uses a program method known as CHEI. This method aggravates immunity against punchthrough by increasing the drain voltage to a level that can trigger CHEI, as shown in Fig. 3-1(a). In addition, the low injection efficiency of the hot electrons generated at the drain side and the high parasitic resistance at the S/D also impose a constraint on scaling the cell size down. Consequently, the lower effective program voltage due to the high parasitic S/D resistance in an extremely scaled cell results in a small V_T window and thereupon retards the program speed. CHEI programming in conventional NOR-type Flash memories also poses a constraint on the choice of the proper gate voltage (V_G) and drain voltage (V_D), as shown in Fig. 3-1(b). A high V_D is necessary to induce a high lateral electric field for the generation of hot electrons. Furthermore, a high V_G is indispensable for attaining a sufficient vertical electric field for the injection of hot electrons into a charge storage node. Simultaneous optimization of the lateral and vertical electric fields is very difficult. Moreover, the high voltage needed to generate an adequate amount of hot electrons for programming consumes a large amount of power.

The source-side injection of hot electrons for programming at low voltage is therefore attractive because of its high injection efficiency and the absence of constraints on the co-optimization of V_G and V_D. Previous reports on source-side injection by the decoupling of hot electrons from the drain field demonstrated a fast low-voltage programming operation (Wu et al., 1986); however, it is difficult to adapt this approach to NOR-type Flash memory as it requires extra processes and different circuitry. In this section, an intensive analysis of NOR Flash memory, where double-gate (DG) DSSB FinFET silicon-oxide-nitride-oxide-silicon (SONOS) devices are employed, is carried out. The program speed is boosted even at a low program bias owing to the improved CHEI, which is enabled by the inherent sharp band bending of the DSSB at the source side. The DSSB structure provides several benefits, including increased lateral and vertical fields, excellent injection efficiency into the charge storage node, and a drain disturbance-free feature against a conventional device composed of diffused p-n junctions.

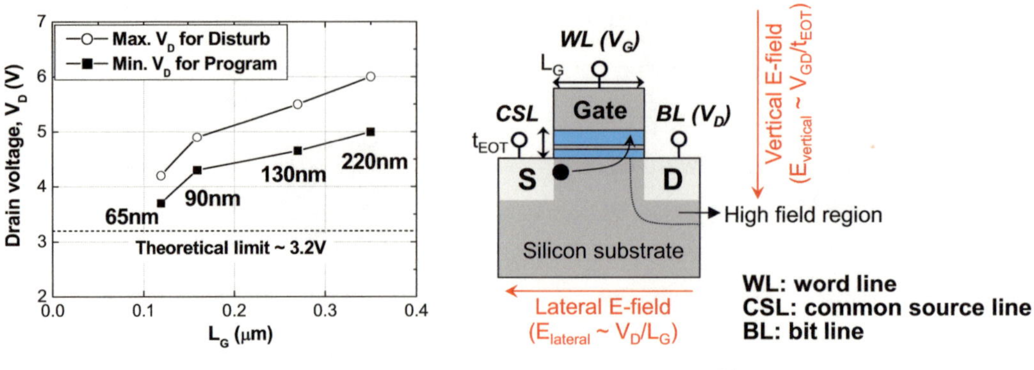

(a) (b)

Fig. 3-1. (a) Scaling trend of drain biases. Minimum bias for programming speed and maximum bias for allowable drain disturbance are drawn for NOR flash generations. (b) Trade-off relations between vertical field and lateral field in the conventional CHEI programming method.

3.1.1 Device fabrication

The process schematics and sequences are summarized in Fig. 3-2. The process flow of the DSSB FinFET SONOS device is the same as that of the conventional FinFET except for the formation of gate spacers and the silicided S/D junctions. Using a shallow implantation of arsenic (As) after the formation of gate spacers, the SB height is effectively modulated by using segregated dopants. During the formation of the gate spacers, the S/D regions are recessed so that they subsequently provide a uniform S/D along the fin depth (vertical direction). This task is challenging with only S/D implantation and activation. Finally, the DSSB S/D was formed by means of nickel silicidation (NiSi) in a two-step rapid thermal processing (RTP), which can minimize the lateral diffusion of NiSi.

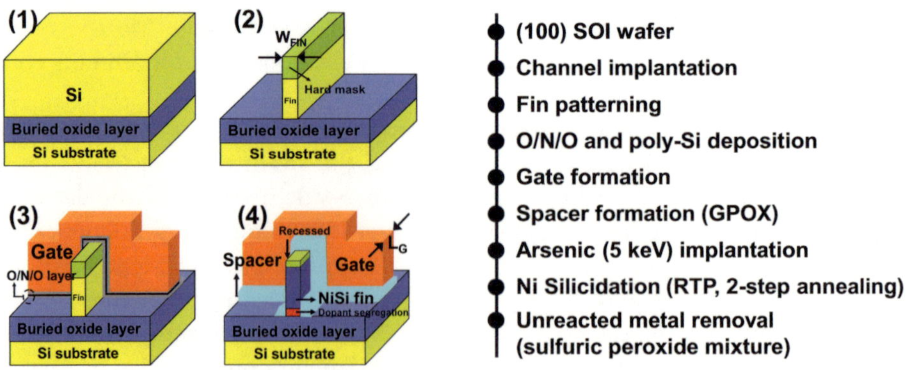

(a) (b)

Fig. 3-2. Flow chart of the DSSB FinFET SONOS device. In the silicidation process, a two-step RTP is used to reduce any overgrowth of NiSi and mitigate lateral diffusion. Since the SB height is effectively modulated by the dopant concentration, a shallow implantation (5 keV) of As was applied.

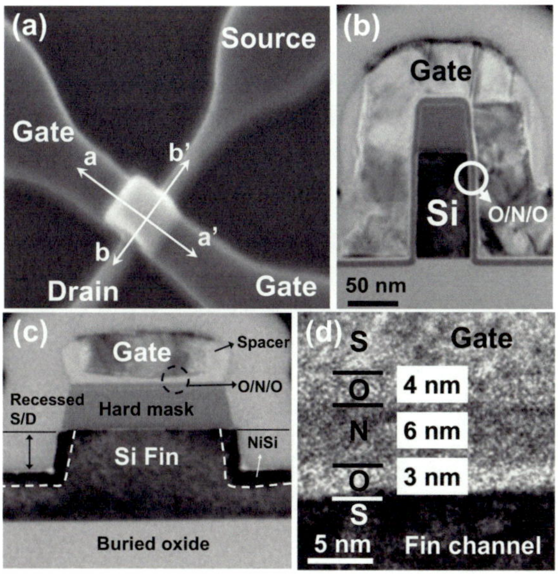

Fig. 3-3. SEM and TEM images of the fabricated devices (Choi et al., 2008).

The SEM photograph in Fig. 3-3(a) shows a bird's-eye view of the fabricated DSSB FinFET SONOS device. Fig. 3-3(b), 3-3(c), and 3-3(d) are cross-sectional TEM images from various points of view of the DSSB FinFET SONOS device. The device has a gate length of 220 nm and a fin that ranges in width from 30nm to 100nm. For the control group, a conventional FinFET SONOS device with a diffused p-n junction was also fabricated. In Fig. 3-4, the results obtained from a scanning TEM image for verification of dopant segregation are shown. Dopant segregation at the interface between the silicon and the silicide is clearly observed.

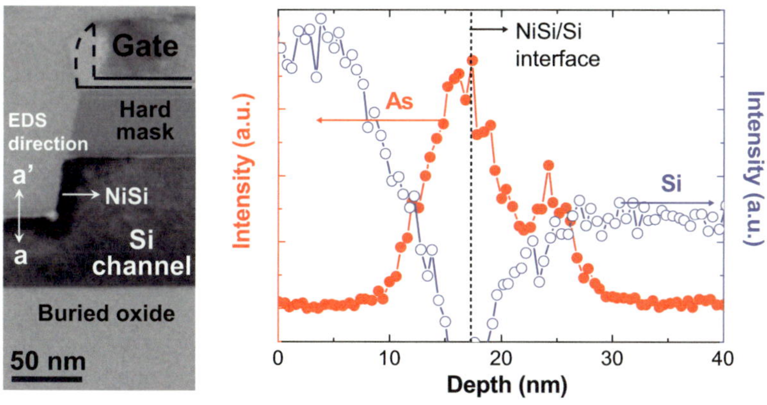

Fig. 3-4. TEM image of DG DSSB SONOS and STEM energy dispersive spectromotry (EDS) analysis. (Choi et al., 2009a)

3.1.2 Memory characteristics

Fig. 3-5(a) schematically illustrates the different injection mechanism of hot electrons for the DSSB Flash memory device and the conventional Flash memory device under the programming bias condition of CHEI ($V_G > 0$ and $V_D > 0$). In the case of the conventional Flash memory device, hot electrons are generated near the drain-side where the device is under a high lateral electric field; the hot electrons are then injected into the drain-side charge storage node. However, the drain-side region has a low vertical electric field due to the low gate-to-drain potential difference ($V_{GD} = V_G - V_D$). As a result, the injection efficiency is lowered. Moreover, due to high V_D, a Flash memory cell that uses a conventional CHEI method is not suitable for applications with low power operation and high density. In contrast to the conventional device, however, the DSSB device has an abrupt band bending capability near the source-side region, and this capability provides a naturally built-in high lateral electric field that generates sufficient source-side hot electrons, even at a low voltage. In addition, this source-side region experiences a high vertical field due to the high gate-to-source potential difference ($V_{GS} = V_G - V_S$, V_S = grounded). As a result, hot electrons are injected into the source-side storage node rather than the drain-side storage node; consequently, the DSSB device has higher injection efficiency than the conventional device. Fig. 3-5(b) shows a simulated energy band diagram for both cases at the programming state. The magnitude of the simulated lateral electric field in a programming state is also shown in Fig. 3-5(c) for different drain voltages. Note that the DSSB FinFET SONOS device has a larger lateral electric field than the conventional FinFET SONOS device under the same programming conditions. This is mainly attributed to the intrinsic sharp band bending of the DSSB junction at the source-side, which is marked by dashed circle in Fig. 3-5(b).

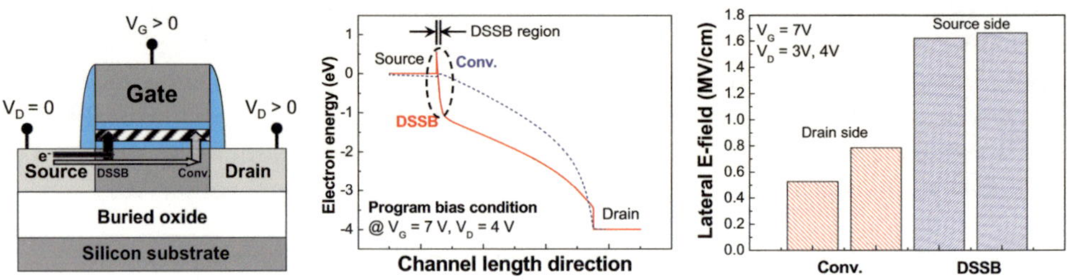

(a) (b) (c)

Fig. 3-5. (a) Comparison of the DSSB device and the conventional device in terms of the charge injection point of hot electrons. (b) Simulated energy band diagrams of both devices at the programming state. The sharp energy band bending should be noted. (c) Simulated lateral electric field for the DSSB device at the source-side and the conventional device at the drain-side. (Choi et al., 2009a)

Fig. 3-6 illustrates the measured programming and erasing transient characteristics. A comparative study was performed with a conventional FinFET SONOS device with the diffused p-n junction as a reference. Under program conditions of V_G = 7 V and V_D = 4 V with t_{PGM} = 350 ns, a V_T shift of approximately 4.5 V is observed in the DSSB FinFET SONOS device. The DSSB FinFET SONOS device and a conventional FinFET SONOS device for programming show a difference of roughly 3.5 V in the V_T shift value at a programming time of 350 ns. This difference is attributed to the high lateral and vertical electric fields at the source-side, which would originate from the sharp band bending caused by the dopant segregated region as well as the intrinsic band profile. In the programming state, electrons injected from the source electrode via thermionic emission or a tunneling process are accelerated by the high lateral electric field and can become hot at the source-side. The electrons can subsequently surmount the tunnel oxide barrier around the source-side. As a result, the programming is more efficient. On the other hand, in the erasing state created by FN tunneling, there is no significant difference between the DSSB FinFET SONOS device and the conventional FinFET SONOS device. However, it can be straightforwardly expected that the erasing characteristics can be enhanced by engineering of the gate stack, such as metal-gate (with high workfunction) or bandgap.

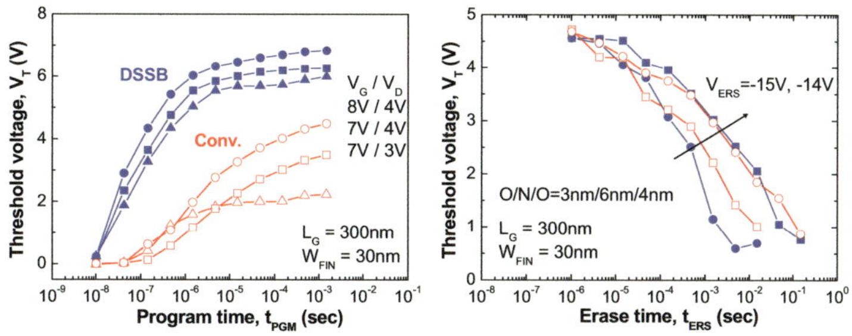

(a) (b)

Fig. 3-6. (a) Program and (b) erase characteristics for DG DSSB and DG conventional SONOS devices (Choi et al., 2009a)

To trace the position of the injected charges experimentally, the transfer characteristics were analyzed after CHEI programming, and the results are shown in Fig. 3-7(a). The observations confirm that hot electrons preferentially inject into the source-side in the DSSB FinFET SONOS device. The behavior of the DSSB FinFET SONOS device is exactly opposite to that of the conventional FinFET SONOS device. After the CHEI programming, the surface potential of the DSSB FinFET SONOS device is more sensitive to V_D in the reverse state than in the forward state because of the source-side injection of hot electrons. Even though the V_T shift as well as the degradation of the subthreshold swing (SS) caused by captured hot electrons at the drain-side is shown in the forward read state (t_{PGM} = 320 ns), the amount of captured electrons at the drain-side is much smaller than at the source-side. As a result, the V_T shift as well as the degradation of SS is not shown in high drain bias of the forward read state. Furthermore, Fig. 3-7(a) shows increased off-state current in relation to V_D during the reverse read operation. As shown in Fig. 3-7(b), the simulated energy band diagrams of the forward and reverse read operation are plotted to explain the V_T shift and the changed off-state current with varying V_D voltage in Fig. 3-7(a). The off-state current in the Schottky-barrier (SB) MOSFET is known to originate from hole tunneling because of the narrowed tunneling width at the drain-side. In a reverse read operation (*i.e.*, the charge trapped region is at the drain-side and read voltage is applied to the drain), the trapped charge can narrow the tunneling width of the drain-side in the off-state. As a result, the off-state current is more sensitive to V_D in the reverse read state than in the forward read state; it also increases in relation to the increment of V_D.

The retention characteristics of the DSSB FinFET SONOS device at various 1k post-cycled programmed states are illustrated in Fig. 3-8. The characteristics are measured at room temperature. The V_T window at t_{PGM} = 1 ms is expected to have a value exceeding 4 V after 10 years.

The drain disturbance of a programmed cell with a relatively high program bias (V_D = 5 V) was also characterized. In Fig. 3-9, the memory architecture in NOR Flash memory is

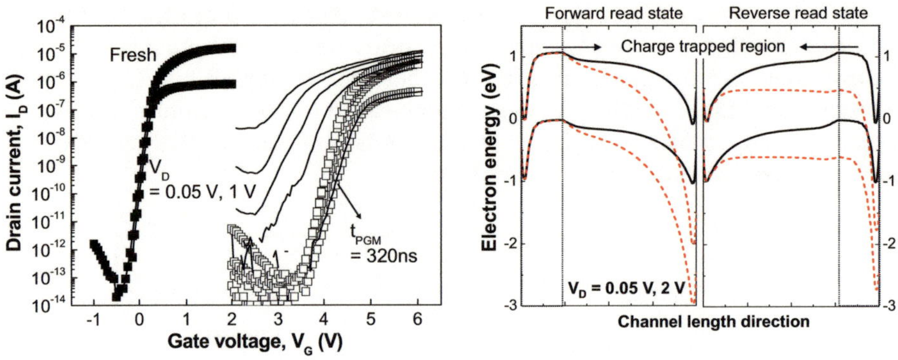

(a) (b)

Fig. 3-7. (a) The I_D-V_G characteristics as a parameter of V_D at the fresh and programmed states in forward and reverse read operations. (b) The simulated energy band diagram of the forward and reverse read state at the off-state. The trapped charges can narrow the tunneling width of the drain-side in the off-state. (Choi et al., 2009b)

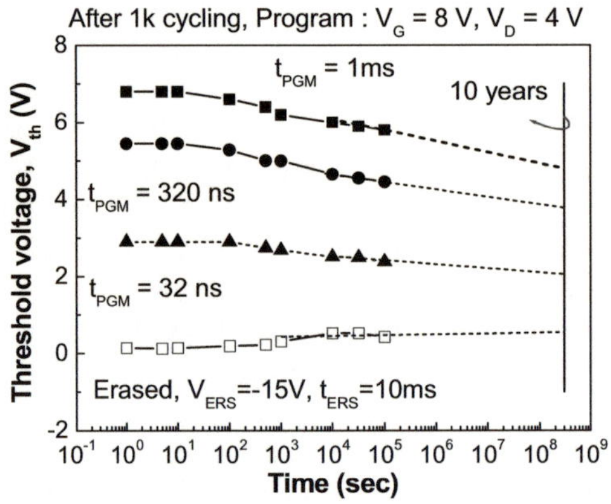

Fig. 3-8. Retention characteristics of a DG DSSB device for MLC in NOR Flash memory operation. (Choi et al., 2009a)

illustrated and the low drain disturbance in DSSB devices is conceptually explained. For the case of cell A (programmed cell), electrons are captured at the source side rather than the drain side. On the other hand, in the case of a conventional device (cell B), trapped electrons at the drain side increase the potential for hot holes to be generated, which results in a drain disturbance (*i.e.*, soft erase). Therefore, improved immunity against drain disturbances is achieved in the DSSB NOR Flash device, as shown in Fig. 3-10. This is primarily due to the trapped electrons located at the source side, as they inhibit hot holes from being injected into the trapped regions.

3.2 Fowler-Nordheim tunneling program in double-gate DSSB MOSFETs

One of the advantages of SONOS type Flash memory devices is natural immunity to floating-gate coupling issues, thereby allowing downscaling to the nano-regime. SONOS-type devices can operate with very few electrons without displaying erratic behavior.

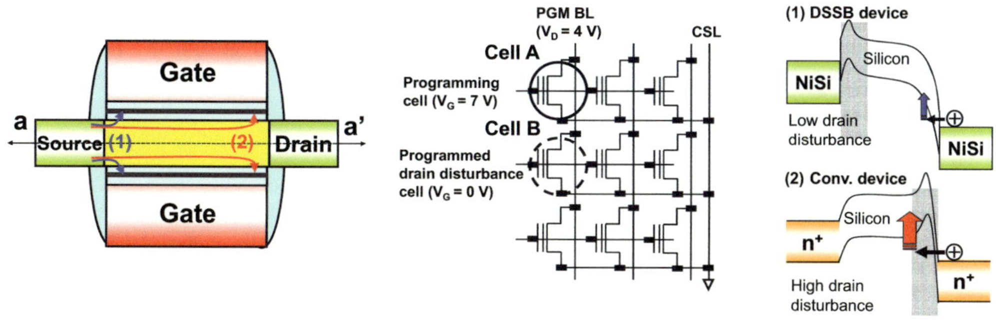

(a) (b) (c)

Fig. 3-9. (a) Schematic of the DG DSSB FinFET SONOS device. (b) Architecture of NOR Flash memory. (c) Conceptually illustrated energy band diagrams at the programmed state for the DSSB and the conventional device. (Choi et al., 2009a)

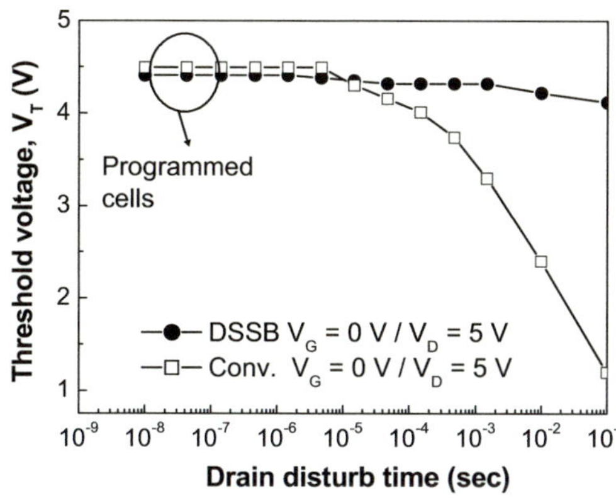

Fig. 3-10. Drain disturbances of DG DSSB and DG conventional devices: Compared to the conventional device, high immunity to drain disturbance is achieved in the DG DSSB device. (Choi et al., 2009a)

However, their programming time is excessively long, falling in a range of $10^{-6} \sim 10^{-3}$ sec due to the Fowler-Nordheim (FN) tunneling mechanism in conventional NAND Flash memory. This makes it difficult for applications requiring high-speed application such as solid-state drive (SSD). In addition, the conventional diffused S/D with deep junctions obstructs further aggressive scaling in the SONOS type memory devices.

Current research on NAND Flash memory is mainly focusing on a 3-D stacking structure realized by deposition of a poly-Si channel. In addition, a junction-free structure, *i.e.*, S/D junctions are not formed, is indispensable, as the formation of S/D junctions is quite difficult due to vertical stacked 3-D Flash memory (Lue et al., 2008). However, this structure cannot be directly applicable to Flash memory with poly-Si channel because of high resistance at the S/D junctions, as aforementioned. Therefore, another method to form S/D junctions is needed. In this section, a novel NAND Flash architecture implemented in the same double-gate DSSB FinFETs SONOS is demonstrated. Fast programming is achieved due to the electrons with extra kinetic energy, *i.e.*, hot carriers, on the dopant segregated

S/D side. These hot electrons require neither high programming voltage nor long programming time. With the same ground voltage on the S/D junction, hot electrons triggered by sharp energy band bending at the edge of silicided S/D junctions are naturally generated.

3.2.1 Memory characteristics

Fig. 3-11(a) explains the operating principle at the programming state. Fast programming is achievable by applying the same ground voltage on both S/D junctions simultaneously (Fig. 3-11(b)). In this case, a locally high lateral of electric field is generated by a sharpened band structure at the dopant-segregated region. Thus, electrons thermally injected or tunneled from S/D edges, *i.e.*, with extra kinetic energy, are energized by this high electric field and are mainly used to program the NAND Flash device. Therefore, fast programming with low voltage is feasible with enhanced tunneling probability. Note that most of trapped electrons in short programming time can be located at the edge of S/D junctions.

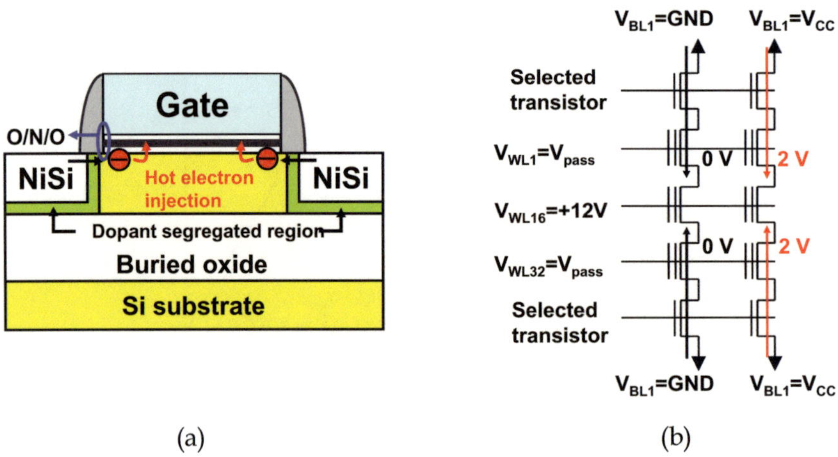

Fig. 3-11. (a) Schematic of the operating principle of the DSSB FinFET SONOS. (b) The hot electrons energized by the DSSB are used to program for a NAND Flash application by applying the ground voltage on the S/D junctions. (Choi et al., 2009c)

Figs. 3-12(a) and 3-12(b) illustrate the programming and erasing transient characteristics, respectively. As a reference, a conventional FinFET SONOS with a diffused p-n junction is compared. The results demonstrate the excellent program efficiency of the DSSB FinFET SONOS. The program conditions V_{PGM} = 12 V with t_{PGM} = 100 ns exhibit a V_T shift of 4.5 V in the DSSB FinFET SONOS. It should be noted that a significant V_T shift for programming was achieved within a few tens of nanoseconds, which is approximately 1000 times faster than the conventional device. The difference in the V_T shift between the DSSB FinFET SONOS and a conventional FinFET SONOS for programming was approximately 3 V at 100 ns programming time. This difference is attributed to hot carrier injection energized by sharp band bending at the dopant segregated S/D junction edge. These outstanding results are among the best results in terms of V_T window and programming/erasing speed reported to date for FinFET structure flash memory devices. However, there is no significant difference in the erase characteristics of the DSSB FinFET SONOS as compared with a conventional FinFET SONOS because electron de-trapping from the nitride to the silicon substrate is not different between them.

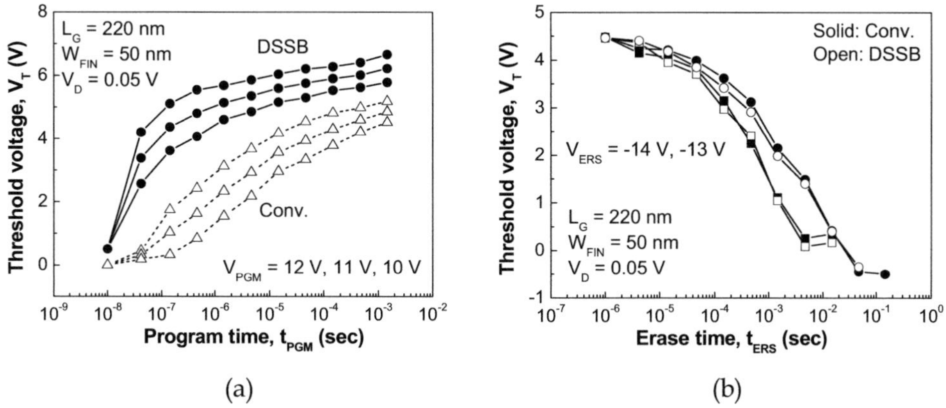

Fig. 3-12. Program (a) and erase (b) transient characteristics with various program voltages. Excellent program efficiency compared to the control group is achieved due to hot electrons energized by sharp band bending at the S/D. (Choi et al., 2009c)

The tunneling oxide of conventional devices may be non-uniform due to the non-uniform etching profile of the narrow silicon channel; therefore the tunneling probability of electrons at the channel fluctuates significantly in conventional devices. However, for the case of DSSB devices, the trapped electrons are mainly located at the edges of the S/D junction. Therefore, a more parallel V_T shift can be achieved in the DSSB device. As shown in Fig. 3-13, a parallel shift among programmed states was found in the DSSB device but not in the conventional device. This implies that two-sided charge injection at the S/D prevails in the DSSB FinFET SONOS device. Note, on the other hand, that an unwanted non-uniform charge injection by FN tunneling occurs in the conventional FinFET SONOS device, resulting in an oblique shift and degradation of the slope.

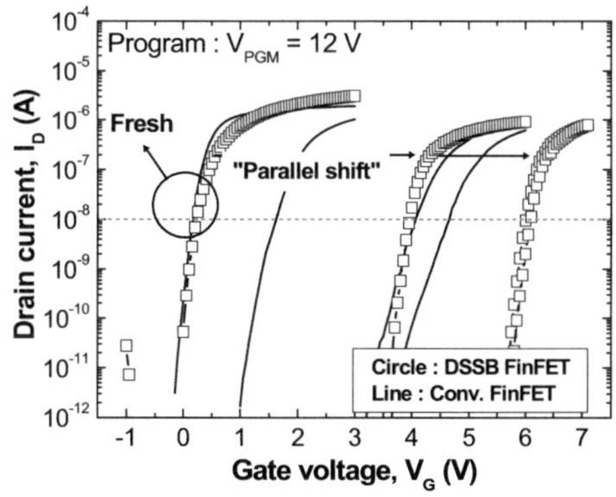

Fig. 3-13. Comparison of the I_D-V_G shift among various programmed states. A two-sided injected charge produces a parallel shift of I-V. (Choi et al., 2008)

The retention characteristics after 1k cycling and P/E cycling endurance of the DSSB FinFET SONOS were compared to the control group, a conventional FinFET SONOS, and the results are presented in Figs. 3-14 (a) and 3-14(b), respectively. These characteristics were measured at room temperature. Fig. 3-14(a) shows that a rapid degradation of the retention characteristics was monitored during longer programming time. Under this condition the stored charges are more likely to be lost due to larger damage by hot carriers, degrading the tunneling oxide quality. Nevertheless, the V_T margin of the DSSB FinFET SONOS after ten years is larger than that of the conventional device. This is attributed to the high efficiency of programming originating from the sharpened energy band bending by the DSSB structure. P/E endurance characteristics are also plotted in Fig. 3-14(b). After 10^5 P/E cycles, only a negligible V_T shift can be seen, thus verifying that the reliability characteristics are satisfactory.

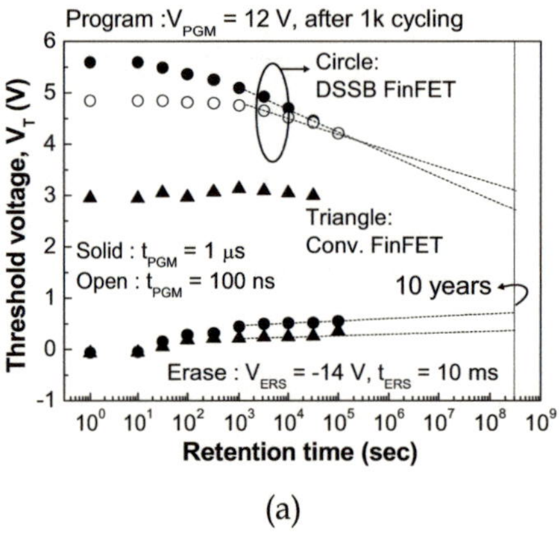

Fig. 3-14. (a) Post cycling retention comparison of the DSSB FinFET SONOS and a conventional FinFET SONOS. Due to damage of hot electrons, the charge loss of the DSSB FinFET SONOS is larger than that of the conventional device. (b) Measured endurance characteristics of the DSSB FinFET SONOS and the conventional device. A negligible V_T shift is observed in the P/E states. (Choi et al., 2009c)

4. Junctionless MOSFETs

Flash memory has recently scaled rapidly down to a 20 ~ 30 nm node. However, with researchers relying on conventional approaches, critical scaling limits are being faced, foreshadowing the possibility that further downscaling will eventually be impossible. Hence, a new and innovative device structure is urgently required. Most importantly, among the crucial limitations, the short-channel effects (SCEs) have increasingly become unavoidable technical challenges, as it is difficult to scale the equivalent oxide thickness (EOT) below 10 nm due to the nature of multi-layered gate dielectrics. Shallow junctions are very important to suppress the SCEs; however, it is difficult to precisely control the junction depth and profile. Moreover, the formation of such shallow junctions becomes a serious concern with 3-dimensional (3D) multi-stacking integration due to the large thermal budget required. For this reason, a "junction-free transistor" based on junction-free virtual S/D for NAND Flash memory was previously reported, and the concept was applied to other types of 3D integrated Flash memory such as Bit Cost Scalable (BiCS) memory (Tanaka et al., 2007), Vertical-Stacked-Array-Transistor (VSAT) memory (Kim et al., 2009), and Terabit Cell Array Transistor (TCAT) memory (Jang et al., 2009), among others (Hubert et al., 2009). However, it can be expected that current flowing through a string of NAND Flash memory will be significantly degraded by pre-existing high resistance regions, *i.e.*, undoped source/drain (S/D) regions, despite that these regions can be transformed into low resistance regions via an inversion process by fringing the field from the gate. This can therefore lead to severe back-pattern dependency or result in the failure of read operations. These challenging issues tend to be more severe in 3-D multi-stacked Flash memory where poly-crystalline silicon (poly-Si) is used as a channel (Walker et al., 2009).

Recently, a nanowire transistor known as a "junctionless transistor" or a "gated resistor" was introduced (Colinge et al., 2010). It consists of n^+ (or p^+ for a p-channel device) homogenously doped silicon nanowire (SiNW), *i.e.*, an n^+ source - n^+ channel - n^+ drain (or a p^+ source - p^+ channel - p^+ drain) for the p-channel device, with a gate electrode. Junctionless transistors have several advantages compared to traditional inversion-mode transistors: (i) they are easily fabricated; (ii) they are free from S/D junctions therefore have less dopant fluctuation; (iii) they can reduce SCEs; (iv) they can reduce mobility degradation by surface roughness scattering; and (iv) they relax the stringent requirements reducing the gate dielectric thickness. These intrinsic strengths make the concept proposed here attractive for application of a junctionless transistor to Flash memory. However, existing junctionless transistors have an inherent limitation in that they primarily implemented on a SOI wafer.

In this section, an all-around-gate (AAG) junctionless transistor is applied to oxide-nitride-oxide (O/N/O) type charge-trapping Flash memory. By utilizing a deep reactive ion etching (RIE) system (Ng et al., 2009), a junctionless transistor with a suspended SiNW channel with a width of 4 nm (W_{NW} = 4 nm) and a length of 20 nm (L_G = 20 nm) is fabricated, where the channel is completely separated from the bulk substrate. The performance is comparable to that of currently reported Flash memory, but it can be scaled down further, below the 20 nm node, due to the simplified process and the advantages inherited from the junctionless transistor.

4.1 Operating principle of junctionless MOSFETs

The operational principle of an n-type junctionless MOSFET is different from that of a standard n-type conventional MOSFET. In the subthreshold region, shown in Fig. 4-1(a), the highly doped channel is fully depleted, and hence it can hold a large electric field. By increasing the gate voltage, the electric field in the channel reduces until a neutral region is created in the center of the channel. At this point, it is possible to define the threshold voltage, because bulk current starts to flow through the center of the channel, as illustrated in Fig. 4-1(b). Then, by further increasing the gate voltage, the depletion width reduces until a completely neutral channel is created, as seen in Fig. 4-1(c). This occurs when the gate voltage equals the flat band voltage. At the onset of this condition, the bulk current reaches its maximum value. Thereafter, by increasing the gate voltage further, negative charges accumulate on the surfaces of the channel, as shown in Fig. 4-1(d). These charges result in surface current, which is similar to the current in a standard n-type conventional MOSFET.

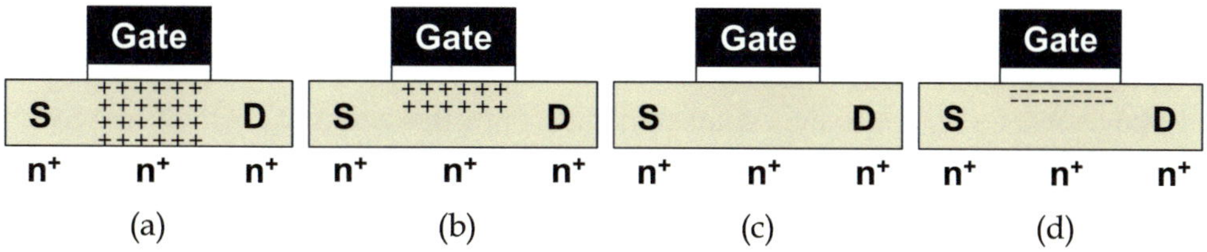

Fig. 4-1. (a) Fully depleted channel in subthreshold mode, (b) semi-depleted channel in bulk current mode, (c) flat band mode, and (d) accumulation mode.

4.2 Device fabrication

A (100) bulk silicon wafer is used as a starting material. First, the top of a silicon bulk wafer is uniformly doped by ion implantation with arsenic for the n-channel devices. The implant energies and doses are chosen to yield uniform doping of 2×10^{19} /cm^3. High doping is required in the junctionless transistor to ensure a high driving current and good source/drain contact resistance. After patterning the active region with W_{NW} = 30 nm, the Bosch process enabled by the RIE system is employed to form the suspended SiNW separated from the bulk substrate. The suspended SiNW via the Bosch process is achieved by balancing anisotropic etching and passivation steps. Details of the Bosch process can be found in the literature (Ng et al., 2009). The scanning electron microscopy (SEM) images in Fig. 4-2 clearly show the suspended SiNWs. The gap distance between the SiNW and bulk substrate is approximately 250 nm. After the formation of the SiNWs, channel stop implantation with boron ions is applied. Subsequently, two iterations of sacrificial oxidation are employed for further reduction of the width (W_{NW} = 4 nm) of the SiNW and to make the channel smooth, followed by the formation of shallow trench isolation (STI). Next, an O/N/O layer with a thickness of 2.8nm/6.2nm/7nm (using a thermal oxide and LP-CVD nitride/TEOS oxide) and an in-situ n^+ poly-Si gate (using LP-CVD poly-Si) are formed sequentially. Afterwards, a gate length (L_G) of 20 nm is patterned. Horizontal and vertical transmission electron microscopy (TEM) images of the fabricated junctionless transistor are also shown in Fig. 4-2.

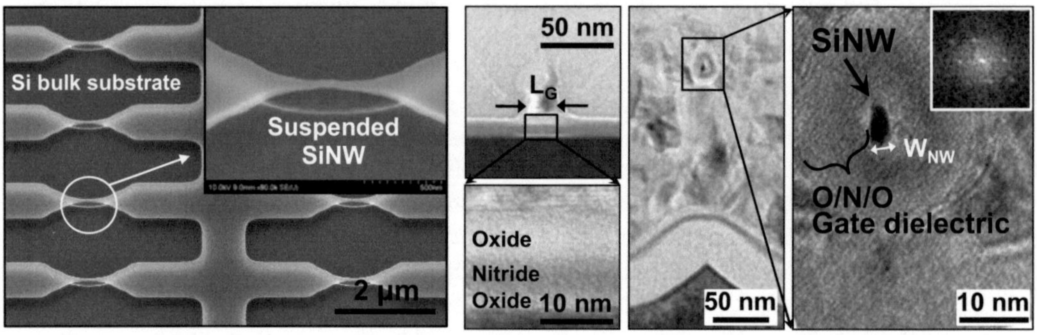

(a) (b)

Fig. 4-2. (a) SEM image and magnified views of the suspended SiNW on the bulk substrate and (b) Horizontal and vertical TEM images in the L_G direction in the AAG junctionless transistor with the O/N/O gate dielectric. The width (W_{NW}) and length (L_G) of the SiNW channel are approximately 4 nm and 20 nm, respectively. The thickness of the O/N/O layers for the charge storage node is 2.8nm/6.2nm/7nm. (Choi et al., 2011)

4.3 Memory characteristics

Fig. 4-3(a) shows the P/E transient characteristics of junctionless AAG SONOS devices with a 20 nm L_G and a 4 nm W_{NW} for various P/E conditions. A large P/E window (ΔV_T) up to 6.5 V was attained with the aid of a GAA structure despite the highly scaled device size, demonstrating the cell suitability for MLC operations. No erase saturation phenomenon was observed, even at -15V, despite the n^+ poly-Si gate. This indicates that there is no need to use a metal-gate or high-k blocking oxide. Moreover, as seen in Fig. 4-3(b), program inhibition is achieved by direct raising of the unselected bit-line potential. It is implicit that there is no need to introduce a complex self-boosting method. A high incremental step pulse program (ISPP) slope (0.7) is also attained, even with a L_G value of 20 nm.

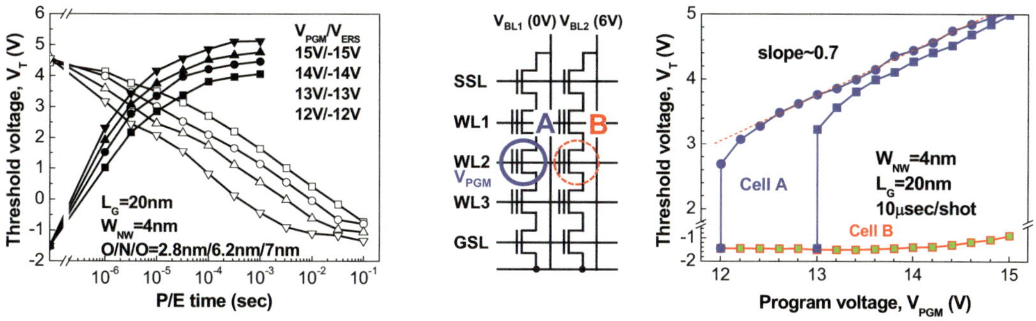

(a) (b) (c)

Fig. 4-3. (a) Program and erase transient characteristics of the junctionless AAG SONOS device. (b) ISPP programming and related inhibit method. Program inhibition is achieved by directly raising the unselected bit-line potential. For a programmed cell, a higher incremental step pulse program (ISPP) slope is also attained, even at 20nm L_G. (Choi et al., 2011)

3D NAND structures with a floating body require careful consideration when designing S/D junctions for enhanced erase characteristics. To fix the floating body potential during erase operations effectively, a sufficient number of holes must be generated by band-to-band tunneling from the S/D junctions. Therefore, the S/D junctions need to be heavily doped, abrupt, and uniform. Unless 3D NAND structures satisfy the aforementioned demands, uniform and efficient erase characteristics cannot be ensured in conventional diffused S/D and junction-free virtual S/D structures (Figs. 4-3(a) and 4-3(b)). Fig. 4-3(c) compares the distribution of the erased V_T for the junctionless and inversion-mode AAG SONOS devices. Contrary to the inversion-mode devices, the S/D of junctionless devices is precisely controlled by the gate electric field. As a result, a uniformly distributed erased V_T is successfully obtained without any V_T correction methods.

Because the conduction of a junctionless device initially occurs in the center of an n^+-doped SiNW channel, the device can be less sensitive to the interface trap generated from P/E cycles compared to a conventional inversion-mode device, as shown in Fig. 4-4. In a TCAD simulation, it is confirmed that the acceptor-type interface trap does not significantly affect the V_T shift in a junctionless device. Note that the higher the doping concentration of a SiNW channel is, the stronger the P/E endurance becomes. Moreover, reasonable post-cyclic data retention characteristics were achieved.

5. Conclusions

In this chapter, as we confront challenges of current Flash memory technology and as the design rule deviates from the historical scaling paradigm, a new type of Flash memory cell based on the structure of dopant-segregated Schottky-barrier (DSSB) MOSFETs, which has an ultra-thin pocket layer with high-dose dopants surrounding the interface between the

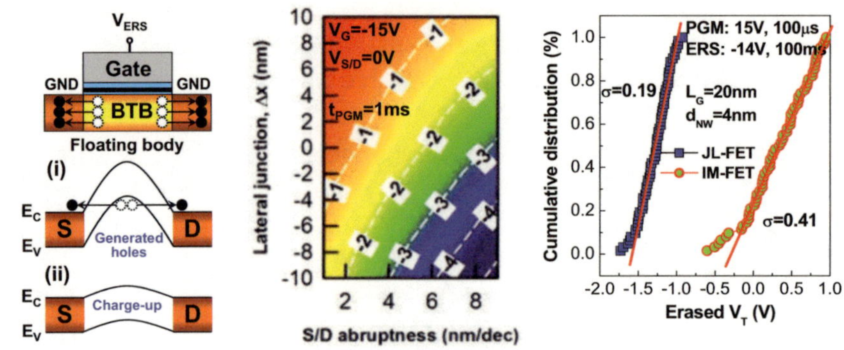

(a) (b) (c)

Fig. 4-3. (a) Erase operations for the 3D NAND structure with a floating body: (i) First, the floating body potential follows the gate potential (V_{ERS}). As a result, holes are generated by band-to-band tunneling. (ii) Second, the generated holes can pin the floating body potential. (b) TCAD simulation of the floating body potential during the erase operation. (c) Distribution of erased V_T values for junctionless and inversion-mode AAG SONOS devices. (Choi et al., 2011)

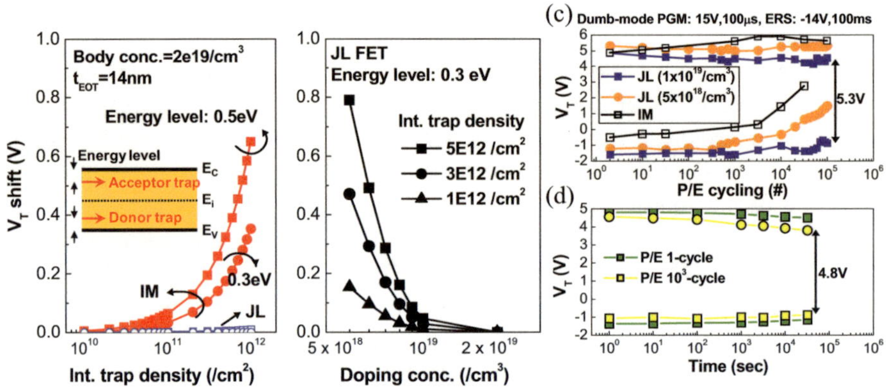

(a) (b)

Fig. 4-4. (a) Simulated V_T shift versus interface trap density (N_{it}) as a parameter of the energy level of both acceptor- and donor-type traps. (b) Simulated V_T shift versus doping concentration of the SiNW channel in the junctionless device. (c) Dumb-mode P/E cycling (without any P/E verify) endurance test. (d) Post-cycling retention characteristics of the junctionless device. (Choi et al., 2011)

metallic silicide material for source/drain (S/D) and the channel, is proposed. The hot carriers intrinsically generated from the shallow DSSB S/D junctions can be utilized for the advancement of both the NAND and the NOR type Flash memory cell. With the aid of hot carriers that can be generated by elevated electric field at the DSSB S/D junctions stemming from the abrupt band bending, the probability to be trapped into a charge storage node of Flash memory, such as polysilicon layer in the floating gate memory device or the nitride layer in the SONOS memory device, is enhanced. Therefore, the DSSB MOSFET shows very fast programming time at low programming voltage, compared to conventional MOSFET based on p-n S/D junctions. Besides, the superior scalability resulting from the abrupt and shallow junctions can also be achieved without the constraint of the parasitic resistance due to metallic silicided material. Therefore, the DSSB devices can be a premier choice for future nano-electronics applications of the logic and Flash memory device since they do not only enable continuation of device scaling due to the improved electrostatics but also provide benefits for an alternative memory cell.

Moreover, a highly scaled AAG junctionless transistor SONOS memory cell with acceptable P/E behaviors, cycling endurance, and data retention is also demonstrated. The junctionless transistor memory cell inherited the scaling advantages of not only the AAG structure but also the junctionless transistor. Therefore, the junctionless transistor memory cell, together with DSSB MOSFETs, is an excellent candidate for the next-generation 3-D NAND Flash memory.

6. Acknowledgment

This work was supported by the IT R&D program of MKE/KEIT [10035320, Development of novel 3D stacked devices and core materials forthe next generation flash memory], the National Research Foundation (NRF) grant funded by the Korea government (No. K20901000002-09E0100-00210), Nano R&D program through the National Research Foundation of Korea funded by the Ministry of Education, Science, and Technology (grant number : 2009-0082583), and Samsung Electronics Co., Ltd.

7. References

Walker, A. J. (2009). Sub-50-nm dual-gate thin-film transistors for monolithic 223 3-D Flash, *IEEE Transaction on Electron Devices*, Vol. 56, No. 11, pp. 2703–2710, IEEE, ISSN:0018-9383

Larson, J. M. et al. (2006). Overview and Status of Metal S/D Schottky-Barrier MOSFET Technology, *IEEE Transaction on Electron Devices*, Vol. 53, No. 5, pp. 1048-1058, IEEE ISSN:0018-9383

Kinoshita, A. et al. (2004). Solution for High-Performance Schottky-Source/Drain MOSFETs: Schottky Barrier Height Engineering with Dopant Segregation Technique, *IEEE VLSI Symp. Tech. Dig.*, pp. 168-169, IEEE, ISBN:4-900784-00-1

Muraka, S. P. et al. (1987). Dopant redistribution in silicide–silicon and silicide-polycrystalline silicon bilayered structures, *Journal of Vacuum Science & Technology*, Vol. 5, No. 6, pp. 1674-1688, ISSN:1071-1023

Uchida, K. et al. (2000). Enhancement of hot-electron generation rate in Schottky source metal–oxide–semiconductor field-effect transistors, *Applied Physics Letters*, Vol. 76, No. 26, pp. 3992-3994, ISSN:0003-6951

Kinoshita, A. et al. (2006). Comprehensive Study on Injection Velocity Enhancement in Dopant-Segregated Schottky MOSFETs, *IEEE IEDM Tech. Dig.*, pp. 1-4, IEEE, ISBN:978-1-4244-237-4

Wu, A. T. et al. (1986). A novel high-speed, 5-volt programming EPROM structure with source-side injection, *IEEE IEDM Tech. Dig.*, pp. 584-587, IEEE, ISBN:978-1-4244-237-4

Choi, S.-J. et al. (2008). High Speed Flash Memory and 1T-DRAM on Dopant Segregated Schottky Barrier (DSSB) FinFET SONOS Device for Multi-functional SoC Applications, *IEEE IEDM Tech. Dig.*, pp. 223-226, IEEE, ISBN:978-1-4244-237-4

Choi, S.-J. et al. (2009a). Performance Breakthrough in NOR Flash Memory with Dopant-Segregated Schottky-Barrier (DSSB) SONOS Devices, *IEEE VLSI Symp. Tech. Dig.*, pp. 222-223, IEEE, ISBN:4-900784-00-1

Choi, S.-J. et al. (2009b). High Injection Efficiency and Low-Voltage Programming in a Dopant-Segregated Schottky Barrier (DSSB) FinFET SONOS for NOR-type Flash Memory, *IEEE Electron Device Letters*, Vol. 30, No. 3, pp. 265-268, IEEE, ISSN:0741-3106

Lue, H.-T. et al. (2008). A novel junction-free BE-SONOS NAND Flash, *IEEE VLSI Symp. Tech. Dig.*, pp. 140-141, IEEE, ISBN:4-900784-00-1

Choi, S.-J. et al. (2009c). Enhancement of Program Speed in Dopant-Segregated Schottky-Barrier (DSSB) FinFET SONOS for NAND-Type Flash Memory, *IEEE Electron Device Letters*, Vol. 30, No. 1, pp. 78-81, IEEE, ISSN:0741-3106

Tanaka, H. et al. (2007). Bit cost scalable technology with punch and plug process for ultra high density Flash memory, *IEEE VLSI Symp. Tech. Dig.*, pp. 14-15, IEEE, ISBN:4-900784-00-1

Kim, J. et al. (2009). Novel vertical-stacked-array-transistor (VSAT) for ultra-high-density and cost-effective NAND Flash memory devices and SSD (solid state drive), *IEEE VLSI Symp. Tech. Dig.*, pp. 186-187, IEEE, ISBN:4-900784-00-1

Jang, J. et al. (2009). Vertical cell array using TCAT (terabit cell array transistor) technology for ultra high density NAND Flash memory, *IEEE VLSI Symp. Tech. Dig.*, pp. 192-193, IEEE, ISBN:4-900784-00-1

Hubert, A. et al. (2009). A stacked SONOS technology, up to 4 levels and 6 nm crystalline nanowires, with gate-all-around or independent gates (Φ-Flash), suitable for full 3-D integration, *IEEE IEDM Tech. Dig.*, pp. 637-640, IEEE, ISBN:978-1-4244-237-4

Colinge, J.-P. et al. (2010). Nanowire transistors without junctions, *Nature Nanotechnology*, Vol. 5, pp. 225-229, ISSN: 1748-3387

Ng, R. M. Y. et al. (2009). Vertically Stacked Silicon Nanowire Transistors Fabricated by Inductive Plasma Etching and Stress-Limited Oxidation, *IEEE Electron Device Letters*, Vol. 30, No. 5, pp. 520-522, IEEE, ISSN:0741-3106

Choi, S.-J et al. (2011) A Novel Junctionless All-Around-Gate SONOS Device with a Quantum Nanowire on a Bulk Substrate for 3D Stack NAND Flash Memory, IEEE VLSI Symp. Tech. Dig., in press, IEEE, ISBN:4-900784-00-1

10

Non-Volatile Memory Devices Based on Chalcogenide Materials

Fei Wang
California State University, Long Beach, United States of America

1. Introduction

Non-volatile memory refers to memory devices that can retain stored information even when electric power is not applied. Usually, non-volatile memories are utilized as secondary storage in computers, long term persistent storage and portable data storage. The most popular portable non-volatile memory nowadays is the Flash memory. The common device structure of a flash memory cell contains a MOSFET with a floating gate. The information storage relies on charge storage on the floating gate. Currently, there exist two types of flash technology: NOR and NAND technology. NAND technology tends to dominate because of its better scaling potential and lower cost. The major concerns regarding the floating gate based flash memory now is its scaling limitations. Challenges, such as cell-to-cell interference and programming disturbance, require closer attention, especially for short gated devices. Solutions have been researched in both software development for flash memory, such as sophisticated reading/writing controller, and physical structure improvement. Nano-floating gate structure is one of the proposed physical solutions to overcome the scaling challenges of flash memory [38]. Instead of using a floating gate, this new proposed structure uses silicon nanocrystals to trap charges. This structure can be used to build devices with much thinner oxide layer, which reduces the size. However, concerns still exist about its data retention capabilities.

Moreover, the current prevailing writing operation for flash memory is called block writing, which includes four steps: 1) Dump the whole block into a buffer DRAM; 2) Write new information into DRAM; 3) Erase old information in Flash; 4) Write information stored in DRAM into Flash. This requirement on buffer DRAM adds complexity to flash memory, which results in more chip space occupation and lower speed.

As the demand for data storage capability increases, memory density and reading/writing speed have become key factors for technology advancement. To overcome or compensate the limitations of flash memory technology, innovative concepts and materials are being investigated. Non-volatile memory devices based on chalcogenide materials are the most promising technology due to its fast reading/writing speed and high scalability. In addition to those, since the information storage for chalcogenide devices are based on phase or electrochemical reaction, chalcogenide based devices display excellent retention characteristic, especially so when compared to flash memories that rely on charge storage.

In general, information storage devices based on chalcogenide materials could be categorized into two types. Phase change memory (PCM) is one of them. The information storage is realized by converting nanoscale grains of chalcogenide materials between an amorphous state and a crystalline state [1]. The conversion requires applying heat onto nanoscale memory grain. This can be done through either optical or electrical methods. Optical phase change memory was developed and commercialized in 1990s. Now it is widely used in rewritable optical data recording (e.g. RW-DVD discs). Electronic phase change memory did not attract much attention at the beginning, mainly due to the vast developemnt of charge-storage memories, such as EPROM and Flash. Not until the recent decade, when scaling limitation raise concerns on charge-storage memories, does electronic PCM re-gain attention of the memory industry. Materials used as active recording layers for PCM are Sb-Te containing alloys, with the most widely used material being the Ge-Sb-Te (GST) system [2-4].
The other type of information storage mechanism is relatively new. It is known as Programmable Metallization Cell memory (PMC). This type of memory device relocates metal ions in a solid state electrolyte using electrochemical methods [5-6]. Therefore, one can control the resistivity of the solid state electrolyte to achieve the data recording purpose. The PMC was first suggested by M. Kozicki [5] in early 2000s. Several research groups and indutrial R&D are inverstigating in this direction now. A variety of names have been given to this type of devices, such as conductive-bridge RAM, nanobridge memory and eletrolytic memory etc. Materials used as active recording films for this category are metal containing chacogenides, such as Ag-Se, Ag-S [7], Ag-Ge-Se [5-6], Ag-Ge-S [8], Cu-S [9] etc. PMC, compared to PCM, has the advantages in terms of short recording time, low recording power as well as better scaling capability [5-6].

2. Chalcogenide materials

Chalcogenide materials used in both PCM and PMC are usually in glassy form. Glass is also called amorphous materials or disordered materials. Not like crystals, glassy materials do not have long range order in their lattice. This kind of disordered structure makes possible some unique properties of glassy materials. Chalcogenide glasses are simply glasses containing elements from group VI of periodic table; usually they are alloys of group IV and/or group V elements together with group VI elements. When heated, solid glass experience three critical temperatures (Fig 1): glass transition temperature (T_g), crystallization temperature (T_c) and melting temperature (T_m). Glass transition temperature is a signature of significant softening of glasses; it is measured by probing the viscosity of glasses. Glasses with temperature above T_g but below T_m are still in solid format, but with lower viscosity. This is significantly different from crystals, which do not have T_g. When temperature increases up to T_c, glasses starts to crystallize, results in poly-crystal in most situations. Increasing temperature above T_m will melt the glasses. Genrallay, crystallizaon process has two states, nucleation state and crystal growth state. At crsystallization temperature, molecules starts to gather into clusters, thus forms nuclei. The crystal will further grow from those nuclei. The crystal growth process needs time, which is material dependent. Glasses are usually obtained by quickly quenching melts. This quenching process forces temperature to by-pass T_c quickly, so that crystallization does not have time to happen. The GST system (Ge-Sb-Te) used in PCM devices has a typical melting temperature of 600°C, and its crystalization temperature is between 100-150°C depend on specific chemical composition.

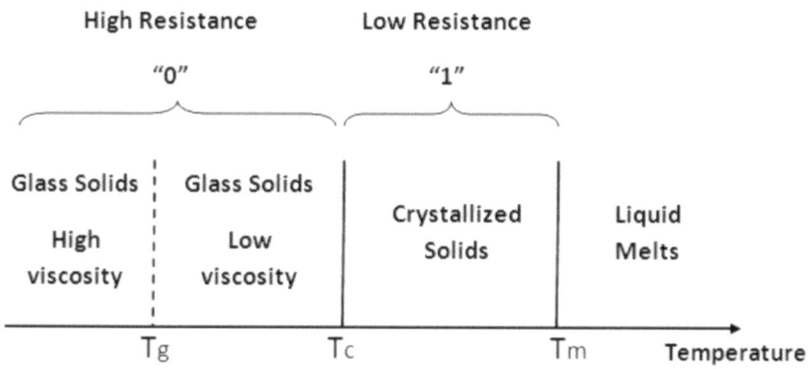

Fig. 1. Phase changes of glassy materials as a function of temperature. Three critical temperatures are observed: glass transition temperature (T_g), crystallization temperature (T_c) and melting temperature (T_m).

Not all compositions can form glasses; some compositions tend to crystallize easily during quenching, those compositions are called poor glass formers. Application of chalcogenide glasses requires their glassy state to be stable, i.e. good glass formers. Boolchand *et. al.* suggested that chalcogenide glasses display three elastic phases as a function of their mean coordination number: floppy phase, Intermediate phase (IP) and stressed rigid phase (Fig 2) [10-22]. Glass compositions in floppy phase and stressed rigid phase are usually poor glass formers due to the high internal stress in their molecular structure. Compositions in IP are usually good glass formers because their molecular networks are nearly stress free. Good glass formers are needed for PCM devices since they can form glass even when temperature is brought down slowly. Therefore, compositions in IP are ideal for PCM devices. Within the glass forming region of Ge-Sb-Te system, increasing composition of Ge usually increases the melting temperature, which is undesireable because of the power concerns. On the other hand, decreasing the Ge content will cause the glass become unstable in glassy states, which causes problem in term of data retention. Therefore, typical compositions selected for PCM

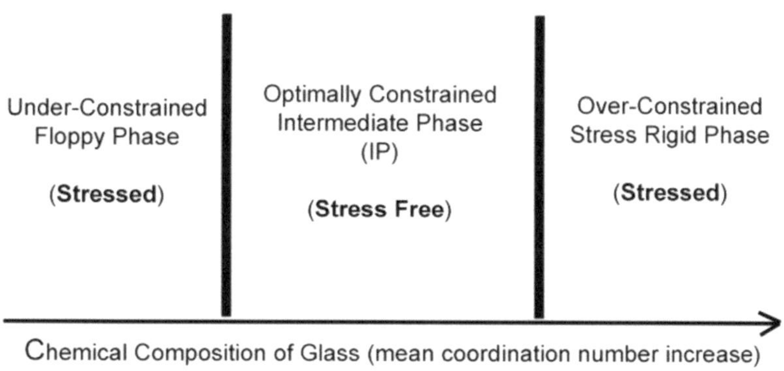

Fig. 2. Elastic phases in chalcogenide glasses as a function of mean coordination number of glasses. Mean coordination number is an indicator of chemical composition.

devices is $Ge_2Sb_2Te_5$ system (GST-225). The GST-225 system have typical melting temperature of 600°C, and its crystalization temperature is around 120°C. Glasses in IP are also ideal for PMC devices. The stress free nature of their network structure makes them good solid state solvent for metal additives, which is necessary for PMC devices.

3. Phase Change Memory (PCM)

3.1 Theoretical background

The operation of PCM devices relies on the resistance difference between the glassy phase (amorphous phase) and the crystalline phase. The materials used in PCM are mostly Tellurium based glasses, i.e. GST systems. As shown in Fig. 1, amorphous phase usually displays high resistance, which corresponds to logic '0'; crystalline phase usually displays lower resistance, which corresponds to logic '1'. The typical high resistance, i.e. Off resistance, is in 10^6 Ω range, and the typical low resistance, i.e. On resistance, is in 10^3 Ω range.

In order to convert the active material from amorphous phase (logic '0') to crystalline phase (logic '1'), one needs to increase the cell temperature above T_c, but below T_m. This corresponds to the SET process in logic memory. However, crystallization process needs time. Depends on the size of the cell, it may take 100~500ns. This somewhat limits the speeds of PCM memory. On the other hand, to convert from crystalline phase to amorphous phase, one needs to increase temperature to a higher level, all the way up to above T_m. Once the cell melts, remove heat and let the cell quench. The cell then returns to amorphous phase, i.e. logic '0'. This process corresponds to the RESET process.

Fig. 3 shows the SET and RESET process of PCM cell. The heating is controlled by cell current. During SET process, cell current is controlled in SET region, this assures the cell temperature is between T_c and T_m. During RESET process, cell current is much higher, at least above I_{RESET_min}, this assures cell temperature is high enough to form melts.

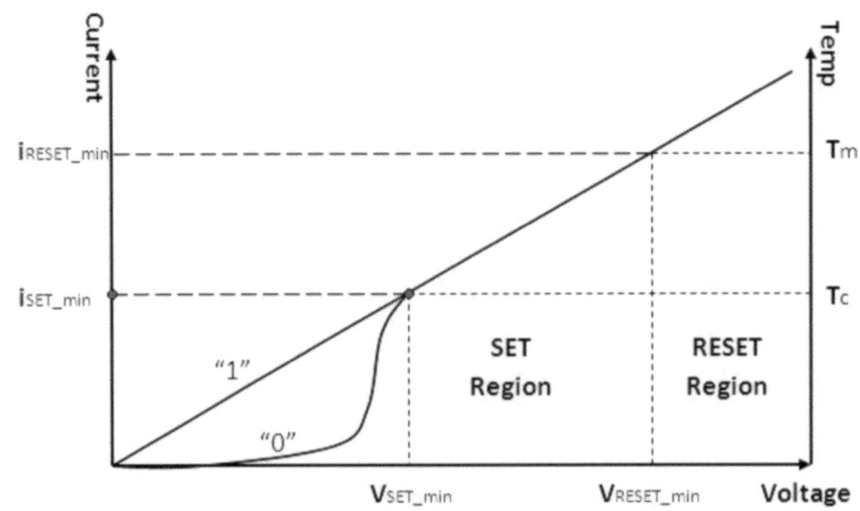

Fig. 3. SET and RESET process of PCM cell. PCM cell temperature is controlled by cell current. i_{SET_min} corresponds to crystallization temperature T_c; i_{RESET_min} corresponds to melting temperature T_m.

3.2 Device structure

Fig. 4 shows a typical structure of a vertical PCM cell. This figure is taken from Woo Yeong Cho et. al.'s IEEE contribution [23]. A PCM cell is composed of an access transistor and an active element, which is usually GST material sandwiched between two electrodes. The gate of the access transistor is controlled by word line. The top electrode (TE) is connected to bit line. Only when both bit line and word line are active, this PCM cell is selected, i.e. current is allowed. In order to improve the heating efficiency, The bottom electrode (BE) is in contact of GST material through a narrow bottom electrode contact (BEC). This BEC structure increases the current density of the cell, therefore, the heating efficiency as well.

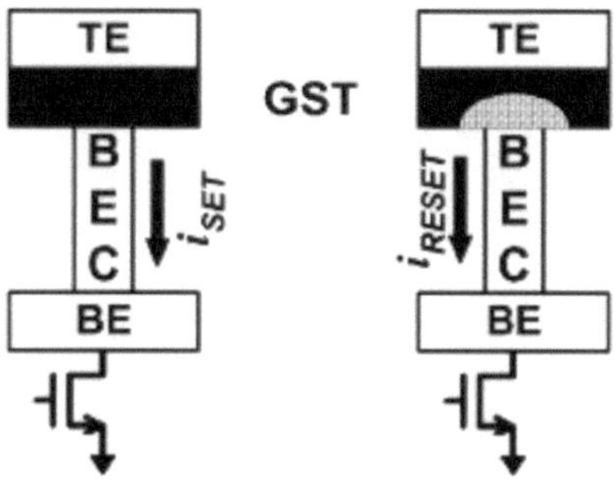

Fig. 4. Typical structure of PCM cell. Left picture indicates a cell during SET process; Right picture indicates a cell during RESET process. Top electrode (TE) is connected to bit line, while the gate of access transistor is connected to word line. [23]

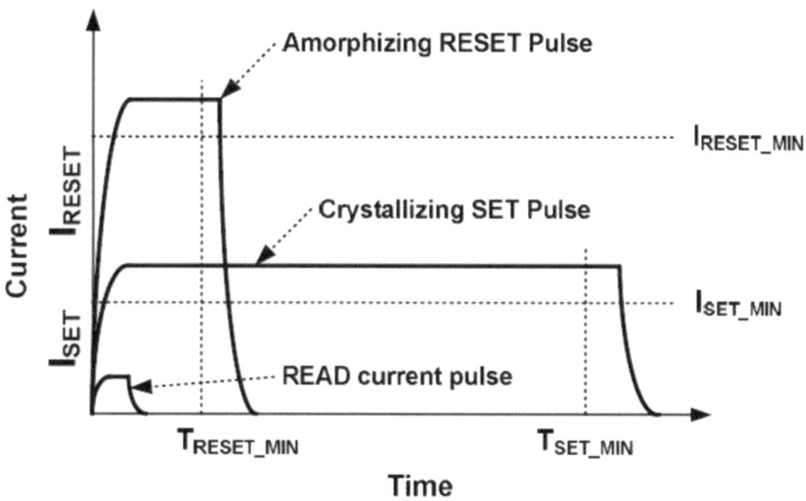

Fig. 5. Current pulses used in reading, SET and RESET processes. [24]

3.3 Reading and writing process

Fig. 5 shows the basic reading and writing process of PCM cell. This figure is taken from Byung-Do Yang et. al.'s IEEE contribution [24]. Writing has two different processes, SET (writing logic '1') and RESET (writing logic '0'). As mentioned earlier, SET process needs lower writing current, but longer time. On the contrary, RESET process needs higher writing current but shorter duration. This is because melting is an instantaneous phase change, but crystallization is a gradual process. Typical SET time is 100~500ns, while typical RESET time is 50-100ns, depends on the size of the device.

Reading is actually a sensing process. During reading process, the phase of active material cannot be affected. Therefore, reading current is much lower than the I_{SET_min}. This assures the cell temperature is always lower than T_c during reading process; therefore, the cell resistance remains in its original category. Typical reading time is around 50ns.

The detailed programming steps are explained as the following [23-24]:

1. RESET

A high voltage is applied on the bit line (BL), while the word line (WL) is active for 50~100ns so that the access transistor is ON during RESET time. This high voltage generate high current, which will melt the GST material. Once RESET time elapses, the current is removed abruptly by de-activate WL. This forces GST material to cool rapidly, hence turns into glass.

2. SET

A medium voltage is applied on BL, while the WL is active for 100~500ns so that the access transistor is ON during SET time. This voltage is not so high to melt the GST material, but is enough to heat it above crystallization temperature (T_c). During SET time, small crystal nucleus form firstly, then grow into larger crystalline structures. Once SET time elapses, heat is removed, proper crystalline phase is formed.

3. READ

A low voltage is applied on BL, while WL is active to turn on access transistor during read time. The stored data is sensed by comparing the BL current with a reference value. If BL current is higher than reference, a logic '1' is identified; if BL current is lower than reference, a logic '0' is identified.

As we mentioned earlier, the programming process of PCM cells heavily relies on resistive heating by elevated currents. This requires the adjacent PCM cells to be isolated properly. Otherwise, disturbances in un-selected cells may cause unwanted writing. On the other hand, reading, SET and RESET current/voltage needs to be carefully calibrated to guarantee 1) they are within design limits; 2) within current/voltage rating of the device.

3.4 Current development in the field

The most widely used information storage media for Phase Change Memory now is $Ge_2Sb_2Te_5$ (GST). Nevertheless, concerns regarding the high SET/RESET threshold and low SET speed of GST material stimulate the efforts in seeking new phase change materials. S. Song et al. [28] recently reported the potential of a low power phase change application using Sb_2Te_3-Ta_2O_5. They claim that the above mentioned material can achieve phase change with lower RESET threshold and shorter pulse width. With a pulse width of 100ns, the RESET threshold is 1.6V, compared to 4.0V for single-layer GST device. This reduction in RESET voltage is due to two factors: 1) The reduced thermal conductivity of Sb_2Te_3-$Ta2O_5$, which is 0.46W/mK compared to 0.54W/mK of crystalline GST. This leads to efficient Joule heating, thereby reducing the voltage required to amorphorize; 2) The lower melting point of Sb_2Te_3-Ta_2O_5 compared to GST. They also found that the Sb_2Te_3-Ta_2O_5 based device could achieve fast programming with pulse width as short as 20ns.

In addition, binary $Sb_{80}Te_{20}$ material is also found to display desirable properties, such as low threshold and fast SET speed. The problem with the pure binary $Sb_{80}Te_{20}$ is its low crystallization temperature, which would be a stability concern. Research has been devoted into doping materials into $Sb_{80}Te_{20}$ [29] or forming a multilayer structure [30] to overcome this issue. Wang et al. [31] recently reported a nano-composite multilayer structure incorporating $Sb_{80}Te_{20}$ and the dielectric material SiO_2. They found by tuning the thickness of $Sb_{80}Te_{20}$ film with respect to SiO_2 layer, one can tune the crystallization temperature, making it higher than that of pure $Sb_{80}Te_{20}$.

With the purpose of increasing the data storage density, research has also been devoted into seeking multi-level storage using a single cell. Y. Gu et al. [32] recently reported that by adjusting the composition of Ge-Sb-Te, one can achieve 3 distinct resistance level by carefully controlling the SET current. They found that $Ge_{15}Sb_{85}Se_{0.8}$ composition display a first resistance shift from $1 \times 10^4\ \Omega$ to $5 \times 10^3\ \Omega$ at 528K and a second resistance shift from $5 \times 10^3\ \Omega$ to $1 \times 10^2\ \Omega$ at 602K. This indicates the possibility to store more than 1 bit of information in the same cell. Y. Yin and S. Hosaka [33] also reported multi-level storage using SbTeN materials. They proved that a 2 bits storage is feasible using the above mentioned material, as shown in Fig. 6. According to their experiment, the SET from R0 to R1 needs 0.4 mA, SET from R1 to R2 needs 0.8 mA, while SET from R2-R3 needs 1.2 mA. The spaces between SET current thresholds are pretty large, so that the manipulation is not hard.

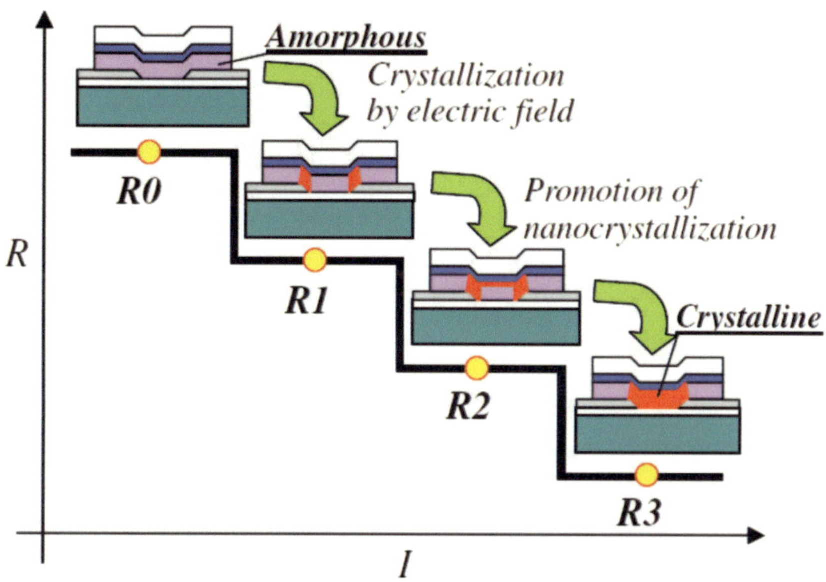

Fig. 6. Multi-level resistance based on promotion of nano-crystallization with programming currents [33]

4. Programmable Metallization Cell (PMC)

4.1 Theoretical background

Active materials forming PMC cells are called solid state electrolytes. They are named so because they are somewhat analogous to liquid state electrolytes. We all know that in liquid electrolytes, ions' mobility is high enough to serve as current carriers. Similarly, solid state

electrolyte also contains ions that are highly movable, majorly they are metal ions that carry positive charges. Many materials can serve as solid state electrolytes. Basically, they can be categorized into two types, chalcogenide-based electrolytes (Ag-Se/S, Cu-Se/S, Ag-Ge-Se/S, Cu-Ge-Se/S [5-9]etc.) and oxide-based electrolytes (WO_3) [25]. We will focus on chalcogenide based electrolytes in this paper.
The process of PMC operation is actually an electro-chemical process. A simple PMC cell is just a thin layer of solid state electrolyte sandwiched between an anode and a cathode. Anode is an electrode that serves as a source of metal ions in active layers. For example, if the solid state electrolyte is silver (Ag) based, i.e. Ag-Se or Ag-Ge-Se, the anode must be Ag. Cathode is an inert electrode, such as nickel (Ni) or aluminum (Al).
A forward voltage bias across the PMC cell will cause the metal ions move towards cathode and eventually be oxidized into metal atoms. Oxidized metal atoms accumulate on cathode, growing towards anode. On the other hand, metal atoms in anode are reduced into metal ions and enter electrolyte to replenish the loss from oxidation. The process is self sustaining until the metal atoms accumulate all the way to anode. This forms a conduction link between two electrodes; therefore, PMC reaches a low resistivity state that corresponds to logic '1'.
A reverse voltage bias will just do the opposite. This time cathode becomes source of reduction. The previous accumulated metal atoms on cathode will be reduced into ions and move toward anode. However, this process cannot sustain since once all metal atoms on cathode are oxidized, there is no longer any oxidation source, and the process will stop automatically. This reverse process dissolves the conduction link between electrodes; therefore, PMC cell returns to high resistivity state, which corresponds to logic '0'.

4.2 Device structure

Fig. 7 illustrates the structure of a PMC cell using silver based solid state electrolyte, as we reported in [26] and [27]. The device is fabricated on a glass substrate using aluminum cathode. We found that the thickness of solid state electrolyte layer has great effects on device performance. We will discuss the thickness dependence in detail in section 4.4. All three layers are evaporated using a thermal vacuum evaporator. In order to avoid spitting during evaporation, a special evaporation boat was designed for chalcogenide layer. The active layer thickness ranges from 8nm to 30nm.

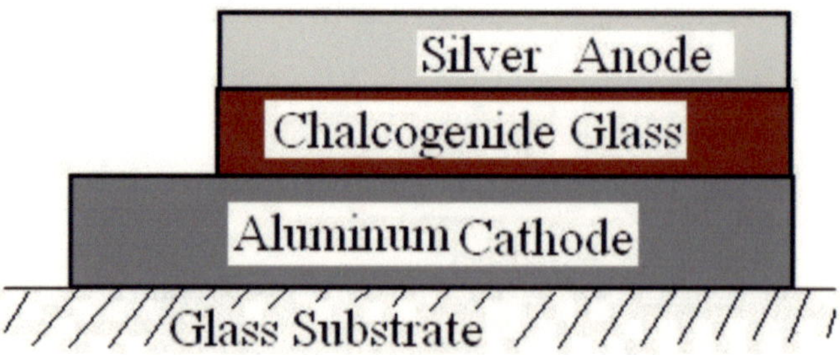

Fig. 7. Cross-section view of a PMC cell structure fabricated on glass substrate. This device is a silver-based PMC. [26]

4.3 Reading and writing process

Fig. 8 shows I-V characteristic of the above mentioned PMC cell. The active layer thickness of the testing device is 15nm. Electric current through PMC cell is measured using a

Keitheley source meter while voltage across device is tuned. Starting from 0V, voltage was increased up to 1V, then decreased to -1V, and finally brought back to 0V. We can clearly observe that the resistance of PMC device switches from high to low at 0.8V (SET voltage); and resistance switches from low to high at around -0.5V (RESET voltage). The measured 'ON" resistance (corresponds to logic '1') is 3 order of magnitude higher than the measured "OFF" resistance (corresponds to logic '0').

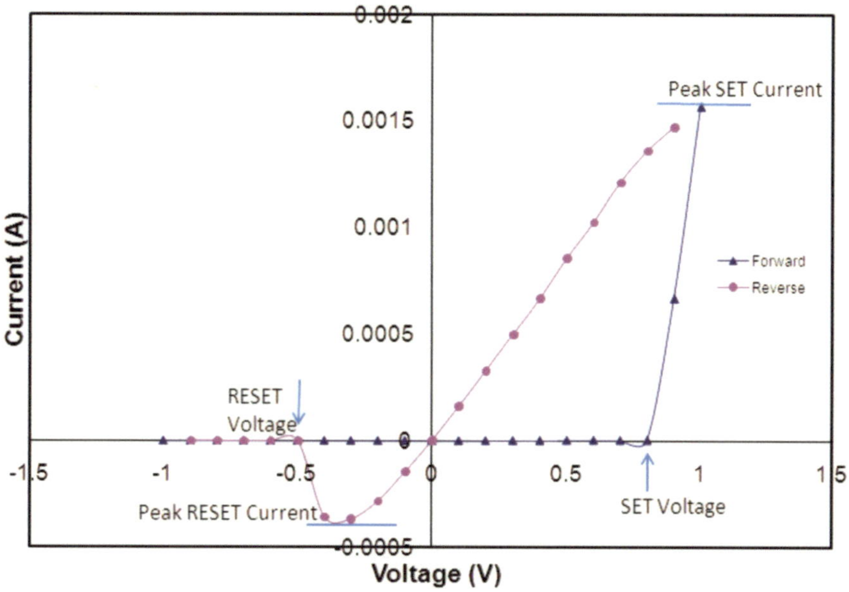

Fig. 8. I-V characteristic of a PMC testing cell. This cell is 100 by 100 μm and 60 nm in thickness. [8]

Therefore, the reading and writing process can be summarized as following:

1. SET

To SET PMC cell, a positive voltage pulse is needed. Since the electro-chemical process only need several ns to complete, a 30-50 ns SET pulse is enough. This, compared to SET pulse of PCM cell, is a significant advantage in term of device speed.

2. RESET

A negative voltage pulse is needed for RESET. This requires the access circuit of PMC cell allows access in both polarities. Therefore, a single access transistor is no longer enough. A possible access structure could be a NMOS transistor plus a PMOS transistor. This somewhat increased the complexity of memory circuit. However, since thermal isolation is not so essential for PMC memory as that for PCM memory, chip spaces for thermal isolation can be saved significantly. Therefore, PMC cell is still a highly scalable solution.

3. READ

A very low voltage pulse, as low as 0.1V, is needed for Reading. Similar to PCM reading, the device current is compared to a reference value. If device current is higher than reference, a logic '1' is identified; if device current is lower than reference, a logic '0' is identified. The typical resistance difference between logic '1' and '0' is at least 2 order of magnitude for PMC cell.

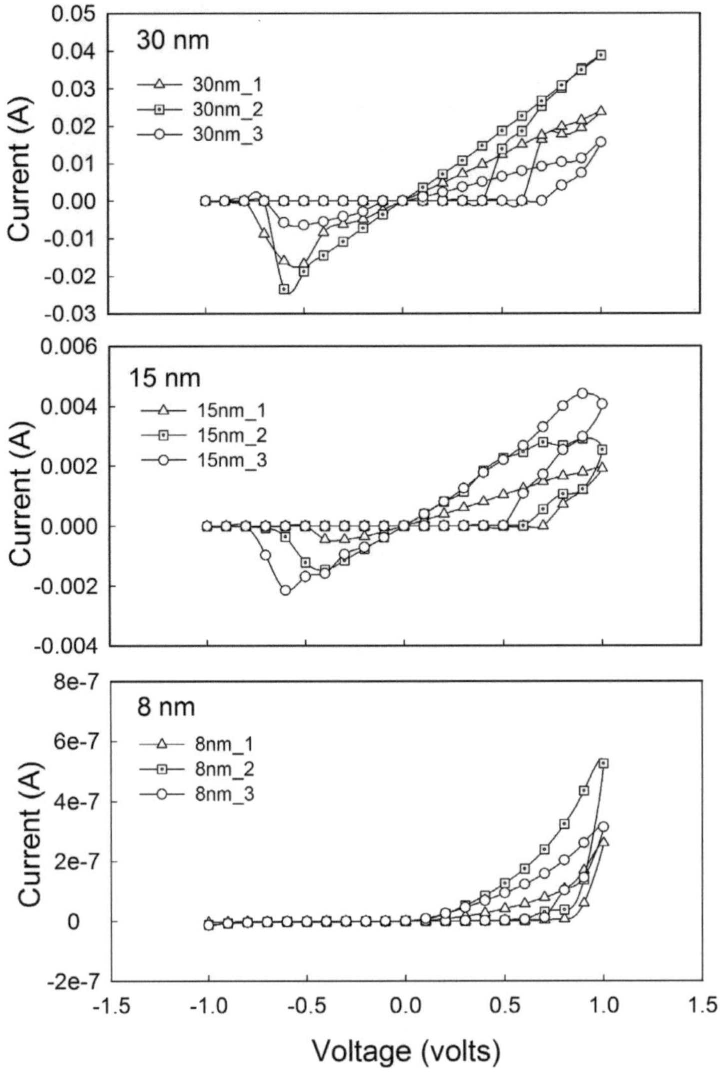

Fig. 9. I-V characteristic of PMC devices with different active layer thickness. Three devices are displayed for each thickness group. [27]

4.4 Effects of active layer thickness

Recently, Wang et. al studied the thickness dependency of PMC devices [27]. They found that the device metrics, such as R_{on}, R_{off} as well as switching threshold, has significant dependency on the active layer thickness. Fig. 9 shows the I-V characteristics of devices with thickness of 8nm, 15nm and 30nm. Table 1 summarizes the essential devices metrics for each thickness group.

From Table 1, one should notice that the devices with 8nm active layer thickness are not effectively conductive. This can be observed from Peak SET Current and Peak RESET Current. The Peak SET Current is less than a micro-ampere, while the Peak RESET Current is in nano-ampere range. The extremely small current is comparable to the parasitic current in reading/writing control circuit, which brings difficulty to reading process. 15nm and 30nm devices do not have this problem.

Device Active Layer Thickness	**8 nm (STD)**	**15nm (STD)**	**30nm (STD)**
Peak SET Current (mA)	4.51E-04 (0.82E-04)	2.356 (1.04)	33.8 (7.92)
Peak RESET Current (mA)	-9.28E-06 (0.10E-06)	-1.123 (0.66)	-17.900 (4.23)
Average R_{off} (MΩ)	30.77 (7.78)	40.88 (9.91)	52.26 (11.12)
Average R_{on} (MΩ)	4.65 (0.69)	0.48 (0.14)	0.003 (0.0009)
Average R_{off}/R_{on}	5.05	137.6	18899.3
SET Voltage (V)	0.71 (0.025)	0.64 (0.054)	0.62 (0.13)
RESET Voltage(V)	0.05 (0.024)	0.46 (0.089)	0.57 (0.025)

Table 1. Average Device Parameters of three batches. Standard deviations are shown in parenthesis. [27]

The Peak SET Current and Peak RESET Current are both increasing as a function of active layer thickness. This is due to the reduced ON resistance (R_{on}) for thicker devices. The formation of conduction links during 'SET' process is an electrochemical deposition process, which always happens at surface first (in this case, electrolyte/cathode surface) [14]. This process relies on the availability of deposition nuclei and the prompt movement of Ag+ ions towards the surface. Therefore, the number of conduction links that can be formed mostly depends on the number of nuclei that can be formed at the beginning of this electrochemical deposition process. According to our previous work on Ag-Ge-S [15], the distribution of Ag+ in Ag-Ge-S electrolyte is not uniform. Rather, Ag+ ions are accumulated in some silver rich islands that are distributed in the backbone. Therefore, at the very beginning, Ag+ ions from islands near the surface tend to form nuclei. Once nuclei are formed, new comers of Ag+ ions would prefer to accumulate around the nuclei. For thinner electrolyte films, the distribution of Ag+ rich islands is dispersed and the size of those islands reduces too. Therefore, for 8nm devices, the formation of deposition nuclei is highly dispersed and not continuous. The result of this discontinuity is that less conduction links can be formed to connect cathode and anode. Moreover, when the active layer is thin, Ag's accumulation at cathodes localizes the Ag ions' movements due to the size of Ag (around 0.32nm in diameter). The overall effect is higher R_{on} for thinner devices.

It is also observed that the R_{off} of all 3 groups are roughly in the same order of magnitude, but slightly increase as a function of thickness. This is obvious since the resistance increases if one extends the length of the resistor. Therefore, the extremely large R_{off}/R_{on} ratio for 30nm devices is majorly due to their low ON resistance.

The SET voltage of the three groups shows very slightly decreasing trend as a function of thickness. This is probably due to the localization of Ag ions' movement in thinner devices. However, since the Ag ions move super fast, the difference among SET voltage is not very significant.

On the other hand, the RESET voltage shows significant discrepancy among three thickness groups. Overall, an increasing trend in RESET voltage is observed as a function of active layer thickness. While the RESET voltage is comparable between 15nm (0.64V) and 30nm (0.62V) devices, the RESET voltage of 8nm devices is significantly lower (0.05V) than that of

15nm and 30nm devices. Our explanation to this phenomenon is thicker devices (i.e. 30nm) have more conduction links once SET; hence, during RESET, more Ag atoms need to be ionized. This requires certainly higher reverse voltage. The 8nm group needs only -0.05 volt to RESET. Also notice, the R_{off}/R_{on} ratio of 8nm devices is only 5.05, significantly lower than that of 15nm and 30nm devices. This indicates that there were very few Ag conduction links formed in 8nm devices during 'SET' process due to dispersed deposition nuclei. Therefore, during RESET, there are not many Ag atoms on cathode to be ionized, which explains the low RESET voltage.

4.4 Current developments in the field

The first generation of programmable metallization cell was built based on metal containing chalcogenide solid electrolytes, such as Ag-Ge-S, Ag-Ge-S and Cu-Ge-S etc, with Ag or Cu as reactive electrodes. People then discovered that using Cu doped SiO_2 as the active medium of PMC is also viable. This new type of device has the advantage of easier integration with the current CMOS technology, since Cu is currently used as the interconnect metal in integrated circuits, while SiO_2 is known as the insulating material. However, unlike chalcogenide based devices, Cu can hardly be photodiffused into SiO_2. Instead, thermal diffusion or ion implantation has to be used to introduce Cu into SiO_2 backbone. Several groups reported the feasibility of fabricating Cu/SiO_2 based devices [34-35].

Approaches aiming to increase the data storage density is also vastly investigated for PMC devices. The research is diverted into two directions; one aims to improve the architecture of the device, i.e. 3-D devices [36] ; the other focuses on multilevel programming of the cell itself [37]. Russo et. al. [37] reported the knetics of the conductive filament's formation and growth during the programming can be controled by limiting the current compliance. The resistance of the cell can be tuned to 4 distinguished resistance states. This suggests the posibility of 2 bits storage of a single PMC cell.

5. Conclusion

In this chapter, we reviewed two non-volatile memory solutions based on chalcogenide glasses. PCM device is a relative mature solution now. PMC is a new concept and still in experimental stage. Non-volatile memory devices based on chalcogenide materials are the most promising replacement of charge-storage based memories due to its fast reading/writing speed and high scalability. In addition to those, since the information storage for chalcogenide devices are based on phase conversion or electrochemical reaction, chalcogenide based devices display excellent data retention characteristic when compared with charge-storage based devices.

6. Acknowledgment

Special thanks go to Dr. Punit Boolchand from University of Cincinnati for helps in bulk sample synthesis; Dr. Jagadeesh Moodera from MIT for helps in fabricating the masks; Dr. Richard Savage from California Polytechnic State University for helps in evaporator and characterization instruments.

7. References

[1] G S. R. Ovshingsky, "Reversible Electrical Switching Phenomena in Disordered Structures" *Phys. Rev. Lett.* 21 (1968) pp1450

[2] T. Ohta, "Phase-change optical memory promotes the DVD optical disk" *J. Optoelectron. Adv. Mater.* 3 (2001) pp609

[3] J. Siegel, A. Schropp, J. Solis, C.N. Afonso, M.Wuttig, "Rewritable phase-change optical recording in $Ge_2Sb_2Te_5$ films induced by picosecond laser pulses" *Appl. Phys. Lett.* 84 (2004) 2250

[4] T. Ohta, E.R. Ovshynsky, in *Photo-Induced Metastavility in Amorphous Semiconductors,* edited by A.V. Kovobov, Wiley-VCH, Weinheim, (2003) p. 310

[5] M.N. Kozicki, M. Yun, S. J. Yang, J.P Aberouette, J.P. Bird, "Nanoscale effects in devices based on chalcogenide solid solutions" *Superlattices and Microstructures,* 27 (2000) No. 5/6, pp485-488

[6] M. N. Kozicki, C. Gopalan, M. Balakrishnan, M. Park, M. Mitkova, "Nonvolatile memory based on solid electrolytes" *Non-Volatile Memory Technology Symposium Proceedings* (2004) 15-17

[7] I. Chaitanya et al. "Metal-semiconductor-metal Junctions with silver sulfide barrier layer" presentation at *American Physical Society March Meeting, Baltimore, MD,* (2006) (unpublished)

[8] Carter De Leo, Senior Project Report, California Polytechnic State University (2007)

[9] Sakamoto et al. "Nanometer-scale switches using copper sulfide" *Appl. Phys. Lett.* 82 (2003) pp3032

[10] S.Chakravarty, D.G.Georgiev, P.Boolchand and M.Micoulaut, "Ageing, fragility and the reversibility window in bulk alloy glasses", *J. Phys. Condens.* Matter, 17, (2005) L1-L7

[11] D.G.Georgiev, P.Boolchand and M.Micoulaut , "Rigidity transitions and molecular structure of As_xSe_{1-x} glasses." *Phys.Rev. B* 62, 14 (2000) pp9268

[12] Tao Qu, D.G. Georgiev, P.Boolchand and M.Micoulaut, "The Intermediate Phase in Ternary GexAsxSe1-2x Glasses" *Mat. Res. Soc. Symp. Proc.* 754 (2003) pp111

[13] Tao Qu and P.Boolchand, "Shift in elastic phase boundaries due to nanoscale phase separation in network glasses: the case of $Ge_xAs_xS_{1-2x}$". *Phil. Mag,* 85, (2005), pp875

[14] D. Selvanathan, W.J.Bresser and P. Boolchand, "Stiffness transitions in Si_xSe_{1-x} glasses from Raman scattering and temperature-modulated differential scanning calorimetry." *Phys. Rev B* 61, (2000) pp15061

[15] P.Boolchand, D.G.Georgiev and B. Goodman , "Discovery of the intermediate phase in chalcogenide glasses" *J.Opto. and Adv. Mater. 3* (2001) pp703.

[16] J.C. Phillips, "Universal Intermediate Phases of Dilute Electronic and Molecular Glasses" *Phys. Rev. Lett.* 88, (2002) 216401

[17] M.F. Thorpe, D.J. Jacobs, M.V. Chubynsky, and J.C.Phillips, "Self-organization in network glasses" *J. Non-Cryst. Solids* 266-269 (2001) pp859

[18] M.Micoulaut and J.C.Phillips, "Rings and rigidity transitions in network glasses" *Phys. Rev. B 67* (2003) 104204.

[19] P.Boolchand, X.Feng, W.J.Bresser, "Rigidity transition in binary Ge-Se glasses and intermediate phase" *J. Non- Cryst. Solids* 293-295 (2001) pp348

[20] X. Feng, W.J. Bresser, P.Boolchand, "Direct Evidence for Stiffness Threshold in Chalcogenide Glasses" *Phys. Rev. Lett.* 78 (1997) pp4422

[21] Fei Wang, S. Mamedov, P. Boochand and B. Goodman, "Pressure Raman effects and internal stress in network glasses" *Physical Rev B.* 71 (2005) pp174210

[22] Fei Wang, P. Boolchand and K. A. Jackson, "Chemical Alloying and light-induced collapse of the intermediate phase in chalcohalide glasses" *J. Phys.: Condens. Matter* 19 (2007) pp226201
[23] Woo Yeong Cho et al. "A 0.18-/spl mu/m 3.0-V 64-Mb nonvolatile phase-transition random access memory (PRAM)" *IEEE Journal of Solid State Circuits,* Vol 40, No. 1 (2005) pp293-300
[24] Byung-Do Yang, Jae-Eun Lee, Jang-Su Kim and Junghyun Cho, "A Low Power Phase-change Random Access Memory using a Data-Comparison Write Scheme" *Proceeding of IEEE International Symposium on Circuit and Systems,* (2007) pp3014-3017
[25] A. Antonaia, M.C. Santoro, G. Fameli and T. Polichetti, "Transport mechanism and IR structural characterisation of evaporated amorphous WO_3 films" *Thin Solid Films,* Vol 426 (2003) pp281-287
[26] P.W. Dunn, Master Thesis, California Polytechnic State University, (2008) (unpublished)
[27] F. Wang, P.W. Dunn, M. Jain, C. De Leo and N. Vickers, "The effects of active layer thickness on programmable metallization cell based on Ag-Ge-S", Solid State Electronics, in press (2011)
[28] S. Song, Z. Song, Y. Lu, B. Liu, L. Wu and S. Feng,"Sb2Te3-Ta2O5 nano-composite films for low-power phase-change memory application", Materials Letters 64 (2010) pp2718-2730
[29] H.Y. Cheng, K.F. Kao, C.M. Lee and T.S. Chin,"Crystallization kinetics of Ga–Sb–Te films for phase change memory „ Thin Solid Films 516 (2008) pp5513-5517.
[30] T.C. Chong, L.P. Shi, R. Zhao, P.K. Tan, J.M. Li, K.G. Lim and L.P. Shi," Phase change random access memory cell with superlattice-like structure„ Applied Physical Letters 88 (2006) pp122144.
[31] C. Wang, S. Li, J. Zhai, B. Shen, M. Sun and T. Lai,"Rapid crystallization of SiO2/Sb80Te20 nanocomposite multilayer films fro phase-change memory applications" Scripta Materialia 64 (2011) pp 645-648
[32] Y. Gu, Z. Song, T. Zhang, B. Liu and S. Feng,"Novel phase-change material GeSbTe for application of three-level phase-change random access memory", Solid State Electronis 54 (2010) pp443-446
[33] Y. Yin and S. Hosaka,"Multilevel storage in lateral phase-change memory by promotion of nanocrystallization", Microelectronic Engineering, in press (2011)
[34] S. Puthen Thermandam, S.K. Bhagat, T.L. Alford, Y. Sakaguchi, M.N. Kozicki and M. Mitkova,"Influence of Cu diffusion conditions on the switching of Cu-SiO_2-based resistive memory devices", Thin Solid Films, 518 (2010), pp3293-3298
[35] Y. Bernard, V.T. Renard, P. Gonon and V. Jousseaume,"Back-end-of-line compatible Conductive Bridging RAM based on Cu and SiO_2", Microelectronic Engineering (2010) in press
[36]C. Kugeler, M. Meier, R. Rosezin, S. Gilles and R. Waser,"High density 3D memory architecture based on the resistive switching effect", Solid State Electronics 53 (2009) pp1287-1292
[37] U. Russo, D Kamalanathan, D. Ielmini, A. Lacaita and M. Kozicki,"Study of multilevel programming in programmable metallization cell memory", IEEE Transaction on Electron Devices, 56, No. 5 (2009) pp1040-1047
[38] R. Bez and A. Pirovano,"Non-volatile Memory technologies: emerging concepts and new materials" , Material Science in Semiconductor Processing, vol. 7 (2004) pp349-355

11

Radiation Hardness of Flash and Nanoparticle Memories

Emanuele Verrelli[1] and Dimitris Tsoukalas[1,2]
[1]*National Technical University of Athens, Dept. of Applied Physics,*
[2]*Insitute of Microelectronics, NCSR "Demokritos",*
Greece

1. Introduction

Recently, the research for new non-volatile memory in the semiconductor industry has become intense, because current flash memory technologies based on the floating-gate (FG) concept are expected to be difficult to scale down for high density, high performance devices (Lankhorst et al., 2005 ; Ouyang et al., 2004 ; Vanheusden et al., 1997). Therefore, a type of non-volatile memory using nanoparticles (NP) as floating gates has attracted much research attention because of its excellent memory performance and high scalability (Tiwari et al., 1996; Park et al., 2002). By utilizing discrete NP as the charge storage element, NP memory is more immune to local oxide defects than flash memory, thus exhibiting longer retention time and allowing more aggressive tunnel oxide scaling than conventional flash memory (Blauwe, 2002; Hanafi et al., 1996). In NP memory, the device performance and reliability depend on many factors, such as the ability to control NP size, size distribution, crystallinity, area density, oxide passivation quality, and the isolation that prevents lateral charge conduction in the NP layer (Ostraat et al., 2001). Thus, NP memory has driven extensive efforts to form NP acting as charging and discharging islands by various methods. Up to now, several techniques have been developed to form uniform NP in gate oxides. For example, Kim (Kim et al., 1999) employed low pressure chemical vapour deposition (LPCVD) to fabricate Si NP with a 4.5 nm average size and $5\times10^{11}cm^{-2}$ average density. King (King et al., 1998) fabricated Ge NPs by oxidation of a SiGe layer formed by ion implantation, and demonstrated quasi-nonvolatile memory operation with a 0.4 V threshold-voltage shift. Takata (Takata et al., 2003) applied a sputtering method with a special target to fabricate metal nano dots embedded in SiO. Various NP memory devices have been made to realize the fast and low-power operation of such devices, mostly using Si NP devices surrounded by SiO (Gonzalez-Varona et al., 2003). The programming efficiency has been improved with program voltages reduced far below 10 V, owing to the scaling of tunneling SiO_2. Among the advantages related with the NP approach to FLASH technologies, worth to emphasize that owing to the discrete nature of the storage nodes, NP memories are expected to behave much better than standard FG devices in radiation environments.
This chapter focuses on this particular issue of the radiation hardness of FLASH, and in particular, NP memory technologies. After a review of the main sources of radiation in space and on earth, we will present a detailed review of the effects of radiation on CMOS electronic devices and discuss the state of the art of radiation effects on standard FG FLASH memories

and NP FLASH memories. In the second part of the chapter, we will present and discuss an extensive study conducted on prototype Si nanocrystal (NC) FLASH memories irradiated with protons.

2. The main sources of radiation

Radiation environments are encountered in military applications, nuclear power stations, nuclear waste disposal sites, high-altitude avionics, medical and space applications. Radiation type, energy, dose[1] rate and total dose may be very different in each of these application areas and require in many cases radiation-tolerant electronic systems.
The space radiation environment poses a certain radiation risk to all electronic components on the earth-orbiting satellites and planetary mission spacecrafts. The irradiating particles in this environment consist primarily of high-energy electrons, protons, alpha particles, and cosmic rays. The weapon environment such as a nuclear explosion (often referred to as the "gamma dot") is characterized by X-rays, gamma, neutrons, and other reaction debris constituents occurring within a short time span. This can cause latchup and transient upsets in integrated circuits such as memories. Although the natural space environment does not contain the high dose rate pulse characteristics of a nuclear weapon, the electronics systems exposed can accumulate a significant total dose from the electron and protons over a period of several years. The radiation effects of charged particles in the space environment are dominated by ionization, which refers to any type of high energy particle that creates electron-hole (e-h) pairs when passing through a material. It can be either particulate in nature or electromagnetic. In addition to creating e-h pairs, the radiation can cause displacement damage in the crystal lattice by breaking the atomic bonds and creating trapping recombination centers. Both of these damage mechanisms can lead to degradation of the electronic performance. The ionizing electromagnetic radiations of importance are the X-rays and gamma rays. Ionizing particulate radiation can be light uncharged particles such as neutrons, light charged particles such as electrons, protons, alpha, and beta particles, and heavy charged particles (heavy ions) such as iron, bromine, krypton, xenon, etc., which are present in the cosmic ray fluences. Gamma rays (or X-rays) basically produce a similar kind of damage as light charged particles since the dominant mechanism is charge interaction with the material. Neutrons have no charge, and react primarily with the nucleus, causing lattice damage. In Fig. 1 is shown a summary of the possible radiation sources and their effects on electronic, optical and mechanical components.

2.1 Space radiation environments

Our planet is surrounded by a radiation rich environment, consisting of mainly energetic charged particles (electrons, protons, heavy ions, see Table 1). They can either be trapped particles, bound to trajectories dictated by the earth's magnetic field, or free, transiting particles originating from the sun or from galactic sources and can be classified in three main categories: the Van Allen belts, the solar cosmic rays (solar flares), the cosmic rays (galactic and not).

---

[1]The dose is the energy deposited per unit mass of the target material by the incident radiation and in the S.I. is measured in Gray, Gy. The unit "rad" (radiation absorbed dose) is related to the abandoned "cgs" system and correspond to 0.01Gy. In this study all the doses are transformed into the correspondent doses in SiO_2.

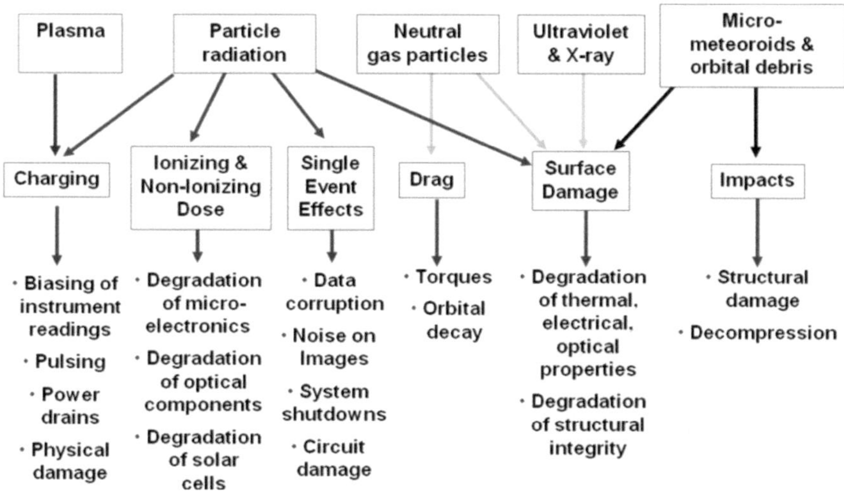

Fig. 1. Radiation sources and their effects on electronic, optical and mechanical components.

Particle type	Maximum Energy
Trapped electrons	10s of MeV
Trapped Protons and Heavy Ions	100s of MeV
Solar Protons	GeV
Solar Heavy Ions	GeV
Galactic cosmic rays	TeV

Table 1. Maximum energies of particles in the space radiation environment (Barth et al., 2002).

2.1.1 The Van-Allen belts

This section discusses natural space environments in which most of the satellites operate, in orbits ranging in altitudes from low earth orbits (150-600 km) to geosynchronous orbits (roughly 35,880 km). Most of the particles in interplanetary space come from the sun in the form of a hot ionized gas called the solar wind; it flows radially from the sun with a speed that in proximity of the Earth varies from about 300 to 1000 km/s, and represents a solar mass loss of about 10^{14} kilograms per day.

The radiation environment of greatest interest is the near earth region, about 1-12 earth radii R_e (where R_e = 6380 km), which is mainly dominated by electrically charged particles trapped in the earth's magnetosphere, and to a lesser extent by the heavy ions from cosmic rays (solar and galactic). As the earth sweeps through the solar wind, a geomagnetic cavity is formed by the earth's magnetic field (Fig. 2).

The motion of the trapped charge particles is complex, as they gyrate and bounce along the magnetic field lines, and are reflected back and forth between the pairs of conjugate mirror points (regions of maximum magnetic field strength along their trajectories) in the opposite hemispheres. Also, because of the charge, the electrons drift in an easterly direction around earth, whereas protons and heavy ions drift westward. Interplanetary space probes such as the Voyager (and Galileo to Jupiter) encounter ionizing particles trapped in the magnetosphere of other planets, as well as the solar flares and heavy ions from cosmic rays.

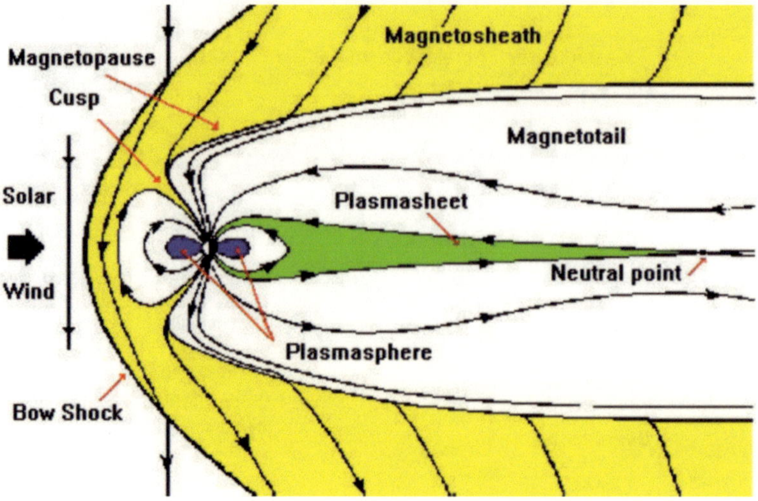

Fig. 2. Interactions between Earth magnetosphere and the solar wind[2]

Electrons in the earth's magnetosphere have energies ranging from low kilo electronvolts to about 7 MeV, and are trapped in the roughly toroidal region which is centered on the geomagnetic equator and extends to about 1-12 earth radii. These trapped electrons are differentiated by "inner zone" (<5 MeV) and "outer zone" (~7 MeV) electron populations. The trapped protons originating mostly from the solar and galactic cosmic rays have energies ranging from a few MeV to about 800 MeV. They occupy generally the same region as the electrons, although the region of highest proton flux for energies $E_p > 30$ MeV is concentrated in a relatively small area at roughly 1.5 R_e. The actual electron and proton flux encountered by a satellite is strongly dependent upon the orbital parameters, mission launch time, and duration. Electrons and protons from the trapped radiation belts on interacting with spacecraft materials produce secondary radiation (e.g., "bremsstrahlung" or braking radiation from the deceleration of electrons). This secondary radiation can extend the penetration range of primary radiation and lead to an increase in dose deposition. Incident electron and proton fluxes are typically calculated from the trapped radiation environmental models developed by the U.S. National Space Sciences Data Center (NSSDC). The trapped particle fluxes responding to changes in the geomagnetic field induced by the solar activity exhibit dynamic behavior.

2.1.2 Solar cosmic rays- solar flares

In addition to the trapped geomagnetic radiation, another contribution to incident particle flux for an orbiting satellite is the transiting radiation from the solar flares. These solar energy particle events (SPE), usually occurring in association with the solar flares, consist mainly of protons (90%), some alpha particles (5-10%), heavy ions, and electrons. This solar flare phenomenon is categorized as an ordinary (OR) event or an anomalously large (AL) event. Particle fluxes from the solar flares can last from a few hours to several days and peak flux during an SPE may be two to five orders of magnitude greater than background, within hours of the event onset. Periods of enhanced flux may last for days, with successive peaks

[2]http://helios.gsfc.nasa.gov/magnet.html

due to multiple events and enhancements during shock passage. AL events (Fig. 3), although occurring rarely, can cause serious damage to ICs. For ordinary solar events, the relative abundance of helium ions can be between 5-10%, whereas ions heavier than He (e.g., carbon, oxygen, iron, etc.), referred to as the "heavy ions," are very small. However, the solar flare protons which contribute to the total ionizing dose radiation are not that significant a factor compared to the trapped radiation environment.

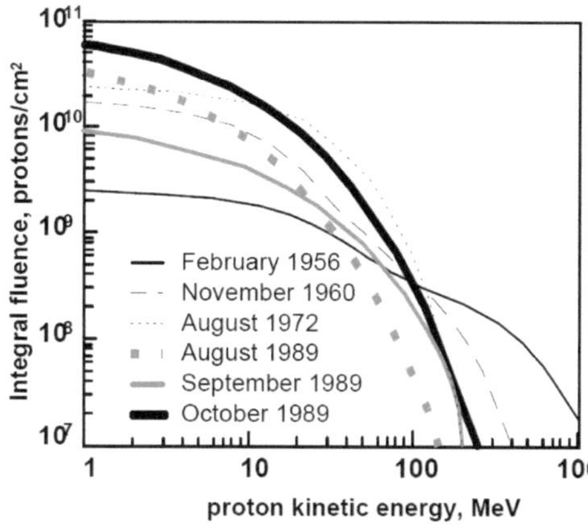

Fig. 3. Distribution in energy of proton fluxes for major past SPEs (free space)

The particles from energetic solar flares (OR events) are heavily attenuated by the geomagnetic field at low altitude and low inclination orbits, such as U.S. Space Shuttle orbits (28.5° inclination). In a 500 km, 57° inclination orbit, some particle fluxes do penetrate. A characteristic of the geomagnetic field which is particularly significant is the South Atlantic Anomaly (SAA), referring to an apparent depression of the magnetic field over the coast of Brazil where the Van Allen radiation belts dip low into the earth's atmosphere. This SAA is responsible for most of the trapped radiation in low earth orbits (LEOs). On the opposite side of the globe, the Southeast-Asian anomaly displays strong particle fluxes at higher altitudes. A polar orbit at any altitude experiences a high degree of exposure, and at geosynchronous orbit, geomagnetic shielding is rather ineffective.

2.1.3 Galactic cosmic rays

Another significant contribution to the transiting radiation is from cosmic rays originating from outside the solar system and consisting of 85% protons, 14% alpha particles, and 1% heavier ions. These galactic cosmic rays (GCR) range in energy from a few MeV to over GeV or TeV per nucleon. The total flux of cosmic ray particles (primarily composed of protons) seen outside the magnetosphere at a distance of earth from the sun (1 AU) is approximately 4 particles/cm^{2}s.

Heavy energetic nuclei, HZE, represent ~1% of the GCR and as shown in Fig. 4, where is presented the distribution in energy of several important HZE nuclei, these particles have very high energies, sufficient to penetrate many centimetres of tissue or other materials. In addition, the HZE nuclei are highly charged and, therefore, very densely ionizing. As a consequence, even though the number of HZE particles is relatively small, they have a significant biological impact that is comparable to that of protons.

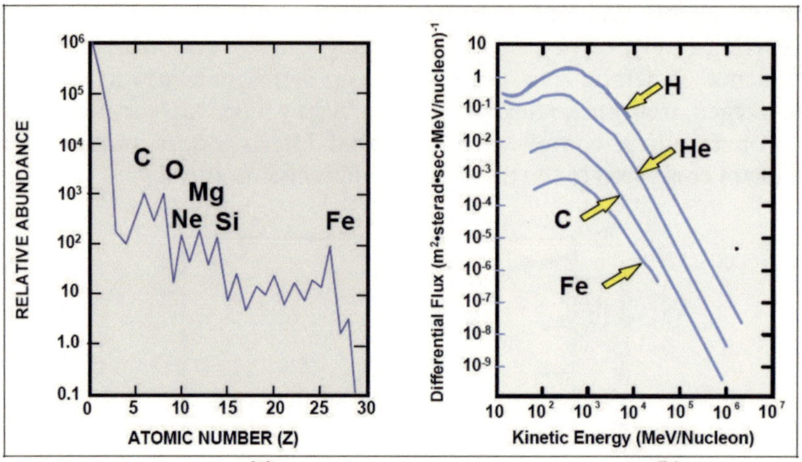

Fig. 4. Abundances (a) and energy spectra (b) of GCR.

3. Ionizing radiation effects on MOS devices

Silicon MOS (metal-oxide-semiconductor) devices are by many decades the mainstay of the semiconductor industry. When these devices are exposed to ionizing radiation, significant changes can occur in their characteristics. Ionizing radiation creates mobile electrons and holes in both the insulator and silicon substrate in MOS devices that may lead to a damage of the device. It is interesting to note that these properties have allowed the use of ionizing radiation damage as a tool for scientific study in a number of areas. Indeed, in the past, the basic mechanisms of carrier transport in insulators have been very effectively explored by using various types of ionizing radiation to create mobile carriers and then monitoring their motion by electrical means. These studies have furthered our understanding of polarons, excitons and trap-hopping processes. The generation of interface traps and oxide trapped charge in large numbers by ionizing radiation has allowed the identification of the atomic structures associated with these defects. By providing a means of altering the trapped charge at the SiO_2/Si interface in a given device, the interaction of mobile charge carriers in the channel of an MOS device with that trapped charge can be explored. By creating trapped charge distributions in the oxide layer which provide traps for carriers, tunneling and carrier capture phenomena can be effectively studied. As the semiconductor industry progresses deep into the ULSI era, the technological impact of ionizing radiation effects becomes more and more important. In order to produce the extremely fine geometries required at high levels of integration, the processes used in the manufacture of the integrated circuits themselves may produce ionizing radiation. At the small geometries of current and future integrated circuits, latchup initiated by normal operating conditions has become a major concern. This trend toward small devices has made normal commercial ICs susceptible to single event upsets caused by ionizing particles created by the decay of residual radioactive material in IC packaging material. Thus many of the concerns for radiation hardened circuits have become a concern for standard commercial products. In addition, in order to make circuits for specialized applications requiring operation in an ionizing radiation environment, significant modifications to the technology employed must be made. There are a large number of specialized applications requiring ICs that have a known, predictable response to ionizing radiation. Satellite systems need electronic components that can operate in the harsh radiation environment around the earth and in space. Without such components satellites would have extremely limited capabilities. Many weapon systems require hardened components to perform their tasks properly trough an operational scenario. Nuclear power plants need instrumentation which can withstand the environment near the reactor and continue to provide reliable data. In the nuclear medicine field, is straightforward the importance of having electronic components with higher performances in radiation environments.

3.1 Damaging mechanisms

The way ionizing radiation affects MOS devices is mainly related to build up of oxide trapped charge, increased amount of density of interface states at the oxide boundaries and to the possibility to have single-event-upsets, SEU (Ma & Dressendorfer, 1989). When ionizing radiation passes through the oxide, the energy deposited creates electron/hole pairs with a generation energy of 18 eV/pair. The radiation generated electrons are much more mobile that holes and are swept quickly out of the oxide. Some of them undergo recombination with holes, depending on many different experimental factors. A final positive charge is then observed into the oxide, resulting from the unrecombined holes generated by radiation that remain trapped in the strained areas of the oxide close to the interfaces with Si or the gate material (Fig. 5). The trap sites responsible for this positive charge build up have been identified as E'centers, deep traps in the bulk of SiO_2 originated by a silicon dangling bond in the oxide matrix. Furthermore, an increased amount of interface states is also observed after irradiation at Si/oxide interface. P_b centers have been found to be responsible of the observed interface states, microscopically related to non bridging silicon atoms between the crystalline silicon substrate and the silicon oxide matrix. This interface bond breaking during irradiation seems to be driven by the excess positive charge and strain present at interface. Finally, in the case of heavy ion irradiation when the incident particle has high enough Linear-Energy-Transfer(LET) transient effects become also important. Indeed the ion along its path inside the device create a dense cloud of electrons-hole pairs generating very intense transient currents that in many cases may result in different kinds of failures of the device itself, even rupture.

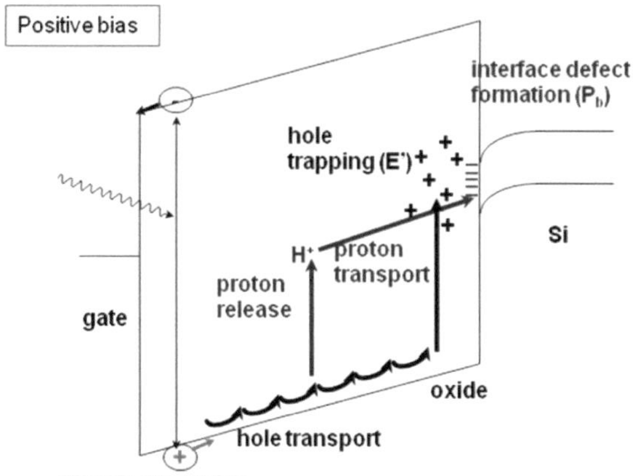

Fig. 5. Detailed representation of the ionizing radiation damage mechanisms into SiO_2.

Thus, when we are interested into the transient response of an MOS component to single events we perform heavy ion irradiations. When on the other hand we are interested into the effect on devices performance of accumulated damage during long time irradiation exposure we perform total ionizing dose (TID) irradiations, using gamma rays or in special cases electrons or protons.

3.2 Performance degradation of FLASH memory devices under irradiation

In MOS microelectronic memory devices, information is stored as quantities of charge. Pulses of ionizing radiation are known to be effective in corrupting the information integrated circuits store. Errors induced by ionizing radiation can be classified in three main classes: soft errors, hard errors and failures. Soft errors are correctable simply by re-entering correct information into the affected elements and can be generated by single ionizing particle or by pulses of ionizing radiation. Hard errors are not recoverable, i.e. are not altered by attempts to rewrite correct information and are caused by single particles like neutrons and heavy ions. Finally, failure events prevent normal device operation and generally are connected to the high transient currents initiated by pulsed ionizing radiation or single events. While RAM can be made insensible to soft errors in many different ways (by design (Liaw, 2003) or by software (Klein, 2005 ; Huang, 2010)), NVMs are susceptible to all three categories of errors above. The lack of any refresh cycle of the stored information make flash memories vulnerable to data loss at each exposure to ionizing radiation. Considering that Flash memories standards impose a retention time for the data stored of 10 years at least and a minimum 10^6 write/erase operations before performance degradation starts, is clear that non-volatile memory cells are in a passive state for most of their lifetime.
Until recently, the effects of radiation in Flash memories have mainly been a concern for the space or aircraft applications. The heavy ions and other high energy particles which are abundantly present at altitudes far above the sea-level cause a variety of problems including the soft errors (mainly SEU, Single-Event-Functional-Interrupts (SEFI)), latchup (If the induced parasitic current levels are sufficiently high, they can cause permanent device failures such as a junction burnout) and hard errors pertaining to oxide degradation due to total dose (irreversible bit-flips due for example to high leakage current in the gate oxide). Recent experiments on current generation Flash memories have however shown that significant amount of radiation effects can be observed at the sea level or terrestrial environments. Previously, the most sensitive component of Flash memory used to be the control circuitry for sense amplifiers and charge pumps. The FG cell array on the other hand was considered to be relatively insensitive to radiation strikes at least at terrestrial levels. This is however changing rapidly because with only ~1000 or fewer electrons stored in the FG, the cells have now become sensitive to charge deposited by the terrestrial cosmic ray neutrons and alpha particles. But most important, because of the conductive nature of the floating gate, in presence of a weak spot in the tunnel oxide, possibly radiation induced, the whole charge stored could be lost with total loss of information. Even in the case that the damage does not generate device failure, data retention and device performance would be dramatically affected by this defect in the tunnel oxide (Oldham et al., 2006).

4. Brief review of radiation effects on FG FLASH memories

In the last decade different teams already investigated the effect of ionizing radiation on FG Flash memories and a summary on the results can be found in the works of Cellere (Cellere et al., 2004a , 2004b, 2004c, 2005) and Oldham (Oldham et al., 2006, 2007).

Cellere investigate the radiation hardness of standard FG memories, under ^{60}Co, X-ray and 100 MeV protons. The result that worth to mention here is that independently (almost) from the radiation used, information loss starts at doses as low as 100 krad(Si).
Oldham investigates TID and SEE effects on commercial 2Gbit and 4Gbit NAND FG memories. TID effects, in reasonable agreement with Cellere, show that static errors rise abruptly above 75 krad(SiO2) while dynamic errors rise quickly at even lower doses. The errors were found to arise from zeroes that could not be erased into ones due to the failure of the erase function. The SEE were monitored in static and various dynamic modes for LET in the range 0-80 MeV cm^2 mg^{-1}. Error Cross sections seem to saturate to a value of $\sim 10^{-12}$ cm^2/bit.

5. Nanocrystal FLASH memory devices under irradiation - A review

NCMs are expected to have better resistance to ionizing radiation: being able to retain information with only a residual fraction of nanocrystals charged, these devices should be quite immune to radiation-induced leakage current, RILC (Larcher et al., 1999; Scarpa et al., 1997; Ceschia et al., 2000 ; Oldham et al., 2005), and they may in principle exhibit high resistance to both single event (SEE) and total ionizing dose (TID) effects. While some works already investigated the effect of ionizing radiation on FG Flash memories, until now, few works have investigated this issue in NC NVMs and will be briefly reviewed in the next.
Petkov (Petkov et al., 2004) report the first results pertinent to the high total dose (TID) tolerance of Si nanocrystal NVM cells studying prototype NC-Si field effect transistors made by ion implantation. Si ions were implanted at 5 keV to a fluence of 1.3 $10^{16}cm^{-2}$ into a bare 15 nm-thick SiO_2 layer, grown on top of p-type doped Si wafer. The ion implantation profile shows a peak depth of 10 nm and a stoichiometry at the peak of 1.75:2. The wafers were annealed at 1050°C for 5 min in dry oxygen, during which time the nanocrystals were formed and the majority of the implantation-induced defects were annealed out. An optically transparent 50 nm poly-Si gate was deposited on top of the wafers. Reference samples without Si NCs were also used. Unfortunately Petkov et al. don't give further details about the final geometry of the device. Radiation experiments were carried out using ^{60}Co and two different conditions were used: (1) V_S = 0 V; V_{DS}=1.5V; V_G=±6V (write/erase square wave potential), and (2) all contacts grounded. They yielded indistinguishable results for the duration of the experiments, in which the maximum achieved dose was 15 Mrad(Si). The typical hysteresis of a device prior to and after irradiation were recorded on 15 NC-Si FETs with write/erase square wave potential applied to the gate. The electrical characteristics of all transistors were virtually unchanged and it is clear that negligible is the effect of ionizing radiation on position and height of the memory hysteresis. In their work, Petkov et al. consider also another set of 6 NC-Si FETs and three conventional FETs, exposed to ionizing radiation environment with all contacts grounded. The control n-channel FET yielded decreasing gate threshold with dose, notably below 1 Mrad(Si) and according to Petkov, this is considered to be consistent with the accepted models for degradation of metal-oxide-silicon structures under irradiation . The lack of change at 2 Mrad(Si) doses is attributed to saturation of interface defect generation and hole trapping. Both of the NC-Si FET show no significant changes in the entire test range of up to 15 Mrad(Si). This is ascribed to the ion-implantation-induced damage and the subsequent reconstruction of the oxide. Petkov et. al. justify this fact with the argument that oxide properties, especially these related to defect density, charge trapping and mobility, can

differ greatly prior to implantation and after reconstruction. They conclude their work suggesting that for NC-Si technologies that do not utilize implantation, we can expect to observe a shift of the erased state upon radiation exposure, as in conventional FETs.

Oldham (Oldham et al., 2005) reported on the exposition to heavy ion bombardment and total ionizing dose of advanced nanocrystal nonvolatile memories. The test chips were experimental 4Mb Flash EEPROM memories fabricated using 0.13 µm design rules, with NAND architecture (Freescale). Channel hot electron (CHE) injection is used to write (that is, to add electrons to the nanocrystal array), and Fowler-Nordheim tunneling to erase (that is, to remove electrons from the array). The nanocrystals are deposited by a CVD process, where the density and diameter of the particles can be controlled by adjusting the deposition conditions. The tunneling oxide and control gate oxide are SiO_2 with thicknesses of 4.3 nm and 5.6 nm respectively while the Si NCs have diameter of 4 nm. The heavy ion testing was done using a Single Event Effects Test Facility, which was tuned to 15 MeV/nucleon, using Ar, Kr, Xe and Au ions. Each exposure was to a total fluence of 10^7 particles/cm^2. Total dose testing was done using a ^{60}Co source with dose rate of 10 rad/s. Oldham et al. performed their tests in three modes: static mode, in dynamic read mode, and dynamic program and erase modes. In the static testing, a pattern was written, and errors counted after the exposure. In dynamic read testing, a stored pattern was read continuously during the exposure, and the errors counted. The write or program mode was tested by continuously doing a write/read cycle. The erase mode was tested by cycling continuously through erase/write/read steps, and counting errors when the pattern read differed from the pattern expected. Patterns that could be written were all zeroes, all ones, checkerboard, and inverse checkerboard. In heavy ion testing, the errors appear to be all static bit flips, zeroes (electrons storage) turned into ones(holes storage). Oldham estimates that about one ion out of 6 that hits the active gate area changes the state of the cell, even at the highest LET tested so far and the observed cross section is about one sixth times the geometric gate cross-section.

Cester (Cester et al., 2006) performed heavy ion irradiation tests on experimental nanocrystal memory cell arrays provided by ST microelectronics based on CAST architecture. Each nanocrystal MOSFET features W/L 0.2µm/0.3µm, with a tunnel oxide 5-nm thick and thermally grown on Si. The external control oxide consists of an oxide-nitride-oxide (ONO) stack with an equivalent oxide thickness (EOT) of 12 nm. Silicon nano-islands were realized by low pressure CVD (LPCVD) process in the Si nucleation regime using SiH as a precursor, followed by a post-deposition crystallization annealing of the islands. A nanocrystal density of 5 10^{11} cm^{-2} was determined by TEM measurements, with an average nanocrystal diameter of 6 nm. On average each cell contains 300 nanocrystals. Irradiations were performed using a tandem van der graaf accelerator. I (301 MeV, LET=64 MeV cm^2 mg^{-1}) and Ni (182 MeV, LET=31,3 MeV cm^2 mg^{-1}) ions were considered at three different fluencies: 0.83 10^8 cm^{-2}, 1.7 10^8 cm^{-2}, 3.3 10^8 cm^{-2}. The devices were unbiased during irradiations. Irradiations induce negligible changes in the drain current without affecting the subthreshold slope (swing). On the other hand Cester et al. observe that as the fluence of ions increases, the gate leakage current also increases being higher for ions with higher LET.

Wrachien (Wrachien et al., 2008) investigated the performance of nanocrystal memories, similar to those of Cester, and floating gate memories when irradiated with protons of 5 MeV and x-rays of 10 keV. The terminals were kept floating during irradiations and some of the devices were in write or erase state. Wrachien observe that X-rays are much more effective than protons in charge removal from charged devices. What arises in the work of

Wrachien et al. is that the nanocrystal memories seem to behave better than the floating gate memories in these environments since higher doses are needed in the former case respect to the latter to observe a certain charge loss. Also the swing is found to behave better for NCM than FG and the charge retention measurements confirm these results indicating much higher retention for NC memories than FG and thus justifies the interest of the radiation effects community on NC NVMs.

6. Fabrication and characterization of Si NC NVMs

The optimized Si NC NVM structures were in the form of capacitors and transistors with Si NCs fabricated according to the ultra-low-energy ion-beam-synthesis (ULE-IBS) technique (Normand et al., 2004). A schematic cross section of the gate area of the devices is shown in Fig. 6. The capacitors had a control-oxide (CO) thickness around 15.5 nm, a tunnelling-oxide (TO) of ~8 nm while the transistors had a CO thickness of 5 nm and TO thickness of 6.5 nm. For both capacitor and transistor structures, the NC layer consisted of Si NCs with mean size of 2-3 nm and density of 5 10^{11} cm^{-2}. Reference devices with no Si NCs have been fabricated as well.

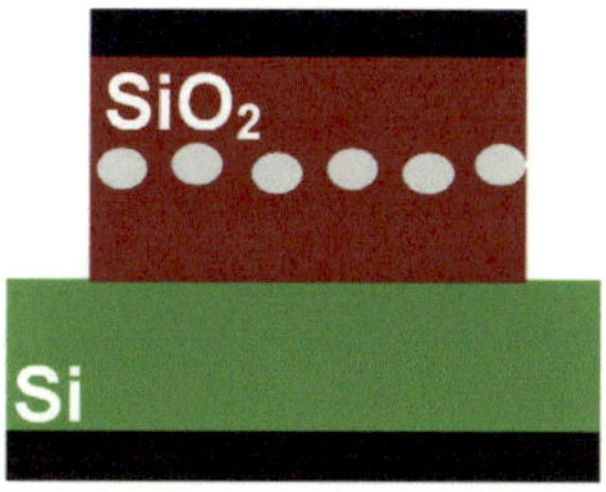

Fig. 6. Schematic of the gate area of the Si NC NVM devices considered in our work.

6.1 The Si NC MOS capacitors

The capacitor structures comprise 3 kind of square gates: 400x400 μm^2, 200x200 μm^2 and 100x100 μm^2. The process flow considered in order to fabricate these devices is the following:

1. p-Si substrate with 9 nm thermally grown SiO^2
2. Si^+ implantation 1 keV, 2 10^{16} cm^{-2}
3. annealing at 950°C/30 min in N_2 (1.5% O_2)
4. deposition 10 nm TEOS oxide
5. annealing at 900°C/15 min in N_2
6. Al evaporation
7. Annealing 320°C/30min in N_2

The TEOS oxide has been added in order to increase the CO thickness and thus improve the retention properties of the devices. The total gate oxide thickness of the implanted samples was ~25.5nm while reference samples (steps 2 and 3 skipped) had a thickness of ~19nm. The electrical properties of the above devices will be briefly presented in the next paragraphs.

The electrical properties of reference (no Si NCs) capacitors are shown in Fig. 7 where the high and low frequency C-V characteristics are presented together with the density of interface states (D_{it}) distribution along the Si band-gap. The oxide thickness extracted from C_{ox} values is ~18.7 nm. The density of interface states throughout the band-gap is extremely low, 2 10^{10} eV^{-1} cm^{-2}, thanks to the very good quality of the SiO_2 oxide thermally grown on Si substrate.

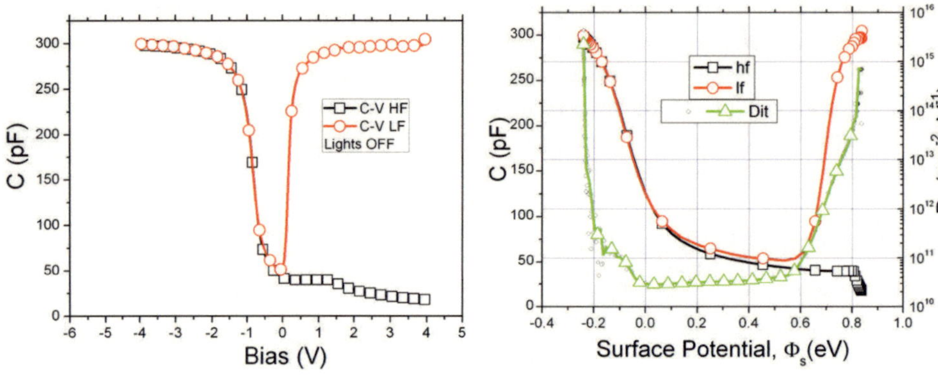

a) b)

Fig. 7. C-V characteristics and D_{it} for a reference MOS capacitor with p-Si substrate (10^{15} cm^{-3}), 18.7 nm SiO_2 and Al gate of 400μm side: a) HF - LF characteristics, b) density of states calculated using the high-low frequency method (the HF and LF C-Vs are also shown)

In Fig. 8 is shown the J-V characteristic of the reference MOS capacitor. It is demonstrated there that the conduction mechanism through the oxide is based on Fowler-Nordheim (F-N) tunneling

$$J = A\,E^2\,e^{-B/E} \tag{1}$$

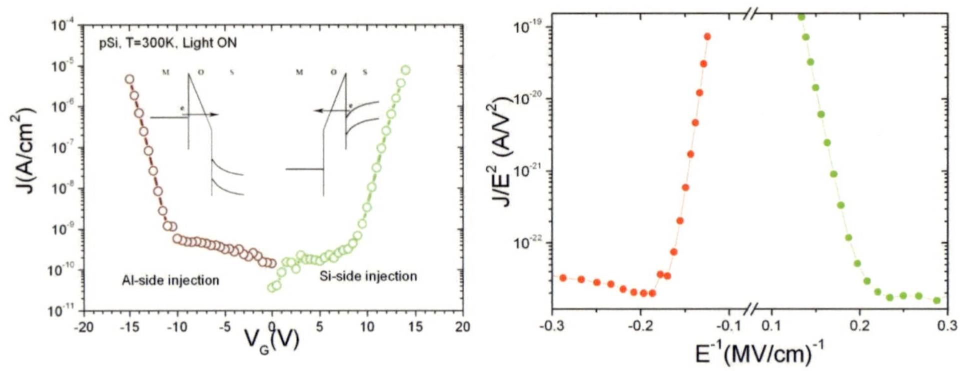

a) b)

Fig. 8. a) Experimental J-V characteristic for a reference MOS capacitor with p-Si substrate (10^{15} cm^{-3}), 18.7 nm SiO_2 and Al gate of 400μm. Probe light was kept on during the measurement in order to ensure a reasonable amount of minority carriers in inversion(green curve), b) F-N plot of the J-V data in which is clear that for E^{-1} below 0.2 $(MV/cm)^{-1}$, i.e. E above 5-6 MV/cm, F-N conduction starts.

and the B parameters extracted from the F-N plot are 194 MV/cm in accumulation (Al-side injection) and 287 MV/cm in inversion (Si-side injection). It should be reminded that the B parameter is related to the effective mass of the tunneling charge carrier and the barrier height. Assuming an electron effective mass in SiO_2 of $0.42m_0$, the extracted barrier heights are 2.7eV and 3.4eV respectively.

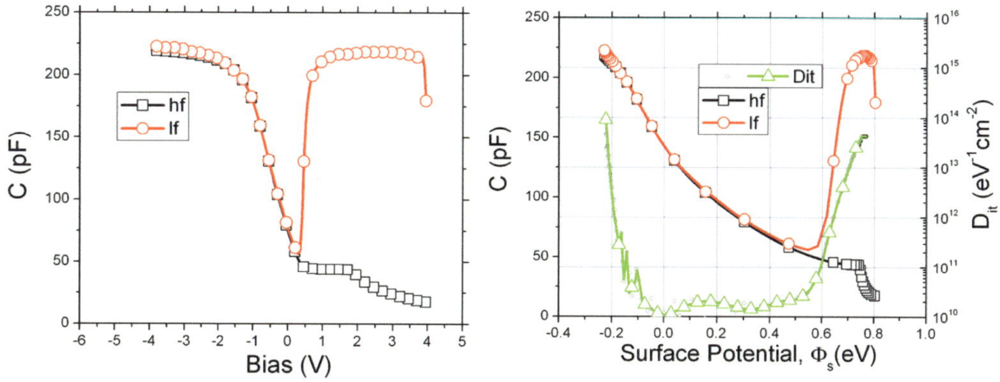

a) b)

Fig. 9. C-V characteristics and D_{it} for a Si NC MOS capacitor with p-Si substrate (10^{15} cm^{-3}), 8 nm SiO_2 TO, 2-3 nm NCs, 15.5 nm CO and Al gate of 400 μm side: a) HF - LF characteristics, b) density of states calculated using the high-low frequency method (the HF and LF C-Vs are also shown).

The Si NC MOS capacitors present similar electrical properties with the reference capacitors. In Fig. 9, the high and low frequency C-V characteristics are shown together with the D_{it} distribution along the Si band-gap. The oxide thickness extracted from C_{ox} values is ~24.5 nm. the density of interface states throughout the band-gap is extremely low, 2 10^{10} eV^{-1} cm^{-2}, thanks to the very good quality of the SiO_2 oxide thermally grown on Si substrate.

In Fig. 10 is shown the J-V characteristic of the reference MOS capacitor. It is demonstrated there that the conduction mechanism through the oxide is again based on F-N tunneling at least in accumulation (Al-side injection) with a B parameter extracted from the F-N plot of 186 MV/cm reasonably comparable with the one of the reference devices. In inversion (Si-side injection) on the other hand the B parameter extracted is very low in comparison with that of the reference capacitor: 100 MV/cm. Fig. 10c can help us in the explanation of this difference since as it is shown there, comparing the leakage current through the reference and the Si NC MOS becomes clear that for the latter conduction starts at much smaller fields in inversion, around 3.5MV/cm. Such a field cannot ignite F-N conduction so the above argument demonstrate that there is another conduction mechanism in competition with (maybe dominates) the F-N tunneling from substrate in the Si-NC memory devices in inversion. Of course the fact that F-N plot shows the characteristic linear behavior of every F-N mechanism is telling us that the mechanism dominating over the F-N injection from the Si substrate should be also an F-N mechanism. This last observation drives to the conclusion that the 100 MV/cm B value should arise from the F-N taking place from the electrons trapped in the NC layer that tunnel toward the gate and ignited by the augmented electric field present in the CO when electrons are present into the NCs while, at the same time, the electric field in the TO is reduced. It can be shown that when the overall, through the dielectric structure, electric field is 4 MV/cm and there is a detectable (in terms of flat-band voltage shifts) negative charge into the NCs, the electric field into the CO is around 5 MV/cm and thus able to ignite F-N. Thus the 100 MV/cm of the B value extracted for the Si-side injection case is related not to the barrier SiO_2/Si-conduction band but SiO_2/NC-Si-conduction band (Fig. 10d). The barrier extracted from the 100 MV/cm value is around 1.8 eV.

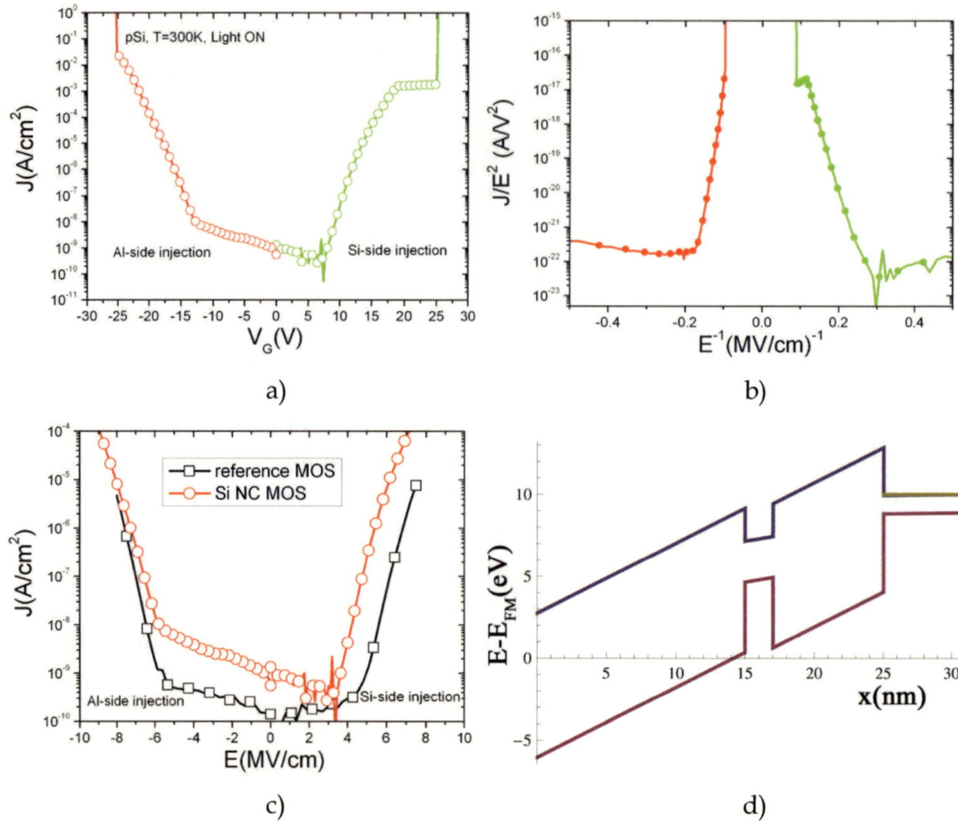

Fig. 10. a) Experimental J-V characteristic for a Si NC MOS capacitor with p-Si substrate (10^{15} cm^{-3}), 8nm SiO_2 TO, 2-3nm NCs, 15.5nm CO and Al gate of 400 μm side. Probe light was kept on during the measurement in order to ensure a reasonable amount of minority carriers in inversion(green curve), b) F-N plot of the J-V data in which is clear that in accumulation F-N conduction starts at -6MV/cm while in inversion it seem to start at 3-4 MV/cm, c) comparison between the J-E characteristic of reference and Si NC MOS capacitors, d) Band diagram of the Si NC capacitor under V_G=10 V without charges into the NC layer.

6.1.1 Memory window

The memory properties of the devices with Si NCs have been recorded with two equivalent ways: gate sweeps and gate pulses. The latter of course is the one in which we are most interested since the memory in its final application is written/erased by voltage pulses.
Gate sweep bias measurements are performed sweeping the the gate voltage circularly i.e. inversion - accumulation - inversion with increasing amplitude of the applied maximum bias. In Fig. 11a are shown the C-V curves obtained with such a measurement; large hysteresis were found for amplitudes above 10V. It should be noted that the hysteresis are counter clock wise, indicating that charging is taking place from the substrate. Upon extraction of the flat-band voltages from the above C-Vs, it is possible to present the data as in Fig. 11b where the memory behaviour of the devices becomes clearer. Electron injection (backward sweeps) seem to start at around 10V, slightly earlier than holes injection (forward sweeps) which start at around 12V while saturation starts at 16V and 18V respectively.

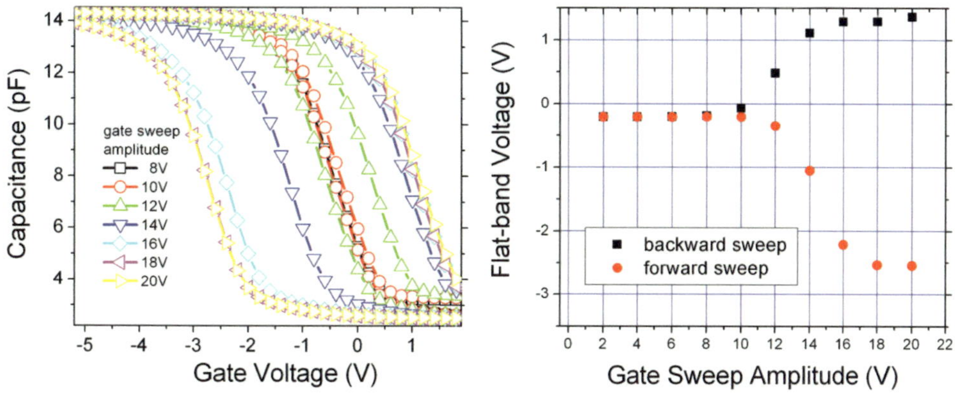

a) b)

Fig. 11. a) C-V characteristics under gate bias sweeps of several amplitudes; Large hysteresis for amplitudes above 10V are shown, b) memory characteristic as extracted from Fig. 11a.

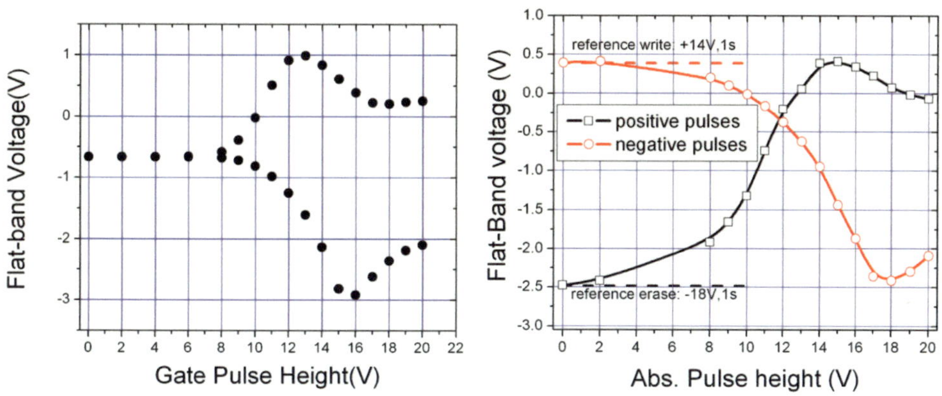

a) b)

Fig. 12. a) memory characteristic extracted from gate pulse measurements (the upper branch refers to positive pulses), b) Memory behavior under repeated positive and negative pulses. The black curve is obtained keeping the constant the erase (negative) pulse and varying the height of the write (positive) pulse, and the opposite is done for the red one.

Gate pulse measurements are performed applying in sequence pulses of increasing height to the gate and measuring at every pulse a C-V characteristic to monitor the flat-band voltage position. In such a way, with pulses of 1s duration, the results shown in Fig. 12a were obtained (where the upper branch refers to positive pulses and the lower branch to negative pulses). There are similarities between the memory behavior under gate bias sweeps and gate pulses like the maximum width and the saturation behavior at high fields, but, also one difference that is the decreasing (increasing) flat-band voltage in order to approach saturation for positive (negative) pulses. The reason of this phenomenon is that when the fields become high enough charges are not only injected into the NCs but also extracted. Actually there is a dynamic equilibrium between this two components at steady regime that

drives to the smooth behavior observed with gate sweep measurements, on the contrary, this equilibrium is perturbed in presence of pulses favoring charge extraction at high fields and this explains the peculiar shape found for the memory characteristic in Fig. 12a.
In its final operation, the memory always switches from write state to erase state and vice versa. Thus, the gate pulse measurement, although gives important informations about the pulsed operation of the memory device, isn't the best one to decide the program and erase condition to be used during its final operation. What should be done is to establish the strength of each positive (negative) pulse starting always from the same erased (programmed) state. This has been done for the Si NC capacitor memories and is shown in Fig. 12b. The most effective programming pulses are +14V and -18V. From now on we will consider as write state or erase state the condition into which is brought the device when programmed with a write pulse +14V,1s or erased with an erase pulse of -18V,1s respectively. The memory window of the device arises then as the difference between the flat-band voltages of the write and erase states. For the Si NC MOS capacitors presented here, the memory window is around 3V.

6.1.2 Charge retention measurements

Charge retention measurements are performed charging a device into one of the two states write or erase and then the evolution with time of the flat-band voltage is recorded for 12 h at least. This is done 1) measuring at regular interval of times the C-V of the device (that was written or erased) in order to obtain a result similar to the example shown in Fig. 13a, and then 2) extracting from the C-Vs the flat-band voltage which is graphed as function of time.

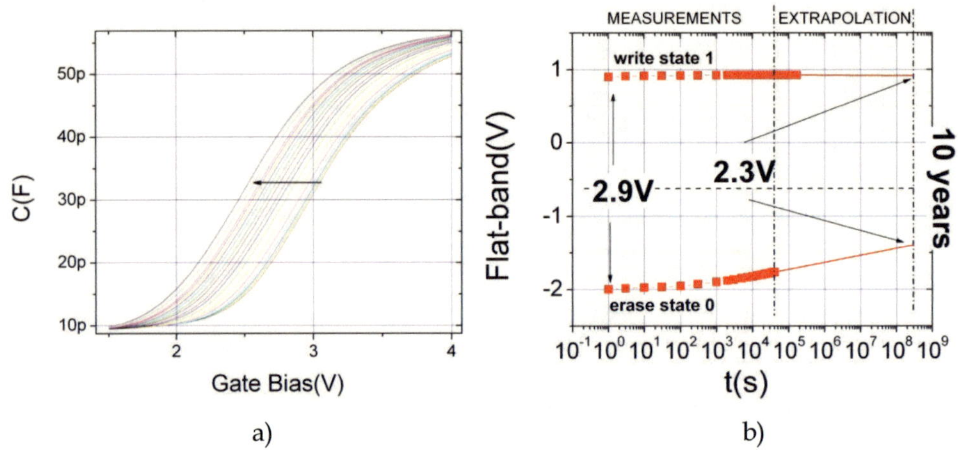

Fig. 13. a) Evolution with time of the C-V characteristic measured at regular interval of times for a Si NC MOS capacitor in the write state. The arrow show increasing time direction. Measurement at room temperature. b) Charge retention measurement in the write and the erase state of the Si NC MOS memory. Measurement performed at room temperature. The electrons loss rate is -4 mV/dec and the holes loss rate is 103 mV/dec.

The above procedure applied to our capacitors drives to the results shown in Fig. 13b where are summarized the measurements for both the write and the erase state. Since the retention curves present in log(t) a linear behavior it is usual to speak in terms of mV/dec loss rate. So, fitting the two curves shown, and assuming that the loss rate will be constant, it is

possible to extrapolate the retention measurements to 10 years. For the erase state the charge loss rate is around 103 mV/dec while for the write state is much smaller, around -4 mV/dec. The charge loss extrapolated at the 10 years retention limit is 20%, thus within the FLASH design standards.
The higher loss rate in erase state (holes retention) than in the write state (electrons retention) has to do with the fact that holes may tunnel back to the substrate by means of imperfections in the TO remained after the implantation and annealing of the Si ions. Electrons on the other hand are not affected by such imperfections and thus the large TO thickness ensures a reliable quantum mechanical barrier against electron loss.

6.2 The Si NC MOSFETs

Si NC MOSFETs were provided in structures of two types: depletion (D) and enrichment (E). Furthermore, both types are provided in various W/L configurations: a) constant W=100µm and L=12,10,8,6,4,2 µm, b) L=100 µm/W=100 µm and constant L=40µm and W=40,20,15,10,8 µm.
Si-NC nMOS transistors were fabricated using a 7 nm thick SiO_2 layer that was Si implanted and annealed under the same conditions as for NC MOS capacitors. No additional TEOS control oxide was deposited. The final gate dielectric stack includes 6.5 nm thick injection oxide, 2.5 nm thick Si NC layer and 5 nm thick control oxide.

6.2.1 Memory window

The memory behavior of the Si NC MOSFETs has been recorded with the gate pulse method mentioned previously. Positive or negative Gate pulses of increasing height are applied in sequence on Fresh devices and after each pulse the Id-VG characteristic is recorded in order to monitor the transistor threshold voltage position. The outcome of such a measurement on

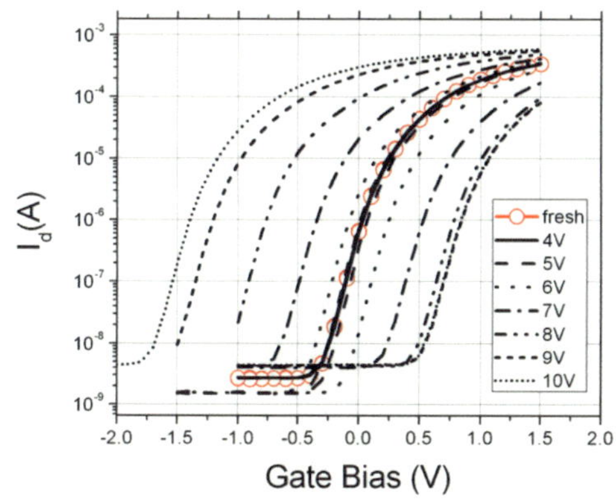

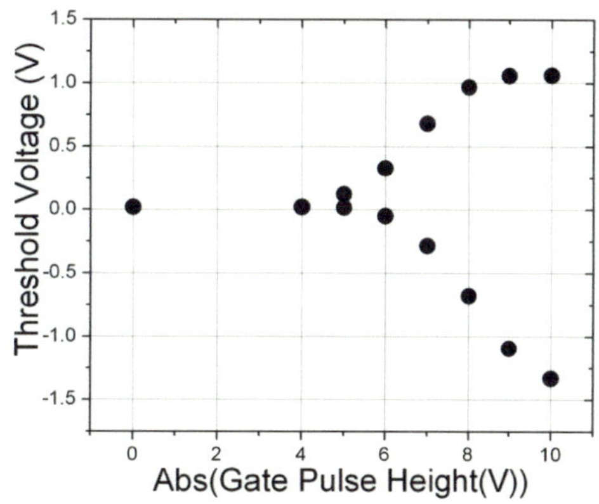

a) b)

Fig. 14. a) Id-V_G characteristics after the application, in sequence, of positive or negative pulses of increasing height (in the legend); the fresh curve refer to the device at the beginning of the measurement i.e. uncharged; on the right of the fresh curve are the characteristics related to positive pulses while on the left are the ones related to negative pulses. b) threshold voltage extracted from a) as function of the gate pulse height; the upper branch is related to positive pulses while the lower branch arises from negative pulses. The pulse duration was constant: 30ms.

our devices, for pulses of 30 ms, is shown in Fig. 14a, while in Fig. 14b the threshold voltages extracted from the Id-V_G characteristics are graphed as function of the gate pulse height. Thus, the write or erase states are defined here as the conditions determined by the application of the write pulse +9 V, 30 ms or the erase pulse -9 V, 30 ms respectively.
Should be mentioned that the swing of the Id-V_G characteristics of such devices is around 127 mV/dec.

6.2.2 Charge retention measurements

Charge retention measurements are performed in a similar manner with the measurement on capacitors except the fact that now Id-Vg characteristics will be monitored instead of C-Vs. The results are presented in Fig. 15. The overall behavior is very similar to that of NC MOS capacitors but the charge loss rates are much higher because of the thinner TO and CO of the transistor with respect to the capacitor structure. Values of -54mV/dec and 150mV/dec have been extracted for electrons and holes loss rates respectively. The overall charge loss extrapolated to 10 years retention is estimated to be ~57%.

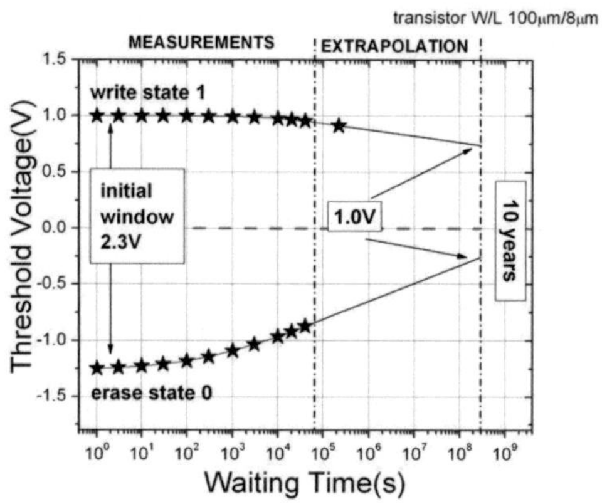

Fig. 15. Charge retention measurement in the write and the erase state of the Si NC MOSFET memory. Measurement performed at room temperature. The electrons loss rate is -54 mV/dec and the holes loss rate is 150 mV/dec.

6.2.3 Endurance to write/erase cycles

In order to perform the measurement within few hours, smaller pulse durations have been considered here. The write and erase pulse are always +9 V and -9 V respectively but the duration is now 15 ms so the memory window will be smaller than ~2 V found with 30 ms. The endurance in these transistor memories is outstanding. Results are presented in Fig. 16a where endurance up to 10^6 W/E cycles demonstrate the robustness of these devices against stress induced leakage currents (SILC). The endurance measurement is a quite stressful operation for the memory device and for this reason is quite common provide, according to FLASH standards, the retention behavior of a transistor memory cell before and after endurance. In our case the comparison is shown in Fig. 16b. After endurance, the charge loss rates are both increased: electrons loss rate before endurance was -54mV/dec while after was -60mV/dec, holes loss rate before endurance was 150mV/dec while after was 172mV/dec. The extrapolated charge loss after 10 year retention is after endurance ~70% i.e. 13% charge lost because of the stress to which the memory underwent.

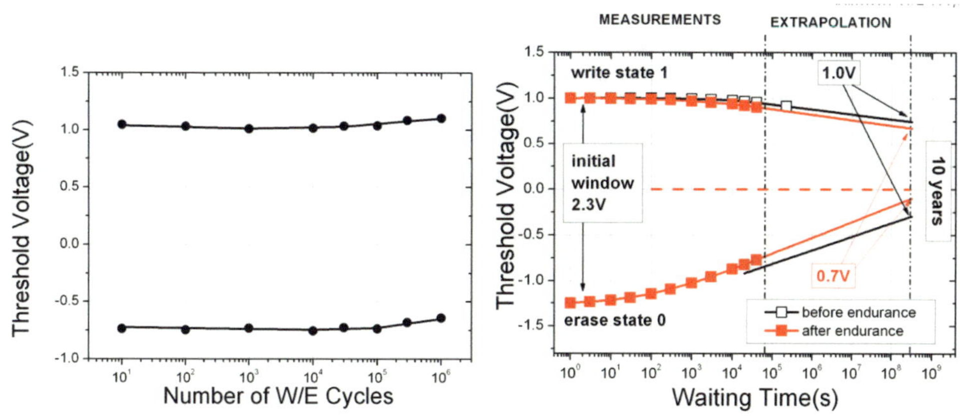

a) b)

Fig. 16. a) Endurance to w/e cycles performed on Si NC MOSFETs. A reduced pulse duration of 15ms has been considered with write pulses of +9V and erase pulses of -9V. b) charge retention measurement before and after endurance.

7. Proton radiation effects on nanocrystal non-volatile memories

The Si NC memory devices, in capacitor and transistor form, presented in section 6, have been irradiated with protons at the Tandem accelerator of the Institute of Nuclear Physics, N.C.S.R. "Demokritos". The energies used ensure that the kind of damage produced is related to TID effects. The ways TID effects alter the operation of NVM cells are essentially two: 1) loss of stored information in the form of bit-flips, and 2) charge retention issues after irradiations (failure to retain the information for 10 years). According to the existing literature on TID effects on standard FG NVMs, briefly reviewed in the previous sections, it is concluded that in FG cells, bit-flips are observed above 100 krad(SiO_2) while retention issues are observed above ~5 Mrad(SiO_2). In the next it will be demonstrated that NC NVM cells present a much higher hardness to TID effects than FG cells (Verrelli et al., 2006, 2007).

7.1 Irradiations details

The protons considered in our irradiation tests had energies of 1.5MeV and 6.5 MeV. The proton fluences (particles/cm^2) and the doses (rad(SiO_2)) considered are shown in Table 2. One important parameter that was constantly monitored during the irradiation was the flux (particles/cm^{2}s) of the particles that was kept at ~5 10^9 protons/cm^{2}s and this was done keeping constant both the proton current driven by the Tandem (200pA) and the beam spot size. It is very important that the flux remain constant during irradiation cause it is known to be related to changes in the effects produced by radiation (Ma & Dressendorfer, 1989) and thus may complicate the interpretation of the results. The samples irradiated have physical dimension of 1.5x1.5 cm^2 while the proton beam spot has been tuned to be the largest possible i.e. 0.5x0.5 cm^2. One sample at a time has been irradiated and upon irradiation of all the samples, their electrical characteristics have been studied in our laboratory. The irradiation and all the electrical measurements took place at room temperature and the characterization of the radiation effects ended within one month period time from irradiation. Actually the fastest the samples are characterized after irradiation the better it is, because the irradiation effects have the property to anneal out with time also at room temperatures (Ma & Dressendorfer, 1989). All the samples have been irradiated with floating terminals except some NC MOS capacitors and transistor which were programmed to "1" or "0".

Irradiation at 1,5 MeV		Irradiation at 6,5 MeV	
CAPACITORS			
FLUENCE (cm^{-2})	DOSE (Mrad(SiO_2)	FLUENCE (cm^{-2})	DOSE (Mrad(SiO_2)
$5*10^{13}$	123	$5*10^{13}$	119
$1*10^{13}$	24.6	$1*10^{13}$	23.7
$5*10^{12}$	12.3	$5*10^{12}$	11.9
$1*10^{12}$	2.46	$1*10^{12}$	2.37
$5*10^{11}$	1.23	$5*10^{11}$	1.19
TRANSISTORS			
$3*10^{11}$	0.74		
$3*10^{12}$	7.42		
$1*10^{13}$	24.6		
$3*10^{13}$	74.2		

Table 2. Fluencies and doses for the samples involved in this experiment. The capacitors were both NC MOS devices and reference devices i.e. MOS capacitors with no NCs. The transistors were NC MOSFET devices only.

7.2 Electrical characterization of the irradiated devices

At first, we should remark that the capacitor and the transistor samples have a main difference: the former work "vertically" while the latter work "horizontally". Indeed, in capacitors, the substrate-gate electric field rules everything while in transistors, Id passes from the source to the drain through the channel formed by the inversion layer in the Si substrate and the whole process is confined into few μm from Si-SiO_2 interface.

SRIM simulations on our structures show that 1.5 MeV and 6.5 MeV protons end their trajectories into the Si substrate at depths from the Si-SiO_2 interface of 80 and 400μm respectively (for this reason irradiation took place with the devices face to the beam i.e. protons always enter the devices from their gates). This represent an important limitation for capacitor structures which work vertically. The reason is that when a particle like a proton with the energies above mentioned penetrate matter, at the beginning of its track it loses energy in small steps slowing down almost entirely through Coulomb interactions with the atomic electrons of the target material. Because of the large number of these interactions, the slowing down procedure is nearly continuous and along a straight-line path. As the particle slows down, it captures electron(s) to form a neutral atom and thus has an increased probability to have nuclear collisions that may induce displacements and vacancies in the target material lattice. The result is that at the end of range of their tracks, protons destroy the Si crystalline structure transforming it into a porous-like material. Of course the above mentioned effect depends from the fluence of protons. It was found experimentally that for fluencies above 10^{14} protons/cm^2 the MOS behavior is completely lost due to the isolation achieved between the Si back contact and the gate of the capacitor. The presence of the damage and its amount can be monitored through the value of the series resistance in C-V measurements which increases as the fluence is increased. As it is demonstrated in Fig. 17, this dependence has been found to be approximately linear with the fluence in both the NC MOS capacitors and the reference (no NCs) MOS capacitors.

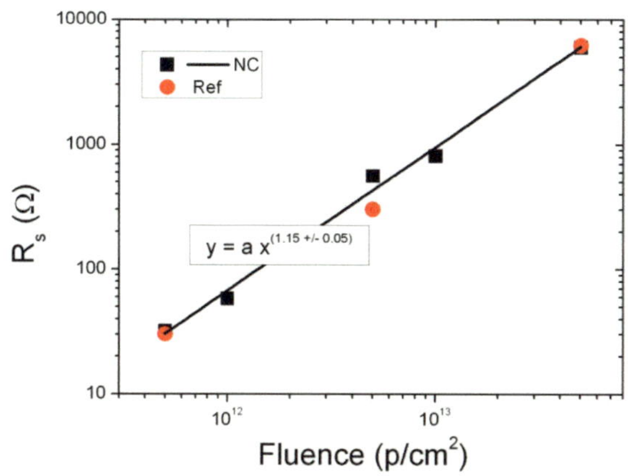

Fig. 17. Dependence upon the fluence of the series resistance measured during C-V measurements on irradiated NC MOS capacitors and reference (no NCs) MOS capacitors.

7.2.1 Radiation effects on the Dit

As mentioned in 3.1, one of the parameter of MOS devices more affected by ionizing radiation is the density of interface states. After irradiation the C-V and G-f characteristics of reference (no NCs) MOS and NC MOS capacitors have been measured in order to estimate the D_{it}. Both methods, high-low frequency and conductance, give similar estimations. An example of the effects on the MOS characteristics is shown in Fig. 18a-18c where the C-V frequency dispersion is shown for some of the irradiated NC MOS capacitors.
The exctracted values of D_{it} at mid-gap have been graphed in function of the dose and are shown in Fig. 18d.
For both reference and NC MOS devices, D_{it} increases sub-linearly with dose. Within the measurement errors, our data are in good agreement with the empirical relationship (Ma & Dressendorfer, 1989) that asserts D_{it} to be proportional to Dose$^{2/3}$. D_{it} distributions were found to be U shaped for the various MOS capacitor samples, with a clear peak in the upper half of the band gap, at around 0.2eV above mid-gap, giving evidence of a sharply distributed electron state in agreement with other observations (Ma & Dressendorfer, 1989).

7.2.2 Effects on F-N injection

One important question to answer was to which extent the radiation effects described above affect the MOS characteristics. In order to determine whether the F-N injection mechanism was altered by the ionizing radiation damage to the SiO_2, the B parameter has been monitored on all the irradiated samples and the result is shown in Fig. 19. This parameter, within experimental errors, does not seem to be affected by the irradiation dose.

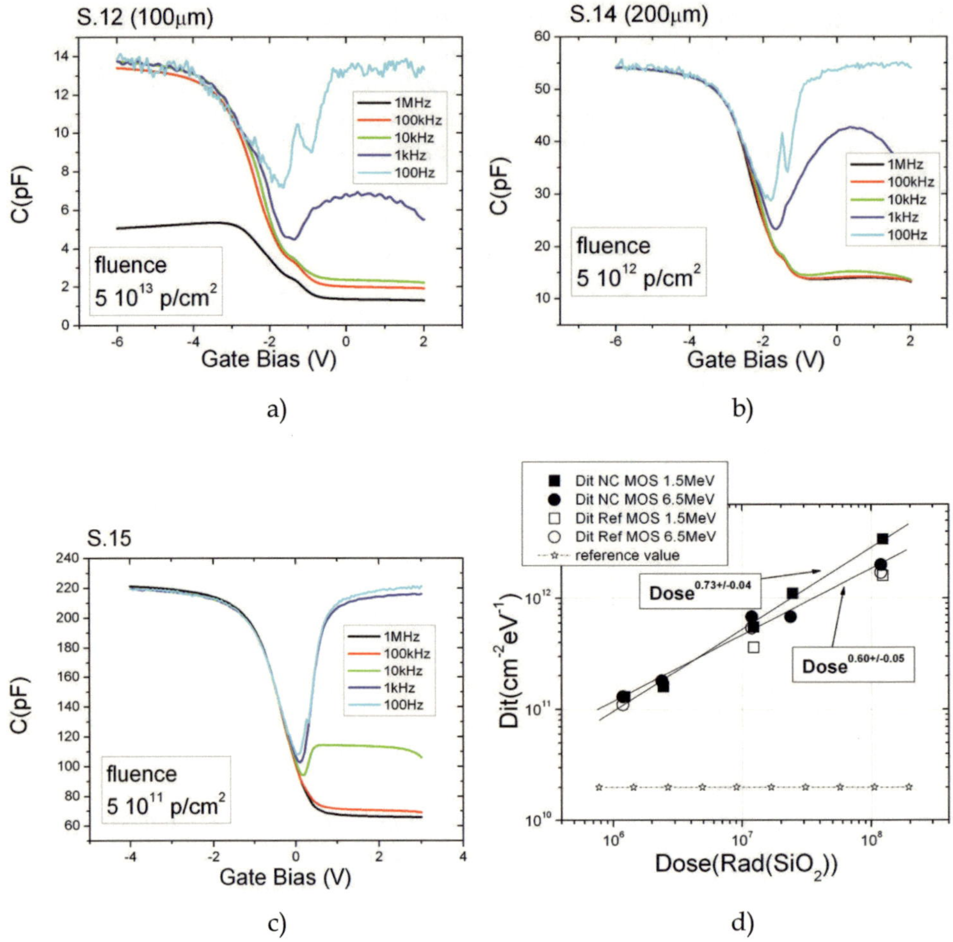

Fig. 18. C-V frequency dispersion for irradiated NC MOS capacitors at different proton fluences: a) 5 10^{13} p/cm^2, b) 5 10^{12} p/cm^2, 5 10^{11} p/cm^2. d) D_{it} versus dose for Reference (without NCs) MOS and NC MOS capacitors irradiated with protons 1.5 MeV and 6.5 MeV. D_{it} reference value for non irradiated devices is also shown. The lines correspond to linear fits of the NC MOS capacitors experimental data to the relationship $D_{it} \sim Dose^b$.

7.2.3 Radiation induced Flat-band/threshold voltage shift

MOS capacitors irradiated with floating terminals exhibit C-V characteristics shifted to lower voltages compared to the characteristics of non-irradiated samples, in agreement to the well-known observation (Ma & Dressendorfer, 1989) that irradiation creates a net trapped positive charge (Q_{ot}) into the SiO_2 layer.

After irradiation of fresh and programmed (+14V/1s write pulse) MOS capacitors, the net positive trapped charge was calculated according to the relation: $Q_{ot} = -\Delta V_{fb} \bullet C_{ox}$ where ΔV_{fb} is the flat-band voltage shift induced by irradiation. The Q_{ot} vs. radiation-dose data shown in Fig. 20 indicate the following:

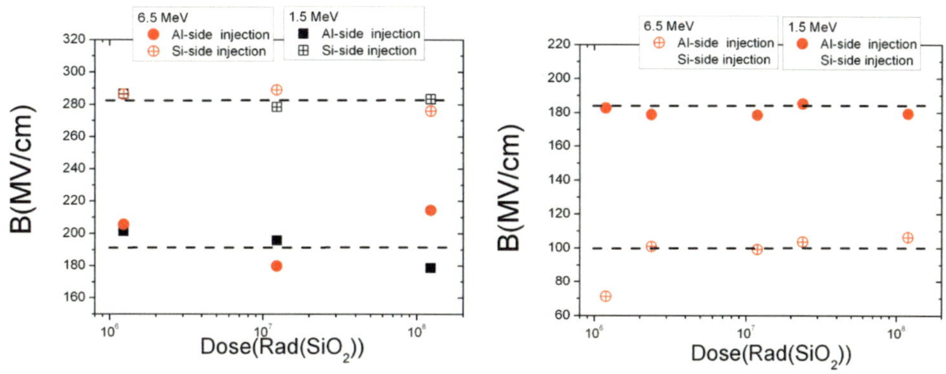

a) b)

Fig. 19. Values of the B parameter related to F-N conduction in (a) reference MOS and (b) NC MOS capacitors after irradiation. The dashed lines correspond to the values observed before irradiation.

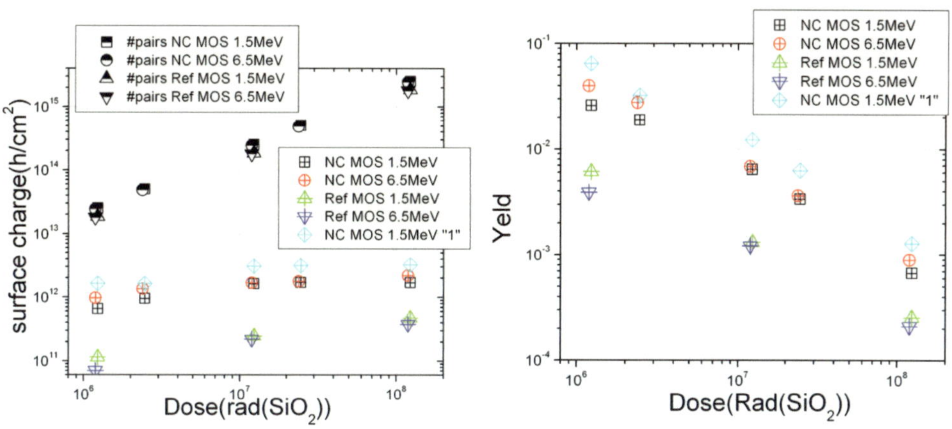

a) b)

Fig. 20. Values of the B parameter related to F-N conduction in reference MOS (a) and NC MOS capacitors (B) after irradiation. The dashed lines correspond to the values observed before irradiation.

1. In all cases, Q_{ot} is well below the number of the created electron-hole pairs, thus indicating that only a relatively small number of holes survive the initial fast recombination process i.e. the radiation yeld is far smaller than unity (Fig. 20b). The number of electron-hole pairs created by irradiation was evaluated as the ratio of the energy lost by the incident protons into the SiO_2 layer (obtained through TRIM simulations) to the 17eV electron-hole pair generation energy (Ma & Dressendorfer, 1989) in silicon dioxide.
2. Programmed NC-MOS capacitors, exhibit increased (~ 2 times) Q_{ot} values compared to capacitors with uncharged NCs. This is attributed to the internal electric field generated by the charged NCs that reduces the hole recombination probability (Ma & Dressendorfer, 1989).

3. The amount of trapped charges in irradiated un-programmed NC MOS capacitors was found to be almost one order of magnitude higher than in the reference MOS samples. This can be related to the extra trapping sites located in the injection and control oxide in the form of excess silicon atoms left behind by the ULE-IBS technique.
4. In all cases Q_{ot} shows saturation for high irradiation doses (Fig. 20a).
5. All the programmed NC MOS capacitors undergo a bit flip 1→0 following irradiation, (Fig. 21b), in agreement with Petkov (Petkov et al., 2004) where bit flip were observed at 150krad.

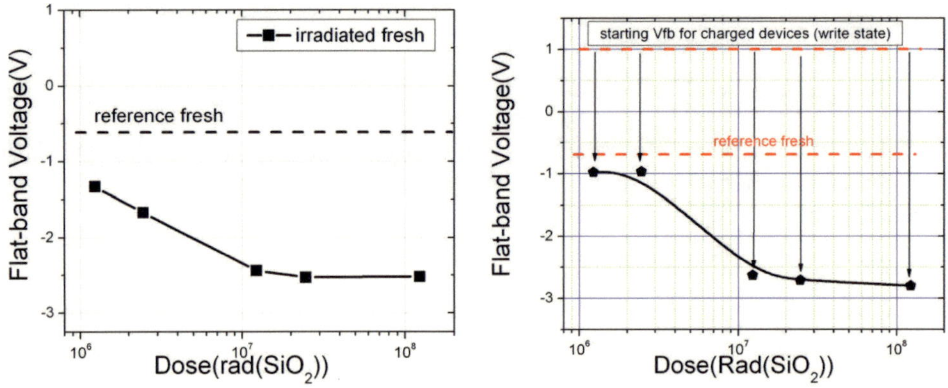

a) b)

Fig. 21. Flat-band voltage after irradiation for a) fresh NC MOS capacitors and b) programmed "1" NC MOS capacitors.

Fig. 21a indicates that under irradiation the induced positive oxide trapped charge results in a shift of the C-V characteristics by 2V (the overall memory window is about 2.9V). If the oxide trapped charge is not removed from the oxide a permanent shift of the memory window would result, causing serious problems in reading the memory state. It was found that our devices could be restored to their initial memory window by tunnel annealing i.e. by electric field stressing (Ma & Dressendorfer, 1989). The memory behavior of 1.5MeV irradiated NC MOS capacitors was examined by symmetrical sweep C-V measurements of increasing width (2→-2→2, 8→-8→8,etc.) and under pulse operating conditions (see Fig. 22a). The initial, dose dependent, radiation induced shift disappears gradually by increasing the voltage sweep. Therefore, the memory window of irradiated devices approaches the memory window of the unirradiated devices, as also reported by Petkov (Petkov et al., 2004). In particular it was found that the radiation induced oxide charge can be removed with 1 write or erase pulse as shown in Fig. 22b.

For what concerns the NC MOSFETs similar results with the one presented above holds. As found for the NC MOS capacitors, the radiation induced oxide charge can be easily removed by electric field stressing (for example 1 write or erase pulse). No bit flip has been observed on charged (write state) devices as shown in Fig. 23. Comparing the V_{FB} shifts observed for the programmed NC MOS capacitors with the Vth shifts for programmed NC nMOS transistors it can be concluded that for the latter devices the effect of radiation induced positive charge trapped into the gate oxide is reduced. It is believed that this effect can be ascribed to the smaller thickness of control and tunneling oxides in the transistor case i.e. to

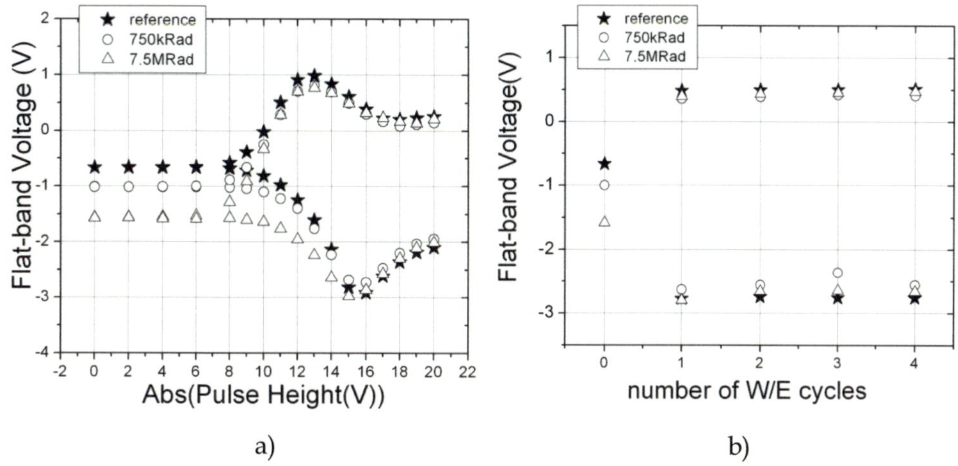

Fig. 22. a) Memory behavior after application of positive and negative pulses (heights from 2V to 20V, 1s duration) on irradiated NC MOS capacitors at 1.5MeV. The initial flat-band voltage differences disappear as higher gate pulses are applied, indicating the removal of the radiation induced positive oxide charge. b) Flat-band voltage evolution during 1s +14V/-16V write/erase cycles on irradiated NC MOS capacitors. The 0 cycle represent the after irradiation flat-band voltage. Differences between the flat-band voltage values of unirradiated and irradiated devices are not observed after the very first write or erase pulse, indicating the immediate removal of the radiation induced positive oxide charge.

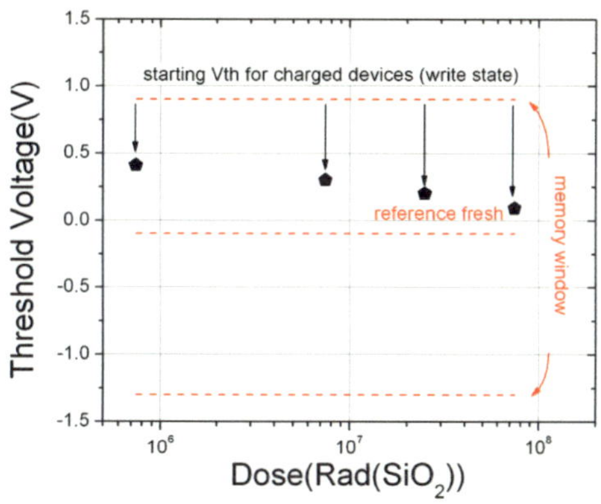

Fig. 23. Threshold voltage measured after irradiation for charged (write) transistors.

the fact that a larger percentage of oxide volume is at tunneling distance from the gate or substrate and thus a smaller volume is left for the radiation induced Q_{ot} (Ma & Dressendorfer, 1989).

The above result indicate that the read failure of irradiated NC transistor cells may appear only at doses above 1-10 Mrad(SiO_2), thus more than 10 times higher than in FG cells.

7.2.4 Effects on charge retention

The charge retention time of the NC non-volatile memory devices is a characteristic of critical importance. What is required is that the write and erase states remain clearly

distinguished after a 10 yrs retention period. Charge retention was here measured through a waiting time of 12h after placing the devices in full write or erase state conditions. In Fig. 24a is presented the overall evolution of the memory window with time, while in Fig. 24b and Fig. 24d are shown the extracted flat-band voltage decay rates, $dV_{fb}/dLog(t)$.
Charge loss rate for the write state is strongly dependent on the irradiation dose while for the erase state no such dependence is observed. It was found that the write state flat-band voltage decay rate depends on irradiation dose as $Dose^{2/3}$, (see Fig. 24b); the same dose

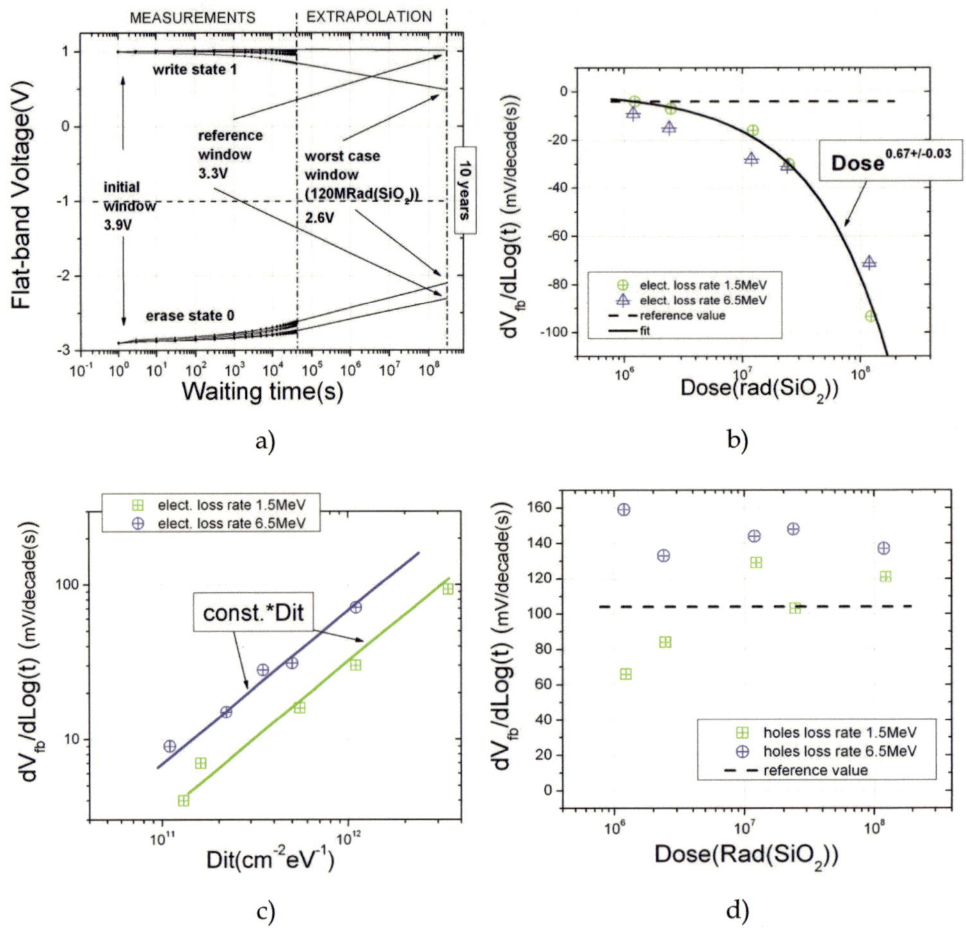

Fig. 24. a) Memory window evolution with time for 1.5MeV protons irradiated NC MOS capacitors. Memory window for unirradiated devices is also indicated. The dashed line is the V_{fb} of fresh unirradiated devices. These results applies also for 6.5MeV irradiations. b) Flat-band voltage decay rates for write state(1s, +14V) vs dose for irradiated NC MOS capacitors with 1.5MeV and 6.5MeV proton energies. The electron loss rate follows the relationship $Dose^{2/3}$, the same valid for D_{it}. c) Flat-band voltage decay rates for write state (1s, +14V) are plotted vs D_{it} and comparison with the relationship $dV_{fb}/dLog(t)$=const*D_{it} is also shown to demonstrate the linear correlation found between electron loss rate and D_{it}. d) Flat-band voltage decay rates for erase state (1s, -16V) vs dose for 1.5MeV and 6.5MeV proton energies. A small increase in the loss rate is observed but not clear is the dependence with dose.

dependence that applies for D_{it}. This strongly suggests that the loss rate of stored electrons is directly related to the damage induced by irradiation at the Si-substrate/SiO_2 interface (Fig. 24c) as it was initially postulated by Shi (Shi et al., 1998). Previous measurements of electron loss at high temperatures revealed that the long-term retention of the present devices is due to the electron storage in NC traps (Dimitrakis & Normand, 2005).

Regarding the erase state (hole storage), the measured flat-band voltage decay rates show a small increase with respect to those of non-irradiated samples and unlike electrons they do not exhibit any clear dependence on dose. These results indicate that the discharging of "0" programmed NC MOS devices is indeed through defects located in the Si-rich injection oxide.

Compared to unirradiated NC devices, the reduction in the extrapolated memory window at 10-yrs of irradiated NC devices does not exceed ~20% (worst case of samples irradiated with 120Mrad(SiO_2)) being ~15% the charge lost by unirradiated devices while for irradiated ones it raises to ~35%.

Concerning the transistors, once again similar results with those presented for the capacitors have been found. Memory window as a function of the waiting time is shown in Fig. 25. It is clear that even in the worst case of NC MOS transistors irradiated with 75Mrad(SiO_2), long time charge storage behavior is still observed. The 10-yrs extrapolated values show that the charge lost is ~74% after irradiation at 75Mrad(SiO_2) with ~17% more charge lost respect to the unirradiated devices.

It should be remarked that both capacitors and transistor structures irradiated with doses up to ~100 Mrad(SiO_2) do not show failure of the retention characteristic. This means that retention failure in NC NVM cells may appear only at doses higher than 100 Mrad(SiO_2), thus more than 10 times higher than in FG cells.

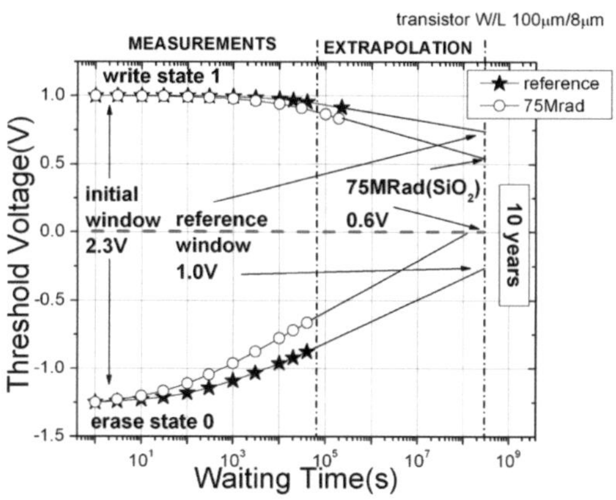

Fig. 25. Memory window evolution for unirradiated and irradiated at the highest dose NC MOS transistors. Extrapolations at 10 years shows that irradiated devices lost 40% of reference window.

7.2.5 Effects onto the endurance to write/erase cycles

Another important specification for non-volatile memories relate to the ability to endure repeated write/erase cycles. Endurance measurements, shown in Fig. 26, were carried out through a 15ms +9V/-9V write/erase pulse regime on all irradiated transistors. Neither degradation, nor drift in the memory window has been observed for all irradiated devices.

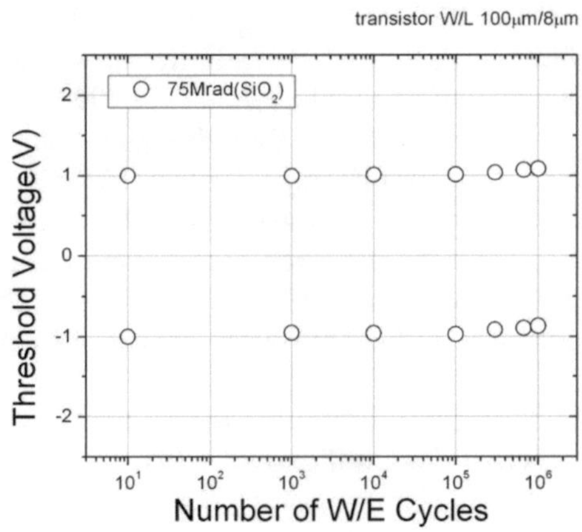

Fig. 26. Memory window evolution for unirradiated and irradiated at the highest dose NC MOS transistors. Extrapolations at 10 years shows that irradiated devices lost 40% of reference window.

8. Conclusions

In this chapter Si nanocrystal non-volatile memory devices were presented and characterized electrically. Memory windows as large as 3-4V have been shown with excellent retention and endurance characteristics. The above devices, in capacitor and transistor configuration, have been used in irradiation experiments with high energy protons and high fluencies showing superior radiation hardness, more than 10 times, respect to standard floating gate memories. It was found that transistor memory cells lose their information only above 10^8 rad(SiO_2) which is outstanding. Furthermore, electron retention is affected by radiation and in particular has been identified a clear relationship between electron loss rate and density of interface states, driving to the conclusion that the Si NC NVMs considered in this work loose stored electrons by tunneling through the interface states. Hole's loss rate doesn't seem to be affected by the radiation. Endurance to w/e cycles remains unaltered after irradiation.

9. Acknowledgments

The authors would like to acknowledge the European Space Agency for financial support. We would like also to thank the collaborators who contributed to this research: Dr. P. Normand, Dr. P. Dimitrakis, Prof. M. Kokkoris and Mr. I. Anastasiadis.

10. References

Barth J.L, C.S. Dyer, E.G. Stassinopoulos, Space, atmospheric, and terrestrial radiation environments, *IEEE Trans. Nucl. Sci.* 50(3), Jun 2003, p. 466-482

Blauwe J., "Nanocrystal nonvolatile memory devices", *IEEE Trans. Nanotechnol.*, vol.1, pp. 72-77, 2002.

Cellere G., A. Paccagnella, , "Charge loss after Co irradiation of flash arrays," *IEEE Trans. Nucl. Sci.*, vol. 51, pp. 2912–2916, Oct. 2004a.

Cellere G., A. Paccagnella, S. Lora, A. Pozza, G. Tao, A. Scarpa, "A review of ionizing radiation effects in floating gate memories," *IEEE – Trans. Device Mater. Rel.*, vol. 4, pp. 359–370, Sept. 2004b.

Cellere G., A. Paccagnella, A. Visconti, M. Bonanomi, P. Caprara, S. Lora, "A model for TID effects on floating gate memory cells," *IEEE Trans. Nucl. Sci.*, vol. 51, pp. 3753–3758, Dec. 2004c.

Cellere G., A. Paccagnella, A. Visconti, M. Bonanomi, A. Candelori, S. Lora, "Effect of different total ionizing dose sources on charge loss from programmed floating gate cells," *IEEE Trans. Nucl. Sci.*, vol. 52, pp. 2372–2377, Dec. 2005.

Ceschia M., A. Paccagnella, M. Turrini, A. Candelori, G. Ghidini and J. Wyss, "Heavy ion irradiation of thin oxides," IEEE Trans. Nucl. Sci., vol. 47, pp. 2648-2655, December 2000

Cester A., A. Gasperin, N. Wrachien, A. Paccagnella, V. Ancarani, C. Gerardi, "Impact of heavy ion strikes on nanocrystal non volatile memory cell arrays", *IEEE Trans Nucl. Sci.*, vol. 53, pp. 3195–3202, Dec. 2006.

Dimitrakis P., P.Normand, Semiconductor Nanocrystal Floating-gate Memory Devices, *Mater. Res. Soc. Symp. Proc.* Vol 830, D5.1.1(2005)

Gonzalez-Varona O., Garrido B., Cheylan S., Pérez-Rodríguez A., Cuadras A., Morante J.R., "Control of tunnel oxide thickness in Si-nanocrystal array memories obtained by ion implantation and its impact in writing speed and volatility", *Appl. Phys. Lett.*, vol. 82, pp. 2151-2153, 2003.

Hanafi H. I., S. Tiwari & I. Khan, "Fast and long retention-time nanocrystal memory", *IEEE Trans. Electron Devices*, vol. 43, pp. 1553-1558, 1996.

Huang C., Method and system for correcting soft errors in memory circuit, United States Patent 7644341, 2010, http://www.freepatentsonline.com/7644341.html

Kim Ilgweon, Sangyeon Han, Kwangseok Han, Jongho Lee & Hyungcheol Shin, "Room temperature single electron effects in a Si nano-crystal memory", *IEEE Electron Device Letters*, vol. 20, pp. 630-631, 1999.

King Ya-Chin, Tsu-Jae King & Chenming Hu, "MOS memory using germanium nanocrystals formed by thermal oxidation of $Si_{1-x}Ge_x$", *IEDM Tech. Dig.*, pp. 115-118, 1998.

Klein D., Method and system for dynamically operating memory in a power-saving error correction mode, United States Patent 6838331, 2005, http://www.freepatentsonline.com/6838331.html

Lankhorst Martijn H. R., Bas W. S. M. M. Ketelaars & R. A. M. Wolters, "Low-cost and nanoscale non-volatile memory concept for future silicon chips", *Nature materials*, vol. 4, pp. 347-352, 2005.

Larcher L., A. Paccagnella, M. Ceschia, and G. Ghidini, "A model of radiation induced leakage current (RILC) in ultra-thin gate oxides," *IEEE Trans. Nucl. Sci.*, vol. 46, pp. 1553–1561, Dec. 1999.

Liaw J., SRAM cell design for soft error rate immunity, United States Patent 6649456, 2003, http://www.freepatentsonline.com/6649456.html

Ma T. P. and P. V. Dressendorfer, Ionizing Radiation Effects in MOS Devices and Circuits. New York: Wiley, 1989.

Normand P., E. Kapetanakis, P. Dimitrakis, D. Skarlatos, K. Beltsios, D. Tsoukalas, C. Bonafos, G. Ben Asssayag, N. Cherkashin, A. Claverie, J. A. Van Den Berg, V. Soncini, A. Agarwal, M. Ameen, M. Perego and M. Fanciulli, Nanocrystals manufacturing by ultra-low-energy ion-beam-synthesis for non-volatile memory applications, *Nucl. Instrum. Meth. B* 216, 228 (2004).

Oldham T.R., M. Suhail, P. Kuhn, E. Prinz, H. S. Kim, and K. A. LaBel, "Effects of heavy ion exposure on nanocrystal nonvolatile memories", *IEEE Trans Nucl. Sci.*, vol. 52, pp. 2366–2371, Dec. 2005.

Oldham T.R., R. L. Ladbury, Member, IEEE, M. Friendlich, H. S. Kim, M. D. Berg, T. L. Irwin, C. Seidleck, and K. A. LaBel, "SEE and TID characterization of an advanced commercial 2Gbit NAND flash nonvolatile memory", *IEEE Trans Nucl. Sci.*, vol. 53, pp. 3217–3222, Dec. 2006.

Oldham T.R., M. Friendlich, J. Howard, M. Berg, H. Kim, T. Irwin, K. LaBel, TID and SEE Response of an Advanced Samsung 4Gb NAND Flash Memory, *IEEE Radiation Effects Data Workshop*, pp. 221–225, 2007.

Ostraat M. L., De Blauwe J.W., Green M.L., Bell L.D., Brongersma M.L., Casperson J., Flagan R.C., Atwater H.A., "Synthesis and characterization of aerosol silicon nanocrystal nonvolatile floating-gate memory devices", *Appl. Phys. Lett.*, vol. 79, pp. 433-435, 2001.

Ouyang Jiantong, Chih-Wei Chu, Charles R. Szmanda, Liping Ma & Yang Yang, "Programmable polymer thin film and non-volatile memory device", *Nature materials*, vol. 3, pp. 918-922, 2004.

Park Nae-Man, Suk Ho Choi, Seong-Ju Park, "Electron charging and discharging in amorphous silicon quantum dots embedded in silicon nitride", *Appl. Phys. Lett.*, vol. 81, pp. 1092-1094, 2002.

Petkov M. P., L.D. Bell, H.A. Atwater, "High total dose tolerance of prototype silicon nanocrystal non-volatile memory cells," *IEEE Trans Nucl. Sci.*, vol. 51, pp. 3822–3826, Dec. 2004.

Scarpa A., A. Paccagnella, F. Montera, G. Ghibaudo, G. Pananakakis, G. Ghidini, and P. G. Fuochi, "Ionizing radiation induced leakage current on ultra-thin gate oxides," IEEE Trans. Nucl. Sci., vol. 44, no. 6, pp. 1818–1825, Dec. 1997.

Shi Y., K.Saito,H.Ishikuro, T.Hiramoto, Effects of traps on charge storage characteristics in metal-oxide-semiconductor memory structures based on silicon nanocrystals, *J.Appl.Phys.* 84(4), 2358 (1998).

Takata M., Kondoh S., Sakaguchi T., Choi H., Shim J.-C., Kurino H., Koyanagi M., "New non-volatile memory with extremely high density metal nano-dots", *IEDM Tech. Dig.*, pp. 553-556, 2003.

Tiwari S., F. Rana, H. Hanafi, A. Hartstein & E. F. Crabbe, A silicon nanocrystals based memory, *Appl. Phys. Lett.*, vol. 68, pp.1377-1379, 1996.

Vanheusden K., Warren W.L., Devine R.A.B., Fleetwood D.M., Schwank J.R., Shaneyfelt M.R., Winokur P.S., Lemnios Z.J.,"Non-volatile memory device based on mobile protons in SiO_2 thin films", *Nature*, vol. 386, 587-589 (1997).

Verrelli E., D. Tsoukalas, M. Kokkoris, R. Vlastou, P. Dimitrakis and P. Normand, Proton Radiation Effects on Nanocrystal Non-Volatile Memories, IEEE T. Nucl. Sc., Vol. 54, No. 4, August 2007.

Verrelli E., I. Anastassiadis, D. Tsoukalas, M. Kokkoris, R. Vlastou, P. Dimitrakis, P. Normand, Proton radiation tolerance of nanocrystal memories, Physica E 38 (2007) 67–70.

Wrachien N., A. Cester, R. Portoghese, C. Gerardi, "Investigation of proton and x-ray irradiation effects on nanocrystal and floating gate memory cell arrays", *IEEE Trans Nucl. Sci.*, vol. 55, pp. 3000–3008, Dec. 2008.

12

Atomistic Simulations of Flash Memory Materials Based on Chalcogenide Glasses

Bin Cai, Binay Prasai and D. A. Drabold
Department of Physics and Astronomy, Ohio University, Athens, Ohio United States

1. Introduction

In the last decade, the market for non-volatile computer storage has experienced rapid growth. However, as the device size scales down, currently used NOR and NAND technology is facing limitations from tunnel oxide and electrostatic interactions between cells (Lacaita & Wouters, 2008). To solve the scaling problems, in the last fifteen years, a number of alternative Flash memory technologies have been proposed and studied. The phase-change memory, solid electrolyte memory, ferroelectric memory, magnetic memory and molecular memory using conducting molecules and carbon nanotubes all are promising candidates to replace technologies that are reaching their limit (Chung et al., 2010; Drabold, 2009).
Vitreous materials involving chemical species from column VI other than oxygen are called Chalcogenide glasses. Chalcogenide glasses have long held interest for applications such as infrared detectors and optical fibers. Recently, chalcogenide glasses attracted further attention due to their promising application in data storage devices. Two of the examples are phase-change memory materials based on tellurium alloys and solid electrolyte memory materials based on metal-doped Ge-Se glasses. In this chapter, by using *ab-initio* molecular dynamics, we introduce the latest simulation results on two materials for flash memory devices: $Ge_2Sb_2Te_5$ and Ge-Se-Cu-Ag. This chapter is a review of our previous work including some of our published figures and text in Cai et al. (2010) and Prasai & Drabold (2011) and also includes several new results. We organized the chapter as follows: we first introduce the simulation method used in all calculations in section 2; in section 3, we show the key findings on $Ge_2Sb_2Te_5$(Cai et al., 2010); then we switch to the study on Ge-Se-Cu-Ag in section 4 (Prasai & Drabold, 2011). For both cases, after forming realistic atomistic models, we analyze the topology and electronic structure, predict their properties, and compare with experimental results.

2. Simulation method

We use the *ab-initio* molecular dynamics method (ab-MD) to generate atomistic models. When such schemes are applied, the initial position of atoms are usually randomized and the system is then annealed or relaxed to seek suitable local energy minima. The final model will be the one with a minimum total energy and agreeing with experimental measurements. One of the popular techniques based on ab-MD is the "Cook and Quench" method, for which the MD simulation is performed at a temperature well above melting point, which will force the system to lose memory of the initial configuration. Finally, the system is equilibrated at a

lower temperature, like room temperature. Then an energy minimization is applied. Many realistic models are made by such a simple but powerful method.
In our work, all of the calculations were carried out using periodic boundary conditions with the Vienna Ab-initio Simulation Package(VASP). VASP is based on density functional theory using a plane wave basis (Kresse & Furthmuller, 1996). For $Ge_2Sb_2Te_5$, we used the projector augmented-wave (PAW) potentials and generalized gradient approximation PBE (GGA-PBE) method (Kresse & Joubert, 1999; Perdew et al., 1996); for Ge-Se-Cu-Ag, we used the local density approximation (LDA) for the exchange correlation energy in conjunction with the Vanderbilt Ultra Soft pseudopotentials (Kresse & Hafner, 1994; Perdew & Zunger, 1981). Both systems were annealed, equilibrated and cooled using molecular dynamic (MD) option of VASP and relaxation is carried out in conjugate gradient (CG) mode. Moreover, to obtain a better estimation for electronic gap, we applied Hartree-Fock (HF) calculation when analyzing the electronic structure of amorphous $Ge_2Sb_2Te_5$. Though HF is known to exaggerate both the optical gap and charge fluctuation in the electron gas. These features are helpful to us for diagnosing the correlations between topology and electronic properties.

3. Phase-change memory material

3.1 Background

For Ge-Sb-Te (GST) alloys, there exists a rapid and reversible transition between crystalline and amorphous states. Controlled modification of electrical conductivity and optical properties of the transition is the basis for promising FLASH and optical memory devices. Akola and Jones (Akola & Jones, 2007) analyzed the structure of liquid and amorphous phases, and compared the electronic structure with the crystal phase. In 2008, Hegedus and Elliott (Hegedus & Elliott, 2008) reproduced the crystal-amorphous transition by MD simulation, and they found that the rapid crystal growth was due to the presence of crystal fragments – four member square rings (so-called "seeds") in amorphous and liquid phases. Their work provided a way to track the dynamic changes of network topology and electronic structure at the same time. Welnic and co-workers (Welnic et al., 2007) studied the origin of optical properties and argued that the optical contrast between amorphous and crystalline phases is due to a change in local order of Ge atoms. Despite this progress, the correlation between topology and electronic structure, most especially the origin of the change in the electronic gap, is still imperfectly understood. One of the challenges is the basic limitation of the LDA for estimating the gap.

3.2 Model preparation

We began our work by creating amorphous $Ge_2Sb_2Te_5$ models by using the Vienna *Ab-initio* Simulation Package (VASP)– a plane-wave DFT code, using a PAW potential and the GGA-PBE method (Hegedus & Elliott, 2008). 63-atom amorphous $Ge_2Sb_2Te_5$ models with lattice constant 12.5 Å were made as follows. The system was first melted and equilibrated at 1000K, followed by a rapid quench to 500K with a quench rate of 16K/ps. Then the system was equilibrated for 20 ps and data collection began at 10ps. For the crystal phase, 108-atom crystal $Ge_2Sb_2Te_5$ cells with lattice constant 21.316Å are generated based on NaCl rock-salt structure with 10% vacancies: 60 Te atoms occupied the Na sites; 24 Ge atoms and 24 Sb atoms randomly occupied the Cl sites which left 10 Cl sites unoccupied. The system was then relaxed under zero-pressure till the minimum total energy was obtained.

	N_{tot}	N_{Te}	N_{Ge}	N_{Sb}
Te	3.4(3.0)	20%(30%)	47%(41%)	33%(29%)
Ge	4.6(4.3)	86%(71%)	5%(13%)	9%(16%)
Sb	4.1(3.6)	69%(62%)	11%(20%)	20%(18%)
N_{seed}	18(1.8)	52%(10%)	69%(12%)	53%(10%)

Table 1. Mean coordinations, bond types and seeds(four member square rings) statistics at 500K. The result obtained at 1000K is listed in brackets (coordination cutoff=3.2Å).

3.3 Result and discussions

3.3.1 Bond statistics

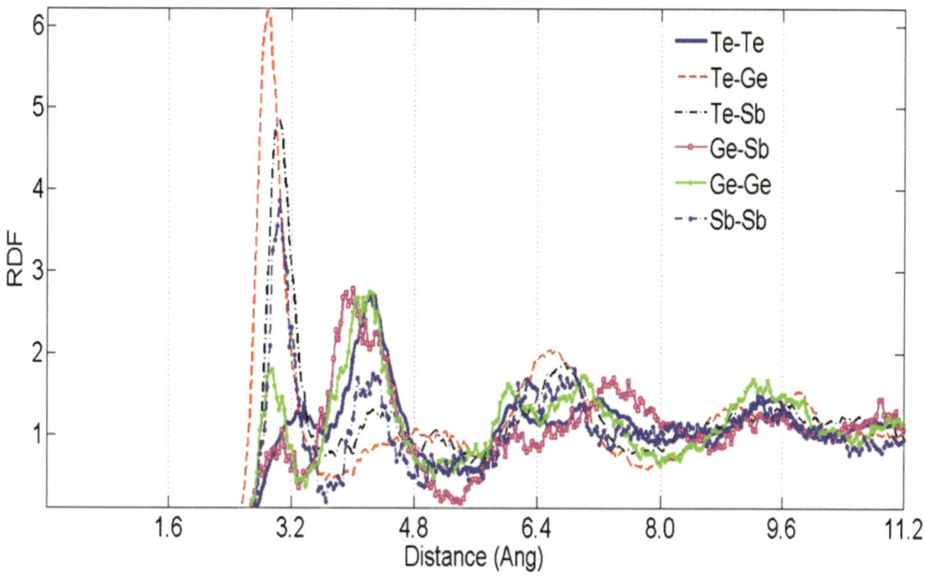

Fig. 1. Partial radial distribution functions for a-$Ge_2Sb_2Te_5$.

The calculated atomic coordinations for a-$Ge_2Sb_2Te_5$(500K) and l-$Ge_2Sb_2Te_5$(1000K) are listed in Table 1 with a 3.2Å cut-off. These results are similar to Akola & Jones (2007), although in our case, the mean coordination of Ge atoms is slightly increased after thermal quench and equilibration, which may be due to the higher equilibration temperature used and/or size artifacts for our smaller model. More highly-coordinated Ge and Sb (5-fold,6-fold) atoms appeared in the amorphous phase, which suggests that a near-octahedral structure may be formed (square-rings and 8-atom cubes). These results indicate that structural ordering is enhanced in the amorphous phase relative to the liquid. Moreover, the number of wrong bonds (Te-Te,Ge-Ge,Sb-Sb and Ge-Sb) are decreased from 1000K to 500K which indicates that the chemical order is also improved. The average number of "seeds" (four member square rings) shows an increase in the amorphous phase and more than 50% of the atoms are involved in "seeds", compared to only 10% in the liquid phase. The calculated partial radial distribution functions are plotted in Fig. 1. The first peak in the Te-Ge and Te-Sb partials are located at 2.81Å and 2.92Å. The shallow first minima imply that the coordination is sensitive to the cutoff value selected. The Te-Ge partial has a broad and weak second peak. However, the Te-Sb partial possesses a second peak with a maximum at 4.4Å which indicates that Ge and Sb atoms differ in local environment relative to Te atoms. Regarding the homopolar bonds, there is a major peak for the Sb-Sb partial centered at 2.9Å. These results are similar to other simulations (Akola & Jones, 2007) and also experimental results (Natio et al., 2010).

3.3.2 Electronic structure

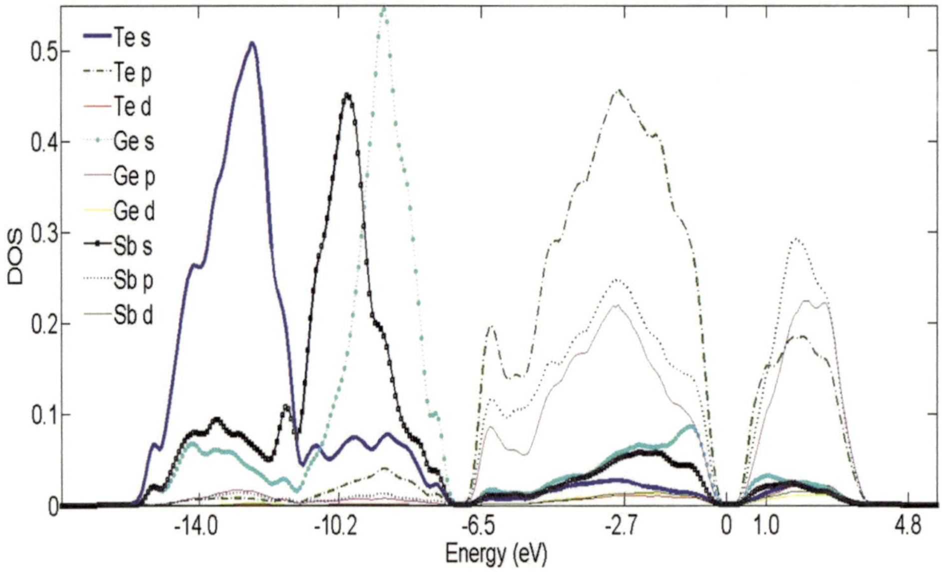

Fig. 2. Electronic densities of states projected onto different atomic species and orbitals. The Fermi level is at 0 eV.

The electronic structure is analyzed through the electronic density of states (EDOS) obtained from Hartree-Fock (HF) calculations. HF is used only to analyze the EDOS, not for forces and total energies. HF is known to exaggerate both the optical gap and charge fluctuations in the electron gas. These features are helpful to us here for diagnosing structural correlations. In the following discussion, the calculated EDOS is averaged over 1000 configurations from the last 2 ps when the cell is in thermal equilibrium at a fixed temperature of 500K. Finally, the averaged HF result of the amorphous phase gives an electronic gap around 0.4eV which is wider than the DFT result–0.2eV (Akola & Jones, 2007) and is closer to the experimental value–0.7eV (Lee et al., 2005). Although the gap is still smaller than the experimental value, it is much improved over LDA, and this may imply that HF provides a better starting point for analysis of the electronic structure.

To correlate topology with electronic structure, we projected the EDOS onto different local sites and are able to attribute the electronic states to specific structural units. We first show the averaged EDOS for different species and orbitals in Fig. 2. The key findings are that, for all three species, p orbitals dominate the gap and tail states; if considering the species, Te-p,Sb-p,Ge-p,Ge-s and Sb-s are important in determining tail states and the magnitude of the gap (Fig. 2). To further correlate structural oddities with electronic states, we also sort atoms with specific features into different groups and accumulate the contribution to EDOS. We briefly report that groups forming homopolar or heteropolar bonds showed that there is a significant difference at a "deep gap" around -7eV below the Fermi level (0eV) in EDOS (atoms involved in heteropolar bonds form a bigger deep gap); however, atoms forming homopolar bonds have a minor impact on tail states and the electronic gap near the Fermi

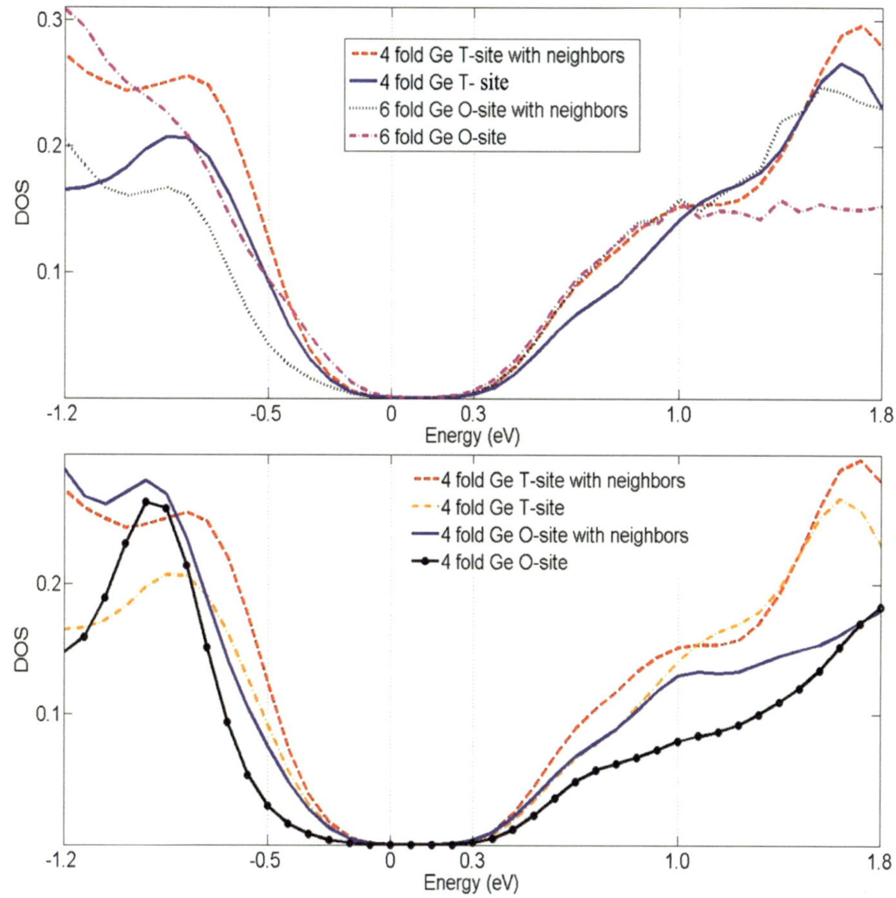

Fig. 3. Projected EDOS on Ge atoms at tetrahedral and octahedral sites. "T" and "O" represent tetrahedral and octahedral sites. The "Ge-T/O site" plot only considers the contribution of Ge atoms to the EDOS, while the "Ge-T/O site with neighbors" plot contains the contribution of Ge atoms and their neighbors. The Fermi level is at 0 eV.

level. Considering the coordination, for Te, 2-fold Te atoms contribute to a narrowed gap and conduction-band tail states appear; for Ge atoms, the contributions for 3, 4, 5 and 6-fold atoms are almost the same; for Sb atoms, the conduction-band tail of 6-fold Sb atoms is pushed to a low-energy level and the valence-band tail associated with 3-fold Sb atoms which satisfy the "8-N" rule is pushed into a higher energy region. While there are differences in electronic tail states and the gap value associated with coordination numbers, the influence is fairly weak. Similarly, sorting atoms involved in "seeds" or not also showed a minor impact on gap magnitude and tail states.

We also considered the "umbrella flip" of Ge atoms. We compared the EDOS of Ge atoms sitting at octahedral sites (O-site) and tetrahedral sites (T-site), as we illustrate in Fig. 3. The projected EDOS on Ge atoms and their neighbors are all considered. The results indicate that 6-fold octahedral Ge and tetrahedral Ge have a similar local gap. However, 4-fold Ge at an octahedral site (4 neighbors with 90 degree angles) have both a shifted valence-band tail and conduction-band tail which may result in a bigger gap. Thus, from our result, sp^3 hybrids introduced by a Ge umbrella-flip may not be the reason for an increased gap in the amorphous phase, but the octahedral Ge existing in the amorphous phase at least would not increase the electronic gap. Analysis of $Ge_1Sb_2Te_5$ showed a similar result (Raty et al., 2010).

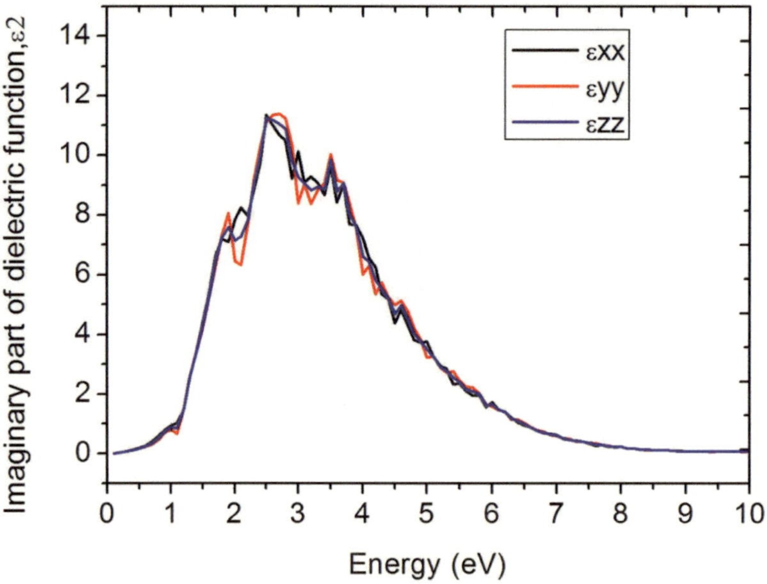

Fig. 4. AC Dielectric function of a-$Ge_2Sb_2Te_5$. Due to finite size effect, the calculation can not predict valid value for small ω ($\omega \lesssim 2eV$).

Finally for this section, we show one last static property – the dielectric function $\epsilon(\omega)$ in Fig. 4. The imaginary part of the dielectric function in three directions are plotted in Fig. 4. ϵ reaches its peak for an energy of about 2.5eV and this spectrum is comparable with both experimental and simulation result (Raty et al., 2010; Wuttig et al., 2007). Notice that due to the finite-size effect, the result is not valid for $\omega \rightarrow 0$. To obtain accurate results for small ω, an extrapolation procedure is required.

3.3.3 Dynamic analysis

Next, we performed a dynamic analysis for a-$Ge_2Sb_2Te_5$. We tracked the structure and the electronic gap during a quench from 1000K to 500K with thermal equilibration at 500K (Fig. 5). Significant structural changes started to occur after 24ps (the temperature was then near 640K). The number of homopolar bonds dropped, the number of 4-membered rings increased, and the mean coordination increased. The changes in topology are similar to those reported by Hegedus & Elliott (2008) and all these shifts signal an increase of both chemical order and structural order. The electronic gap, which we take to be the difference between LUMO and HOMO levels, increased overall, but we observed that there are considerable fluctuations, even for the well-equilibrated system. Local geometry may have huge consequences on the gap.

To study how changes in the local environment at a specific site affected the electronic gap, we tracked a specific unit in the system during equilibration and we show such an evolution for

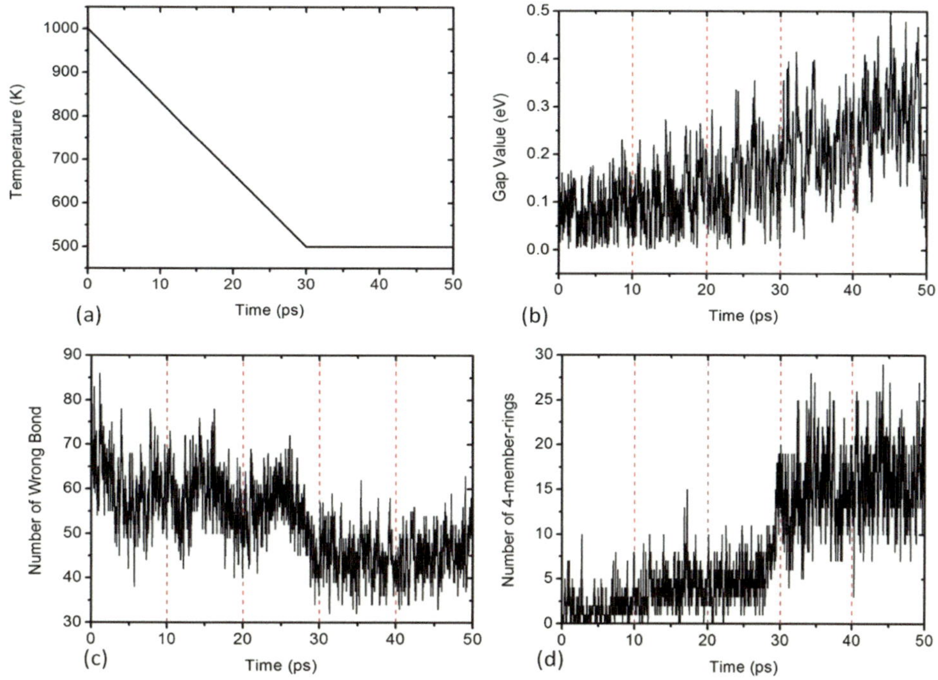

Fig. 5. Dynamic change of temperature, gap value, number of wrong bonds and squares (seeds).

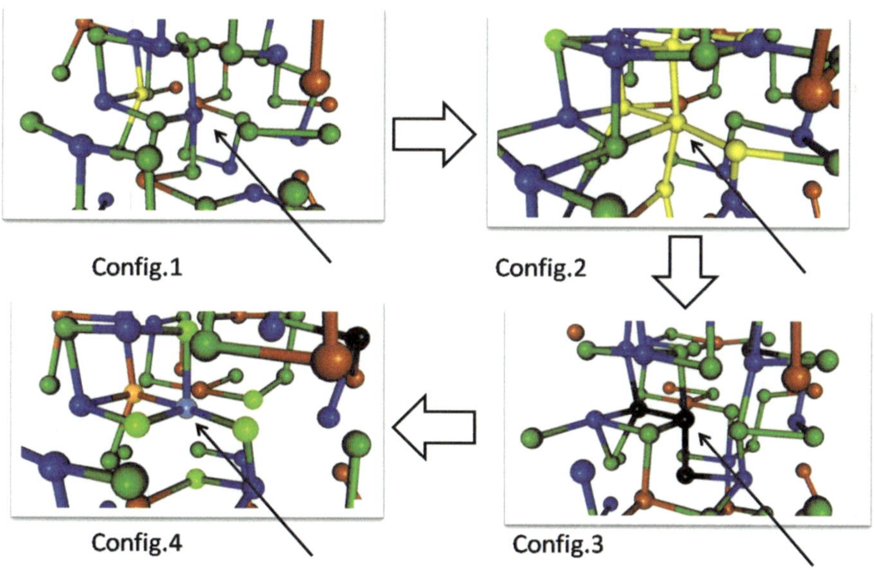

Fig. 6. Snapshots of topology changes for one Ge atom and its six neighbors (Ge-blue, Sb-brown, Te-green). The central Ge atom is identified by black arrows. The valence-band tail states appear in Config.2 and are localized on yellow atoms. The conduction-band tail states appear in Config.3 and are localized on black atoms.

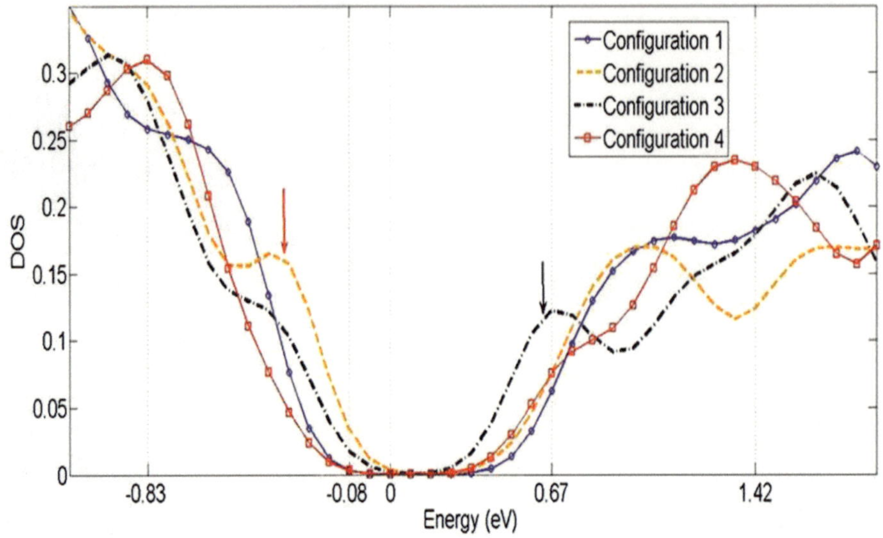

Fig. 7. Instantaneous snapshots of EDOS correlated with the configurations of Fig. 6. A smaller gap appear in Config.2&3. The valence-band tail states (orange arrow) are associated with yellow atoms in Config.2 of Fig. 6. The conduction-band tail states (black arrow) are associated with black atoms in Config.3 of Fig. 6. The Fermi level is at 0 eV.

both the topology and the electronic structure in Fig. 6 and Fig. 7. We mainly focused on one Ge atom which occupied a near-octahedral site (6 nearest Te neighbors with around 90 degree bond angles, indicated by a black arrow in Fig. 6) and its six nearest neighbors. We correlated their local bondings and electronic density of states for many time steps. Configurations 1 and 4 exhibit the biggest gap. However, at intermediate steps between configurations 1 to 4, tail states appear. At configuration 2, a valence-band tail state was present and it was mainly localized on the central Ge atom and four of its nearest neighbors (yellow atoms in Config.2 of Fig. 6); at configuration 3, a conduction-band tail appears, mainly localized on the center Ge atom and two of its nearest neighbors (black atoms in Config.3 of Fig. 6). We should emphasize that from configurations 1 to 4, the whole network did not experience a major change, but the electronic gap fluctuates. Thus, the appearance of valence-band and conduction-band tails are strongly associated with distortions at this Ge site. Our simulations emphasize the dynamic nature of the electronic band tails in $Ge_2Sb_2Te_5$.

3.3.4 Relaxation analysis for crystal phase of $Ge_2Sb_2Te_5$

In this section, we discuss relaxation effects for crystalline $Ge_2Sb_2Te_5$ with 10% vacancies. As mentioned above, the 108-atom cell was obtained based on the NaCl rock-salt structure. We show the electronic density of states for both unrelaxed and relaxed models in Fig. 8 obtained through HF calculations. For both models, Te atoms have a major effect on the valence tail which may be due to the vacancies; Sb atoms contribute more to conduction tail. We could see clearly that the electronic gap opened up after relaxation. Moreover, we tracked the dynamic change of the Highest Occupied Molecular Orbital (HOMO) and Lowest Unoccupied Molecular Orbital (LUMO) and plot them in Fig. 9. It is clear from the plot that the total energy is reduced and both HOMO and LUMO levels are shifted. The HOMO level is pushed away by 0.1eV and the LUMO level is pushed up by 0.2eV.

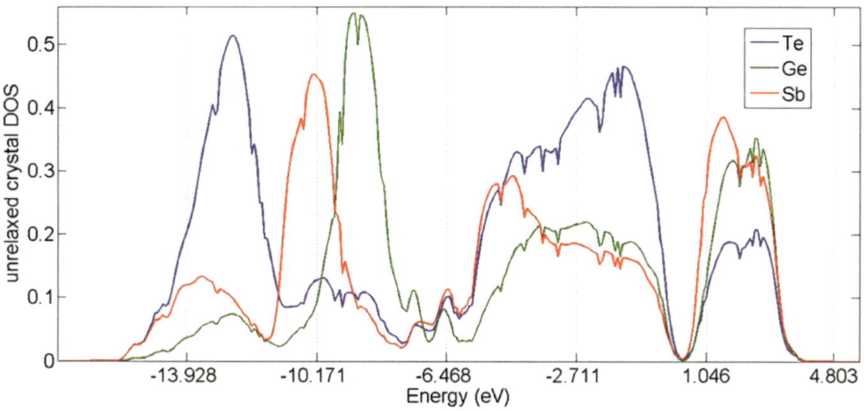

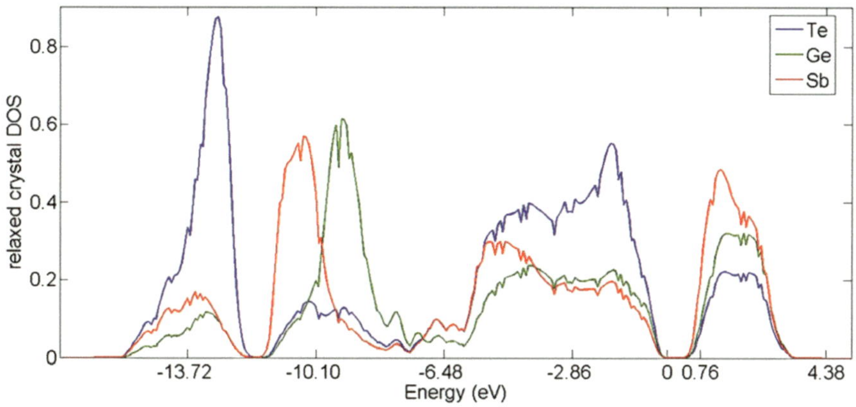

Fig. 8. Electronic density of states of crystal models projected onto different species of atoms. Unrelaxed crystal model with vacancies (top-panel). Relaxed crystal model (bottom-panel). The Fermi level is at 0eV.

Since the crystal model has 10% vacancies, the relaxation actually introduced slight distortion into the network. The structural statistics indicate that the mean coordination of Te, Ge and Sb atoms all decreased. The mean coordination of Te are decreased from 4.8 to 4.28, Sb and Ge dropped from 6 to 5.47 and 5.23 correspondingly. The angle distribution, especially the X-Ge-X and X-Sb-X angle distributions, are also changed. This result indicates that the existence of vacancies and the distortion happened to the network will have a impact on gap. Thus, by controlling the concentration of vacancies and distortion, we may obtained different electronic gap values. This result is similar to results on other Ge-Sb-Te alloys (Wuttig et al., 2007).

3.3.5 Conclusions on $Ge_2Sb_2Te_5$

We made $Ge_2Sb_2Te_5$ models with a 'quench from melt' method. HF calculations give a 0.4eV electronic gap for the amorphous phase. We found that Te-p, Sb-p, Ge-p, Ge-s and Sb-s orbitals are most important to tail states. 6-fold octahedral Ge and 4-fold tetrahedral Ge give rise to similar gaps but 4-fold octahedral Ge results in a bigger gap with both shifted valence-band and conduction-band tails. The study also reveals a large fluctuation in gap value during thermal equilibration which is partially due to the appearance and disappearance of conduction-band and valence-band tail states. Such fluctuations could be

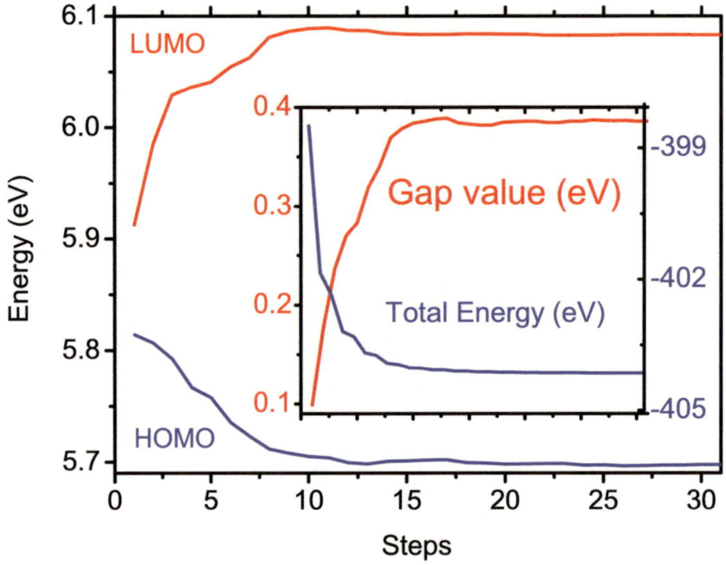

Fig. 9. Change of LUMO, HOMO level, gap value and total energy during relaxation.

associated with the local structural change/distortion of Ge atoms, which introduce localized tail states and have an impact on the electronic gap. Also, the relaxation analysis on crystal phase of $Ge_2Sb_2Te_5$ indicates that vacancies and distortions may play an important role in determining the electronic gap.

4. Electrolyte materials

4.1 Background

Electrolytes are materials with high ionic conductivity and high electrical resistivity. When doped with metals like Ag, chalcogenide glasses (e.g. Ge-Se) become solid electrolytes offering high ionic conductivities. Such electrolytes are getting attention for their technological importance with the application in "conducting bridge" (flash) memory devices (Mitkova & Kozicki, 2002). It has been believed that a variety of different coordination patterns of Ag^+ ions in the glassy host with tiny energy differences is the basic reason why Ag^+ is mobile. Since the properties of chalcogenide glasses accrue from their structure, the knowledge of the structure of these glasses is an essential precursor for further study. From a material point of view it is interesting that an amorphous material should allow rapid motion of a transition metal ion through the network, and a great deal of energy has been devoted to understanding this phenomenon. Such diffusive processes in glasses have been studied for decades with a variety of experimental methods. There have also been several approaches to modeling such diffusive behavior.

There have been a wide range of experimental studies on the atomic structure of the amorphous state of electrolyte material and some computer simulations, typically on Ge-Se glasses doped with transition metals. Ge-Se-Ag based electrolyte materials have been studied experimentally using various techniques. For example, X-ray (Piarristeguy et al., 2000) and neutron (Cuello et al., 2007; Dejus et al., 1992) diffraction, and other experimental methods

have been used to study the structure of Ge-Se-Ag glass. There have also been some computational studies to model the structure. Tafen et al. (Tafen et al., 2005) reported two *ab-initio* models; $(GeSe_3)_{0.9}Ag_{0.1}$and $(GeSe_3)_{0.85}Ag_{0.15}$with short range order consistent with the experimental results. It has also been reported that Ag atoms prefer to sit at trapping center (TC) which is near the midpoint of a line joining two host atoms (Ge or Se) separated by a distance between 4.7 and 5.2 Å with the bond length of Ag to the host atoms ranging between 2.4-2.6 Å (Chaudhuri et al., 2009) for low Ag concentration. The simulation work has been also extended by introducing Cu into the network (Prasai & Drabold, 2011).
Beside structural studies, there have been quite a few studies on the conductivity of Ag doped chalcogenide glasses including both experimental and simulation work. $Ag_x(GeSe_3)_{100-x}$ glasses have been particularly studied for the ionic conductivity within a wide range of x (10 to 25%). Ureña et al. (Ureña et al., 2005) predicted that the ionic conductivity follows an Arrhenius law. Tafen et al. presented a molecular dynamics(MD) simulation on $Ag_x(GeSe_3)_{100-x}$ with $x = 10$ and 15% (Tafen et al., 2005) at different temperatures. In recent work, we have also presented a MD simulations on these glasses with the addition of Cu and illustrated the motion of the ions on the accessible time scales (tens of picoseconds) (Prasai & Drabold, 2011). Some of the results will be discussed in the following sections.

4.2 Simulation of properties of electrolyte materials

The models of Ag- and Cu-doped chalcogenide glasses discussed here were generated using the melt-quenching method. A cubic supercell is constructed with a fixed volume and a fixed number of atoms in order to reproduce the experimental density according to the desired stoichiometry. The atoms were randomly placed in the supercell with minimum acceptable distance between two atoms set to 2Å. The calculations were carried out under periodic boundary condition using the Vienna *Ab-initio* Simulation Package(VASP)(Kresse & Furthmuller, 1996), with Vanderbilt ultrasoft pseudopotentials. We used the local density approximation (LDA) for the exchange correlation energy. The details of the model generation can be found in the reference Prasai & Drabold (2011). Beside the models discussed there, two more models $(GeSe_3)_{0.8}Cu_{0.2}$ and $(GeSe_3)_{0.8}Cu_{0.1}Ag_{0.1}$ have been added to the discussion.

4.3 Results and discussion

4.3.1 Structural properties

Fig. 10 shows the calculated total radial distribution functions (RDFs) and structure factors for the models; g-$(GeSe_3)_{0.9}Ag_{0.1}$, g-$(GeSe_3)_{0.8}Ag_{0.2}$, g-$(GeSe_3)_{0.9}Cu_{0.1}$and g-$(GeSe_3)_{0.77}Cu_{0.03}Ag_{0.2}$. The first peak of the RDF is the contribution from Ge-Se and Se-Se correlations whereas the second peak is due to Se-Se and Ge-Ag/Cu correlations(Fig. 11 and Fig. 12). There is not much variation in the short range order (SRO) i.e. nearest neighbor distance and second nearest neighbor distance for the different models. We observed a slight change in the nearest neighbor distance for the Ag rich model and Cu rich model. The average bond length and the mean coordination numbers are presented in Table 2. We did not detect Ge-Ge bonds in any of our models as seen previously in g-$(GeSe_3)_{0.9}Ag_{0.1}$(Tafen et al., 2005). We also observed that both Ag and Cu preferred to have Se as neighbor with only 16% of Cu/Ag bonded with Ge in our models. These results are very close to bond lengths measured by Piarristeguy et al. (Piarristeguy et al., 2000). We also obtained the silver and copper coordination number for each model. The coordination number 3.1 of silver at 20% is as predicted(3.0) by Mitkova et al. (Mitkova et al., 1999). The coordination number 4.67 of copper at 10% is much higher than 2.16 of silver (found to be 2.0 by Tafen et al. (Tafen et al.,

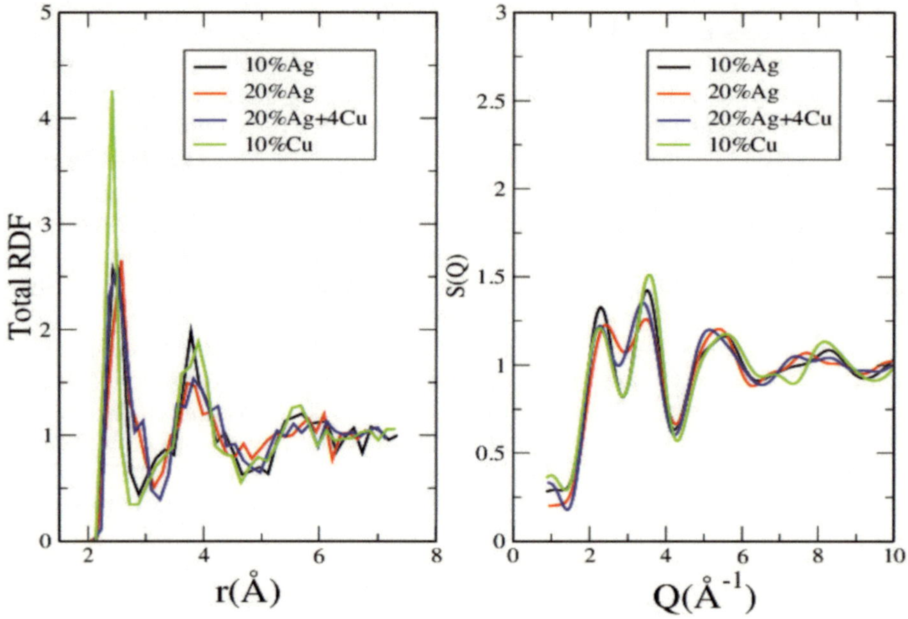

Fig. 10. Comparison of total radial distribution functions and static structure factors for all amorphous models

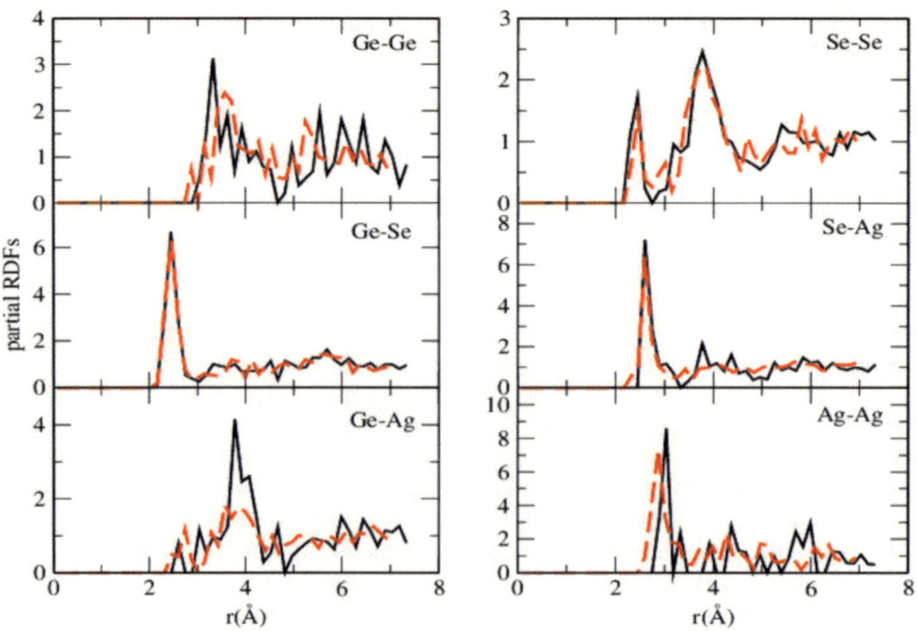

Fig. 11. Partial radial distribution functions for amorphous $(GeSe_3)_{0.9}Ag_{0.1}$(black) and $(GeSe_3)_{0.8}Ag_{0.2}$(red/dashed line)

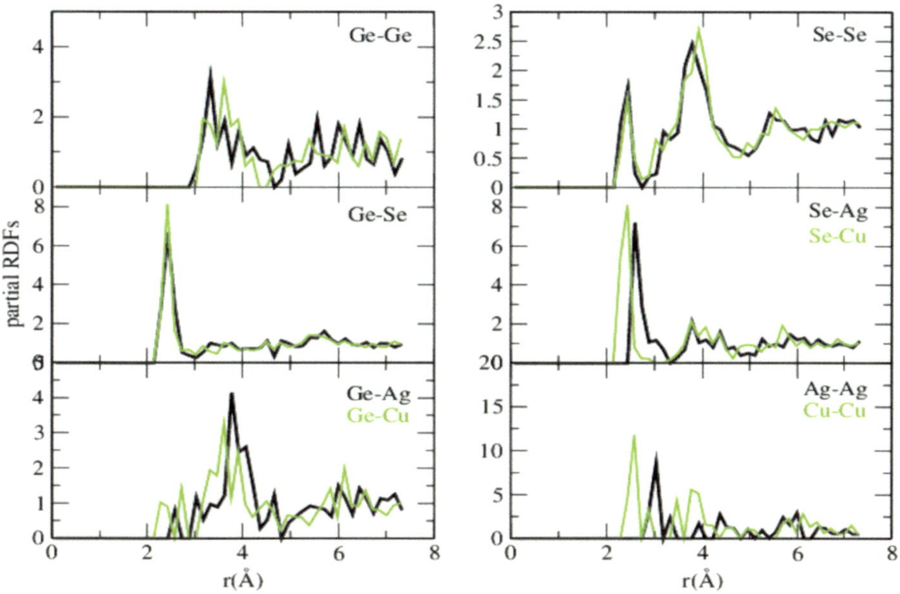

Fig. 12. Partial radial distribution functions for amorphous $(GeSe_3)_{0.9}Ag_{0.1}$(black) and $(GeSe_3)_{0.9}Cu_{0.1}$(green/thin line)

	NN(Å)	NNN(Å)	CN
$(GeSe_3)_{0.9}Ag_{0.1}$	2.49	3.75	2.50
$(GeSe_3)_{0.8}Ag_{0.2}$	2.51	3.80	2.92
$(GeSe_3)_{0.77}Cu_{0.03}Ag_{0.2}$	2.45	3.80	2.9
$(GeSe_3)_{0.9}Cu_{0.1}$	2.40	3.83	2.8

Table 2. Short range order; nearest neighbor distance(NN), next nearest neighbor distance(NNN) and mean coordination number(CN).

2005)) for the same concentration. We detected a few 3-fold Ge and 3 and 4 fold Se that we interpret as a structural defect in our models. Detailed bond parameters can be found in Prasai & Drabold (2011).

We also compared the static structure factors for our models (Fig. 10). There is no significant change in the position of the first two peaks. We observed a weak peak in S(Q) slightly above 1 Å $^{-1}$. This peak, which is a precursor to the first sharp diffraction peak (FSDP), varies as a function of Ag concentration and the peak disappears as Ag concentration increases, also shown by Piarristeguy et al. (Piarristeguy et al., 2003). We did not observe any particular correlation contributing to this peak as the partial structure factors shows that the peak has contribution from all of the partials. We compared partial structure factors for $(GeSe_3)_{0.9}Ag_{0.1}$ and $(GeSe_3)_{0.9}Cu_{0.1}$ and observed the only differences in correlation of Ag-Ag and Cu-Cu as well as in Se-Ag/Cu.

We performed thermal MD simulation at 1000K for 25ps in order to obtain well-equilibrated liquid systems. We calculated the total and partial radial distribution functions (RDF). The RDFs are averaged over the last 2.5 ps. The major peak positions in total RDF are 2.45 Å for $(GeSe_3)_{0.9}Cu_{0.1}$, 2.48 Å for $(GeSe_3)_{0.9}Ag_{0.1}$ and 2.53 Å for $(GeSe_3)_{0.8}Ag_{0.2}$ and

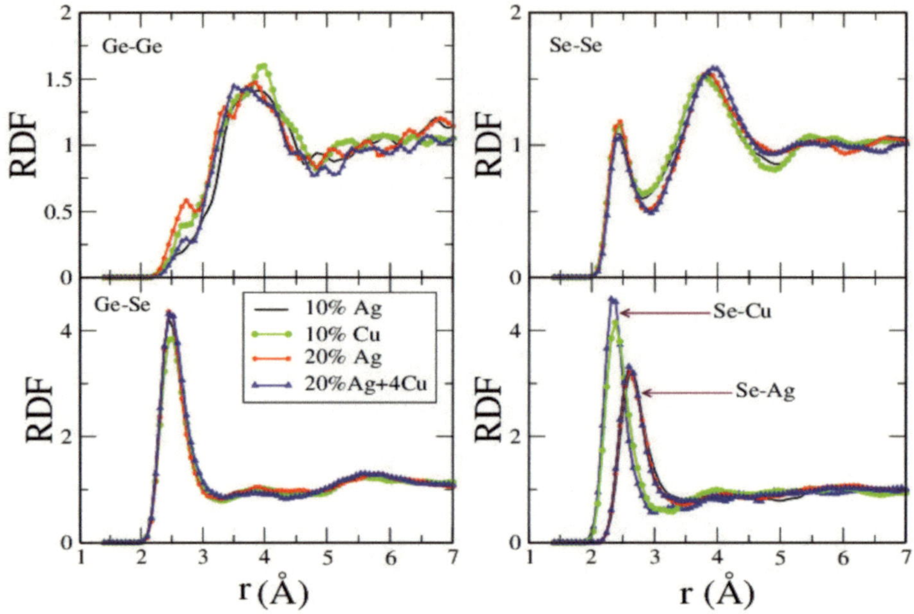

Fig. 13. Comparison of partial radial distribution functions for all liquid models at 1000K

$(GeSe_3)_{0.77}Cu_{0.03}Ag_{0.2}$. We present partial radial distribution functions in Fig. 13 showing Ge-Ge, Ge-Se, Se-Se and Se-Ag/Cu correlations. All of our models except $(GeSe_3)_{0.9}Ag_{0.1}$(2.6Å) confirm the presence of Ge-Ge homopolar bonds with peak position at 2.71 Å in contrast with the glass. We also observed Se-Se and Ge-Se bond distances of 2.47Å and 2.50 Å, respectively. We observe no concentration dependence on the first peak position of Ge-Se,Se-Se and Se-Ag/Cu correlations. The major contribution to the first peak of the total RDF is from Ge-Se,Se-Se and Se-Ag/Cu correlations with Se-Ag/Cu correlation causing the shifts on the first peak positions. The second peak of the total RDF is mainly due to Se-Se correlation.

4.3.2 Ion dynamics

We studied the dynamics of Ag and Cu ions in the $GeSe_3$ host by computing the mean square displacement (MSD) for each atomic constituent as:

$$\langle r^2(t)\rangle_a = \frac{1}{N_a}\sum_{i=1}^{N_a}\langle|\vec{r}_i(t) - \vec{r}_i(0)|^2\rangle \tag{1}$$

where the quantity in $\langle\rangle$ is the calculated statistical average over the particular atomic species α. We carried out constant temperature MD calculations at three different temperatures 300K, 700K and 1000K in order to study ion dynamics in our the amorphous as well as the liquid systems.

4.3.2.1 Amorphous Ge-Se-Cu-Ag

As expected, at 300K none of the ions showed measurable diffusion. In order to investigate the diffusion in the solid place, we chose $T = 700K$ and present the MSD for each species for each system calculated at this temperature in Fig. 14. At 700K Ag^+ ions show significant

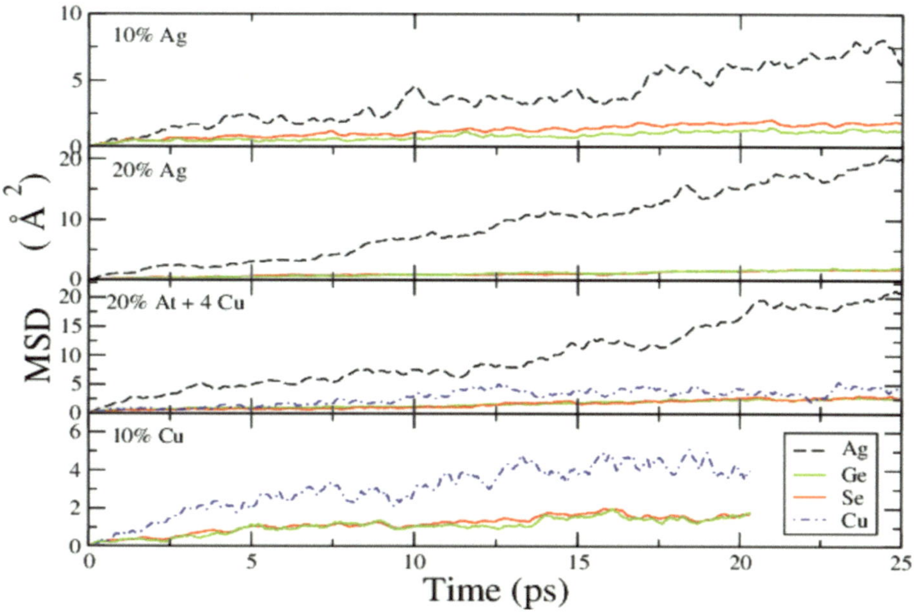

Fig. 14. Mean square displacement of atoms in amorphous $(GeSe_3)_{0.9}Ag_{0.1}$, $(GeSe_3)_{0.8}Ag_{0.2}$, $(GeSe_3)_{0.77}Cu_{0.03}Ag_{0.2}$and $(GeSe_3)_{0.9}Cu_{0.1}$(top to bottom respectively) glasses at $T = 700K$. Ag(black) Ge(green), Se(red) and Cu(blue)

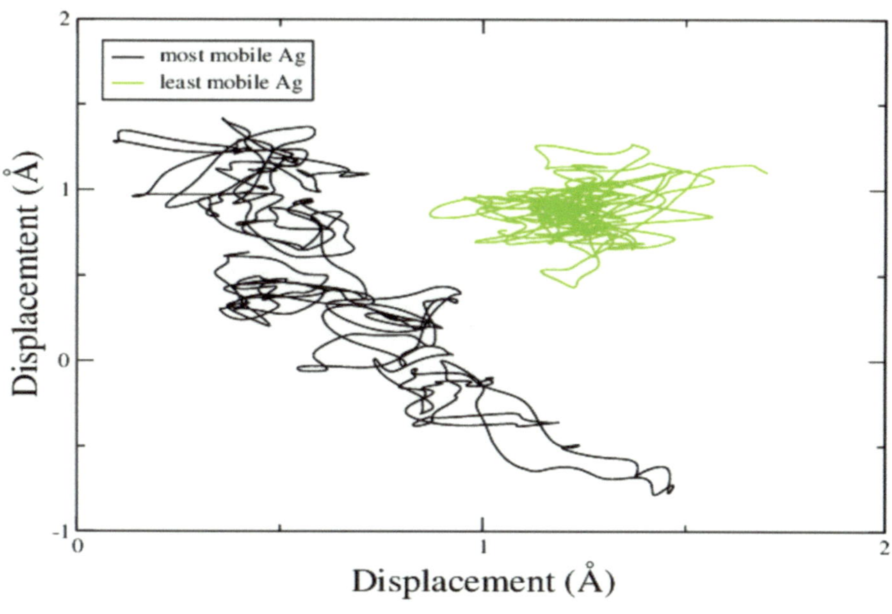

Fig. 15. Trajectories of the most and the least diffusive Ag ions at 700K as a function of time in amorphous $(GeSe_3)_{0.9}Ag_{0.1}$.

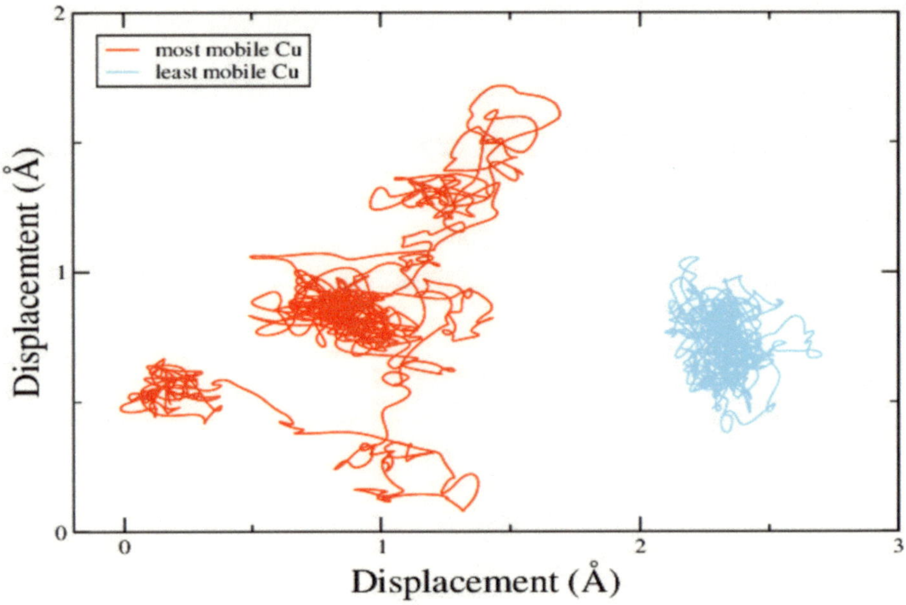

Fig. 16. Trajectories of the most and the least diffusive Cu ions at 700K as a function of time in amorphous $(GeSe_3)_{0.9}Cu_{0.1}$.

diffusion consistent with the previous result(Tafen et al., 2005) in contrast to Cu ions that do not diffuse much. To elucidate the diffusion of these ions we examine the trajectories for 20ps. Fig. 15 and 16 show two dimensional projections of the trajectories of the most and the least diffusive ions in $(GeSe_3)_{0.9}Ag_{0.1}$ and $(GeSe_3)_{0.9}Cu_{0.1}$. The trajectories illustrate the wide range of diffusion for the ions with displacement ranging 1Å-3.87Å in $(GeSe_3)_{0.9}Ag_{0.1}$, 2Å-6.71Å in $(GeSe_3)_{0.8}Ag_{0.2}$ and 1Å-3.74Å in $(GeSe_3)_{0.9}Cu_{0.1}$. For the mixed-ion model $(GeSe_3)_{0.77}Cu_{0.03}Ag_{0.2}$, this displacement ranges between 1.73Å-2.82Å for Cu and 1.41Å - 8.06Å for Ag. For Ag rich models more than 60% of the ions exhibit displacements greater than the average displacement (2.36Å in $(GeSe_3)_{0.9}Ag_{0.1}$ and 4.47Å in $(GeSe_3)_{0.8}Ag_{0.2}$) whereas for Cu, the majority has displacement smaller than the average(2.11Å). The wide range of diffusion can be attributed to variation in the local environment of the ions. To illustrate this we calculated the local densities of the most and the least mobile ions. We employed a sphere of radius 5.0Å around the ion and calculated the mean density of atoms inside the sphere. We observed that the most diffusive ion is located in the region with lower local density. In other words the most mobile ions have the wider variation of the local density as compared to that of the least mobile ion.

4.3.2.2 Liquid Ge-Se-Cu-Ag

One of the essential properties of a liquid is the high diffusivity of atoms in the system. To illustrate this, we calculated the mean square displacements for each species at 1000K in all of our models. The diffusion plots as presented in Fig. 17 shows that the MSD of each species increases rapidly as compared to that at 700K. We observe Ag diffusion still significantly larger than the host particles however; Ge and Se atoms are also diffusing rapidly. As before Cu still does not show high diffusion as Ag does compared to the host atoms.

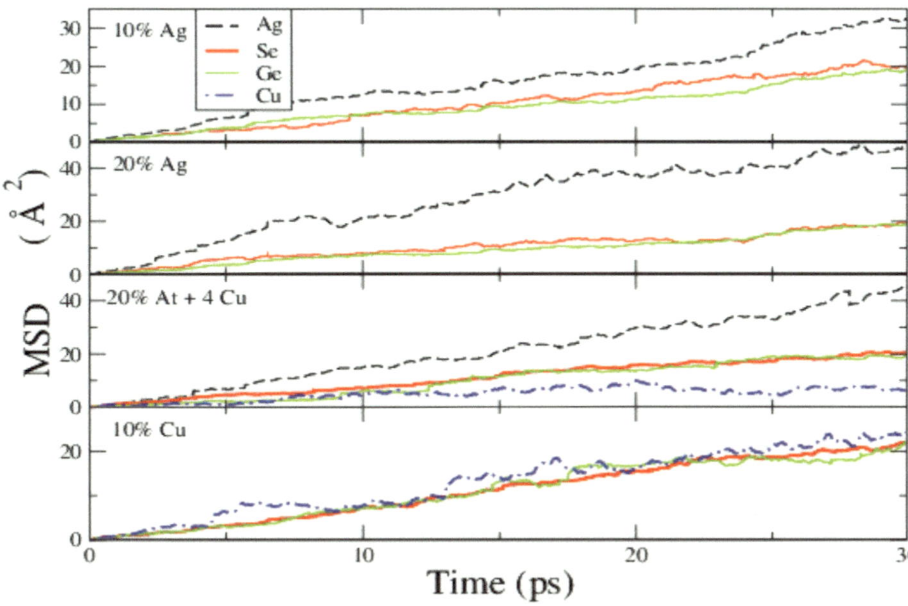

Fig. 17. Mean square displacement of atoms in liquid $(GeSe_3)_{0.9}Ag_{0.1}$, $(GeSe_3)_{0.8}Ag_{0.2}$, $(GeSe_3)_{0.77}Cu_{0.03}Ag_{0.2}$and $(GeSe_3)_{0.9}Cu_{0.1}$(top to bottom respectively) glasses at $T = 1000K$. Ag(black) Ge(green), Se(red) and Cu(blue)

Based on the plots we calculated diffusion coefficients using Einstein relation (Chandler, 1987). The Einstein relation for self-diffusion is given by:

$$\langle|\vec{r}_i(t) - \vec{r}_i(0)|^2\rangle = 6Dt + C \quad (2)$$

where C is a constant and D is the self-diffusion coefficient. The conductivity can be calculated from the equation

$$\sigma = \frac{ne^2D}{k_BT} \quad (3)$$

where n is the number density of ions. The temperature dependence of the diffusion is shown in Fig. 18 and the values of diffusion coefficients and conductivities at different temperatures are presented in Table 3. We did not find experimental results for the conductivity of Cu ions; however Ag conductivity is close to ones reported by Ureña et al.(Ureña et al., 2005).

4.3.3 Trap centers and hopping of ions

To illustrate the different ionic transport properties of Ag and Cu, it is essential to study the local environment of Ag and Cu in our models. Fig. 19 shows the local environment for Ag and Cu in $(GeSe_3)_{0.9}Ag_{0.1}$ and $(GeSe_3)_{0.9}Cu_{0.1}$respectively. In the relaxed networks, most of the Ag ions(58.3%) are found to occupy the trap centers, between two of the host sites as also predicted by the previous workers (Chaudhuri et al., 2009; Tafen et al., 2005) but this is not the same case with Cu. Cu is always surrounded by more than two host atoms that makes the traps for Cu more rigid than for Ag. In Ag rich systems at 300K, we observed that Ag is basically trapped with only a few hopping events. At 700K the lifetime of the trap decreases and hopping occurs. We observed the lifetime of the traps varying from 1ps

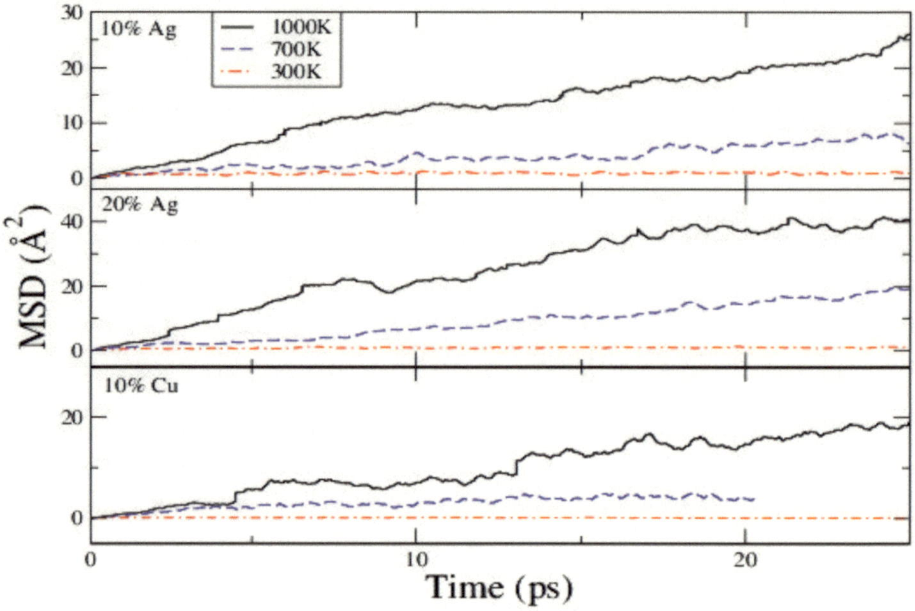

Fig. 18. Temperature dependence of conductivity of ions for different models

	T(K)	D(cm^2/s)	σ(Scm^{-1}) This work	Expt.Ureña et al. (2005)
10%Ag	300K	1.15×10^{-9}	2.63×10^{-5}	1.3×10^{-5}
	700K	4.53×10^{-6}	4.44×10^{-2}	2.07×10^{-2}
	1000K	1.23×10^{-5}	8.45×10^{-2}	8.98×10^{-2}
20%	300K	1.16×10^{-8}	5.3×10^{-4}	7.5×10^{-5}
	700K	1.20×10^{-5}	2.35×10^{-1}	6.57×10^{-2}
	1000K	2.53×10^{-5}	3.47×10^{-1}	2.584×10^{-1}
10%Cu	300K	7.3×10^{-10}	1.67×10^{-5}	
	700K	3.3×10^{-6}	3.23×10^{-2}	
	1000K	1.13×10^{-5}	7.75×10^{-2}	
0.77%Cu	300K	D_{Ag}=1.06×10^{-8}	4.85×10^{-4}	
		D_{Cu}=7.16×10^{-9}	1.63×10^{-5}	
	700K	D_{Ag}=1.30×10^{-5}	2.54×10^{-1}	
		D_{Cu}=1.16×10^{-6}	3.8×10^{-3}	
	1000K	D_{Ag}=2.42×10^{-5}	3.32×10^{-1}	
		D_{Cu}=5.24×10^{-6}	1.2×10^{-2}	

Table 3. Self diffusion coefficient D and conductivity σ at 300K, 700K and 1000K for $(GeSe_3)_{0.9}Ag_{0.1}$(10%Ag), $(GeSe_3)_{0.8}Ag_{0.2}$(20%Ag), $(GeSe_3)_{0.9}Cu_{0.1}$(10%Cu) and $(GeSe_3)_{0.77}Cu_{0.03}Ag_{0.2}$(0.77%Cu)

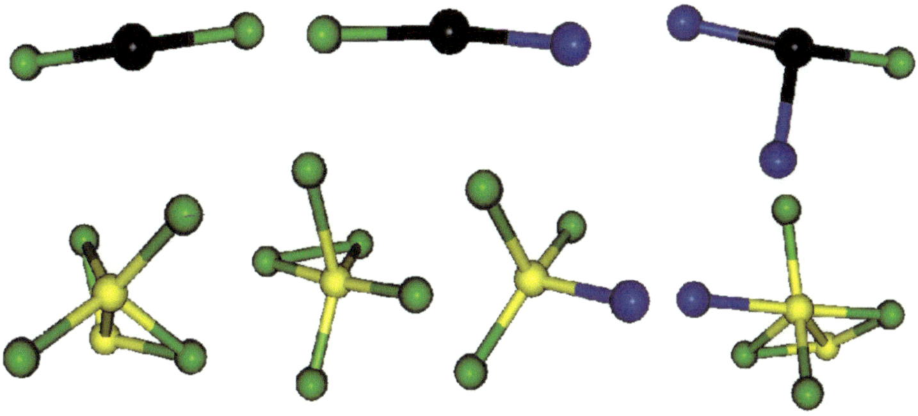

Fig. 19. Local environments of Ag atoms(top) and Cu atoms (bottom). Black, green,blue and yellow colored atoms respectively represent Ag, Se, Ge and Cu

- 3.5ps. However at 1000K we failed to observe well defined hopping events because of the high the diffusion of the host itself. In the Cu rich system the story is completely different. Even at 700K we could observe only a few hopping events with much larger trap life time. It has also been shown by previous workers that the nature of trap or cage depends mainly on coordination number, nearest neighboring distance and angular distribution of the nearest neighbors (Kraemer & Naumis, 2008). The low coordination number of Ag makes it easy to escape the trap whereas for Cu, high coordination number, smaller neighbor distance and a more uniform angular distribution makes it more difficult to escape from the trap.

4.3.4 Mixed ion conductivity

One big challenge in these materials is to fully understand the effect on the dynamic properties such as ionic conductivity when one of the mobile ion is partially substituted by another type of mobile ion. There is a non-linear change in ionic mobility when two or more than two types of mobile ions are mixed in ion conducting glasses and crystals, and the effect is known as mixed ion effect. This section reveals that the mixed ion effect in Ag and Cu doped $GeSe_3$ glasses is present in our simulation. Constant temperature MD simulations were carried out in $(GeSe_3)_{0.8}(Ag_{1-x}Cu_x)_{0.2}$ where $x = 0, 0.5$ and 1 at two different temperatures of 700K and 1000K. The calculated ion conductivities are presented in Fig. 20. The figure shows a drastic drop in the ionic conductivity when both Ag and Cu ions are present in the system. This result implies a mixed ion effect in Ag/Cu doped chalcogenide glass, where Ag^+ conduction is greatly reduced by the presence of Cu^+. It is encouraging to see a mixed-ion effect in our simulations; its atomistic origin is under study.

4.4 Conclusion: Fast ion conducting glasses

We prepared different Ag and Cu doped $GeSe_3$ glass and liquid models by *ab initio* simulation using the 'melt-quench' method and analyzed their structural and electronic properties. We also simulated dynamics of Ag and Cu ions using molecular dynamics. We were able to reproduce structural data as provided by X-ray diffraction. From the electronic density of state we observed that the increase in Ag concentration widens the optical gap whereas increase in Cu concentration narrows the gap. We were also able to see the metallic behavior for the liquid systems with the gap closing completely at 1000K. We were able to show the diffusion

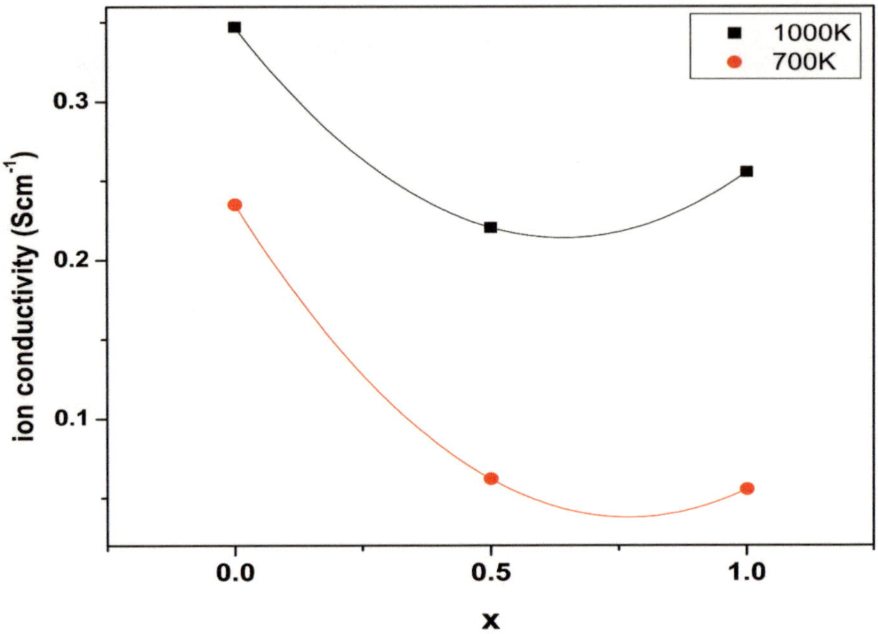

Fig. 20. Mixed ion effect: comparison of ion conductivities $(GeSe_3)_{0.8}(Ag_{1-x}Cu_x)_{0.2}$ glasses as a function of x.

of the ions even in our time scale and predict the conductivity close to the experimental data. We also studied the trap and found that Cu traps are more rigid that those for Ag making very hard for Cu to diffuse.

5. Conclusion

By using molecular dynamic simulations, we generate the atomistic models of $Ge_2Sb_2Te_5$ and Ge-Se-Ag-Cu and analyzed their topology and electronic structures. Both phase-change and electrolyte solid materials show the promising properties as candidates to replace the contemporary technologies in Flash memory. With further development, we believe the new generation of the computer storage device will eventually appear with much smaller size, higher speed and more reliable features. We show that computer simulation can lend insight into promising technologies.

6. Acknowledgement

The authors would like to particularly thank Professor S.R. Elliott and Dr. J. Hegedus for an introduction to phase-change memory materials and collaboration on GST work. DAD thanks Professor M. Mitkova and M. Kozicki for years of advice and collaboration. The authors also want to thank Prof. Gang Chen and Dr. Mingliang Zhang for their assistance and suggestions. This work was partly supported by the US NSF grant DMR-09033225, DMR-0844014 and DMR-0903225.

7. References

Akola, J. & Jones, R.O. (2007). Structural phase transitions on the nanoscale: The crucial pattern in the phase-change materials $Ge_2Sb_2Te_5$ and GeTe, *Physical Review B* Vol. 76, 235201.

Akola, J. & Jones, R.O. (2007). Density functional study of amorphous, liquid and crystalline $Ge_2Sb_2Te_5$: homopolar bonds and/or AB alternation? *Journal of Physics: Condensed Matter* Vol.20, 46103.

Cai, B., Drabold, D.A.& Elliott, S.R. (2010). Structural fingerprints of electronic change in the phase-change-material:$Ge_2Sb_2Te_5$, *Applied Physics Letters* Vol. 97, 191908.

Chandler, D. (1987). *Introduction to Modern Statistical Mechanics* (Oxford University Press, New York) pp. 249-250.

Chaudhuri, I., Inam, F. & Drabold, D.A. (2009). *Ab initio* determination of ion traps and the dynamics of silver in silver-doped chalcogenide glass, *Physical Review B* Vol. 79, 100201(R).

Chung, A., Deen, J., Lee, J.-S. & Meyyappan, M. (2010). Nanoscale memory devices, *Nanotechnology* Vol. 21, 412001.

Cuello, G., Piarristeguy, A., Fernández-Martínez, A., Fontana, M. & Pradel, A.(2007). Structure of chalcogenide glasses by neutron diffraction, *Journal of Non-Crystalline Solids* Vol. 353, 729-732.

Dejus, R., Susman, S., Volin, K., Montague, D. & Price, D. (1992). Structure of vitreous Ag-Ge-Se, *Journal of Non-Crystalline Solids* Vol. 143, 162.

Drabod, D. (2009). Topics in the theory of amorphous materials, *The European Physical Journal B* Vol. 68, 1.

Hegedus, J. & Elliott, S.R. (2008). Microscopic origin of the fast crystallization ability of GeĺCSb-Te phase-change memory materials, *Nature Materials* Vol. 7, 399.

Kraemer, A.S. & Naumis, G.G. (2008). Use of the cage formation probability for obtaining approximate phase diagrams, *Journal of Chemical Physics* Vol. 128, 134516.

Kresse, G. & Furthmüller, J. (1996). Efficient iterative schemes for *ab-initio* total-energy calculations using a plane-wave basis set, *Physical Review B* Vol. 54, 11169; http://cmp.univie.ac.at/vasp/.

Kresse, G. & Hafner, J. (1994). Norm-conserving and ultrasoft pseudopotentials for first-row and transition-elements, *Journal of Physics: Condensed Matter* Vol. 6, 8245, 1994

Kresse, G. & Joubert, D. (1999). From ultrasoft pseudopotentials to the projector augmented-wave method, *Physical Review B* Vol. 59, 1758.

Lacaita, A.J. & Wouters, D. J. (2008). Phase-change memories, *Physica status solidi(a)* Vol. 205, No.10, 2281.

Lee, B.S., Abelson, J.R., Bishop, S.G., Kang, D.H., Cheong, B. & Kim, K.B. (2005). Investigation of the optical and electronic properties of $Ge_2Sb_2Te_5$ phase change material in its amorphous, cubic, and hexagonal phases, *Journal of Applied Physics* Vol. 97, 093509.

Mitkova, M., Wang, Y. & Boolchand, P. (1999). Dual chemical role of Ag as an additive in chalcogenide glasses, *Physical Review Letters* Vol. 83, 3848.

Mitkova, M. & Kozicki, M.N. (2002). Silver incorporation in Ge-Se glasses used in programmable metallization cell devices, *Journal of Non-Crystalline Solids* Vol. 299-302, 1023.

Natio, M., Ishimaru, M., Hirotsu, Y., Kojima, R. & Yamada, N. (2010). Direct observations of $Ge_2Sb_2Te_5$ recording marks in the phase-change disk, *Journal of Applied Physics* Vol. 107, 103507.

Perdew, J.P. & Zunger, A. (1981). Self-interaction correction to density-functional approximations for many-electron systems, *Physical Review B* Vol 23, 5048.

Perdew, J.P., Burke, K. & Ernzerhof, M. (1996). Generalized gradient approximation made simple, *Physical Review Letters* Vol. 77, 3865.

Piarristeguy, A., Mirandou, M.,Fontana, M. & Arcondo, B.(2000). X-ray analysis of GeSeAg glasses, *Journal of Non-Crystalline Solids* Vol. 273, 30-35.

Piarristeguy, A., Fontana, M. & Arcondo, B. (2003). Structural considerations about the $(Ge_{0.25}Se_{0.75})_{100-x}Ag_x$ glasses, *Journal of Non-Crystalline Solids* Vol. 332, 1-10.

Prasai, B. & Drabold, D.A. (2011). *Ab initio* simulation of solid electrolyte materials in liquid and glassy phases, *Physical Review B* Vol. 83, 094202.

Raty, J.Y., Otijacques, C., Gaspard, J.P., Bichara, C. (2010). Amorphous structure and electronic properties of the $Ge_1Sb_2Te_4$ phase change material, *Solid State Sciences* Vol. 12, 193.

Tafen, D. N., Drabold, D.A. & Mitkova, M. (2005). Silver transport in Ge_xSe_{1-x}:Ag materials: *Ab initio* simulation of a solid electrolyte, *Physical Review B* Vol. 72, 054206.

Ureña, M.A., Piarristeguy, A., Fontana, M. & Arcondo, B. (2005). Ionic conductivity (Ag^+) in AgGeSe glasses, *Solid State Ionics* Vol. 176, 505.

Welnic, W., Botti, S., Reining, L. & Wuttig, M. (2007). Origin of the Optical Contrast in Phase-Change Materials, *Physical Review Letters* Vol. 98, 236403.

Wuttig, M., Lusebrink, D., Wamwangi, D., Welnic, W., Gilleben, M. & Dronskowksi, R. (2007). The role of vacancies and local distortions in the design of new phase-change materials, *Nature Materials* Vol. 6, 122.